THE PARKS AND WOODLANDS OF LONDON

THE PARKS AND WOODLANDS OF LONDON

by
ANDREW CROWE

FOURTH ESTATE
LONDON

First published in 1987 by
Fourth Estate Limited, 113 Westbourne Grove, London W2 4UP
Telephone: (01) 727-8993

Photographs by Andrew Crowe
Maps by David Stevens

British Library Cataloguing in Publication Data

Crowe, Andrew
The parks and woodlands of London.
1. Parks—England—London—Guide-books
2. London (England)—Description—1981–
—Guide-books
I. Title
914.21'04858 DA689.P2

ISBN 0-947795-61-8

Typeset in Palatino by
MC Typeset Limited, Chatham, Kent
Printed and Bound by
Richard Clay (The Chaucer Press) Ltd, Bungay, Suffolk

This book is dedicated to all those individuals who have in some way fought to provide and preserve public open land within the capital, in particular to Lord Eversley, founder of the Commons Preservation Society, and Miss Octavia Hill, founder of the National Trust.

Contents

Acknowledgements

My thanks first of all to all my friends who gave me much needed encouragement and support, in particular to Vicky White and Bridget Bishop. Next, I would like to acknowledge the often considerable help given to me by the staff of the thirty-five or so libraries with which I dealt during the course of the research, in particular to the librarians at 'Woodlands' in Greenwich and the hard-worked staff of my local library in Balham who uncomplainingly followed up for me requests for more than one hundred (often obscure) books and articles.

As to the many borough parks departments, helpfulness varied considerably from those (an alarmingly large proportion) who unconcernedly lost my correspondence without trace, to those who always showed remarkable thoroughness and enthusiasm in my dealings with them. In particular I would like to thank Mr J.G. Berry (now retired) of Merton Borough's Recreation and Arts Department.

Also particularly helpful during the book's research phase was Mr Philip Daniell of Environment Bromley and Mrs Joyce Bellamy of the Green Heritage Service.

For information and help on a London-wide basis, I owe a great deal to the Greater London Council: to the council's Recreation and Arts Information Officer, Mr L.R. Prescott, and to the librarians of the GLC's research library at County Hall and the Greater London Record Office and History Library at Clerkenwell.

Introduction

Renowned the world over for its rich and varied parkland, Greater London has in all sixty-seven square miles (174 square kilometres) of public open land, covering almost eleven per cent of the city's total area. Though the exact number of these parks, woodlands, commons, greens and squares is not known, those over one acre alone together number almost 1700, ranging from the small ecological reserves such as Camley Street Natural Park just a few yards from King's Cross station, to the 6000-acre expanse of ancient woodland, grassland, heath and marsh of Epping Forest, and from such tiny horticultural gems as the Chelsea Physic Garden on the Chelsea Embankment, to the 300-acre international showpiece – the Royal Botanic Gardens at Kew.

For some, an exploration of London's parks will mean visits to such classically landscaped masterpieces as Syon Park in Brentford and Chiswick House Gardens in Chiswick, or a stroll around some of the city's more modern horticultural attractions – the Coombe Wood garden in Croydon for example, the Isabella Plantation in Richmond Park or The Rookery garden at the top of Streatham Common. Others may be drawn more to the wilder, uncultivated areas – areas which, with the increasing destruction of our traditional countryside, are coming to be more widely appreciated. Such places would include Hampstead Heath, Oxleas Woodlands and Selsdon Wood Nature Reserve, all of which provide pockets of unspoiled countryside, many so rich in their variety of wildlife that they have been designated SSSIs (Sites of Special Scientific Interest). Among these are many remnants of ancient woodland known to have been continuously wooded from as far back as the last Ice Age – Ruislip Woods, Kenwood and Sydenham Hill Wood being examples of this.

Whatever your interest in London's parks – whether it is primarily horticultural or ecological, or just a need for some fresh air and exercise – the city has a surprising amount to offer.

History

The general history of London's public open spaces can be said to begin with the city's common land – places such as Hampstead Heath, Epping Forest, Blackheath and Wimbledon Common.

There is a popular misconception that our commons have been public property since ancient times; in fact, they were all originally privately owned by the local lord of the manor. The lord's tenants enjoyed certain common rights which usually included the right to graze cattle, sheep, horses and pigs, to gather firewood and dig gravel. Such rights are typically described by an early seventeenth-century Act of Parliament (referring to the Hackney commons); the copyholders, it says, are entitled to:

> lop and shred all such trees as grow before their houses . . . upon the waste ground and the same convert to their own use, without any offence, so the said trees stand for defence of their houses, yards, or gardens; and also may dig gravel, sand, clay and loam, upon the said waste grounds, to build or repair any of their copyhold tenements . . . so always as every of the said copyholders do fill up so much as shall be digged by him or them.

A less well-known variation was the existence in some parts of lammas lands – land to which common rights applied only on a seasonal basis, between 12 August and 15 April. Such seasonal commons included what is now Millfields, London Fields, Hackney Downs, Hackney Marsh and Lammas Park.

For at least eight centuries common land provided a more or less stable form of land tenure for subsistence agriculture, but with the growing urban pressures of the early nineteenth century, firewood began to be replaced by coal as a source of fuel, and the production of milk and meat became more centralized. The commons were at that time still widely used for such homely practices as carpet beating and clothes drying but the land was fast appreciating in value as a source of gravel, brick clay and real estate for the building of railways and houses. With alarming speed the lords of the manors enclosed the city's (and indeed the whole country's) common land, often with no regard at all for the rights of existing commoners. Between 1727 and 1844 alone, seven million acres of common land in England and Wales were enclosed, inevitably arousing that sense of injustice so memorably expressed in an eighteenth-century rhyme:

The law imprisons man or woman
Who steals the goose from off the common,
But lets the greater villain loose
Who steals the common from the goose.

The problem was perhaps most acute in and around London, where the real turning point came with the announcement in 1864 of plans to sell off one-third of Wimbledon Common. This scheme proved to be the last straw, leading to the passing of an Act of Parliament – the Metropolitan Commons Act, 1866 – which succeeded in making further enclosure of the city's commons practically impossible. In the final rush to sell before the Act came into force, hundreds of acres of Epping Forest, Plumstead and Tooting Commons were enclosed, but the Act had at last given conservationists the legal muscle they so badly needed. (The often colourful stories of how individual commons were finally saved are told under the respective commons – see, for example, Epping Forest, Hampstead Heath, Plumstead Common and Wimbledon Common.) Equally important at this time was the forming in 1865 by George John Shaw-Lefevre (later Lord Eversley) of the Commons Preservation Society – a society which to this day (under its modern name, the Open Spaces Society) continues to play a crucial role in the protection of public open land. It is, in fact, from this historic society that the National Trust came into being, having been formed by one of the society's members, Miss Octavia Hill, in 1895 in response to the need to purchase and hold places of beauty, as well as to campaign to save them. Joining the movement in 1878 was the Kyrle Society (founded mainly also by Miss Octavia Hill) which campaigned and raised funds to 'place subjects of beauty within the reach of the poor', and the Metropolitan Public Gardens Association which, since its founding in 1882 by Lord Brabazon (later Earl of Meath), also played an important role in providing 'gardens for the gardenless'.

The need to provide Londoners with public parks was not in fact *officially* recognized until 1833, when a parliamentary committee announced their realization that 'the spring to industry which occasional relaxation gives, seems quite as necessary to the poor as to the rich'. The committee, which had been appointed to consider 'the best means of securing Open Spaces in the Vicinity of populous Towns, as Public Walks and Places of Exercise, calculated to promote the Health and Comfort of the Inhabitants', led Parliament to the conclusion that no less than five parks should be laid out in the poorer parts of London. The committee's report pointed out that most of the working classes earned their living 'shut up in heated Factories' and that, for health's sake, they needed 'on their day of rest to enjoy the fresh air and . . . to walk out in decent comfort with their families'. Providing public parks, it was suggested, might also serve to draw the labouring classes away from such 'low and debasing pleasures' as 'drinking-houses, dog fights, and boxing matches'.

Six years later Parliament's lofty proclamation had come to nothing and the only parks in London freely open to the public remained the royal parks, none of which were in or even near the poorer areas of the city. It was not until the publication in May 1838 of the public health reports of William Farr to the Registrar-General that the government was finally spurred to action. Farr's historic report linked, for the first time, 'the source of the higher mortality in cities' to 'the insalubrity of the atmosphere'. He argued that 'wide streets, squares, and parks with spacious houses, would render ventilation easy, and secure the dilution of poisonous emanation' and that 'the epidemics which arise in the east end of town, do not stay there; they travel to the west end, and prove fatal in wide streets and squares'. 'The registers', he wrote, 'show this: they trace diseases from unhealthy to healthy quarters, and follow them from the centres of cities to the surrounding villages and remote dwellings.'

Finally, in 1842, without any debate, funds were made available by a royal grant for the city's first true public park – Victoria Park – to be created in London's East End. Government officials had at last been compelled to think in terms of London as a whole, even though there was as yet no system of London-wide government. Thus, in spite of the fact that Victoria Park was never used by the royal family, it was initially a royal park, maintained by HM Commissioners of Works out of national taxation. Along the same lines followed the Act for the creation of Battersea Park in 1846 and in 1852 Kennington Common was converted into what is now Kennington Park. Local authorities, however, still lacked the necessary power to provide public open spaces themselves, but in 1855 came the Metropolitan Board of Works (later becoming the London County Council, later still the Greater London Council), and it is from this body that the city's first truly municipal parks came into being – Finsbury Park in north London and Southwark Park at Rotherhithe.

The Open Spaces Movement can be said to have been motivated by three main concerns: health, spiritual salvation and social reform. Besides the link that Farr's report provided between the lack of open spaces and the appalling disease epidemics of the early and mid-nineteenth century, there was also a deep religious conviction in the power of Nature to reform – the belief being that a country-like environment would 'instill a hallowed calm, and a spirit of reverence into the mind and heart of man'. Some of this concern for the 'common man' sprang from an analysis of the prevailing atmosphere of social unrest, in which it was argued that parks for the poor would distract them from the vices of the city – drinking, prostitution and crime – and help bring the 'lower orders' into contact with their 'natural superiors'.

That there should have been parks at all for the labouring classes was hotly contested by many as an extravagance, especially since these new parks – Southwark Park and Finsbury Park – were situated in areas not yet built up. It was a sore point, too, that Battersea, Victoria and Kennington Parks and Bethnal Green Gardens were all still being maintained out of national taxation, and in 1886 the House of Commons expressed its discontent by refusing to vote through the annual funding. Thus, these parks too were passed to the Metropolitan Board of Works, which itself lasted only two more years before being superseded by the London County Council.

The new council got off to a good start, for in its first year of office, 1889, two exceptionally generous landowners came forward to donate land for the creation of further parks – William Minet who donated Myatt's Fields and Sir Sydney Waterlow who presented Waterlow Park. Other public-spirited landowners soon followed and fund-raising campaigns were set up to enable the council to buy further land, some of which was already attractively landscaped as private estates, though more often it required first a good deal of laying-out work. The campaign for the preservation of commons was, of course, already well underway, while the Metropolitan Public Gardens Association involved itself in the valuable work of converting many of the city's disused burial grounds to public gardens, often in some of London's most densely populated areas.

Meanwhile, outside the old County of London (but mostly still within the modern boundaries of Greater London) the Corporation of the City of London had also been active. In 1878 the corporation was authorized by an Act of Parliament to acquire land within twenty-five miles of the City 'for the recreation and enjoyment of the public' and to preserve its natural state. Epping Forest was, in 1878, the first of these open spaces to be acquired, followed in 1883 by the four Coulsdon Commons, in 1885 by Highgate Wood and Queen's Park and later West Wickham Common and Spring Park.

To this, the London Squares Preservation Act (1931) contributed several hundred more acres, so that by 1955 the London County Council alone had under its control no less than 140 parks and open spaces together covering more than 7000 acres.

One of the greatest benefits such a system of London-wide government has conferred on Londoners over the past 130 years has been the provision and maintenance of public parks irrespective of the social class or wealth of the inhabitants of the immediate neighbourhood, and the establishment of a London-wide standard of what an adequate provision of open space might be. It was, however, becoming increasingly clear that with the growth of London the administration of its parks needed some decentralization. The London Government Act of 1963 paved the way for the inception of the Greater London Council in 1965, which, in 1971, handed over many of the old London County Council's parks to the new London boroughs, generally retaining only those which served an area significantly beyond the borough in which they fell. Thus, the GLC was left with such strategic open spaces as Hampstead Heath, the Oxleas Woodlands of Eltham, Trent Park near Cockfosters, Hainault Forest near Chigwell, Holland Park in Kensington, Crystal Palace Park at Sydenham and the ambitious new park in Walworth – Burgess Park. This last park is one of the best examples of the benefits the city has reaped from the existence of a London-wide governing body, for here the council (first the LCC and later the GLC) identified an area severely lacking in public open space and set about creating parkland out of what was at that time mostly bombed and demolition sites. Such a scheme would have been hard enough for a wealthy borough to achieve, but in such a poor area a local authority alone would have found such a project quite impossible.

By the time this book is printed, this elected London-wide governing body – the GLC – will have been abolished by the national government. Not only is such a move of concern politically, but it also makes future projects such as Burgess Park and Mile End Park practically impossible to implement while it threatens many of London's larger municipal parks. Will Oxleas Woodlands still be able to resist having a four-lane highway cut through the middle of it (as the Department of Transport proposes at present to do), and will development of the GLC's newer parks ever be carried to completion?

In the outer boroughs, the local councils were also active, often with substantial financial help from either the Middlesex County Council or the London County Council – purchasing old estates, tracts of wild land, farmland or former commons, many of these acquisitions being in response to the far-sighted Green Belt (London and Home Counties) Act (1938).

During the Second World War, many of London's parks were turned to food production or bases for air-raid shelters, trenches, anti-aircraft guns, barrage balloons, searchlights and ammunition stores. Iron railings and gates disappeared and prefabs went up to house the homeless. In 1940 alone, fourteen tons of tomatoes were produced in the LCC's greenhouses, while the following year nine parks were disced, ploughed and cultivated to grow potatoes, yielding 655 tons of tubers which, like the tomatoes, were distributed to various local hospitals and schools. Production increased from year to year, much of it with the help of schoolchildren and Austrian refugees. In 1942 these parks produced over 20,000 lettuces, eight tons of onions, approximately a ton of herbs and several tons of beetroot, carrots, turnips and parsnips.

The war brought terrible destruction, but in the years that followed, the parks were gradually returned once again to their peacetime uses, with low-lying areas such as Hackney Marsh raised for better drainage by infilling with rubble from bombed sites. With this destruction came also the opportunity to create new parks, many of them within the old City itself. The most ambitious new projects came out of the County of London Plan of 1943, in which standards were laid down for what could be regarded as an adequate provision of public open land.

The Future

This brief history of the setting up of our enviable system of parks might lead one to assume that the battles and campaigns are at last all over and that we need now only go out and enjoy all this open space. Sadly, this is not the case. Of the 80,000 acres or so of green belt zoned land within Greater London, an average of about thirty acres is lost every year. Local councils from time to time announce plans to build over existing parks and woodland – areas such as Sydenham Hill Wood in south London and Jubilee Gardens in Southall (the latter receiving a reprieve at the last minute, even after the development contract was signed). Just as the powerful railway companies of the last century frequently had the political influence necessary to route their tracks through much of our common land, so now the Department of Transport (DOT) threatens to cut roads through many of our parks and woodlands. At the time of writing, the DOT has its eyes on slices of Highgate Wood and Oxleas Wood, both significant wildlife reserves; this, in spite of the fact that Oxleas Wood has been declared an SSSI, that it is acknowledged as one of Britain's few surviving fragments of ancient woodland and that it is a key part of the *Green Chain* – a strip of parkland specifically protected from development. In a sense we have only exchanged our lord of the manor for what one author describes as 'the faceless destroyers': local or national government departments. The need for independent conservation organizations is as great now as ever it was, both in protecting our open spaces from adverse planning applications and in ensuring that standards of maintenance are preserved. Several parks now have their own such organizations: for example, the Friends of Wanstead Parklands, and the Friends of Brockwell Park; and some councils have introduced subscription tree-planting or have shown their preparedness to co-operate with such voluntary conservation groups as Environment Bromley, the RSPB (Royal Society for the Protection of Birds), the Ecological Parks Trust, the London Wildlife Trust and the Brent River and Canal Society.

Conservation and wildlife bodies have in recent years achieved some significant successes, such as ensuring that the M25 motorway was routed *under* Epping Forest rather than through it; saving such interesting pockets of wild land as the Gunnersbury Triangle near Chiswick and helping to create new reserves such as the Camley Street Natural Park by King's Cross. The growth of interest in the city's wilder open spaces is reflected in the membership of such organizations as the London Wildlife Trust. Meanwhile the Ecological Parks Trust has pioneered the concept of artificially created wildlife reserves. In 1977 it created the first such park out of two acres of inner city wasteland just a stone's throw from Tower Bridge. This former warehouse site and lorry park was completely transformed by shrub planting and the creating of an artificial lake to provide an attractive refuge for wildlife which, in its later stages, supported up to 350 plant species, over 200 invertebrate species and a good range of birds and butterflies. This new park – the William Curtis Ecological Park – was so successful that it soon drew over 13,000 visitors a year, many of them schoolchildren who came here to learn about urban wildlife. Though the park has since had to close down to make way for development, it did pave the way for other similar schemes.

With this growing interest in urban wildlife has come a greater appreciation of such ecological corridors as railway and canal embankments, by which both animals and plants migrate in and out of the city and surrounding countryside. There is now a better understanding of the need to mow some areas of parkland on a less frequent basis and less severely in order to foster the growth of wildflowers, and to leave patches of stinging nettles as food plants for the small tortoiseshell, peacock, comma and red admiral butterflies.

Many of London's public open spaces are appreciated now more for their wildlife and likeness to rural countryside than for their recreational facilities or ornamental gardens – a fact which helps in the preservation of such ecologically unique areas as ancient woodland, relict heathland and London's fast-dwindling marshland habitats.

But a fascination for wildlife need by no means displace an appreciation of the city's more formal beauty handed down by England's long gardening tradition, in particular by the landscape movement of the eighteenth century.

London contains the whole range of landscape styles from the formal rectangular 'canals' and straight avenues of Hampton Court, to the more 'natural' style which later replaced it. The work of landscape architects of this new school can be seen at Syon Park, Danson Park and Kew Gardens, all designed at least in part by Lancelot 'Capability' Brown; and Chiswick House Gardens and Gunnersbury Park – the work of William Kent; and Golders Hill Park and the grounds of the Kenwood estate – both designed by Humphry Repton. There is much still to be learned today from the work of these men, much of which was succinctly summed up by Alexander Pope in 1713, when he advocated 'the amiable simplicity of unadorned Nature' with the advice that 'all the rules of gardening are reducible to three heads; the contrasts, the management of surprises and the concealment of bounds.'

Scope of this book

The scope of the present book perhaps calls for some explanation. Considering that even within the historic City boundary (the 'Square Mile'), there are 400 green spaces ranging in size from a suburban sitting room to three football pitches, there has been a need to be quite selective about which parks to include. Thus, the scope of the guidebook is restricted to what I consider to be the best, or most interesting, 100 of London's larger parks, appended with a reference section of a further 200 or so smaller parks, many of them of more local or historical interest. With a few important exceptions the 'top 100' have been selected from parks over one hundred acres (forty hectares) in the outer boroughs, and over twenty-five acres (ten hectares) in Inner London, i.e. the old County of London. For the appendix section, the parks have been selected (with the exception of the Tradescant Garden by Lambeth Palace) from those over two acres (about one hectare). As it stands, the book required research into about 400 parks, involving around one thousand written references, correspondence with about one hundred interested bodies, and visits to almost 250 of the city's parks, gardens, woodlands and commons. Hopefully, another writer will tackle the many smaller refuges within and close to the City, but for me London's inspiration will always remain in its opportunities for a sense of rural space, with all the soft lines and colours of the natural world.

Key to London's Major Parks and Woodlands

	Building of interest	Children's playground	Classical landscaping	General historical interest	Good walking	Museum or information centre	Nature trail	Ornamental gardens	Refreshments	Site of Special Scientific Interest	Specimen trees	Water feature	Wildlife	Woodland	Page
Alexandra Park	•	•		•				•				•	•		37
Avery Hill Park	•	•		•				•	•						39
Barnes Common & Putney Lower Common					•					•		•	•	•	41
Battersea Park		•		•				•	•		•	•	•		43
Bayhurst Wood Country Park					•	•	•		•	•			•	•	46
Beckenham Place Park	•	•		•		•	•	•	•		•		•	•	48
Beddington Park				•				•	•			•			51
Bedfords Park				•	•		•		•				•	•	53
Belair Park	•	•		•				•			•	•			55
Belhus Woods Country Park					•	•						•	•	•	57
Bentley Priory Park				•	•					•		•	•	•	60
Blackheath				•								•			63
Bostall Heath & Woods					•		•						•	•	66
Brent River Park	•	•			•			•	•			•			69
Brockwell Park	•	•		•								•			72
Burgess Park		•				•		•				•			74
Bushy Park		•	•	•	•			•				•	•	•	77
Cannizaro Park	•		•	•				•			•	•		•	80
Chelsea Physic Garden				•		•		•	•		•				82
Chiswick House Gardens	•		•	•		•		•	•		•	•		•	84
Clapham Common		•							•			•			86
Clissold Park	•	•		•				•	•			•			88
Colne Valley Park					•	•	•		•	•		•	•	•	90
Coombe Wood & Addington Hills	•			•	•			•	•				•	•	93
Coulsdon Common					•		•						•	•	95
Crystal Palace Park		•	•	•					•		•	•			97
Danson Park	•	•	•	•				•	•			•			100
Dulwich Park		•					•	•	•		•	•			102
Epping Forest	•			•	•	•	•		•	•		•	•	•	104
Farthing Down				•	•		•		•	•					108
Finsbury Park		•						•	•			•			110
Forty Hall Estate	•		•	•	•	•		•	•			•		•	112
Fryent Country Park					•		•					•	•	•	114
Fulham Palace Grounds & Bishop's Park	•	•		•				•	•		•				116
Golders Hill Park			•	•			•	•	•		•	•	•		118

	Building of interest	Children's playground	Classical landscaping	General historical interest	Good walking	Museum or information centre	Nature trail	Ornamental gardens	Refreshments	Site of Special Scientific Interest	Specimen trees	Water feature	Wildlife	Woodland	Page
Green Park				•							•				120
Greenwich Park	•	•	•	•		•		•	•		•	•	•		122
Gunnersbury Park	•	•	•	•		•		•	•			•		•	125
Hainault Forest					•		•		•			•	•	•	127
Hall Place	•			•		•		•	•			•			130
Ham Common					•							•	•	•	132
Ham House Grounds	•		•	•		•		•	•		•				134
Ham Riverside Lands					•								•	•	136
Hampstead Heath		•		•	•		•		•	•		•	•	•	139
Hampton Court Park	•		•	•	•	•		•	•		•	•	•		143
Happy Valley Park		•			•		•			•			•	•	145
Havering Country Park					•		•						•	•	147
Hayes Common					•								•	•	150
High Elms Estate				•	•	•		•	•				•	•	152
Highbury Fields		•							•						155
Highgate Wood & Queen's Wood		•			•				•				•	•	157
Holland Park	•	•		•				•	•			•	•	•	160
Horniman Gardens	•			•		•	•	•	•			•			162
Horsenden Hill		•			•		•						•	•	164
Hounslow Heath		•		•	•					•		•	•		167
Hyde Park		•		•					•		•	•	•		169
Joyden's Wood					•		•						•	•	172
Kennington Park		•		•				•	•						175
Kensington Gardens	•	•	•	•				•	•		•	•	•		178
Kenwood	•		•	•	•	•		•	•	•	•	•	•	•	180
Kew Gardens	•		•	•		•		•	•		•	•	•	•	182
King's Wood													•	•	184
Ladywell Fields		•			•				•			•			185
Lee Valley Park		•			•	•				•		•	•	•	187
Lesnes Abbey Woods	•			•	•		•	•	•	•			•	•	190
Maryon Park & Maryon Wilson Park		•						•	•			•		•	193
Mitcham Common					•				•			•	•		195
Monken Hadley Common					•							•	•	•	198
Morden Hall Park & Ravensbury Park	•	•		•							•	•			200
Osterley Park	•		•	•	•	•			•		•	•	•	•	202

	Building of interest	Children's playground	Classical landscaping	General historical interest	Good walking	Museum or information centre	Nature trail	Ornamental gardens	Refreshments	Site of Special Scientific Interest	Specimen trees	Water feature	Wildlife	Woodland	Page
Oxleas Woodlands		●			●		●		●	●			●	●	205
Parkland Walk		●			●	●	●						●		209
Peckham Rye Common & Park		●						●	●			●			212
Petts Wood					●								●	●	214
Plumstead Common		●		●	●							●			216
Primrose Hill		●													219
Ravenscourt Park	●	●		●				●	●			●			221
Regent's Park	●	●	●	●				●	●		●	●	●		223
Richmond Park	●	●		●	●			●	●		●	●	●	●	225
Ruislip Woods & Reservoir		●			●		●		●	●		●	●	●	229
Ruskin Park		●						●	●			●			233
St James's Park		●	●	●				●	●		●	●	●		235
Scadbury Park				●	●		●						●	●	238
Selsdon Wood					●								●	●	241
Southwark Park		●						●	●			●			244
Springfield Park	●	●		●				●	●		●	●			246
Stanmore Common					●					●		●	●	●	248
Streatham Common, The Rookery & Norwood Grove	●	●		●	●			●	●				●	●	250
Sydenham Hill Wood & Cox's Walk					●		●						●	●	254
Syon Park	●		●	●		●		●	●	●	●	●	●		256
Tooting Commons		●			●		●		●			●	●	●	258
Trent Park				●	●		●		●		●	●	●	●	260
Valentines Park	●	●		●				●				●			263
Victoria Park		●		●				●	●		●	●			265
Wandsworth Common		●			●	●	●		●			●	●	●	268
Wanstead Park			●	●	●							●	●	●	270
Waterlow Park	●			●				●	●			●	●		274
Welsh Harp Park		●		●	●					●		●	●		276
Whitewebbs Park	●			●	●		●		●			●	●	●	279
Wimbledon Common & Putney Heath	●			●	●	●	●		●	●		●	●	●	282

Regional Index

The regional index is designed to make it easier to see which parks are in your area. It is *not* divided up by postal districts, as these are notoriously illogical (with SE districts west of the City, SW districts north of the river and no NE or S). The parks have instead been grouped according to the London boroughs in which they fall. The two central regions represent the old County of London, while the outer boroughs are divided into five similarly-sized areas, three north of the river and two south. Bold type indicates entries in Major Parks and Woodlands, the remainder are to be found in the Appendix.

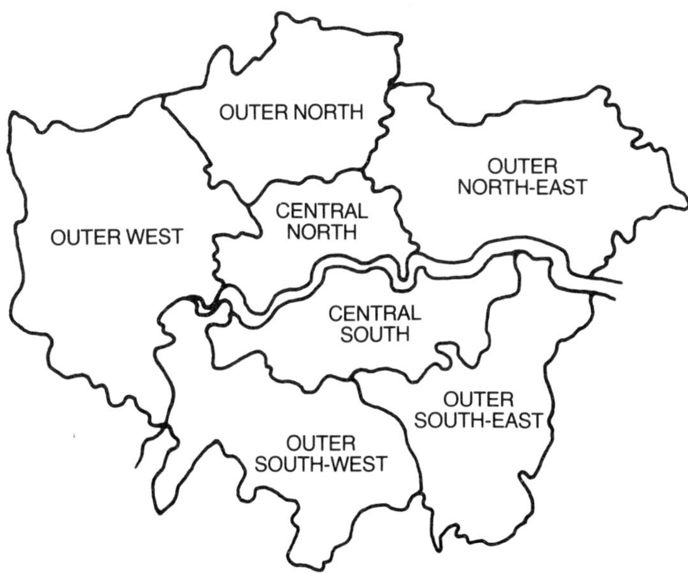

Outer West

The London Boroughs of Hillingdon, Ealing, Harrow, Brent, Hounslow and that part of Richmond north of the Thames

The two Royal Parks by Hampton Court Palace – Hampton Court Park and Bushy Park – together give a taste of the variety of London's parkland, ranging from wilderness right through to such formal seventeenth-century features as a rectangular canal and *patte d'oie*. Syon Park and Chiswick House Gardens, though not so well known, certainly deserve to be, especially to anyone with a serious interest in English garden design, and Syon Park's Butterfly House cannot fail to fascinate both children and adults alike. Other formal attractions at this end of the city include the York House Gardens and Marble Hill Park down by the Thames and, near Brentford, Boston Manor Park, Osterley Park and Gunnersbury Park. For wildlife enthusiasts there is the Ruislip Woods, Bayhurst Wood, Bentley Priory Park, Stanmore Common or the shores of the Welsh Harp Reservoir, or, on a more modest scale, Ten Acre Wood, Crane Park, Harrow Weald Common and the newly opened Gunnersbury Triangle. Covering some forty square miles on the city's western boundary is the Colne Valley Park – an area of countryside and reservoirs which functions as something between a stretch of green belt and a park in the more conventional sense, while a little closer to the city is the Brent River Park which links together enough recreational riverside land to be of interest to walkers and naturalists alike.

Outer South-West

The London Boroughs of Croydon, Sutton, Merton, Kingston upon Thames and that part of Richmond south of the Thames

Any prizes here must surely go to the Royal Botanic Gardens at Kew. Whatever the season and however bad the weather, Kew Gardens always has something to offer. Much less well known, but certainly worth travelling for, is Cannizaro Park just off Wimbledon Common, the little Coombe Wood gardens near Croydon and the seventeenth-century grounds of Ham House. For a breath of the countryside Richmond Park seems to ramble endlessly, with such a rural feel that one can scarcely credit it with being a part of London at all. Clustered around the royal deer park are many other worthwhile open spaces – Ham Common, East Sheen Common, Wimbledon Common, Ham Riverside Lands and – towards Richmond itself – the lovely Terrace Gardens. Equally well endowed is the area south of Croydon, where the extensive cluster of wild land includes the Coulsdon Commons, Selsdon Wood Nature Reserve, King's Wood, Croham Hurst and so on, together offering some excellent possibilities for long walks.

Outer South–East

The London Boroughs of Bromley and Bexley

For wild daffodils, Lesnes Abbey Woods is said to be unsurpassed in the south of England, and for heraldic topiary (the art of pruning evergreen shrubs and trees into imitative shapes) Hall Place is unique within the city. At Danson Park is an example of the work of Lancelot 'Capability' Brown, while at Sydenham, Crystal Palace Park (with its prehistoric monsters) continues to attract visitors from far afield, long after its huge glass exhibition hall was destroyed by fire. For wildlife, High Elms Estate and the newly opened Scadbury Park have much to offer, as do the adjoining woodlands of Chislehurst and St Paul's Cray Commons and Petts Wood. In spite of heavy use, the ponds at Keston Common continue to be both attractive and rich in wildlife, with some good opportunities for walking in the nearby woods of Hayes and West Wickham Commons. Of the region's smaller parks, perhaps the most varied and aesthetically designed would be Kelsey Park in Beckenham and the Church House and Library Gardens behind the Bromley Central Library.

Beckenham Place Park / Cator Park / Chislehurst Common / Church House and Library Gardens / **Crystal Palace Park / Danson Park /** Elmstead Wood / Frank's Park / **Hall Place** / Hawkwood Estate / **Hayes Common / High Elms Estate / Joyden's Wood** / Jubilee Park / Kelsey Park / Keston Common / **Lesnes Abbey Woods / Petts Wood** / Priory Gardens / St Paul's Cray Common / **Scadbury Park** / Shoulder-of-Mutton Green / Sidcup Place / Southmere Park (see Thamesmead Parks) / Spring Park / Thamesmead Parks / West Wickham Common / Woodland Way (see Thamesmead Parks)

Outer North-East

The London Boroughs of Havering, Redbridge, Waltham Forest, Newham and Barking

Though many of the parks in the north-east are rather plain, Valentines Park and Wanstead Park equal those in any of London's better-endowed suburbs. There are some excellent wild areas too, such as Bedfords Park, the northern part of Hainault Forest, and the whole 6000 acres of Epping Forest from Wanstead Flats right out to beyond the town of Epping. There have been some interesting new developments in the north-east too, with the opening of the wooded Havering Country Park at Havering-atte-Bower, the Fairlop Country Park, recently laid out on part of the former Fairlop Plain, and the 10,000-acre Lee Valley Park, which stretches for some twenty-three miles along the Lee Navigational Canal from London's East End right out to Ware in Hertfordshire. This last park offers some interesting long walks and a surprising range of wildlife in its various reservoirs and marshland habitats.

Barking Park / **Bedfords Park / Belhus Woods Country Park** / Bretons Outdoor Recreation Centre / Central Park, E6 / Central Park, Dagenham / Dagnam Park / Duck Wood / **Epping Forest** / Fairlop Country Park / **Hainault Forest** / Harrow Lodge Park / **Havering Country Park** / Highams Park / Hornchurch Country Park / Larkswood / **Lee Valley Park** / Lloyd Park / Lyle Park / Mayesbrook Park / Parsloes Park / Plashet Park / Roding Valley Linear Park / Royal Victoria Gardens / St Chad's Park / Tylers Common / Valence Park / **Valentines Park** / Walthamstow Marshes (see **Lee Valley Park**) / Wanstead Flats (see **Epping Forest**) / **Wanstead Park** / West Ham Park

Outer North

The London Boroughs of Barnet, Enfield and Haringey

On the northern edge of Greater London are some of the city's most attractive country estates – Forty Hall Estate, Whitewebbs Park, and Trent Park with its woodland trail for the blind. Further to the west stretches one of London's more densely wooded commons – Monken Hadley Common – and two remnants of the former Moat Mount Estate – Scratchwood and Moat Mount Open Spaces. A little closer to town, Alexandra Park is achieving new popularity through its connection via a walk along a disused railway line (the Parkland Walk) to Highgate and Queen's Wood and on to Finsbury Park – one of the city's oldest municipal parks. Hampstead Heath, to the west, is so accessible and varied that it must surely rank as one of London's most attractive stretches of open land, linking, as it does, several former private estates – Golders Hill Park, The Hill garden and Kenwood. Practically unknown outside its immediate neighbourhood is the Avenue House Grounds in Finchley which, for its wealth of specimen trees, is well worth a trip from much further afield.

Alexandra Park / Arnos Park / Avenue House Grounds / Big Wood / Brent Reservoir (see **Welsh Harp Park**) / Broomfield Park / Bruce Castle Park / Cherry Tree Wood / Coldfall Wood / Downhills Park / **Finsbury Park / Forty Hall Estate / Golders Hill Park** / Grovelands Park / **Hampstead Heath / Highgate Wood** / Hilly Fields Park / **Kenwood / Lee Valley Park** / Moat Mount Open Space / **Monken Hadley Common /** Oakwood Park / **Parkland Walk** / Priory Park / Pymmes Park / Queen's Wood (see **Highgate Wood**) / Scratchwood Open Space / Town Park / **Trent Park / Welsh Harp Park / Whitewebbs Park**

Central North

The London Boroughs of Hammersmith & Fulham, Kensington & Chelsea, Camden, Islington, Hackney, and Tower Hamlets and the Cities of London and Westminster

Besides including all the central royal parks – St James's, Green Park and Hyde Park, Kensington Gardens, Regent's Park and Primrose Hill – this area contains London's first 'People's Park' (Victoria Park) and England's second oldest botanic garden (Chelsea Physic Garden). Other deserved favourites are Waterlow Park in Highgate, Holland Park in Kensington, Springfield Park near Stoke Newington and the little Hill garden tucked away within the wilder acres of Hampstead Heath. Also good for wildlife and long walks is the Lee Valley Park, in particular the Walthamstow Marshes, and the old Abney Park Cemetery in the centre of Stoke Newington. Among the more imaginative recent innovations in the area is the successful little community park at Meanwhile Gardens in Kensal Town and the ecologically orientated Camley Street Natural Park near King's Cross station.

Abney Park Cemetery / Bethnal Green Gardens / Bishop's Park (see **Fulham Palace Grounds**) / Brook Green / Bunhill Fields / Camley Street Natural Park / **Chelsea Physic Garden** / Clapton Common / **Clissold Park** / Coram's Fields / Eelbrook Common / **Fulham Palace Grounds** / Furnivall Gardens / Geffrye's Garden / **Green Park** / Hackney Downs / Hackney Marsh / **Hampstead Heath** / **Highbury Fields** / The Hill garden (see **Golders Hill Park**) / **Holland Park** / Hurlingham Park / **Hyde Park** / Island Gardens / **Kensington Gardens** / **Kenwood** / Kilburn Grange Park / King Edward Memorial Park / **Lee Valley Park** / Limehouse Churchyard / Lincoln's Inn Fields / London Fields / Meanwhile Gardens / Meath Gardens / Mile End Park / Millfields / New River Walk / Paddington Recreation Ground / Parliament Hill (see **Hampstead Heath**) / Parson's Green / **Primrose Hill** / **Ravenscourt Park** / **Regent's Park** / Royal Hospital South Grounds / Russell Square / St George's Gardens / **St James's Park** / St John's Church Wood Gardens / St Luke's Garden / St Pancras Gardens / Shepherd's Bush Common / **Springfield Park** / Stepney Churchyard / Stoke Newington Common / Tower Hamlets Cemetery / Victoria Embankment Gardens / **Victoria Park** / Victoria Tower Gardens / **Waterlow Park** / Well Street Common / Wormwood Scrubs

Central South

The London Boroughs of Wandsworth, Lambeth, Southwark, Lewisham and Greenwich

Central though Battersea Park is, it often gets overshadowed by its northern royal neighbours, but the erection here in 1985 of the London Peace Pagoda placed it once again in the limelight. Dulwich Park has long been a favourite for its rhododendrons, azaleas and crocuses (though few know of its wealth of specimen trees) and Greenwich Park remains famous for its old observatory; but there are many more excellent parks which remain more or less undiscovered – the Avery Hill winter garden near Eltham, Horniman Gardens behind the Horniman Museum and The Rookery garden at the top of Streatham Common, plus many smaller parks such as Manor House Gardens, Sydenham Wells Park, Myatt's Fields and Well Hall Pleasaunce. For wildlife, Bostall Heath and Woods and Oxleas Woodlands are just two of the many stretches of open land making up the Green Chain, which links the Thames Barrier and Thamesmead with Cator Park, New Beckenham. Interesting new developments south of the river include the ambitious new Burgess Park at Walworth, the tiny ecological parks at Lavender Pond and Dulwich Upper Wood and the gardens behind the Tradescant Trust Museum of Garden History, by Lambeth Palace.

Archbishop's Park / **Avery Hill Park / Battersea Park / Beckenham Place Park / Belair Park /** Birchmere Park (see Thamesmead Parks) / **Blackheath** / Blythe Hill Fields / **Bostall Heath and Woods** / Brenchley Gardens / **Brockwell Park** / Brookmill Park / **Burgess Park** / Camberwell Green / Castle Wood (see **Oxleas Woodlands**) / Charlton Park / Chinbrook Meadows / **Clapham Common** / Cox's Walk (see **Sydenham Hill Wood**) / **Dulwich Park** / Dulwich Upper Wood / Eaglesfield / Eltham Common (see **Oxleas Woodlands**) / Eltham Park (see **Oxleas Woodlands**) / Falconwood Field (see **Oxleas Woodlands**) / Faraday Garden / Forster Memorial Park / Garratt Green / Geraldine Mary Harmsworth Park / **Greenwich Park** / Hilly Fields / Hornfair Park / **Horniman Gardens** / Jackwood (see **Oxleas Woodlands**) / Jubilee Gardens / **Kennington Park** / King George's Park / **Ladywell Fields** / Lavender Pond Ecological Park / Manor House Gardens / **Maryon Park** / Maryon Wilson Park (see **Maryon Park**) / Mayow Park / Mountsfield Park / Myatt's Fields / Norwood Park / One Tree Hill / **Oxleas Woodlands / Peckham Rye Common and Park / Plumstead Common** / Putney Lower Common (see **Barnes Common**) /

London's Major Parks & Woodlands

Alexandra Park

Alexandra Park Road, N22

How to get there: by train to Alexandra Palace (previously known as Wood Green) station. By bus: W3.
Origin of the name: named in honour of Princess Alexandra of Denmark who married the Prince of Wales and became Queen Alexandra when her husband came to the throne as King Edward VII.
Area: 194 acres (79 hectares).
Owned and maintained by: London Borough of Haringey.

This hill is the former commercial pleasure grounds of the famous Alexandra Palace, or 'Ally Pally', erected here by the Alexandra Park Company between 1864 and 1873. Just sixteen days after the public opening ceremony, the palace caught fire and was burnt to the ground. Not easily thwarted, the owners immediately began the construction all over again and within two years the People's Palace had been entirely rebuilt. In July 1980, however, this too was almost completely destroyed by fire. Now, for the third time, the old entertainment complex is under construction – this time with the hope of serving as an exhibition and conference centre.

Of the many events that were staged in the palace grounds, balloon ascents, horse racing and firework displays by the famous firm of James Pain were some of the most popular. One of the more spectacular of these pyrotechnic displays was a show entitled 'The Last Days of Pompeii', first produced here in 1888. For the event, the boating lake was decorated to represent the Bay of Naples, with boats and gondolas, while the island became Pompeii with its temples, palaces, squares, columns and amphitheatres; all dominated by an enormous canvas of Mount Vesuvius. A cast of 200 played the parts of soldiers, slaves, priests and flower girls as the story of Ione and Glaucus was enacted. In the tremendous finale Vesuvius erupted, flames burst from the palaces and temples, with columns and buildings crumbling and crashing to the ground. All this was followed by a gigantic firework display.

In the same year, balloon ascents from Alexandra Park were also taking on a new dimension. An American gymnast known as Professor Baldwin, anxious to give added interest to his balloon ascents, began making parachute jumps that would demonstrate how he, the parachute and the balloon could all land back in the same spot within the park. Unfortunately these feats were not always successful. Once the performer landed in France, while other landings were made on the roofs of nearby houses. Occasionally Baldwin would land in trees or find himself trying to avoid the trains on the nearby main line. All a part of good nineteenth-century entertainment.

Alexandra Park's attractions are today perhaps a little less spectacular but the park is still popular for its elevated views out to the south and east, to Telecom Tower, Crystal Palace Tower and beyond. Behind the palace is the boating lake, a children's playground and an artificial ski-slope. To the eastern end of the park lies a delightful nature reserve with its own wildlife pond. To enrich the pond's ecological diversity a number of wetland plants have been transferred here by members of the British Trust for Conservation Volunteers from the Welsh Harp Reservoir when some of the reservoir's fringing vegetation needed to be cleared to improve the conditions for its wildfowl.

Over the years 120 bird species have been sighted within Alexandra Park, of which forty-six are known to breed here, and the park's range of butterflies is at least as impressive as that of the nearby Parkland Walk. This unusual walk, which follows the old Alexandra Palace railway line, links the Palace with Finsbury Park via Queen's and Highgate woods, providing one of London's most interesting ecological corridors. This, of course, contributes to the park's wildlife as does the rail link on the park's eastern side, which provides a migration route for both fauna and flora between Hertfordshire and King's Cross.

Alexandra Palace and Park were purchased 'for the free use of the people for ever' by the local authority in 1900, with the ownership passing to Haringey Borough Council in January 1980, just six months before the most recent fire.

Avery Hill Park

Avery Hill Road, SE9

How to get there: by train to Falconwood station and a half-mile walk. By bus: 124, 124A, 132, 228 or 299.
Origin of the name: apparently a corruption of the nineteenth-century name Aviary Hill.
Area: 96 acres (39 hectares) including the 19-acre (8-hectare) nursery.
Owned and maintained by: London Borough of Greenwich.

The magnificent domed winter garden here houses many hundreds of exotic trees, flowers, shrubs, cacti, palms and ferns from all over the world. The garden consists of three temperature-controlled glasshouses – temperate, cool and tropical – each designed to have at least some plants in bloom at all times of the year.

The winter garden entrance takes one first into the central temperate house under the main ninety-foot-high dome, with a towering Chinese palm at its centre. The palm, which was donated by the Royal Botanic Gardens at Kew when the garden was reopened to the public in 1962, is now well over one hundred years old. Arranged around this are trees from India, along with various plants from South America and Africa, lemons, tangerines, grapefruit and – just to the left as you enter – an attractive display of flowering house plants.

Through the door to the right is the cool house with camellias, oleanders and acacias surrounding an ornamental pool with fountains, at the centre of which is a sensuous white marble statue of the Greek goddess Galatea, carved in 1880 by the Italian sculptor Leopoldo Ansiglioni.

Perhaps most interesting is the tropical house, with its Bluefield bananas, Arabian coffee, Mexican breadfruit, pineapples, Joseph's coat-of-many-colours and elephant's ears. As in the cool and temperate houses, the plants here are chosen for their interest to the general public rather than for any specialist or scientific value, and a few are included in the collection as examples of specimens suitable for growing as house plants.

Originally the brainchild of Colonel John Thomas North, the winter garden was built in about 1890 in order to 'render the Colonel and his family independent of outdoor exercise during inclement weather'. Colonel North – also known at one time as the Nitrate King – had acquired his wealth through the building of a business empire based on nitrates, coal, water, cement, steel, gold and railways. The Colonel acquired the lease of the original twenty-acre Avery Hill Estate in 1882, but as his business empire grew so too did his estate, and by October 1891 the extent of property here either leased or owned by him had reached over 671 acres.

Colonel North had the old house pulled down, retaining just one room which he then incorporated into his magnificent new fifty-room mansion. Forming part of this 'most lavishly fitted and decorated' new house was a handsome conservatory and winter garden, fernery, mushroom house, fruit room, vineries and special greenhouses for the culture of peaches, figs and cucumbers. All this luxury was, however, short-lived, for less than six years later the Colonel died of a heart attack while attending a board meeting at his office in Grey Church Street on 6 May 1896. He was aged fifty-four and had UK assets of over £500,000.

In 1902, the London County Council purchased eighty-four acres of the estate along with the Colonel's mansion and winter garden – the mansion and its immediate grounds being later set apart for their present use as a teacher training college, while the parkland and winter garden were opened for public recreation in May 1903.

The winter garden itself, which is thought to be the only one of its kind in Greater London, was seriously damaged by a flying bomb during the Second World War, and it was not until 1962 (when the central Chinese palm was donated by Kew Gardens) that it was reopened to the public. The winter gardens are now open all the year round, except on Christmas Day and the first Monday of each month. Opening is generally restricted to the afternoons between 1.00 p.m. and 4.00 p.m. (Portable ramp access for wheelchairs is provided.)

Most of the rest of the park is flat, open grassland used as playing fields, though there are some attractive trees and parts of the huge plant nursery area are open to the public. There is also a pleasant walled-in formal rose garden and a pretty bed of assorted purple and white heathers, both situated next to the winter garden.

Teas and snacks are available in the refreshment house from March to September (wheelchair-accessible loos adjacent) and a spacious car park is provided next to the college, off the entrance to the nursery.

Barnes Common and Putney Lower Common

Queens Ride, SW13

How to get there: by train to Barnes station. By bus: 22, 33, 37, 74, 264, or 265.
Origin of the name: in the eleventh century the name Barnes was spelt in the singular Berne, meaning 'the barn'. Putney Lower Common is so called to distinguish it from Putney Upper Common (i.e. Putney Heath), Putney meaning 'Putta's quay or landing place'.
Area: Barnes Common is 123 acres (50 hectares); Putney Lower Common is 40 acres (16 hectares).
Owned and maintained by: Barnes Common is owned by the Church Commissioners and maintained by the London Borough of Richmond upon Thames. Putney Lower Common is under the care of the Conservators of Wimbledon and Putney Commons.

Though much wilder than many London commons, Barnes Common is still said by some to be one of the city's best kept open spaces. Up until the end of the last century it was quite marshy with a lush vegetation and rich variety of fauna, but while drainage work carried out here around 1880 would certainly have improved the common's recreational appeal, it did take its toll on the wildlife. And yet Barnes Common has still sufficient richness and variety in its fauna and flora to warrant the protective designation of Site of Special Scientific Interest (SSSI).

Among the rough, uneven grassland are clumps of gorse and broom amidst patches of oak and birch and tangles of blackberry bushes. There are trifid bur-marigolds, horse radish, cow parsley, periwinkle, St John's wort, white campion, lesser celandine, ragwort and lovely shows of the lilac flowers of rosebay willowherb. There are even a few bluebells, the odd heather plant and – rather rare for this part of Britain – the burnet rose.

Since the late nineteenth century, many trees have been planted – often either in formal avenues or in single rows. Apart from oak and birch, these include lime, London plane, horse chestnut and black poplar. Elsewhere the common's wilder character resumes with any amount of elder, hawthorn, holly and sycamore. While the noise of the railway and road serves as a reminder of the urban setting, the dense foliage of summer still offers attractive seclusion to visiting picnickers. Overhead, kestrels soar or hover and herons occasionally pass by, while on the common itself jays and magpies frequently nest and chaffinches and nuthatches are not uncommon.

Putney Lower Common to the east is, by comparison, much flatter and more open. Though the distinction between the two commons might today seem academic, the precise boundary between them has long been a subject of contention. At least as early as 1589 the folk from the township of Barnes were refusing those of Putney the right to use their end of the common and would impound any of their cattle found on it. To stop the offending cattle from straying, a manorial ditch was dug along the boundary and, although this has since largely been filled in, traces (especially at the northern end) can still be seen. The gatekeeper, whose job it was to allow traffic along Mill Hill Road while preventing cows from straying between the commons, lived at the small cottage at the south-western corner of Putney Cemetery.

This central road acquired its name from the mills which once stood on the common: a post-mill built here in 1740 and blown down in 1780, and a tower mill that was demolished in 1838.

Though the old Putney Cemetery remains to this day enclosed from the common by a high wall, Barnes Cemetery to the north of this was appropriately returned to the common when the mortuary and porter's lodge were demolished in 1967.

Barnes Common has been remarkably free of the battles over common rights that have involved most of London's commons. For over 1000 years the Dean and Chapter of St Paul's had been the lords of the manor here under a grant made long before the Norman Conquest. It is to their credit that they made arrangements for the proper care of the common for posterity without insisting on any purchase from them of manorial rights.

The case with Putney Common was, however, not so simple. In 1864, the Lord of the Manor, Lord Spencer, in an attempt to override common rights, announced his plans to sell 300 acres of common land for building development. It was only after much campaigning and argument that Putney Lower Common was finally protected under the Wimbledon and Putney Commons Act, 1871.

Probably the most attractive part of Putney Lower Common is a less well-known riverside strip following the Beverley Brook, which provides a pleasant pedestrian link between these two commons and the river Thames. In fact, following this brookside path down to the river forms the first leg of an enjoyable walk along the Embankment, over Putney Bridge and into Bishop's Park and the grounds of Fulham Palace – a distance of about one and a half miles.

Battersea Park

Queenstown Road, SW8

How to get there: by train to Battersea Park station. By bus: 19, 39, 44, 45, 49, 137 or 170.
Origin of the name: from the eleventh-century name of the parish Batrices ege, meaning 'Beaduric's island', referring to the fact that the area was slightly higher than the surrounding riverside marshes.
Area: 200 acres (81 hectares).
Owned and maintained by: London Borough of Wandsworth.

Battersea Park is noted for its remarkable variety of mature trees, boasting this country's tallest recorded black walnut tree (five metres higher than the one at Marble Hill Park) and the largest hybrid buckeye tree (in both height and girth). The park is also renowned for its exceptionally fine examples of maidenhair tree, Chinese thuja, black Italian poplar, Italian alder, whitebeam, Kentucky coffee tree, red horse chestnut, narrowleaf ash, Chinese privet and foxglove tree. Sadly, though, the removal of fences and shrubs in recent years has led to a marked loss in bird life, especially of spotted flycatcher, willow warbler, blackcap and long-tailed tit, and a noticeable reduction in numbers of blackbird, song thrush and robin.

The Festival Gardens, a little north of the centre of the park, retain some of their original features, notably the formal flower gardens. The gardens were created in 1951 as part of the Festival of Britain celebrations, attracting eight million visitors in that year alone. Other attractions within the park include the children's zoo and the boats for hire not far from the café at the north-eastern end of the lake. Less well-known is the excellent and comprehensive herb garden on display within the staff courtyard at the north-western corner of the park and the recently-formed nature reserve – Mist's Pitch – named after the London Wildlife Trust's honorary park warden, Brian Mist. These two acres near the park's north-eastern corner are rich in both fauna and flora, especially with regard to butterflies. There have even been plans for the repair of the old Pump House by the lake for use as a wildlife education centre. For the disabled, Battersea Park is one of the more accessible, with both good internal roads and toilets with wheelchair access (adjacent to the ladies' toilets at the athletics pavilion). There is a demonstration garden especially designed for wheelchair-users and ramps for access to the bowling green.

For many, the park's most inspirational feature is the majestic new London Peace Pagoda – the first major monument in central London to be dedicated entirely to peace. It was a gift to the capital from the late Most Venerable Nichidatsu Fujii and the Buddhist Order, Nipponzan Myohoji, and was formally presented to the people of London on 14 May 1985. As a Buddhist stupa based on ancient Japanese and Indian designs, the pagoda depicts various scenes from Lord Buddha's life. On the south side, the gilded Buddha statue shows his birth at Lumbini in the Himalayas; the eastern niche – his enlightenment at Buddhagaya; to the north, facing the river Thames – his first sermon at Sarnath; and finally, in the west-facing niche – Buddha's death at Kushinara.

Until about 1560, most of the land now occupied by Battersea Park was under water at high tide. Around that date Battersea Fields, as it was then known, was reclaimed from the Thames by means of a rough embankment and added to the common land of the manor of Battersea. It was not, however, for another 300 years that the land was opened as a public park – one of the first of its kind in London.

Meanwhile, the land had been partly under cultivation, but mostly used for grazing, pigeon-shooting and gypsy encampments. Battersea Fields was also the site of several public houses, the most notorious of which was the Red House which, though said to have been quite aristocratic in its early days, was later to acquire a rather scandalous reputation in connection with its Sunday fairs. Every summer, during the early nineteenth century, these bawdy events were regularly held here, shocking the likes of Thomas Kirk, a city missionary, who wrote:

> And surely if ever there was a place out of hell that surpassed Sodom and Gomorrah in ungodliness and abomination, this was it. Here the worst men and the vilest of the human race seemed to try to outvie each other in wicked deeds. I have gone to this sad spot on the afternoon and evening of the Lord's day, when there have been from 60 to 120 horses and donkeys racing, foot-racing, walking matches, flying boats, flying horses, roundabouts, theatres, comic actors, shameless dancers, conjurers, fortune-tellers, gamblers of every description, drinking-booths, stalls, hawkers and vendors of all kinds of articles. It would take a more graphic pen than mine to describe the mingled shouts and noises and the unmentionable doings of this pandemonium on earth.

By the 1840s, events here had apparently degenerated to such a state that the government decided to step in, closing several of the pubs and acquiring the Fields to be laid out as a public park.

As yet, London had neither municipal parks nor the legislation to create them, so it required a special Act of Parliament to authorize, in 1846, 'the Commissioners of Her Majesty's Woods to form a Royal Park in Battersea Fields, in the Parish of Saint Mary, Battersea, in the County of Surrey'. Note that Battersea Park is referred to here as a royal park – a designation which reflects the fact that the setting up of the park (like Victoria Park in the East End) pre-dated any form of metropolitan government and hence required royal assent, even though neither park was in fact created for, or belonged to, the Crown.

A large part of the original 320 acres purchased for the new park was then leased out for building as a way of paying for the extensive laying-out work, which involved both the building of a new embankment and the raising of the entire park by dumping several hundred thousand cubic yards of earth fill here – most of this came from the Victoria Docks extension works. The park's design was to the plans of Sir James Pennethorne and most of the important features of his original design still remain – for example, the carriageways, lake and central avenue.

Though little now remains of the old sub-tropical garden laid out in 1864 to the west of the lake with tree ferns, palms and giant grasses, the Old English garden at the north-western corner (by the staff yard) still survives. This tranquil little garden remains (in spite of recent neglect) one of the park's finest features.

Following its formal opening by Queen Victoria in 1858, Battersea Park became a centre for the late nineteenth-century cycling craze. Not only did it become one of London's most popular places for folk to learn to ride their new machines, but it became for a time quite the fashionable place (especially for ladies) to take a morning promenade – followed by an elegant park breakfast by the lake. In fact, Battersea Park remains to this day one of the few central parks where cycling is freely permitted.

Bayhurst Wood Country Park

Breakspear Road, Uxbridge

Map: see Ruislip Woods and Reservoir, page 229.
How to get there: by bus: 114, 128 or E2 to Reservoir Road and then take the public footpath (for one mile) along the southern boundary of Mad Bess Wood.
Origin of the name: believed to be derived from the personal name Baega and the Old English word *hyrst*, meaning 'wooded hill' – hence 'Baega's wooded hill'.
Area: 98 acres (40 hectares).
Owned and maintained by: London Borough of Hillingdon, with some assistance from the Countryside Commission and Colne Valley Regional Park Authority.

This area of ancient woodland, covering the crown of a hill on the eastern side of the Colne valley, is one of a number of recreational areas known collectively as the Colne Valley Park. To the east, the wood is linked by footpaths through Mad Bess Wood, Copse Wood and Ruislip Common to Ruislip Lido and Park Wood, which together form an extensive stretch of public woodland and water covering some 760 acres. Together, these woods provide an important wildlife habitat, in particular for a vast variety of fungi; in fact, over a number of visits by the British Mycological Society, a total of about 450 different species had been recorded here by 1981 – a fact which has contributed to the designation of Bayhurst Wood and the neighbouring Ruislip Woods as Sites of Special Scientific Interest.

Bayhurst Wood itself consists mainly of pedunculate and sessile oaks, beech, sweet chestnut and hornbeam (a number of which show signs of former coppicing). Of the remaining trees perhaps the most interesting is the relatively rare wild service tree – a tree whose presence is generally confined to ancient woodlands such as this and neighbouring Ruislip Woods, i.e. woods which have for the most part been under more or less continuous tree cover since the last Ice Age. Wild service – the name apparently derives from the use of the fruit by the Romans for flavouring beer (*cerevisia*) – has lobed leaves rather like the sycamore, with white flowers in May and greenish-brown apple-shaped berries in October.

The country park originally formed part of a large estate, which for some time was in use as a game reserve. Just north of the centre of the wood a few bricks from the original gamekeeper's cottage can still be seen and nearby a patch of stinging nettles which, since these generally grow only on ground that has at some time been cultivated, probably indicates the whereabouts of what was once the gamekeeper's garden.

On the wood's south-western perimeter a small pond has been created by the country park staff in order to enhance the park's wildlife interest, and this now provides a habitat for a number of aquatic plants and some interesting fauna including geese, swans, herons and ducks.

A more recent innovation is the open-air woodland craft museum – an area of some five acres devoted to demonstrating the trades once associated with such woods as Bayhurst. Though the ecological significance of traditional woodland management – coppicing and pollarding – is well illustrated in some other parks, this museum is, to my knowledge, the first project within Greater London to be aimed primarily at demonstrating its economic significance. This novel idea is the brainchild of Bayhurst's head warden, George Mist, who, since 1982, has been developing the museum site to demonstrate charcoal burning, broom-, rake- and hurdle-making, woodcutting, thatch-making and wood turning. The charcoal burner's encampment shows the various stages of kiln construction and the style of the turf huts in which the charcoal burners used to live. Nearby is a reconstruction of one of the traditional and fascinatingly simple pole lathes, a saw gantry and a practical, if basic, hurdle-maker's vice. The new museum is scheduled to be open on occasional weekends.

Bayhurst Wood is well equipped with facilities for the picnicker, with excellent car parking space, toilets (including those with wheelchair access), piped water and barbecue grills (which can be booked by contacting the lettings officer, Uxbridge 50111 ext. 3454). There is a riding trail round the park's perimeter and a one-and-a-quarter-mile waymarked nature trail for the use of the general public, leaflets for which are available from Hillingdon libraries and from the park's own information centre/refreshment kiosk. This kiosk, which serves tea and coffee, is open (weather permitting) every Sunday from Easter to October.

Beckenham Place Park

Beckenham

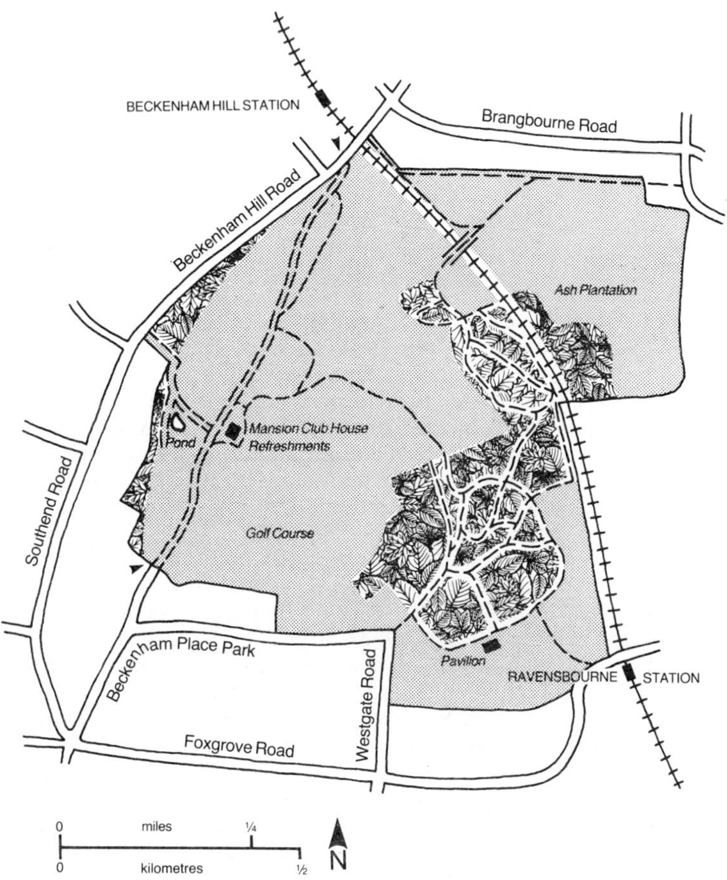

How to get there: by train to Beckenham Hill station. By bus: 54.
Origin of the name: Beckenham means 'Beohha's village'. The park itself is named after the manor house which is today still the park's focal point.
Area: 213 acres (86 hectares).
Owned and maintained by: London Borough of Lewisham.

Beckenham Place Park is one of the gems of this part of London and is best appreciated from the high ground by the mansion, from where the spacious rolling grassland of the golf course can be seen stretching to a distant wooded horizon.

The mansion was built by the timber merchant John Cator, shortly after he became Lord of the Manor of Beckenham in 1773. It is built of Portland stone in the Classic style with an imposing portico, the Ionic columns of which were brought here from another mansion at Wricklesworth, Blackheath.

John Cator was the Sheriff for Kent in 1781 and Member of Parliament for Ipswich – until he lost his seat for bribery in 1784. His contemporaries described him as 'a purse-proud Tradesman coarse in his Expressions, and vulgar in Manners and Pronunciation, though very intelligent, and full both of money and good sense' (quoted from Mrs Thrale of Dr Johnson fame).

Cator was responsible for the planting of many of the trees here, as apparently was the famous Swedish botanist Linnaeus, whom Cator is said to have entertained here.

Both the mansion and the manor were to remain in the Cator family until the acquisition of the grounds by the London County Council in 1927. The Cator estate was then opened as a public park two years later, on 27 May 1929.

Today, Cator's former mansion houses an all-year-round cafeteria, golf club facilities and the Green Woodpecker Nature Centre. The centre, which is designed to introduce the visitor to the park's ecology, features various displays relating to the park's plant, animal and insect life. The nature centre's opening hours are subject to seasonal changes but it is open by appointment during weekdays for organizations and school parties. (For further details telephone the warden on 01-650 6695.)

Although over the past twenty-five years or so the park's bird population has declined (from the sixty-five species then recorded), Beckenham Place Park still supports, or at least attracts, over forty-five species. Within the park at least sixty different wildflowers can still be found and among the park's estimated 15,000 trees, a remarkable sixty different species are represented. There are some magnificent oaks, as well as black mulberry, swamp cypress, Atlas cedar, Persian ironwood and sweet gum. In fact the woodland and copses together cover around sixty of the park's total 213 acres.

The largest portion of the park, however, is devoted to an eighteen-hole golf course – the first municipal golf course in London and today so popular that in spite of opening every day of the year, the demand for bookings at weekends is such that these need to be decided by ballot.

Across to the east of the railway the park continues. Though mostly flat grassland serving as playing fields, there is a small continuation here of the ash plantation west of the railway which up until about forty years ago still used to be coppiced. The main woodland, however, is an area to the south-east of the mansion known as Summerhouse Hill Wood, which is well managed with the judicious use of low, open fencing and some new planting where natural woodland regeneration is failing to get a foothold.

Close by the mansion (to the west) is the park's only pond, some thirty feet deep, beneath which is a well that is believed to have once supplied water to the house and stables via conduits. I am told that the surrounding mud is like quicksand, and that in some places one could be sucked under in a few minutes – which is why the pond is so securely fenced!

Also nearby are the more formal gardens and rockeries of roses and of heathers, with plenty of wooden benches from which to enjoy the view. And wheelchair users will no doubt be heartened to discover here that thought has been given to the provision of access ramps.

Those with more energetic interests may be interested to learn that Beckenham Place Park forms part of the newly planned Green Chain Walk which now links Cator Park just to the west with Thamesmead and the new Flood Barrier on the river Thames. For further details refer to the walks section. Within the park itself there is also a number of nature trails, for which informative guide booklets are available from the Engineer and Surveyor's Department, Deptford Town Hall, New Cross Road, SE14 6AE (01-692 1288).

Beddington Park

Croydon Road, Wallington

How to get there: by train to Hackbridge station. By bus: 151, 213, 234, 403, 408, 716 or 726.
Origin of the name: Beddington means 'farm or estate associated with Bēada'.
Area: 149 acres (60 hectares).
Owned and maintained by: London Borough of Sutton.

This consists of two adjoining properties: one, Beddington Park proper; the other, an old private botanical garden known as Grange Park – both of which were formerly part of the Carew estate and both of which have the Wandle as their main feature. Beddington Park itself consists mainly of gently rolling grassland scattered with mature trees; the smaller Grange Park, by contrast, is more formal with such attractive features as an elaborate pergola, a three-and-a-half-acre ornamental lake and a restaurant. A little further to the north, over the park boundary, is a further stretch of open land – Beddington Sewage Farm – which serves to enhance the parks' wildlife interest by effectively functioning as a bird sanctuary for a number of such uncommon species as little ringed plovers, turtle doves and stonechats.

The Carew family first came to Beddington in 1350, following the outbreak in England of the Black Death epidemic, and continued to live here for the next 500 years. Their estate, which at one time extended north as far as Streatham and as far south as Epsom, was once famous for its hunting – in fact deer were to be seen roaming in Beddington Park until 1855.

Through this park Sir Walter Raleigh used to ride while courting Elizabeth Throgmorton (Sir Francis Carew's niece) and several monarchs – Henry VIII, Queen Elizabeth I and James I – were at various times entertained here. The following seventeenth-century account gives some idea of the remarkable extent of the Carews' hospitality when Queen Elizabeth came to visit the estate in August 1600:

> Here I will conclude with a conceit of that delicate knight, Sir Francis Carew: who, for the better accomplishment of his royall entertainment of our late Queen of happy memory, at his house at Beddington, led her Majesty to a cherry tree, whose fruit he had of purpose kept back from ripening, at the least one month after all cherries had taken their farewell of England. This secret he performed, by straining a tent or cover

> of canvas over the whole tree, and wetting the same now and then with a scoop or horn, as the heat of the weather required; and so, by withholding the sun-beames from reflecting upon the berries, they grew both great, and were very long before they had gotten their cherry colour: and when he was assured of her Majesties comming, he removed the tent, and a few sunny dayes brought them to their full maturity.

Apart from extending the cherry season, Sir Francis was also credited with being the first person successfully to cultivate orange trees in England – his orangery here producing in its best years over 10,000 fruit. Sir Francis's pomegranates also became a subject of celebrity, for when John Evelyn visited the estate in 1658, he remarked how even these trees bore fruit.

Just over two hundred years later, on the break-up of the Beddington estate in 1864, the old mansion was purchased for use by the Female Orphan Asylum (later known as the Royal Female Orphan Asylum) and has since been used as a school.

Of Gothic Revival style, the present building dates mostly from the eighteenth century, though some remains of the historic seventeenth-century orangery adjacent to this still survive, as does the late fifteenth-century Great Hall.

The first thirteen acres of the present park were opened 'as a public open space for all time' in 1925, growing by the mid-1930s to ninety-seven acres and then extended again by the public opening of Grange Park in April 1936.

The Grange Park gardens, which at one time were renowned throughout Surrey, were created by Alfred Smee and were the subject of a classic 650-page work on horticulture written by him in 1872 entitled over-modestly *My Garden*. The Grange itself – a Tudor-style mansion – was built by Smee in 1879, though this burnt down in 1960 and has since been replaced by the present restaurant building.

Bedfords Park

Lower Bedfords Road, Romford

How to get there: by train to Romford station and then take the 103 bus. By tube to Dagenham East on the District Line and then take the 103 bus. By bus: 103, 339 or 712 to Chase Cross.
Origin of the name: from its having formed part of the property held in the Middle Ages by the family of Robert de Bedeford.
Area: 215 acres (87 hectares).
Owned and maintained by: London Borough of Havering.

This semi-natural parkland consists of undulating slopes rising steeply to over 300 feet above the Thames valley to provide extensive views across east London towards the Kentish hills. Random strips of oak and hawthorn divide this grassland into a number of warm south- and west-facing meadows, offering an interesting sequence of views either south-west to Shooters Hill, west towards the City, or a little north of west towards neighbouring Bower House and Bower Wood. The park has plenty of wildlife interest too, with a number of small ponds, scattered woodlands and a rich variety of wildflowers. The park's focal point, though, is a small deer sanctuary at the centre of the property and, just to the north of this, overlooking much of the pleasant scenery, an attractive modern cafeteria.

Bedfords Park, as we know it today, was originally enclosed in the late fifteenth century for use as a farm by Sir Thomas Cooke, one-time Lord Mayor of London and resident of nearby Gidea Hall. Along with several other large estates in the area, the property remained in the Cooke family for almost two hundred years. The park's modern history began with its acquisition in 1771 by John Heaton – one of the area's most influential men – who built the manor house of Bedfords on the site of the present café. In the latter half of the nineteenth century this original two-storey brick mansion was enlarged, while the surrounding hilltop was laid out with gardens and various exotic trees, such as monkey puzzle and cedar of Lebanon – many of which are still to be seen today.

Havering Council purchased the estate in 1933 and opened the grounds to the public as a park in June 1934. At first Bedfords House was used as a museum and art gallery, housing a collection of British and foreign birds, tapestries and some 300 paintings but, following the Second World War, the mansion fell into such a state of disrepair that in 1959 it was demolished, thereby making way for the present hexagonal-shaped café built in 1964.

The deer pen opposite this was originally set up in the early 1930s with the idea of building up a herd of red deer for subsequent release into the park. However, the cost of the iron railings needed to enclose the entire park proved so prohibitive that the park's management had to content themselves with a mere extension to the original pens. Unfortunately, this first herd of six deer brought here in 1934 had by 1947 all either died or been destroyed under veterinary advice; the present herd originates from a donation of a further two animals in 1949.

To encourage the appreciation of the park's wildlife, an interesting waymarked nature trail has been developed by the council, with help from the Countryside Management Service, the Essex Naturalist Trust and the Havering Conservation Volunteers. Copies of trail leaflets are available from the Town Hall, Mercury House and all local public libraries.

Among the park's other facilities are a cricket square, two football pitches (north of the car park by Broxhill Road) and provision for angling at the small rectangular lake by Bedfords Road. The café is open every day during the summer months, and weekends during the rest of the year (telephone Romford 752043).

Belair Park

Gallery Road, SE21

How to get there: by train to West Dulwich station. By bus: 3.
Origin of the name: Belair was a popular name in the eighteenth century, used here to suggest that this was a healthy and attractive place to live.
Area: 25 acres (10 hectares).
Owned and maintained by: London Borough of Southwark.

Though Belair is marked on very few maps and is not well known even locally, it is certainly worth visiting for its trees alone, if not for its serpentine lake which forms the only stretch of the ancient river Effra still to remain above ground.

The park's 140 or more trees represent at least forty-three different species, many of them quite rare. Of these, a handsome old cork oak tree, near the rosebed by Gallery Road, is one of the more interesting. The cork oak, which is the same tree from which commercial cork is harvested in Portugal, Spain and Algeria, is fairly rare in this country and this one, with a height of fifteen metres, is regarded as one of Britain's finest specimens. Another tree of particular interest at Belair is the white mulberry, the food plant of the silk worm, and a native of China – a tree which does not generally grow well in Britain.

Perhaps the park's most attractive area is the banks of the long narrow winding lake, already mentioned as being a remnant of the river Effra which is elsewhere, like so many of London's historic rivers, now confined to underground pipes. Tradition declares that Queen Elizabeth I, on at least one occasion, sailed along this river in her state barge.

The lakeside is mostly lined with willows, but also supports quite a variety of other trees such as alder, hawthorn, oak, ash, horse chestnut, elm, holm oak, whitebeam and sycamore. The birdlife around the lake is equally varied, even apart from such waterfowl as swan, mallard and muscovy ducks, moorhen and coot.

The old Georgian mansion, after which the park is named, was built in 1780 and is attributed to the architect and surveyor John Adam. Until 1938 it was a private house with attached park, farm and kitchen gardens, the most recent of its wealthy occupants being Sir Evan Spicer, head of the paper-producing firm of Spicer's Ltd. During his residence, Sir Evan had been leasing the property from the Governors of Dulwich College estates and they, after Sir Evan's death, tried unsuccessfully for seven years to find a new squire to replace him, meanwhile turning down proposals for the development of the mansion site variously as modern flats, a nursing home, and a large hotel. The house and its grounds were acquired finally on a ninety-nine-year lease by the Southwark Borough Council in 1945 and on 19 July 1947 the Belair estate was formally opened as a public park.

During the Second World War, Belair House had been commandeered by the army and used as headquarters for a vehicle park, during which time it was badly damaged and, by 1960, the council decided to demolish it. The governors, however, objected since part of the original lease contained a restoration agreement which obliged the council to repair the building. Unfortunately, parts of the old mansion needed to be completely rebuilt, especially when it was discovered that the whole house had been built over a well which would first need to be filled in; much to the council's dismay, the bill for the whole project finally ran to £54,000.

The now restored Belair House still houses the original spiral Adam staircase, famed for the fact that its weight is designed to be entirely supported by its lowest step. Incorporated also on the ground floor are a restaurant, kitchen and buffet, with changing rooms and showers in the basement. The top-floor rooms can be hired for meetings, classes and various other functions.

Belhus Woods Country Park

Aveley Road, Upminster

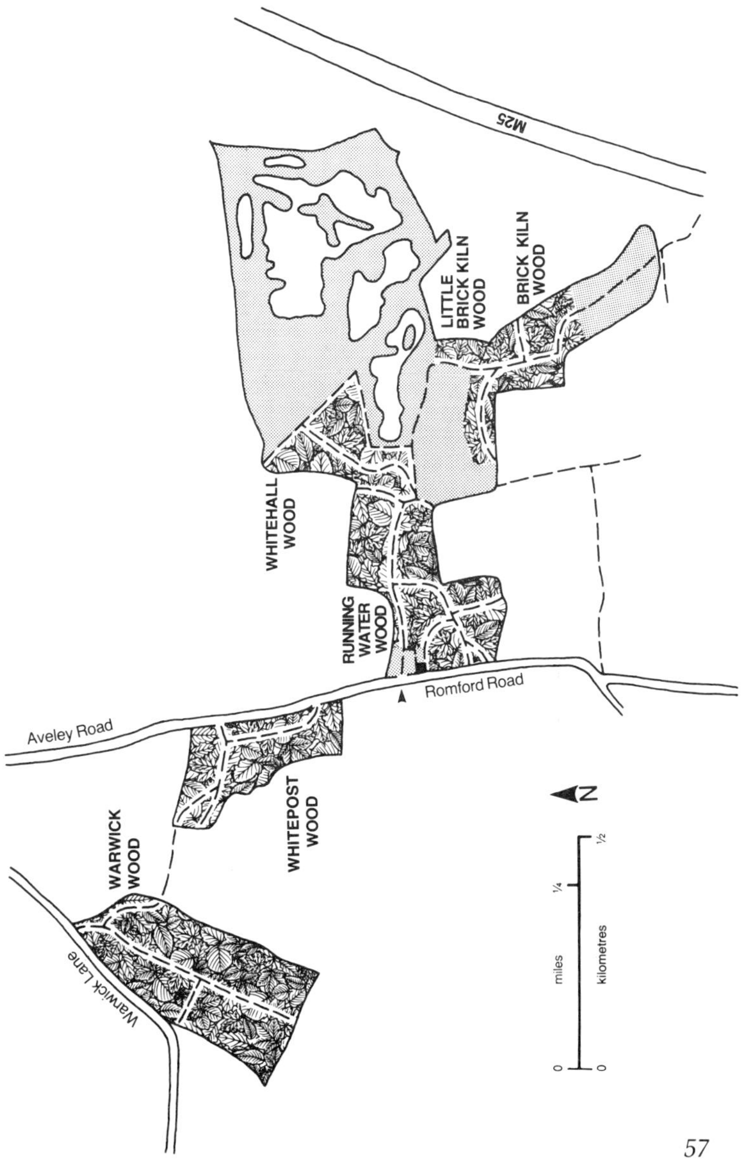

How to get there: not easy by public transport. By bus: Thames Weald Company, or 373, 375 or 389. (373 and 375 stop at Rainham railway station.)
Origin of the name: the name derives from the family of Nicholas de Belhus (from Ramsden Bellhouse) who appear to have settled at Aveley in around 1327.
Area: 155 acres (63 hectares).
Owned and maintained by: Essex County Council (though in fact it is situated largely in the London Borough of Havering).

Approaching Belhus Woods from London, this country park marks the first refreshing breath of true countryside.

The property consists of three separate though interlinked plots of land: Warwick Wood on Warwick Lane, Whitepost Wood on the western side of Aveley Road and the main part of the park to the east of Romford Road, just north of Running Water Brook. While the first two areas are entirely wooded, the larger eastern section embraces a mixture of open grassland, mixed woodlands and several lakes. Near the entrance (which is signposted by Romford Lodge) a car park, toilets and visitor centre have been provided.

Continuing from here into the park, the first woodland one comes to is Running Water Wood, where several areas of hazel have been restored to the traditional coppice management. This involves cutting a number of woodland plots in rotation, allowing the freshly-cut stumps to resprout, thus providing a self-sustaining source of timber. The first plot was cut here in the winter of 1977 and the eighth and final plot in the winter of 1984. This eight-year cycle will then be continuously repeated, providing good straight hazel poles for making spars and pegs which are both still in demand for the old woodcraft of thatched roof making. Besides providing a renewable source of timber, this type of management also encourages a much more diverse wildlife by creating a mosaic of woodland plots of different ages and environments. Each time a plot is cut, a flood of light and warmth is let through on to the woodland floor, thereby stimulating the growth of a new range of plants. One such plant here at Running Water Wood which is benefiting from coppice management is the pink-flowered ragged robin.

In spite of the generous provision of paths, it is quite possible to miss completely the large group of artificial lakes to the north-east, since these are in many places hidden from view by their surrounding embankments. These lakes, with that most beautiful of marsh plants – the reed mace – attract hundreds of coot and several swans. The surrounding landscape is open enough here for one to enjoy long views to uncluttered horizons and to appreciate the extent of the surrounding farmland. Anglers will be glad to learn that public fishing is likely to be permitted in these lakes from 1986 onwards.

The name of the next woodland plot to the south, Brick Kiln Wood, refers to what was once one of this area's main industries. As far back as 1619 there were brickfields in Belhus Park and a local brickmaker, Mrs Perry, is mentioned in local records in 1736, though the wood apparently did not acquire its present name until 1842.

Following the path south through the wood brings one to the M25 motorway and the park's southern boundary, though a footbridge does link the park with another interesting woodland known as the Ash Plantation. The Long Pond here can sometimes be a good place to watch herons – descendants, it is said, of those from the great heronry of the former Belhus Park estate. These birds were then bred to be hunted by falcons and hawks as one of the traditional sports of the wealthy and of royalty.

Most people using the park today appear to live locally for I have noticed several visitors here greet each other by name, but no doubt the new visitor centre will soon be attracting users from further afield.

Bentley Priory Park
Uxbridge Road, Stanmore

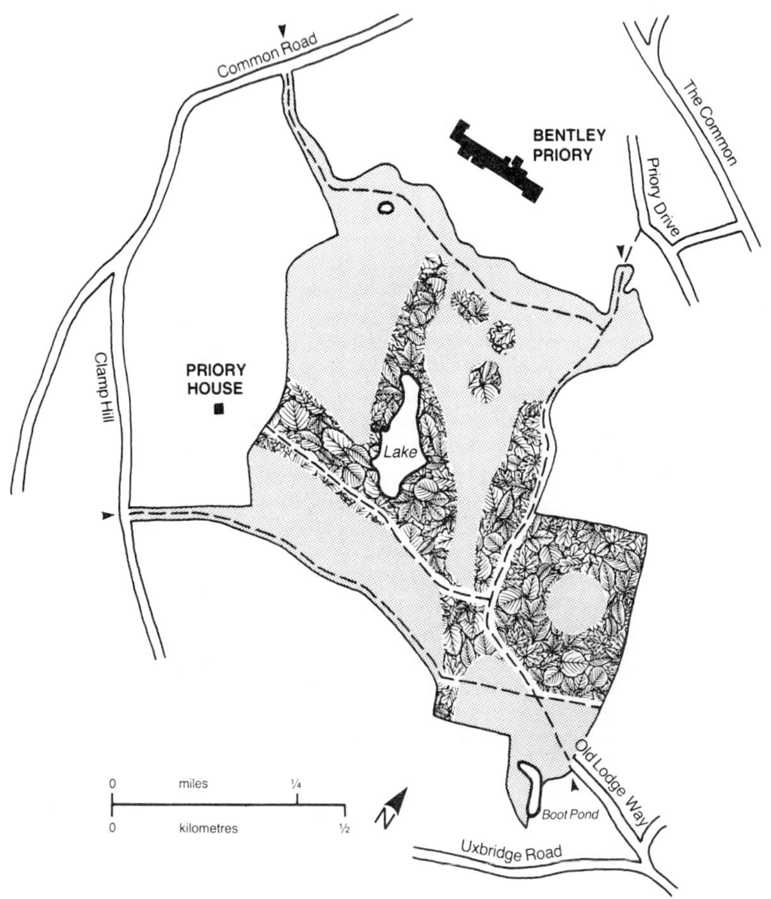

How to get there: by tube to Stanmore station on the Jubilee Line (the entrance to the park is just under one mile to the west and along Old Lodge Way off Uxbridge Road). By bus: 286 to the Old Lodge Way entrance; 258 to the rather obscure Common Road entrance; or 142, 708 or 719 to the Priory Drive entrance.
Origin of the name: the name Bentley dates back at least to AD 1243 and means woodland pasture where 'beonet' grass grew, in reference to a type of coarse grass of the *Agrostis* genus.
Area: 163 acres (66 hectares), including the 9-acre nature reserve.
Owned and maintained by: London Borough of Harrow.

The original priory is believed to have been founded here in the early thirteenth century by the Archbishop of Canterbury in honour of Mary Magdalene and, until its dissolution by Henry VIII in 1536, it housed a community of Augustinian priors.

The present hilltop building dates, however, from 1766 and was designed for James Duberly by Sir John Soane, architect of the Bank of England, with some major alterations made between 1788 and 1798 for the Marquess of Abercorn.

The Priory has since changed hands several times, being for a time a rather unsuccessful private residential hotel and then a school, before the break-up of the estate in 1925. The Priory building with some forty acres of land then went to the Air Ministry while other parts of the estate went to forming the present public park. The Priory itself was later to become the centre from which Air Marshal Sir Hugh Dowding (later Lord Dowding) controlled the Battle of Britain in 1940 and this part of the estate remains under the control of the Ministry of Defence.

The park itself, south of the old priory, has long been of particular interest to naturalists for its unusually varied flora and fauna and, in recognition of this, has been designated by the Nature Conservancy Council (along with neighbouring Harrow Weald Common and Stanmore Common) as a Site of Special Scientific Interest (SSSI). At least eighty bird species have been recorded here of which almost fifty, including all three British woodpeckers, are known to breed within the park. Also known to breed here are kestrel, redpoll, little grebe, willow tit and lesser whitethroat, while the great grey shrike, redstart and whinchat have all been seen to visit.

The park's vegetation is equally varied, with areas of heathland to the west, a sizeable tract of gorse and broom to the north and elsewhere many patches of oak, beech, hornbeam and hawthorn woodland. In all, there are at least 200 species of flowering plants, ranging from rhododendron (which was probably introduced in the nineteenth century) to the much less common greater burnet saxifrage, great horsetail, monkey flower and cowslip.

Grey squirrels and rabbits are both common, as are foxes. There are woodmice, short-tailed and bank voles, common shrews and moles, and the occasional harmless grass snake.

Probably the two regions of greatest wildlife interest are Boot Pond at the park's southern tip and the nine-acre Bentley Priory Nature Reserve near the centre of the property.

Boot Pond, so named from its almost perfect Wellington boot shape, is about ninety-nine per cent spring-fed, supporting mainly cyperus sedge and great reed mace, with perch, common carp and three-spined stickleback and, in March, any number of frogs. The total count of plant species in the immediate vicinity numbers at least 152, with fifty-six different kinds of animals, including the more obvious coot, moorhen and mallard.

About half a mile to the north-west is another stretch of water – the four-and-a-half-acre Summerhouse Lake – which, as part of the formally declared Bentley Priory Nature Reserve, is well fenced off from public access by several rather ugly strands of barbed wire. The purpose of limiting access is to give protection to the wildlife, but anyone with a serious interest can apply for entry by contacting A.A. Tinsey, 124 Kings Road, South Harrow. Otherwise, from the outside one can still enjoy many beautiful glimpses between the rhododendrons to the lake itself and the reserve's many birds.

In spite of its natural appearance, Summerhouse Lake is in fact artificial, having been formed by damming the Edgware Brook near its source. The old summerhouse after which it was named was at one time used by Queen Adelaide, and Sir Walter Scott apparently corrected the proofs for his poem *Marmion* here.

It was not only the lake's beauty but also its scientific importance which led the council formally to declare this a reserve in 1975. At the time it was noted as being the nearest place to London where the kingfisher and grey heron could be seen. Today, the reserve is managed by the Hertfordshire and Middlesex Trust for Nature Conservation in association with the Harrow Natural History Society.

Walking further north still, one comes to higher, more open ground with views south over London and to the north glimpses between the trees of the elegant and stately Italianate Priory – a view unfortunately rather marred now by various ugly military structures. From here, paths connect the park via an avenue of rhododendrons with Harrow Weald Common to the west, and to the north along the eastern boundary of the RAF grounds to Stanmore Common – both also important wildlife habitats.

Blackheath

Shooters Hill, SE3

How to get there: by train to Blackheath station. By bus: 53, 54, 75, 89, 108, 108B or 402.
Origin of the name: black heathland, referring to the colour of the soil.
Area: 272 acres (110 hectares).
Owned and maintained by: London Boroughs of Greenwich and Lewisham.

Blackheath is a vast, treeless plateau intersected by several main roads and offering good breezy views over much of Greater London. Though visually bleak, the heath does have a fascinating history, much of which derives from its strategic position, both with regard to its commanding view and to its being situated on the ancient Roman Watling Street which was once the main route between London and the Channel coast.

One good way to explore this history is to study the names so aptly given to many of the roads which intersect the heath. Duke Humphrey Road, for example, commemorates Henry VI's uncle, to whom the King gave permission in 1432 to enclose 200 acres of the heath to form what is now Greenwich Park – surely one of the few examples where the citizens of London have actually benefited from a private enclosure of common land. The royal park is today still separated from the heath by a high brick wall running along Charlton Way, and Duke Humphrey Road leads directly to one of its entrance gates.

Wat Tyler Road, to the west, commemorates one of the many peasant revolts that have gathered on the heath. This particular protest in 1381 was over the imposition of poll tax – a flat tax of one shilling levied on everyone over the age of fifteen. The Kentish contingent of the poll tax rebellion was led by a blacksmith from Dartford named Wat Tyler, and the Essex folk by Jack Straw (after whom the famous pub at Hampstead is named). From this spot a crowd of over 100,000 people marched on the city and succeeded in occupying the Tower of London, burning the Temple library and destroying the Monastery of St John of Jerusalem at Clerkenwell. Eventually, though, the rebellion failed: Wat Tyler was stabbed by the Lord Mayor, and Jack Straw, along with many of his companion rebels, was beheaded.

Similarly in 1450 there was the Blackheath Petition: Jack Cade (after whom Cade Road is named) along with 20,000 of his followers met here before setting out to 'punish evil ministers and procure a redress of grievance' by beheading the Lord Treasurer and destroying title deeds in their search for equality. And again in 1497 there was a protest here by 6000 Cornishmen against taxes being levied on them to pay for Scottish wars, in which the protesters fought the army of King Henry VII . . . and lost.

Another street, Goffers Road, commemorates just one of the heath's many royal associations, when James I introduced the ancient Scottish game of goff, or golf, to Blackheath in the early 1600s. This was later to lead to the formation of the country's first golf club – the Royal Blackheath Golf Club – which has since moved south to Eltham.

The heath has always been a popular place with sportsmen and women, ranging from the British Amazons, an eighteenth-century team of women archers, to the various Blackheath Pedestrians, like George Wilson who undertook in 1815 to walk 1000 miles in 1000 hours on the heath. In 1911, one of the earliest model aeroplane clubs in the country was formed here, and Blackheath has seen the launching of at least one balloon.

George Whitefield is commemorated not only by the road of that name, but also by Whitefield Pond and Whitefield Mount, both at the junction of Goffers Road and Mounts Pond Road. Whitefield was, like his friend Wesley, a Methodist who preached popular field sermons to enormous crowds here in the eighteenth century.

At that time, the heath looked completely different with none of its present neatly shorn grass. It was, in fact, quite thickly wooded both with trees and with gorse and covered with gravel pits and hollows. The wildlife was then much richer than it is now, but this varied terrain also provided excellent hideouts for highwaymen and women, who terrorized local people and travellers along the Dover Road. When they were caught, these thieves would often be hung on the gibbet at Shooters Hill.

The Second World War was to bring with it many changes to the heath – some of them permanent. Searchlights, anti-aircraft guns, prefabricated houses and even a barrage balloon that could be stored, fully inflated, below ground level inside one of the old gravel pits – these were all here. After the war, most of the heath's gravel pits were filled in with rubble from the bombed sites, and grassed over, leaving Blackheath a treeless plateau with little of interest to the naturalist beyond stag beetles and the occasional fox from Shooters Hill, the odd woodpecker, jay, squirrel or hedgehog. Certainly a far cry from the days when the exquisite beauty of the flowering gorse here inspired Linnaeus to fall down on his knees in thanks to God; or even in more recent times when the heath boasted a number of newly discovered plant sub-species and more types of wild grass than anywhere else in southern England. Today, the heath with its bowling greens, twenty-eight football pitches and five cricket fields seems by comparison quite barren.

Being ancient common land, Blackheath has been vulnerable to the same encroachments suffered by similar land in other parts of London. But two factors in particular have helped to save it: at first, its poor fertility protected it from enclosure for agriculture, and later when the building boom was underway, the heath was already bordered by the fine houses of those with the will and influence to conserve it. Then in 1871, not long after the passing of the Metropolitan Commons Act, Blackheath finally received official protection to remain a public open space for ever.

Bostall Heath and Woods

Bostall Hill, SE2

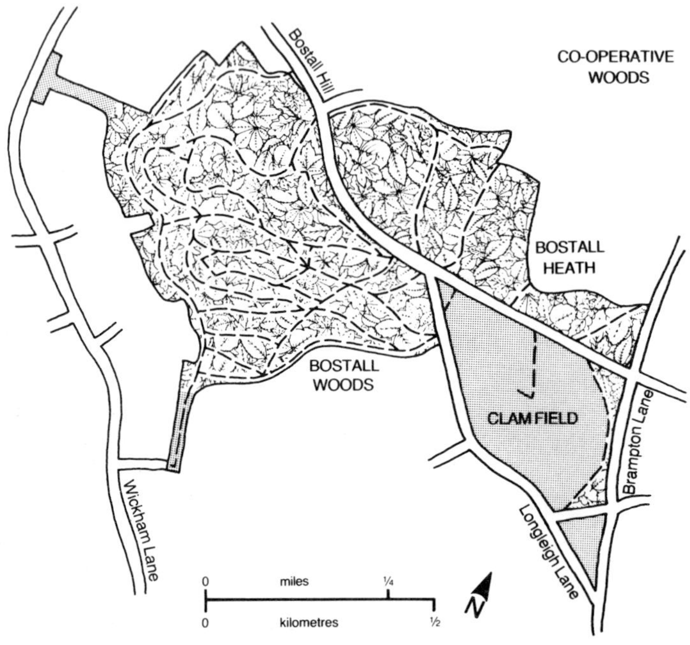

How to get there: by train to Abbey Wood station and half a mile walk (one can avoid the traffic by taking the woodland path to the east of, and parallel to, Knee Hill). By bus: 99.
Origin of the name: the name Bostall comes from the Old English *borg steall* meaning a 'safe place' or 'place of refuge'.
Area: 159 acres (64 hectares).
Owned and maintained by: London Borough of Greenwich.

Bostall Heath and Woods, along with the adjoining Lesnes Abbey Woods, rise steeply above the surrounding houses and streets to over 200 feet above sea level to form one of the largest and most beautiful areas of woodland in London. The woods consist now mostly of beech plantations, self-sown birch and oak with smaller areas of pine, some of which were planted to replace those destroyed in a black pine beetle epidemic at the turn of the century. There are also a number of interesting specimen trees such as sweet gum, narrow-leaved ash and blue Atlas cedar, which have been planted by the staff yard near the junction of Bostall Hill and Longleigh Lane. Across Bostall Hill Road to the north the land is by contrast rougher and more open, with the occasional grassy glade studded with handsome gorse bushes.

Originally the land was two separate properties – the heath, which was part of the common or waste land of the Manor of Plumstead, and the woods, which were previously the property of Sir Julian Goldsmid. The story behind their preservation is a dramatic one, described more fully under Plumstead Common

The struggles began in 1866, when Queen's College, Oxford, (the Lords of the Manor of Plumstead) put up a post and rail fence around the whole of Bostall Heath and attempted to sell it as private property. This, along with other similar enclosures, led the local commoners to take the college to court. Although in 1870 the locals did eventually win the case, the following year neighbouring Plumstead Common was then under threat – this time by the War Office, which proceeded to destroy the vegetation and natural beauty of the common by exercising troops there in preparation for the Franco–German war. Feelings were still running high from the earlier injustices and before long the commoners started to make their feelings known through a campaign of civil disobedience. The series of events which followed was eventually to lead to the arrest and imprisonment of the campaign's leader, John de Morgan.

The climax of all this was de Morgan's release from prison on 5 November 1876, the anniversary of Guy Fawkes' Gunpowder Plot. The timing of de Morgan's release was most appropriate as far as the commoners of Plumstead were concerned and he was given a somewhat riotous hero's welcome amid celebratory bonfires and an estimated crowd of 30,000. Within a year, both Plumstead Common and Bostall Heath had been purchased from the college by the Metropolitan Board of Works, thus putting an end at last to the threat of speculation and the abuse of manorial privilege.

That is the story behind the heath – but its size was soon to double, when the London County Council extended the common with the purchase of the adjoining Bostall Woods in 1893. At that time, the new property was already well wooded with oak, ash, birch and chestnut, with a plantation of Scotch firs and larch, belonging to Sir Julian Goldsmid. Sir Julian had been one of the campaigners who had fought against the Queen's College's abuse of its rights in the enclosure of the heath and he now wanted to complete his good work by selling his own property to the Council for the generously low price of £12,000.

Both the woods and heath are well supplied with footpaths, offering a variety of views along the wooded valleys and over the Thames to the north. At the southern corner is Turpin's Cave, reputed to have been one of the many hiding places of the notorious early eighteenth-century highwayman, Dick Turpin. This cave is one of many of its kind to be found around London, known as 'dene holes', all of which have much the same structure with a central shaft leading to an underground chamber. These pits are thought to have been constructed originally to excavate chalk, possibly for use in marling the soil for agricultural purposes.

Besides provision for some of the more common sports, such as bowls, cricket and football, there is here a permanent course for a new sport called orienteering – described as being a kind of competitive navigation on foot. (Details from the Lesnes Abbey Park Office.) In summer, refreshments are available from the café near the abbey ruins in Lesnes Abbey Woods – just over half a mile's walk to the north-east. Unisex toilets for the disabled are situated both here by the Lesnes Abbey café and 300 yards from Bostall Heath car park.

Brent River Park

W7

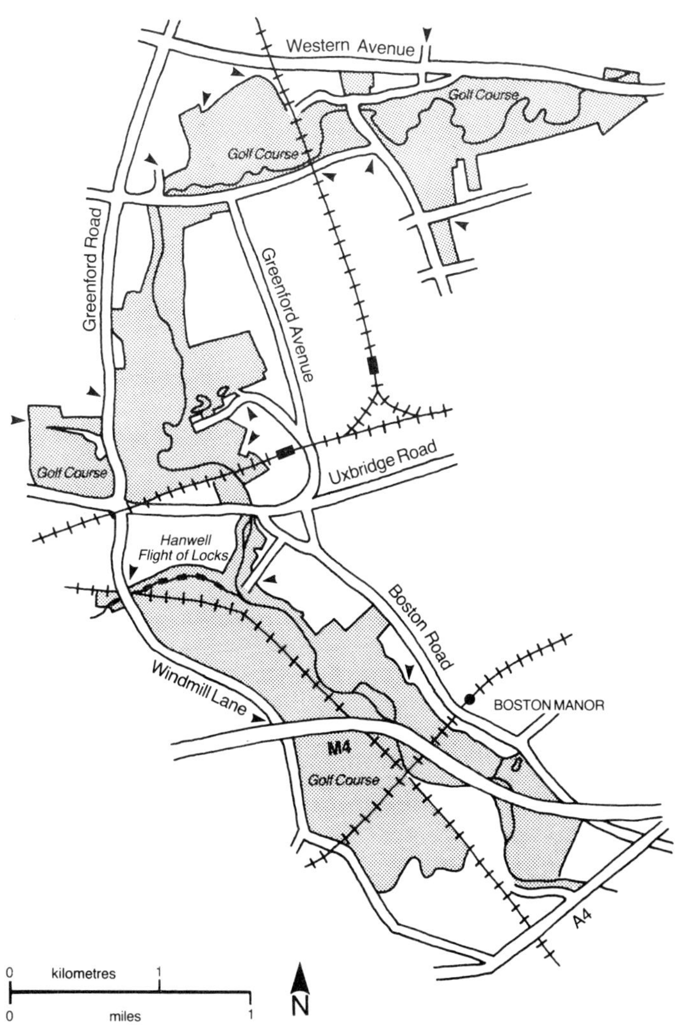

How to get there: By train to South Greenford or Hanwell stations. By tube to Hanger Lane or Perivale stations on the Central Line, or to Boston Manor station on the Piccadilly Line. By bus: E1, E2, E3, 83, 91, 92, 207, 274 or 282.
Origin of the name: the river's name is derived from the Old British word *brigantia*, meaning 'holy one'.
Area: approximately 850 acres (345 hectares).
Owned by: mostly the London Borough of Ealing, though some parts are either under private ownership or owned by the London Borough of Hounslow.
Administered by: the Brent River Park Steering Group.

The idea for the park is a new one, effectively linking a whole chain of open spaces along the banks of the river Brent, stretching from near Hanger Lane tube station at the northern end to the point where the Great West Road (A4) crosses the Grand Union Canal. Most of the land is either public parkland, playing fields or golf courses, which together form a park some four and half miles long and varying in width from about 200 yards at its narrowest point to one mile at its widest.

The river park scheme originated in 1973 with the founding of the Brent River and Canal Society which has, for its tenth anniversary, published an excellent guide to a number of the park's riverside walks. This handy booklet, entitled *Walks in the Brent River Park* (available from the society's chairperson, Jenny Vallance, 17 Sutherland Road, Ealing W13, 01-998 9785) gives details of five circular walks, each with a route map and directions, accompanied by historical notes. String these five walks end to end and you have a trail running almost the entire length of the park.

In spite of its urban setting, the park does have some delightfully rural and secluded stretches, often with quite rich wildlife interest. Perhaps one of the most interesting of these is a three-acre fragment of ancient woodland by the M4 motorway, known as Long Wood. This prehistoric wood provides a habitat for many of the classic woodland plants such as bluebells and dog violets, along with such birds as owls and woodpeckers. Elsewhere along the park, there is a wide range of flora – plenty of elderberries in summer if you make your own wine, sloes in autumn to make sloe gin or blackberries for jam. In fact, the area known as Blackberry Corner, by the Hanwell Flight of Locks and Brunel's famous Three Bridges, is every bit as good picking as its name suggests.

These bridges are worth a visit, too. In spite of the name, the Three Bridges are in fact only two – one to carry the Grand Union

Canal over the railway cutting and another carrying the road (Windmill Lane) over the canal. Another impressive sight just here is the Hanwell Flight of Locks, which together form a kind of aquatic stairway in the canal, raising the water level fifty-three feet in a distance of 600 yards.

Not far north of here is another interesting feat of engineering – the Wharncliffe Viaduct – also designed by Brunel, in 1837. It is said that, in order to enjoy the view across the valley and Churchfields from the top of the viaduct, Queen Victoria used to make special arrangements to have her train stop here.

Of the parks included within the Brent River Park, several are quite attractive in their own right, particularly Boston Manor Park and Pitshanger Park, where the path skirts between the trees along the banks of the river. There is also Perivale Park which, though largely devoted to golf and elsewhere rather bleak, is being gradually improved by tree planting. Also included are Brent Lodge Park, Churchfields, Scotch Common and Elthorne Park.

The idea of developing all these parks, the golf courses and playing fields as one unit is not only to promote their recreational value, but also to help protect them from the further encroachment of building development. Until recently, much of the land had been spared from development largely through its vulnerability to flooding. With the advent of the Greater London Council's Flood Alleviation Scheme, planning for the area's recreational use in a more cohesive way may well prove to be a vital factor in its future protection.

The Brent River and Canal Society's plans depended of course on the co-operation of the Ealing Borough Council, to whom credit is due for their acceptance of the society's proposals and for their setting up in 1976 of the Brent River Park Steering Group, in which the society has continued to play an important and active role.

To date – as a result of the Brent River Park scheme – a great number of trees have been planted, fencing improved and detrimental planning applications opposed, while some attractive historic buildings, such as St Mary's Church, Perivale, and Rectory Cottage, Hanwell, have been saved. Several new footpaths have also been opened and supplied with seats and signposting.

With continued good management, particularly screen tree planting, the park is likely to continue to grow in popularity for walking, bird watching and plant spotting.

Brockwell Park

Dulwich Road, SE24

How to get there: by train to Herne Hill station (just a few yards from the park's eastern entrance). By bus: 2, 3, 37, 68, 172 or 196.
Origin of the name: not known, but possibly derived from the Old English words *broc* and *wella*. 'Broc', meaning 'stream' or 'brook', in reference perhaps to the old river Effra; and 'wella', meaning a 'spring', 'stream' or 'well'.
Area: 126 acres (51 hectares).
Owned and maintained by: London Borough of Lambeth.

Although Brockwell Park is well known for its views from the hill where the mansion now stands and for its attractive chain of ornamental lakes near the western entrance, one of its finest features is easily overlooked. This – the Old English garden – is situated near the lakes on the site of the former walled-in kitchen garden and was the first of its kind to be laid out in a municipal London park, cultivated now with roses, golden yews, wisteria and honeysuckle.

If you are confused by the different kinds of waterfowl commonly found in London parks or want to help children learn about them, the largest of the three lakes here has an information board illustrating and naming them: Canada geese, tufted ducks, moorhens, coots, mallards and mute swans. Also by the lake is a small aviary and nearby it will not be hard to spot some of the park's many grey squirrels bounding up the trunks of the lakeside trees.

Although at least ninety old elms have in recent years had to be felled owing to the outbreak of Dutch elm disease, there is still a good number of mature trees scattered around the park. Especially beautiful in spring is the avenue of flowering cherries through which one enters the park from the Tulse Hill gates.

The land which now forms Brockwell Park at one time belonged to the medieval Hospital of St Thomas – that is, until 1538 when they were forced to surrender it to Henry VIII, who subsequently subdivided the land and sold it off. Its modern history begins with the purchase of the estate in the early nineteenth century by a wealthy glass manufacturer, John Blades, who built the present hilltop mansion between 1811 and 1813. The estate came into public ownership as a park through Blades's grandson, Joshua John Blades Blackburn, who had initially planned to sell the land to developers. Meanwhile, though, a popular campaign was underway to acquire a public park for the Brixton area. At the time, the campaign group already had another site in mind – the ten-acre grounds of Raleigh House on Brixton Road – and had obtained a special Act of Parliament (the Raleigh Park Act, 1888) for the purpose of authorizing a contribution from the Metropolitan Board of Works towards its purchase. Although the Brockwell estate was, because of its size, much more expensive, it represented so much better value that, at a 'large and enthusiastic' meeting at the Effra Public Hall in April 1889, it was decided that the campaign should instead be diverted towards the acquisition of the Brockwell Hall estate.

Brockwell Park was formally opened by Lord Rosebery on Whit Monday 1892, but sadly, during the opening ceremony, the one man who had done most to secure the park for the public – Thomas Bristowe – died suddenly from a heart attack. Until 1958, a memorial drinking fountain stood near the Herne Hill entrance in his memory, with the inscription: 'Thomas Lynn Bristowe, MP for Norwood 1885–1892. Ready to every good work, he led the movement for the acquisition of these broad acres as a public park, with great tact and energy, and died suddenly in the very moment of his unselfish triumph . . .'

The old standing clock by the mansion commemorates another of Brockwell Park's key figures: Charles Ernest Tritton, a member of the committee who helped to negotiate the purchase of a forty-three-acre extension at the park's northern end, an area which includes the site of the present open-air swimming pool.

Apart from this open-air pool, the park today has a good range of sporting facilities, including tennis courts, cricket pitches, a putting green and, at the top of the hill, netball courts.

Three other particularly interesting parks are situated nearby – Belair, Dulwich and Ruskin Park – all within about a mile's walk and all notable for their unusually good variety of mature trees.

Burgess Park

Albany Road, SE5

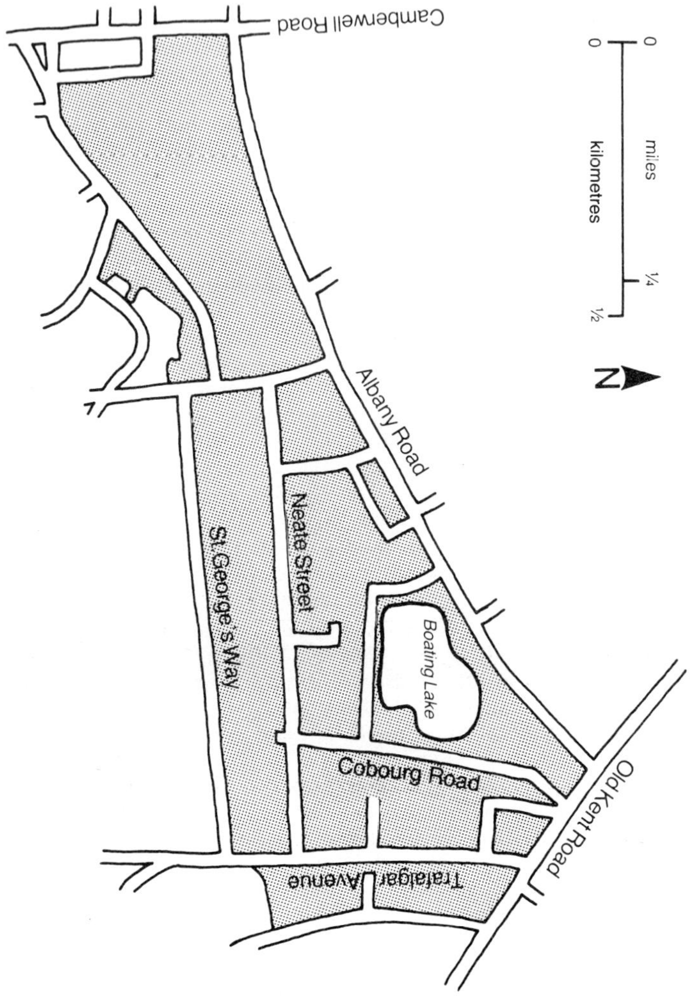

How to get there: by bus: 12, 21, 35, 40, 42, 45, 53, 63, 68, 78, 141, 171, 176 or 184.
Origin of the name: after the late Jessie Burgess, a Camberwell councillor and alderwoman.
Area: 100 acres (36 hectares) at present, though planned to reach 135 acres (55 hectares) by the 1990s.
Owned and maintained by: London Borough of Southwark.

While all other major parks in London have been made possible through defending the land against the encroachment of building development, roads and railways, at Burgess Park the process has been reversed. Where once there were schools, factories, churches, thirty streets and over 900 dwellings, there is now a substantial stretch of open space complete with large boating lake, gardens, trees, nature area, festival site, sports facilities and children's playgrounds.

This part of London had long been acknowledged as being short of open space, but it was not until 1943 that a group of planners saw the opportunity to create out of an expanse of bombed and demolition sites a large new park. From the outset, it was clear that such an ambitious project could take as much as fifty years to complete; individual properties needed to be acquired by compulsory purchase or bought up as each became vacant. 'North Camberwell Open Space' (as it was then known) was started in 1950, growing steadily in area to just over fifteen acres by 1965, and planned finally by the year 2000 to cover the whole area bounded by Albany Road, Camberwell Road, St George's Way, Glengall Road and Old Kent Road.

Like a jigsaw puzzle the pieces are being put together, with facilities being moved as new areas become available for public use. It may take another fifteen years before the park is complete, but the greatest possible use is being made of the land already available. After all, there are around 100,000 people living in the high-rise council flats just next door and the nearest alternative parks of a comparable size are some two miles away.

The most interesting development of late has been the creation of a brand new eight-acre lake, opened to the public at the 1982 May Day Festival. It is the first recreational lake to be created in inner London this century and the first ever to be constructed on land which used to be occupied by roads, houses and factories. The water is held in by a series of ten-metre-wide polyethylene sheets – believed to be the longest in the world – welded together side by side to make a continuous waterproof lining capable of holding twelve million gallons of water. After protecting this lining with a thick layer of gravel, the lake was stocked with

11,000 fish, mostly roach, carp and rudd, and since 1983 the lake has been open for public fishing with access provided for disabled anglers. Likewise, of the sailing dinghies and pedaloes for hire on the lake, three boats are reserved for people with disabilities and, nearby, wheelchair-accessible toilets have been provided.

Yet to come are the restaurant complex, entertainment centre, golf nets, changing rooms, bridleways and nature trails. Burgess Park is primarily a place of activity – of sports and games – yet it has its quiet secluded areas too, with flowerbeds and roses, along with nature areas which are gradually being developed through the sowing of wildflower seeds and bulbs; already you can find bluebells here in spring. Many of the park's trees have been planted by local schoolchildren, who are encouraged to chart their growth and the insects found on them. The greenhouse (by the Information Centre on Cunard Street/Albany Road) is also open to schools, as well as to members of the general public seeking advice on growing indoor plants. Both this and the information centre are open to the public every day of the week.

It may indeed be true that no one else in the world has ever bulldozed so much urban landscape to create a public park, but some reminders of the past have nevertheless been allowed to remain. For example, a number of Georgian and Regency houses along Trafalgar Avenue and Glengall Road are to be preserved in spite of the difficulties of incorporating them into the park's design. And, not far from Victory Square, at the western end of the park, are the renovated remains of an old lime kiln, used during London's rapid growth in the nineteenth century to provide a kind of material known as Roman cement. On a line to the east of this used to be the Camberwell Arm of the old Surrey Canal, though this unfortunately had to go because of its poor state of repair and lack of water supply.

At the time of writing, the Conservative government has abolished the GLC, the administrative body that has made all this possible. What happens to Burgess Park from now on is likely to be a test of any alternative management this government might propose.

Bushy Park

Hampton Court Road, East Molesey

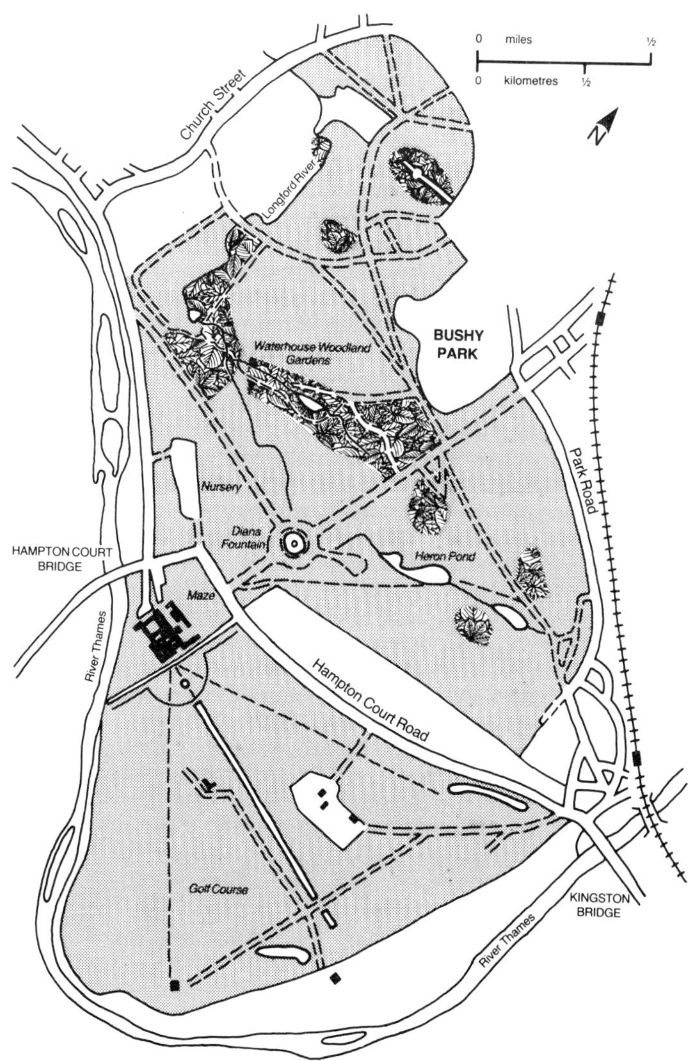

How to get there: by train to Teddington or Hampton Court stations. By bus: 111, 131, 216, 267, 461, 715, 716, 718 or 726.
Origin of the name: a reference to the park's shrubby vegetation.
Area: 1100 acres (445 hectares).
Owned by: the Crown.
Maintained by: Department of the Environment.

Although Bushy Park and Hampton Court Park share much of the same history, in character they are quite different. Bushy Park, like its southern neighbour, was enclosed in the early sixteenth century by Cardinal Wolsey to provide himself with a place to which he could escape from city business. By 1529, however, Henry VIII had grown so envious of the grandeur of Wolsey's estate that he banished the Cardinal and immediately took over the palace and both the parks for himself.

While successive monarchs spent a good deal of time and money on forever changing the immediate palace grounds to suit their various tastes, for the most part they were content to leave Bushy Park in its naturally wild state. Two monarchs did, however, make their mark. One was Charles I, who made possible the Waterhouse Woodland Garden by introducing running water to the park; he had a watercourse cut all the way from the river Colne to create a natural-looking stream, the Longford river, which now flows through the park and under Hampton Court Road via the Long Water and into the Thames.

The elements of formality found in the central Chestnut Avenue and Diana Fountain were arranged for subsequent monarchs, Mary II and William III, by Sir Christopher Wren as part of a scheme to create a grand northern approach to the palace. This mile-long double row of 274 horse chestnuts is at its best in May when the millions of candle-like white and pink blooms provide one of the park's most spectacular features. In fact, from the mid-nineteenth century until quite recently, this was the destination for special excursions from the city to celebrate the once famous 'Chestnut Sunday'.

My favourite part of Bushy Park, though, is the little-known Waterhouse Woodland Garden which stretches westward from Chestnut Avenue. This three-quarter-mile woodland strip, covering an area of some one hundred acres, comprises three sections each enclosed by wooden fencing to protect it from browsing deer. Here the emphasis is on rhododendrons, azaleas and camellias, so the best season in which to visit is April to June, but the design is so good that the gardens are definitely worth seeing at all times of the year. Although created from two copses believed originally to have been planted by Charles I, the idea for the gardens was not conceived until some 300 years later, by J.W. Fisher, superintendent of Hampton Court garden, in 1949. The more interesting trees here include a particularly fine dawn redwood – a tree which was thought to be extinct until its rediscovery in the Hupeh province of China in 1941 – and Persian ironwood, with its spectacular autumn colours.

These gardens feel so far away from any hint of London. Beneath the tall trees are wooden benches from which to absorb the sense of woodland, the stream and birdsong. Woodpeckers, treecreepers and nuthatches are plentiful; in the spring – flycatchers, willow warblers, whitethroat and even kingfishers.

In all, Bushy Park supports around fifty breeding species of birds, which rates it as being second only to Richmond among the royal parks. Here too are the occasional fox, rabbit, weasel, pygmy and common shrew and plenty of grey squirrels, voles and hedgehogs. Of the wild plants, slender cudweed and upright chickweed are among the more interesting. Then, of course, there are the fallow and red deer (320 of them) whose heads can frequently be seen poking above the high bracken.

It is the western end of the park which is the wildest and generally most attractive to wildlife, but even in the well-used eastern section great crested grebes are not uncommon visitors in spring. Here too are a number of migratory wading birds, such as greenshank and common sandpiper.

Just as Richmond Park has its folk hero (John Lewis), so too does Bushy Park. The battle of which Timothy Bennett is the local hero was over a right of way through the park from Hampton Wick to Hampton Court Gate – a right which was denied to the public by the park ranger in the mid-eighteenth century, George Montague, Earl of Halifax. Timothy Bennett, a seventy-five-year-old local shoemaker, refused to take 'No' for an answer and before long was in a head-on confrontation with the Earl, following which Lord Halifax did finally give in. Through Bennett's courage and persistence, this public path was preserved until the palace and both the parks were opened to the public by Queen Victoria in 1838.

Montague's action was by no means the only threat to Bushy Park, for almost exactly one century earlier, Bushy and Hampton Court Parks were both put up for auction and sold to the highest bidder. They might well have disappeared altogether had not they been promptly repurchased when Oliver Cromwell subsequently decided to make Hampton Court Palace his family home.

Much of the park today is suitable for wheelchairs and wheelchair-accessible toilets are provided by the children's playground and tea house near the Hampton Court Gate.

Cannizaro Park

West Side Common, SW19

How to get there: by train to Wimbledon station, then by bus. By tube to Wimbledon station on the District Line, then by bus. By bus: 80, 93 or 200.
Origin of the name: after a nineteenth-century tenant of the estate, Francisco Platamone, Duke of Cannizaro.
Area: 34 acres (14 hectares).
Owned and maintained by: London Borough of Merton.

Although Cannizaro Park is not well known, even among those living in south-west London, it is surely equal in interest and beauty to any of the more famous royal parks. Here, on the edge of Wimbledon Common, tucked away behind Cannizaro House, is one of the finest collections of rhododendrons and azaleas in the south of England. Even apart from these, there are here well over four hundred flowering trees, shrubs and herbs, many of these either nationally or locally rare.

Entering the park along the narrow walkway to the right of the house, between elaborate displays of Victorian-style bedding plants, one emerges to a charmingly rural view across the rolling six-acre lawn towards distant hills and the spire of Richmond church. To the right, among mature red Japanese maple trees, is an unusual white-and-gold-painted aviary in the style of Pisa cathedral and inhabited by rather noisy budgerigars. To the left is the eighty-five-year-old Cannizaro House and, beyond this, one of the park's spring highlights – the sunken garden.

Continuing on round to the southern wooded end of the park, one comes to Lady Jane's Wood, the main feature of which is its magnificent azalea dell. Throughout the long spring flowering season, the whole wood appears to be in flower. Look out here also for the magnolia and the Chilean flame tree (which flower in late May/June). A little to the north, a curving flight of steps leads through one of the early plantings of deciduous azaleas which have since been laced together to form a tunnel, or pleached alley. Over towards the boundary wall of the old kitchen garden is an equally pleasant path – the Laburnum Walk – which leads north to the pond.

Continuing in this direction past the end of the main lawn, one arrives eventually at the Keir Garden and Guide's Chapel, both at the northern extremity of the park. The chapel was built in the early nineteenth century originally to provide living quarters for the estate's resident priest. Nearby are several interesting trees including New Zealand's national symbol, the yellow-flowered kowhai, along with a pomegranate, loquat and an old mulberry tree.

At Cannizaro Park there is floral colour to be enjoyed even in the coldest months, but if it is camellias you want to see, then visit in May, for magnolias either March or April, while the main rhododendron plantings start to bloom in April and continue to flower until the early summer.

The gardens as we see them today are the result of plantings by generations of owners, though most of the more interesting mature trees and shrubs were planted here between 1920 and 1947 by the late E. Kenneth Wilson, a keen member of the Rhododendron Society. Following the council's purchase of the estate in 1948, the park underwent a fairly major overhaul to make up for a period of serious neglect during and after the war. In making new plantings a sense of surprise and intricacy was sought, providing mass effects likely to appeal to the non-specialist, while interplanting these with smaller groups of rare and interesting species to intrigue the more knowledgeable. The obvious success of this effect is an on-going tribute to the care and enthusiasm of the borough's Parks Department.

Though the present Cannizaro House is by no means old (dating from 1900 when the original residence was accidentally destroyed by fire) the history of the estate can be traced back to the early eighteenth century. Probably the first person to contribute significantly to the park's present appearance was Henry Dundas, Viscount Melville (1742–1811). The wood, which to this day bears his wife's name – Lady Jane's Wood – was planted by him, as were several of the large beeches, and both the old kitchen garden and pond are known to date at least from the time of Dundas' residence here.

The next tenant of interest was Francisco Platamone, Count St Antonio, later Duke of Cannizaro, a Sicilian nobleman who lived here for a few years in the early nineteenth century following his marriage to Miss Johnstone, the wealthy daughter of Commodore George Johnstone, Governor of West Florida. Though the Duke's connection with the estate was both brief and rather tenuous (much to his wife's dismay, he spent most of his time living with a lover in Milan) the house and park have borne his name ever since.

Chelsea Physic Garden

Swan Walk, SW3

How to get there: by train – one mile from Victoria station. By tube – a ten-minute walk from Sloane Square station on the District and Circle Line. By bus: 39 (Mon.–Sat.).
Origin of the name: it is thought that Chelsea means 'chalk landing place'; 'physic' refers to the original role of the garden in growing plants for both medicinal and general scientific use.
Area: 4 acres (1½ hectares).
Owned and maintained by: Trustees of Chelsea Physic Garden.

Chelsea Physic Garden, like the Royal Botanic Gardens at Kew, was set up originally as a centre for the scientific study of plants. It was founded by the Worshipful Society of Apothecaries in 1673, making this England's second oldest botanic garden, forty-one years younger than the one at Oxford and nearly a hundred years older than the Botanic Gardens at Kew.

Though founded by the Society of Apothecaries and termed a physic garden, these grounds were not devoted solely to the growing of medicinal plants. In the seventeenth century, the word 'physic', it is thought, referred originally to things natural rather than specifically medicinal; and, in any case, the apothecaries were at that time still influenced by the Paracelsian belief that *every* plant had a medicinal use – even though some had not yet been discovered.

Though the garden has continued to this day to function primarily as a centre for botanical research and education, the present trustees, who took over in 1981, decided to raise funds by restricted opening of the grounds to the public and by hiring out part of the buildings to gardening and botanical societies for lectures. As a result of this, the garden is now open Wednesday and Sunday afternoons from mid-April to late October, and an admission charge is made. (For up-to-date details, telephone 01-352 5646.)

In this most compact of plant collections (just one mile from Victoria station) are several of London's most notable trees, including New Zealand's kowhai – this specimen is said to be a grandchild of the original plant brought here by Sir Joseph Banks from Cook's first voyage on the *Endeavour*. Here, too, is one of London's few specimens of the cork oak and Britain's largest olive tree, along with a rare and magnificent specimen of the Chinese willow pattern tree. There are black mulberries, maidenhair (or ginkgo) trees, pomegranate and an example of one tree which until 1941 was thought to have been extinct for some two million years: the dawn redwood. In all there are here over 7000 different plants attractively arranged in rectangular beds, most of them grouped either according to their botanical family or to their country of origin.

A major function of the garden is still, however, to support research. The University of London, for example, is growing millet and sorghum here to find ergot-resistant strains for tropical countries, and Chelsea College is conducting extensive medical research into the effects of feverfew on migraine sufferers. Likewise, the international exchange of plants continues; in 1981, for example, over 6100 packets of seeds were sent out and 1200 species received.

Two of the better known plants in whose history Chelsea Physic Garden has played an important role are cotton – the seeds of which were sent from here to Georgia, subsequently providing that state's staple crop – and Madagascan periwinkle, which arrived at Chelsea from Madagascar via the Paris Jardin des Plantes and later escaped to roadsides in many tropical countries before being found to be useful in the treatment of cancer.

In order to continue such important botanical research and education here, the trustees are appealing for donations and sponsorship of specific projects. For more information, contact the Appeals Director, Chelsea Physic Garden, 66 Royal Hospital Road, London SW3 4HS (01-352 5646).

Chiswick House Gardens

Burlington Lane, W4

How to get there: by train to Chiswick station. By bus: 290 or E3.
Origin of the name: Chiswick means 'cheese farm'.
Area: 67 acres (27 hectares).
Owned and maintained by: London Borough of Hounslow. (The house is maintained by the Department of the Environment.)

To anyone with a fascination for the history and development of English gardening, this is one of London's most interesting and varied parks. Chiswick House Gardens represents an important turning point in the English garden style, between the rigid geometrical designs of the age of Wren and the freer, more natural curves which typify the work of Lancelot 'Capability' Brown – such as can be seen at Danson Park, Syon Park and Kew Gardens. Up until the creation of Chiswick House Gardens, English landscape gardening had largely been inspired by Louis XIV's gardener, Le Nôtre, in the manner of Hampton Court and Greenwich Park – often with straight avenues and long rectangular canals laid out on a grand and imposing scale, evoking a sense rather of formality than of any love of the natural world.

In fact, it was such a garden that Lord Burlington had originally planned for Chiswick before his second visit to Italy. Partly inspired on his overseas trip by the spirit of nature as portrayed in poetry and painting, and partly as a result of personal observation, Lord Burlington returned to England to set about the ambitious new design, in around 1716, for the grounds of Chiswick House. Although it is thought that Alexander Pope helped in this early period and some features of the garden are known to be the work of Charles Bridgeman, the present layout is largely the work of Burlington's protégé – the famous architect and designer, William Kent.

Just as these grounds mark a new departure from the prevailing fashion of the time, so too does the villa. Chiswick House, which was built between 1725 and 1729, also by the third Earl of Burlington, has survived as one of the finest examples of English Palladian architecture. Though modelled on Andrea Palladio's sixteenth-century Villa Capra, near Vicenza, it was never intended as a residence, but rather as a 'temple' – a kind of ornamental gallery and library – in which Lord Burlington could entertain, and house his paintings, ornaments and books.

The house itself is open to the public daily, though closed on Mondays and Tuesdays during the winter. There is an admission charge, and wheelchair access to the ground floor. (Telephone 01-994 3299 for further details.)

A walk around the grounds reveals the essentially geometrical layout of radiating straight paths, mellowed by the irregular distribution of statues and garden buildings, the informal planting of trees and the faintly serpentine form of the canal or river, which flows the length of the grounds. Taking the avenue which leads north-west away from the garden-front of the villa, one arrives at a small obelisk standing in the centre of a circular pond, within a turf amphitheatre, facing into which is a small Ionic temple. Here the path divides into three, each path picking out its own visual focus in the form of a garden monument. The western branch leads to James Wyatt's Classic Bridge, built in 1788 and adorned with various cherubs and urns – the far side of this bridge connecting in turn with another straight path leading south to a taller obelisk, erected over a Roman tombstone, believed to date from the second century. From this point, the eighteenth-century fascination for geometrical design continues to be evident, as this obelisk reveals itself as a focus for further paths radiating out into the park – one to the Ionic temple (by the circular pond) and one to the Chiswick House villa itself.

As one explores around the grounds, there are several interesting trees to look out for, including the original cedars of Lebanon, maidenhair, stone pine and one of this country's largest narrow-leaved ash trees.

Over at the eastern end of the gardens is the Inigo Jones gateway, brought here from Beaufort House, Chelsea, in 1736, and the nineteenth-century Italian Garden and Conservatory. This last is an addition by Samuel Ware, designer of the Burlington Arcade in Piccadilly, and famous today for its camellia collection. And about 150 yards south of here, over towards the villa's main entrance from Great Chertsey Road, perhaps the small cafeteria will prove a welcome discovery.

Clapham Common

SW4

How to get there: by train to Clapham or Clapham Junction stations which are both a little over half a mile from the common. By tube to Clapham Common or Clapham South stations on the Northern Line. By bus: 35, 37, 45, 88, 118, 131, 137, 155, 189 or 755.
Origin of the name: Clapham means 'village on or near a hillock'.
Area: 204 acres (82 hectares).
Owned and maintained by: London Borough of Lambeth.

Clapham Common was originally two commons – the western half being part of the manor of Battersea and Wandsworth and called Battersea East Common, and the eastern half belonging to the manor and parish of Clapham. Disagreement between the two parishes over where the boundary lay led to no end of argument and finally to a very lengthy lawsuit. At one point – in 1716 – the parishioners of Battersea were so fed up that they dug a ditch and bank across the common to keep out cattle belonging to the Clapham folk. Then when the Clapham commoners responded by filling the ditch back in and levelling the bank, the Lord of the Manor of Battersea, Lord Viscount St John, tried unsuccessfully to sue them for trespass.

Considering how central it is within London, Clapham Common has withstood enclosures remarkably well – a fact which is largely due to the large number of wealthy and influential people who once lived along its boundaries and who had the means to protect it. A quick glance at a map of London will demonstrate how Clapham Common is, for example, one of the very few large metropolitan commons not to have been cut up by the laying of railways.

Of course, there were some enclosures, and a couple of these are still very obvious today: the Holy Trinity Church, built in 1774–6, and the Windmill Inn, which dates back to 1729, along with the terraced houses behind it. The inn takes its name from the old post-mill which stood here at least as early as 1629, the houses behind the inn surrounding the site of the old windmill pond.

The common did not come into the protection of public ownership until it was purchased from the lords of the two manors (the Bowyer family and Lord Spencer) by the Metropolitan Board of Works in 1877. But as early as 1722 there was a scheme of management led largely by a local magistrate, Christopher Baldwin, who arranged to drain the land and plant a variety of trees here. In fact something of Clapham Common's present park-like appearance can be attributed to him.

Over the years, the common's appearance has changed considerably; the heather and gorse have been replaced by mown grass and with them have gone the hedgehogs and polecats that once found refuge here. The sheep and cattle of the commoners, and later of local butchers, have of course also long since gone, as have the cartmen's horses and donkeys, though one pleasantly unkempt wild area has been allowed to remain at the north-western end, along with a few scattered patches of hawthorn.

A few of the old ponds still remain. Mount Pond, south-west of the bandstand, was one of the old gravel pits, excavated to provide gravel for the main London to Tooting road. In the 1740s it was almost lost from the common as private property when a crafty Lombard Street banker, Mr Henton Brown, enclosed the pond for a private lake. The Long Pond near Rookery Road has continued to be used for the sailing of model boats, though no longer for watering horses. Its former name of Boat-house Pond refers to a boat-house built on its banks by the lord of the manor. Both this and Eagle Pond were probably excavated originally to build the road now known as Clapham Common South Side. Eagle Pond was originally called Eagle House Pond from the mansion which once faced it. Like Mount Pond, this is popular for fishing. And finally, Cock Pond, over by Holy Trinity Church, which, though now a paddling pond, was once dangerously deep, having been excavated to provide material for raising the ground where the church now stands. Its name is derived from an adjoining inn.

The common's focal point, however, is surely the brightly and tastefully painted bandstand, designed by Captain Francis Fowke, the architect of the original Albert Hall. It was one of a pair that were erected in the Royal Horticultural Society garden in South Kensington in 1861 and was moved to Clapham Common (do not ask how!) in 1890 when the society's garden was abandoned.

Clissold Park

Stoke Newington Church Street, N16

How to get there: by tube to Manor House station on the Piccadilly Line and then a half mile walk south along Green Lanes. By bus: 73, 141 or 171.
Origin of the name: named after the previous owner of the estate, the Rev. Augustus Clissold.
Area: 55 acres (22 hectares).
Owned and maintained by: London Borough of Hackney.

Clissold Park's history centres round the old mansion at the eastern end of the park, which now houses the cafeteria. This mansion, a listed building, dates back to the 1790s and was the home of the Crawshays and later of the Rev. Augustus Clissold, after whom the park is now named.

The Rev. Clissold's association with the park can be said to have begun when he fell in love with one of Mr Crawshay's two daughters – unfortunately a match of which Mr Crawshay was violently to disapprove. Apart from having a particular hatred for parsons, Crawshay also had an unusually bad temper, and, as a result of this, the local curate was forbidden to visit the house. In response to the imposed ban, the couple resorted to communicating through messengers, whom Crawshay then threatened to shoot and, as a last resort it is said, he even increased the height of the walls to prevent the couple from catching glimpses of each other. The couple's patience was eventually rewarded with the old man's death and they married, thus making the curate the new owner of Crawshay's Farm, whose name he subsequently changed to Clissold's Place or Park.

At the northern end of the park the two lakes, in a sense, tell the rest of the park's history. In the 1890s these ornamental sheets of water were locally christened Beckmere and Runtzmere, in honour of the leaders of the movement by which the park was preserved for public use. After Clissold's death, the property had reverted to another member of the Crawshay family who, in spite of assurances to the contrary – written by George Crawshay and published in *The Times* – sold his interest in the entire estate to the Ecclesiastical Commissioners who, it was known, already had plans to subdivide the land for building. An influential committee, in which Joseph Beck and John Runtz were particularly active, fought for three years to ensure the preservation of the estate as open space for the public, finally succeeding in persuading the Metropolitan Board of Works to acquire the park in 1887. The two lakes, which had by this time been filled in, were, in response to the campaigners' victory, immediately re-excavated and informally named in honour of the park's two benefactors. Clissold Park was formally opened to the public by the first chairman of the London County Council, the Earl of Rosebery, on 24 July 1889.

Having been a private estate, Clissold Park already had the advantage of being well planted with mature trees and of possessing the two ornamental lakes which, incidentally, were originally dug to provide clay for making the bricks for the mansion. In addition to these was what appears now to be a linear lake, in front of the mansion, but which is in fact an above-ground remnant of the New River, dug originally between 1609 and 1613 to supply fresh water to London from springs at Amwell. To complement these natural attractions, Clissold Park became one of the first of London's municipal parks to have an aviary and a miniature zoo, both of which it still has today.

Apart from the ubiquitous London plane tree and several horse chestnut, there are here silver birch, flowering cherry, Caucasian wingnut, scarlet oak, willow and tree of heaven. Mixed shrub beds in the centre of the park have the pleasing effect of subduing any bleakness that one might otherwise encounter in long views over mown grass. The park's ducks, coots and geese, along with the fallow deer, help further to lend a rural atmosphere. The park has also an attractive bowling green, various sports facilities, a children's playground, paddling pool, one o'clock club and toilets with wheelchair access.

To ramble further afield, from Clissold Park it is only a half mile walk up Green Lanes to Finsbury Park and thence to the start of Parkland Walk. To Highbury Fields is likewise only half a mile: along Collins Road, Kelross Passage, Kelross Road and left along Highbury Park.

Colne Valley Park
Uxbridge

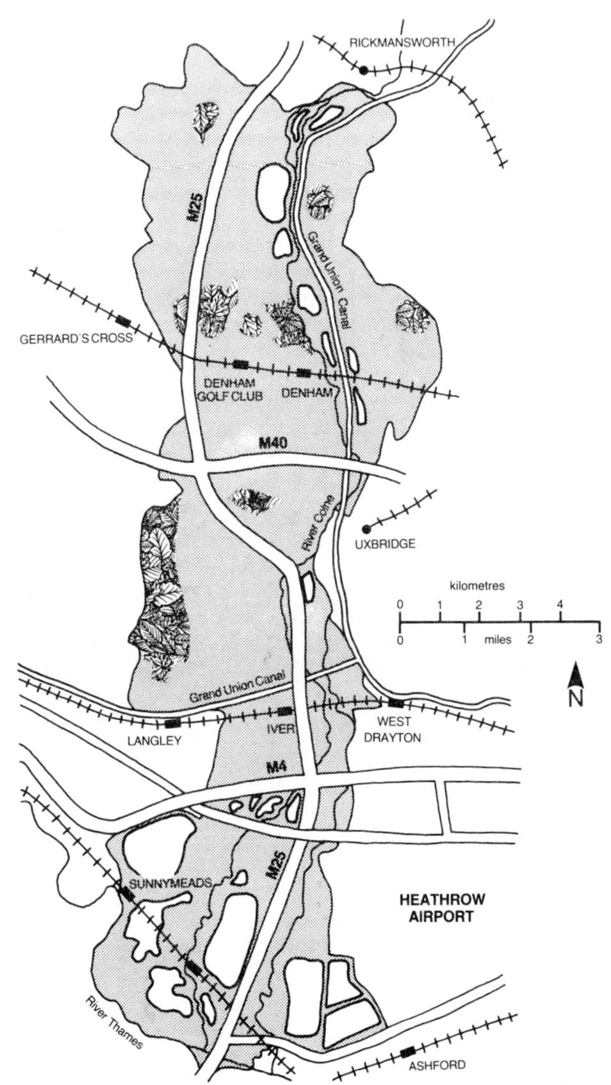

How to get there: by car on the A40/M40, the A4/M4 or the A30. By train from Marylebone to Rickmansworth or Denham stations; from Paddington to Iver; from Waterloo to Wraysbury or Sunnymeads. By tube to Rickmansworth on the Metropolitan Line; to Uxbridge on the Metropolitan or Piccadilly lines. By bus: Green Line to Slough, Uxbridge or Rickmansworth (704, 705, 711 or 724).
Origin of the name: Colne means water. Such a simple name reflects the fact that the river Colne was, for part of its course, the historic boundary between Middlesex and Buckinghamshire.
Area: more than 40 square miles (more than 100 square kilometres) of which about one-quarter lies within Greater London.
Owned by: mostly in private ownership, though large areas are owned by the respective local authorities.
Administered by: Colne Valley Working Party.

This three-mile-wide and fourteen-mile-long park, which lies on the inner edge of the green belt, stretching along the western boundary of Greater London from Rickmansworth to Staines, is really more analogous to the green belt itself than a park in the traditional sense of the word. Before the Second World War, the area was gradually urbanized until planning restrictions, including the green belt policy, were introduced. Although the idea for the forty-square-mile park was first conceived in the 1960s, it was not until 1972 that the first strategy for its development was actually published. Apart from protecting the area from unwelcome building projects, the park is being developed as a recreational zone, with the provision of visitor facilities, the planting of over 20,000 trees, and improvements to the existing footpaths, bridleways and the Slough arm of the Grand Union Canal.

Despite its proximity to central London, the Colne Valley Park is rich in wildlife, with several areas – Bayhurst Wood Country Park, Fray's Farm Meadows, Harefield Moor and Old Park Wood – being designated Sites of Special Scientific Interest (SSSI). The park has several heronries, including one of the largest in the London area, a fact which has led to the choice of this bird as the park's emblem. During migration time, several species of bird stop off on the way to their northern breeding grounds in Europe, Russia, Greenland and Canada during the spring, and again on their return journey each autumn. In winter, too, the gravel pits and reservoirs provide wildfowl refuges of national importance, at which time it is possible to spot the great northern diver, red-necked grebe, even smew and eider.

For broadleaved woodlands, the northern end of the park is best: Denham Marsh Wood, Oakend Wood, Caps Wood and Bayhurst Wood Country Park. For coniferous woodland, visit Black Park on the western side. One excellent introduction to the Colne Valley Park is a walk along the towpath of the Grand Union Canal from Rickmansworth to Denham (both points accessible by train from Marylebone station), or from Rickmansworth to Uxbridge if you prefer to use the tube.

Good circular walks are also possible within various regions of the park, for example from Gerrards Cross railway station in the north (through Oakend and Denham Marsh Woods and Great Halings Wood); or from Uxbridge tube station near the centre of the park (following part of the Colne Brook to Iver and returning along the Grand Union Canal). Or at the park's southern end, from Wraysbury railway station, around the Wraysbury gravel pits (a good site for spotting water birds). You can, of course, also plan your own walks with the help of Ordnance Survey maps which mark the public footpaths. For more detailed information, leaflets on the park's walks, wildlife, fishing and sailing facilities are sometimes available from local council offices, public libraries, travel centres and tourist offices.

As far as fishing goes, there are about fifty angling clubs which use the park, plus several public fishing venues, and about nine sailing clubs are licensed to use the various reservoirs and lakes.

Coombe Wood and Addington Hills

Coombe Lane, Croydon

How to get there: by train to East Croydon or West Croydon stations, then by bus. By bus: 130, 130B, 353, 355 or 357.
Origin of the name: Coombe is derived from the Old English word *cumb*, meaning 'hollow on the side of a hill' or a 'steep valley'. The place name of Addington dates back to at least 1086 and means 'estate in Aedda's territory'.
Area: Coombe Wood – 14 acres (6 hectares). Addington Hills – 130 acres (53 hectares).
Owned and maintained by: London Borough of Croydon.

The beauty of the Coombe Wood gardens is striking the moment you walk through the gate – a delightful effect which continues to enchant as you walk on around the grounds.

The first feature, facing the Conduit Lane entrance, is the Terrace Garden, once used as a fernery, but today planted with an attractive display of seasonal bedding plants. To continue around the gardens, take the uneven path to the left past the nineteenth-century pond with its bog primulas, water lilies, monkey flowers, umbrella plants and giant rhubarbs, to the rock garden planted with primulas, ornamental onions, mullein, thyme, astilbes and hellebores. The narrow path winds on between the old Coombe Wood House and stable block to emerge into the rose garden, and thence the winter garden with its formal beds of heaths and heathers.

From here the woodland itself begins, with its network of narrow and often very steep paths covering most of the southern side of the grounds, and providing an attractive contrast to the cultivation and formality of the gardens themselves. The woodland paths curve around towards Conduit Lane again, emerging into what was once the Coombe Wood House kitchen garden, now known as the Broad Walk and planted with flowering cherries, pillar roses, delphiniums, giant asphodels, bear's breeches and sweet peas.

Coombe Wood is one of those few examples in London where the public have actually benefited in the long run from the enclosure of common land. Up until the turn of the eighteenth century, Coombe Wood had formed part of Broadcombe Common, but following the enclosure of the common, this part was acquired by James Bourdieu Senior (of neighbouring Coombe House) in 1801. Coombe Wood House was, however, not built until almost a century later by Mr Arthur Lloyd in 1898, and it was presumably around this time that the first gardens here were laid out. The house now serves as a restaurant, while the old stable block adjacent to it has been turned into a café. Both are open to the public seven days a week.

For more rugged walking, cross Coombe Lane to the north to enjoy the wilder, less contained atmosphere of Addington Hills. Here, some 130 acres of rambling woods and heathland cover a 465-foot plateau, which falls steeply away to the north-west, with extensive views towards, and occasionally beyond, London. Apart from a wealth of regenerating trees such as birch and oak, there is also a good number of beech, pine and sweet chestnut – the result of various improvement plantings carried out here from as far back as 1878.

To reach the viewpoint from Shirley Hills Road, take the turning for the Shirley Hills Licensed Restaurant and then walk on a few yards further to the north. (Unfortunately, wheelchair access at this point is frustrated by five steps leading up to the small viewing platform.) A detailed direction indicator here points out such distant features as Amersham thirty-two and a half miles away, Windsor Castle and Epping Forest, though perhaps easier to see are Telecom Tower, the Crystal Palace TV mast and the skyscrapers of central Croydon.

The original viewpoint was a few hundred yards west of here, by the old Addington Reservoir, where the former Valve House Café was one of the added attractions – that is, until a typhoid outbreak in 1937 was traced to one of the reservoir water supplies: Addington Wells. The reservoir was then promptly fenced off, the café closed and the present restaurant opened at a respectable distance.

While exploring the hills, you are likely to come across several numbered green-painted posts. These mark the checkpoints or 'control sites' on a permanent orienteering course set up by Croydon Parks Department and the London Orienteering Klubb. (Orienteering maps and details are available from either the Addington Hills or Coombe Wood café, or from the borough's Parks Department.)

Apart from the obvious recreational value of the hills, this former common has also long been of interest to scientists, in particular to geologists studying the juncture between the south-western end of the Blackheath pebble plateau and the Woolwich clay beds, and to archaeologists who have frequently unearthed prehistoric tools along the plateau. To the naturalist, Addington Hills has a particularly interesting association of plant species, 200 of which were listed during a survey carried out in 1911.

Coulsdon Common

Coulsdon Road, Coulsdon

How to get there: by bus: 409, 411, 411A or 419.
Origin of the name: from the nearby town, whose name means 'Cudroed's hill'. (There has been speculation that one of the Saxon skeletons unearthed on Farthing Down was that of the original Cuthred or Cudroed.)
Area: 125 acres (51 hectares).
Owned and maintained by: Corporation of the City of London.

Being contiguous with Happy Valley Park and Farthing Down, Coulsdon Common forms part of a three-mile arc of some 500 acres of open countryside, stretching from Kenley Aerodrome to just short of Coulsdon South railway station. Coulsdon Common is one of four local commons purchased by the Corporation of the City of London in 1883, in order to solve a legal dispute between the Coulsdon commoners and the Lord of the Manor, Squire Byron. Like many of the lords of the manor of his time, Mr Byron had been steadily enclosing these commons – Coulsdon and Kenley Commons, Farthing Down and Riddlesdown – with a complete disregard for existing common rights. Opposition by the commoners was led by the Messrs Hall who, at great personal expense, took the lord of the manor to court and finally won the case against him. The Corporation of the City of London – well before any formal recognition of the need for a green belt policy – then stepped in and purchased the four commons to protect them for the public recreation of future generations. To this day, though fifteen miles from the City itself, all four commons have remained in the corporation's care and ownership – a fact which only serves to remind us of their great foresight over a century ago.

As common land, local people had for hundreds of years enjoyed the right to graze their pigs and cattle here, both on the grassland and in the woods, and the right to dig gravel for building or road repairs. Some of the old gravel pits can still be seen today, notably Gravel Pond, near the junction of Stites Hill Road and Rydons Lane, which has subsequently been cleaned and enlarged to attract birds such as finches which now come to drink and bathe.

Near The Fox public house is the site of another pond, now dried up, known as Sisters Pond. This was originally excavated in 1834, apparently to provide a water supply for the villagers. Although it no longer holds water, the earthen banks are still easily discernible by Fox Lane, opposite the car park.

The pub itself and the nearby block of houses, known as 'Newlands', are both early encroachments on to the original common. The present pub building dates from 1890, though this replaced an earlier ale house, a picture of which (dated 1760) is on display inside. Newlands was, at the beginning of the nineteenth century, the site of the Coulsdon Workhouse, of which one building near the centre of the plot still exists. Later, in 1830, it became the site of the first 'paupers' cottages', or almshouses, seven of which were built here by the local vestry at the cost of £140 each. Two of these can still be seen on the Coulsdon Road frontage.

About 150 yards north is the site of one of Coulsdon's two windmills, built about 1777 and demolished in 1924. This one was the village flour mill, as distinct from the smaller and older corn mill, which stood north of Stites Hill Road where Windmill House now stands. This smaller mill dated at least from the second half of the seventeenth century, but was demolished in 1880. Both were of the rather clumsy post-mill construction – that is, a type of heavily built mill which needed to be turned round each time the wind changed. All that remains of the old mills today is the hedged enclosure south of Stites Hill Road, and the miller's old cottage. There is also a small grindstone in the wall of 'The Granary' to the left of the entrance to Windmill Farm Kennels, and a 'peak stone' set in the grass at the gateway.

Oak and birch woodland accounts for about half the common, with several grassy clearings, one of which, along the northern side of Stites Hill Road running out to the east, has a strangely regular shape. This grassy corridor, much loved by winter tobogganists, resulted from the felling of trees in order to lay the Coulsdon gas main through the woods in the late 1960s.

Numbered posts at the western end of the common refer to points on a nature trail, designed by Croydon Borough Council in conjunction with the City Corporation in response to European Conservation Year in 1970. Detailed guide booklets for the trail can be obtained from Croydon Parks Department or Public Library.

For refreshments visit either The Fox pub on Fox Lane (car parking provided nearby) or the tea rooms by Ditches Lane on Farthing Down.

Crystal Palace Park

Crystal Palace Park Road, SE26

How to get there: by train to Penge West or Crystal Palace stations. By bus: 12, 12A, 157 or 227.
Origin of the name: from the enormous glasshouse, originally erected in Hyde Park for the Great Exhibition of 1851 and brought here in 1852.
Area: 106 acres (43 hectares) excluding the area occupied by the National Sports Centre.
Owned and maintained by: London Borough of Bromley.

The Crystal Palace was built by Sir Joseph Paxton originally in Hyde Park to house the Great Exhibition of 1851, but when the exhibition ended the palace was re-erected by popular demand at Sydenham Hill. Part of Paxton's task here was somehow to match the grandeur of the palace with an equally elaborate design for the grounds, so that Crystal Palace Park, in its original form, was laid out with imposing terraces, gardens, wide gravel walks, hundreds of statues and an awesome array of fountains. Some impression of the scale of this design can be grasped from the fact that with the whole of the fountain system on display, no less than 11,788 jets were in operation, pumping 120,000 gallons per minute and consuming for each grand display six million gallons of water.

The Crystal Palace and Park, which was to function as a kind of Victorian Disneyworld, with funfairs, spectacular firework displays, exhibitions, music, theatre and sporting events, was formally opened to the public by Queen Victoria to a crowd of 40,000 spectators and a choir of 1000 on 10 June 1854.

Today, over a century later, only scattered traces of this former grandeur and magnificence remain, for Crystal Palace was, like Alexandra Palace in north London, to be plagued by serious accidental fires. The north transept and part of the north wing were destroyed by fire in 1866, and in 1923 there was a fire in the south wing. Finally, on Monday 30 November 1936, Crystal Palace was completely destroyed by a fire so fierce that in spite of an all-out effort involving ninety fire engines, the glow could be seen from as far away as Brighton and from ships in the English Channel. By the following morning only the flanking water towers remained. The fire is thought to have been caused by a repairman's blowtorch accidentally setting fire to the paint store.

Without doubt, the most colourful aspect of the original park still to survive today is a collection of life-sized reproductions of prehistoric monsters which appear to lurk among the trees and climb out of the water at the southernmost end of the park. This antediluvian scene captures the imagination of adult and child alike in a way no ordinary palaeontological museum ever could, effectively illustrating the evolution of these animals from the early primitive creatures at the western end of the lake to the more advanced ones at the eastern end.

One curious aspect of these monsters is that although the models conform exactly to the knowledge of prehistory current in the mid-nineteenth century, in the light of subsequent discoveries they are now known to contain a number of inaccuracies. For example, the two Dicynodons at the western end of the lake are now known not to have had protective shells on their backs, and the horn shown on the nose of both the Iguanodons is now known to have been its thumb! If you should ever wonder what the old models are made of, the following is a list of what went into one of the Iguanodons: four iron columns, 600 bricks, 650 half-round drain tiles, 900 plain tiles, thirty-eight casks of cement, ninety casks of broken stone, 100 feet of iron hooping and twenty feet of cube inch bar.

In the mid-nineteenth century, when the boating lake formed the lowest and largest reservoir of the grand waterworks system, the level of water could be seen fluctuating so dramatically during a full display of the fountains that this came to be known as the 'Tidal Lake'.

Also of interest by the Tidal Lake is the popular children's zoo and, not far from this, the Penge cafeteria, serving sandwiches, cakes and teas from Easter to October.

Continuing on round the eastern side of the park, the next two lakes one comes across were originally the park's intermediate reservoir (now popular with anglers) and, in the northernmost corner near the BBC television mast, the upper reservoir, the remains of which have since given way to a covered reservoir. Scattered around the grounds also are a number of interesting trees thought to date from Paxton's original design for the park – among these are a couple of specimens of the rather unusual weeping beech.

Of the hundreds of statues which once stood either within the palace or its grounds, few now remain. That of Dante is to be found by the northern corner of the lower terrace, and a huge bust of Sir Joseph Paxton (1803–65) is situated about halfway between here and the railway station, facing the turnstiles to the National Sports Centre. Prior to its recent labelling by the Crystal Palace Foundation, this was frequently taken to be an intended likeness of either Beethoven or Karl Marx.

For many, the park's highlight is the series of open-air concerts at the Crystal Palace Concert Bowl, where the country's leading symphony orchestras have been giving performances every summer since 1961.

An interesting new development is the setting up in around 1981 of the Crystal Palace Foundation – a voluntary organization which has undertaken restoration and conservation of the palace and grounds, organizing exhibitions, talks and walks and publishing historical research. The foundation is also now in the process of setting up a Crystal Palace Museum on Anerley Hill in the building which housed Britain's first school of engineering (for further details telephone 01-650 8534).

Danson Park

Danson Road, Bexleyheath

How to get there: by train to Welling or Bexleyheath stations. By bus: 89, 96, 132 or 402.
Origin of the name: spelt Densington in the fourteenth century, earlier still as Denesiging tūn, meaning 'Denesige's farmland'.
Area: 186 acres (75 hectares).
Owned and maintained by: London Borough of Bexley.

Prior to its opening as a public park in 1925, the Danson estate had, for over three centuries, been a gentleman's country seat. Probably its most influential owner was Alderman John Boyd, an affluent City merchant whose wealth came largely from his directorship of the East India Company and his ownership of sugar plantations on the West Indian island of St Christopher. It was Boyd who commissioned Sir Robert Taylor to build the present Danson House – a Palladian mansion of Portland stone, built between 1763 and 1773 – and he who, at about the same time, commissioned Lancelot 'Capability' Brown to landscape much of the present park.

Perhaps the most ambitious of Brown's alterations was the building of the stone-lined earthen dam across the Danson stream to form the present twenty-acre boating lake – a project which involved flooding the site of the original mansion, along with its adjacent small rectangular sheet of ornamental water, known as The Canal.

Danson Park, along with the mansion and stables, was purchased by the Bexley Urban District Council in 1924 and formally opened then to the public on 13 April 1925 by HRH Princess Mary Viscountess Lascelles – an event which is commemorated by a memorial stone behind the house.

In front of the house is a delightful enclosed Old English Garden, well tended, with wooden benches pleasantly shaded beneath rose pergolas. To the west of this are the old stables which, though still standing, are in too dangerous a condition for public access. Just to the south of the house are magnificent rose beds planted in an awesome array of colours.

Descending the hill to the head of the long boating lake, one arrives at another enclosed garden, this time much more informal in character. This has been designed around the old Store Ponds and includes a water garden, rockery and heather garden. The rockery was inspired largely by the success of an earlier and smaller one at Hall Place, and constructed here between 1961 and 1962, using almost 300 tons of individually selected Kentish ragstone.

The park is well provided also with sporting and play facilities. Rowing and paddle boats can be hired from Easter to late September and licences purchased for dinghy sailing too. Anglers will perhaps already be aware that the lake is renowned for roach, and for perch, carp, tench and gudgeon; wheelchair access to the water's edge has been provided. (Wheelchair-accessible toilets are situated by the mansion.) Tennis courts, a bowling green, a grassy children's playground, fitness trail and open-air swimming pool all add to the park's attractions, as does a small refreshment kiosk contained within the Boat House building.

Each July Danson Park becomes the venue for the Bexley Show, attracting in some years as many as 30,000 people. Apart from the more traditional sideshows, typical attractions here include aerial stunt teams, parachute jumps and water-skiing. Since May 1983, Danson Park has also been the launching site for Bexley's annual hot-air balloon rally.

Dulwich Park

College Road, SE21

How to get there: by train to North Dulwich or West Dulwich stations, which are both only half a mile's walk. By bus: 12, 63, 78, 176, 185 or P4.
Origin of the name: Dulwich means marshy land or damp meadow on which the medicinal herb dill grew.
Area: 72 acres (29 hectares).
Owned and maintained by: London Borough of Southwark.

Dulwich Park can boast of having one of the best ranges of tree species of any park in London and of having several trees that are regarded as being among the finest British specimens of their species. Examples of such trees are the park's white birch, pin oak, Japanese pagoda tree, Kentucky coffee tree, tree of heaven and Cappadocian maple. Several of the oak trees here are believed to be over 200 years old and, because of their arrangement, are thought to mark ancient field boundaries. Although Dulwich Park had the advantage of having many mature trees even before it was first opened to the public almost a hundred years ago, a wide range of trees from all over the temperate world have been planted since then. A leaflet entitled *Dulwich Park Tree Trail* provides a guide to thirty-two species of the park's trees and this is on sale at the park manager's office.

The land was presented as a free gift to the public by the governors of Dulwich College in 1885; they in turn had been given the land in the early seventeenth century by Edward Alleyn, a friend of Shakespeare. Alleyn himself referred to this as 'God's gift' – an appropriate description, considering that he is supposed to have been frightened into making his generous bequest by 'an apparition of his satanic majesty among six theatrical demons' in a play in which he was taking part. There is perhaps a certain justice in this, since much of the land had previously formed part of Dulwich Common which had been filched a hundred or so years earlier. This common once stretched from Dulwich Park's main entrance (opposite the art gallery in College Road) almost down to Dulwich Wood, though all that now remains to remind us of its existence is the road by that name along the park's southern boundary.

When Dulwich Park came into public ownership in May 1885, it consisted of a series of undulating meadows covered with old oak trees, and had first to undergo major redesigning in the Victorian style, with an encircling tree-lined carriage drive and irregularly shaped boating lake, before its ceremonial opening by the first chairman of the London County Council in June 1890.

This three-acre lake, situated at the south-western end of the park, while only just deep enough for the paddle boats which are for hire here, supports a good variety of waterfowl, including Canada geese, mandarin ducks and teal. Also displaying a good range of bird species is the aviary – another of the park's original nineteenth-century features – which is situated at the eastern end of the lake. The café just to the north of this sells snacks and teas from March to October and is convenient for the popular children's playground, the bowling green, tennis courts and one of the park's two ecology areas. Another attractive feature dating back to the 1890s is the azalea and rhododendron garden, which Queen Mary used to visit regularly, and for which Dulwich Park is still famous today. This is situated at the eastern end of the park, near Rosebery Gate, and is at its best in May. (In early April the park's carpet of crocuses and daffodils is also worth seeing.)

Dulwich Park has the advantage of not having direct frontage on any main roads, so it seems unfortunate that vehicular traffic should be permitted through the park itself. Although there is little doubt that this detracts from the park's otherwise secluded atmosphere, it does mean good access for the physically disabled. There are wheelchair-accessible toilets in the cricket pavilion and by the café, access ramps for wheelchair-players on the bowling green, and a series of new 'touch' maps for the blind and visually handicapped, situated at each of the park's entrances.

Dulwich Park retains something of the aristocratic air of its early days, when Lieutenant-Colonel Sexby commented that: 'It is particularly free from the loafing population, which lolls upon the grass in St James's Park thick as windfalls in an orchard. Though open to all, it is specially frequented by a superior class of visitors from the immediate neighbourhood.' Before long, though, as the park became better known, it was better used, and today, superior or not, the park's visitors on a fine Sunday can number anything up to 15–20,000.

Within a quarter mile's walk are two other parks worth visiting – Belair Park off Gallery Road and Cox's Walk (starting at the junction of Lordship Lane and Dulwich Common) which provides a peaceful and beautiful approach to Sydenham Hill Wood .

Epping Forest

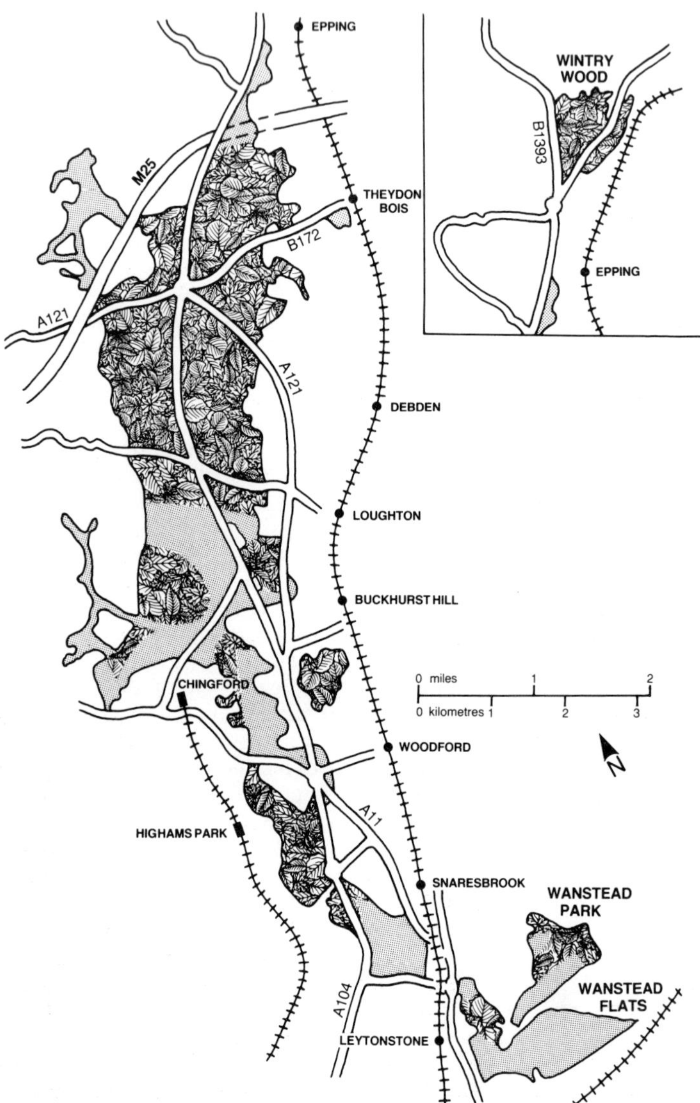

How to get there: by train to Manor Park, Wanstead Park, Wood Street, Highams Park or Chingford stations. By tube to Snaresbrook, Loughton or Epping, which are all on the Central Line.
Origin of the name: from the Old English *yppingas* meaning the 'people on the upland'.
Area: 6000 acres (2428 hectares).
Owned and maintained by: Corporation of the City of London.

'London's Back Garden', as Epping Forest is sometimes known, is equal in size to all London's royal parks put together; it stretches in a continuous twelve-mile arc of woodland and pasture from Wanstead Flats to beyond the town of Epping. Perhaps the best way to appreciate its extent and variety is to follow what is known as the Epping Forest Centenary Walk – a walk of some fifteen miles from Manor Park railway station to Epping tube station. (Guide booklets are available from the Conservation Centre, behind the King's Oak pub at High Beach.)

Some two-thirds of the total area is wooded, most of this lying north of Chingford, the rest being largely grazing land and ponds. The diverse habitats – ancient woodland, grassland, heath, marsh and over 150 ponds – support a great variety of wildlife. For example, a remarkable 144 bird species have been spotted in the area and some 300 species of flowering plants, including several that are quite rare. Apart from adder's tongue, cuckoo flower, heather, cross-leaved heath, gorse and broom, there are the rarer cotton grass and insect-eating sundew. In the lighter soils beech and birch are the main trees, with mostly oak and hornbeam elsewhere. Less common are wild service tree, field maple and butcher's broom, all of which indicate the wood's ancient origin, i.e. the fact that Epping Forest has been continuously wooded since the last Ice Age. Perhaps less obvious to the casual visitor, but something for which Epping Forest is famed in natural history circles, is the well over 1200 different species of beetle. In all, the forest clearly deserves the designation given to it in 1953 by the Nature Conservancy Council of Site of Special Scientific Interest (SSSI).

Human habitation in the forest is known – from remains of an ancient shelter found near High Beach – to date back at least to the Mesolithic Age some 10,000 years ago. Also of prehistoric times, and much more easily seen, are two iron-age earthworks, both thought to have been constructed as refuges in times of war: Ambresbury Banks (opposite the junction of Crown Hill and Epping Road) and the rather less conspicuous but more impressively sited Loughton Camp (about half a mile north-east of the Robin Hood public house on Epping New Road).

Around the time of the Norman Conquest, Epping Forest (then known as the Forest of Essex) extended to some 60,000 acres and was used as a royal chase for hunting. In fact, the forest strain of black (or very dark brown) deer is still kept here – nowadays within a special sanctuary on the edge of the forest – and Queen Elizabeth's Hunting Lodge has survived as the Epping Forest Museum. The museum, which houses a fine collection of forest animals, plants, birds, butterflies, moths and other exhibits, is open to the public from 2 p.m. to 6 p.m. (or dusk) Wednesday to Sunday, and is by the Royal Forest Hotel on Ranger's Road.

Fulfilling a similar function is the Epping Forest Conservation Centre at High Beach, behind the King's Oak pub at the junction of Manor Road and Wake Road. Established by the Corporation of London as their contribution to European Conservation year in 1970, the centre is managed by the Field Studies Council. It provides an environmental education service for primary and secondary school and university students, but also has an information desk, exhibition area and guided walks for the general public. (For further details telephone 01-508 7714.)

Even before the forest was used as a royal chase, local commoners grazed their cattle and collected firewood here, and it is from this time that the forest was managed by the system of pollarding which is so evident in the distorted forms of many of the older trees today. In order to collect firewood, the commoners had the right, during the lopping season, to cut branches from specified trees in their manor, and it is partly through the exercising of this ancient right that Epping Forest was eventually saved as a public open space.

In the mid-nineteenth century, like so many other commons, Epping Forest was fast disappearing; from 1850 to 1871 its extent had been reduced from 5500 to 2000 acres or less. When well over 1000 acres was enclosed by the squire and rector of Loughton, the Rev. John Whitaker Maitland, for sale as building plots, a local seventy-three-year-old labourer, Thomas Willingale, decided to make his protest.

To maintain the ancient lopping rights, custom had it that the loppers had to light a fire on Staple's Hill at midnight on 11 November each year. On that night in 1865 a large banquet with plenty of ale was said to have been staged at the King's Head pub by Maitland in the hope that the woodcutters would be too drunk to perform their annual ceremony. Tom Willingale and his two sons, however, stayed sober and slipped out just before midnight to perform the crucial ritual and returned to present a branch to the furious Reverend.

The Commons Preservation Society stepped in to offer Willingale financial help in the ensuing legal battles, but it was not until the City of London Corporation took the Lord of the Manor of Loughton to court in 1874 that the enclosures were finally stopped. Protection was finally bestowed on the forest by the Epping Forest Act (1878) and with much ceremony, on 6 May 1882, Queen Victoria declared: 'It gives me the greatest satisfaction to dedicate this beautiful forest to the use and enjoyment of my people for all time.'

Not only does the forest today provide for walking, horseriding and nature study, but also for boating, bathing, fishing, football and golf. On Wanstead Flats you may even see parascending – a sport in which the participant wears a modified parachute and is towed up into the wind behind a motor vehicle. At the more secluded western end of the Flats you are likely to come across cattle grazing – an odd sight for London. They belong to local commoners who have continued, in co-operation with the City Corporation, to exercise one of the traditional rights that have played such an historic role in the life and eventual preservation of Epping Forest.

Farthing Down

Ditches Lane, Coulsdon

How to get there: by train to Coulsdon South railway station. By bus: 190 or 411.
Origin of the name: the hill on or near a farthing (i.e. a fourth part) of a particular piece of land.
Area: 121 acres (49 hectares).
Owned and maintained by: Corporation of the City of London. A further 7-acre (3-hectare) strip of land, known as the Farthing Down Tree Belt, belongs to the London Borough of Croydon.

This common runs along the crest of a downland ridge some 480 feet above sea level, offering attractive rural views across deep valleys both to the east and west, and views north over Croydon towards Crystal Palace. To the south, Farthing Down adjoins the more densely wooded Happy Valley Park and Coulsdon Common , together forming a three-mile arc of recreational countryside stretching from near Coulsdon South railway station to as far east as Kenley Aerodrome.

For its natural beauty and walks alone, Farthing Down is well worth visiting, though it is perhaps more renowned for its archaeological remains, for clear evidence is still visible here of the down having been used by the Celts for farming and later by the Saxons for burying their dead.

Along the entire length of Farthing Down a network of low ridges divides the ground into small rectangular plots – most of these less than two and a half acres in area. These ridges, known as 'lynchets', mark ancient field boundaries where narrow strips of land between each ploughed plot would be left uncultivated, just as such strips can be seen between modern vegetable allotments today. These lynchets, which create noticeable humps in the road where they cross it, have survived from the first and second centuries AD, when the Romano-British settlers cultivated this hilltop for growing wheat. Owing to the primitive nature of their ploughs, the Celts had to confine their farming to areas naturally sparse in vegetation, but as ploughs improved the Saxons moved the sites of their farms down into the valleys where the soil is richer. It was during this period – the sixth and seventh centuries – that Farthing Down was turned into a cemetery, and many of these original Saxon burial mounds, or barrows, can still be seen, especially in winter when the grass is short.

The entire cemetery is thought to have contained some thirty barrows, all of which were excavated between 1770 and 1948, revealing skeletons, knives, swords, utensils and personal ornaments. The bodies were apparently all buried with their heads towards the west, suggesting the beginnings of Christian influence in this part of Surrey. There has been speculation that one of these skeletons, found in a barrow near the centre of the down, may have been that of the Cuthred, or Cudroed, after whom Cudroed's Down (i.e. Coulsdon) was named.

Following its use as a cemetery, Farthing Down became waste or common land used for grazing and the gathering of fuel and turf, and so it continued until it was acquired by the Corporation of the City of London, along with the other Coulsdon commons, as a public open space in February 1883.

Today it is provided with two car parks, toilets, tea rooms and a numbered nature trail, which links the down with Happy Valley Park. A series of trail guides for the different seasons is available from Croydon Parks Department.

In recognition of the need to preserve the unique and interesting nature of the down, it has been declared both an Area of Special Character (ASC) and a Site of Special Scientific Interest (SSSI).

Finsbury Park

Endymion Road, N4

How to get there: by train to Finsbury Park station. By tube to Manor House station on the Piccadilly Line or Finsbury Park station on both the Piccadilly and Victoria lines. By bus: 4, 19, 29, 106, 141, 171, 210, 221, 230, 236, 253, 259, 279, 279A, 735, W2, W3 or W7.
Origin of the name: the park was originally intended for the inhabitants of the old Borough of Finsbury, the name of which means 'Fin's manor'.
Area: 115 acres (46 hectares).
Owned and maintained by: London Borough of Haringey.

Although Southwark Park can, since it was opened almost two months earlier than Finsbury Park, claim the distinction of being London's oldest municipal park, the conception of Finsbury Park actually pre-dates that of Southwark by almost fifteen years.

By the mid-nineteenth century, the notion was fast gaining ground that the provision of public parks was conducive not only to public health but to the moral improvement of society and that, with the rapid expansion of London, the royal parks could no longer meet London's needs. In 1850, a meeting of Finsbury inhabitants resolved 'that a park on the borders of a district so large as the borough of Finsbury, and containing a dense industrial population of nearly half a million is universally admitted to be a public necessity.' With this historic declaration the campaign for the acquisition of Finsbury Park began, but it was not until nineteen years later, on 7 August 1869, that the present park was finally declared open 'to the public for ever'.

One reason for the long delay was the fact that the Metropolitan Board of Works (the first equivalent of the Greater London Council) did not yet exist and neither did the legislation which would later enable it to acquire land for public parks. It is to these campaigners' eventual triumph over red tape that we owe most of London's present parks, for it is they who helped clear the legal channels by which subsequent parks could be provided.

The most central and, at over 140 feet above sea level, the highest point of the park is the attractive boating lake with its ducks, gulls and geese. This occupies the site of an earlier lake dating from the days when Finsbury Park was part of the grounds of the old Hornsey Wood Tavern. Prior to the laying out of the park, this tavern and its surrounding tea gardens had been one of London's most fashionable places for pigeon shooting, that is until the sport shifted to Hurlingham and the Welsh Harp. A sense of the atmosphere of those days is felt in the words of one contemporary poet:

> A house of entertainment – in a place
> So rural, that it almost doth deface
> The lovely scene; for like a beauty-spot
> Upon a charming cheek that needs it not,
> So Hornsey Tavern seems to me. (*Hone*)

By the mid-1800s tea drinking in the tavern gardens had declined to such an extent that one of the first things to be undertaken in laying out the new park was the demolition of the old tavern.

The ground surrounding the lake slopes gently away, permitting an expansive view over rolling grassland and avenues of mature London planes and horse chestnuts. A good variety of young trees has been planted in the more open grassland in recent years and it is hoped that in time this may increase the park's attractiveness to breeding birds. For although sixty-three species of bird have been sighted in the park, only sixteen of these are known to be breeding here – a fact which is largely due to the lack of variety of trees and other vegetation. By contrast, the nearby Parkland Walk, with its wide range of birds and butterflies, and the banks of the New River at the northern end of the park, both provide good examples of the contribution to wildlife that even relatively small wilderness areas can make.

Other attractions within the park are the American or shrub gardens by Endymion Road at the north-western corner, and the nursery and training area nearby which, though fenced off from public access, is still admired through the iron railings. The small rose gardens adjacent to this provide a secluded place to sit, particularly popular with the elderly. Apart from the usual amenities of tennis courts and cricket grounds, there is a running track, bowling green (ramps provided for wheelchair players), adventure playground, café (open March to October) and toilets accessible to the disabled (near the car park).

Part of the nineteenth-century appeal of the park was its freedom from the smoke of London which would invariably ruin many of the flowers grown further south. Today it provides a convenient starting point for the Parkland Walk – a relaxing nature trail which follows a disused railway line, running from the railway bridge by the lake, right up to Alexandra Park via Queen's and Highgate Woods.

Forty Hall Estate
Forty Hill, Enfield

Map: see Whitewebbs Park, page 279.
How to get there: by train to Turkey Street station. By bus: 191, 231, 217, 217B, 310, 316, 360 or 735. By car – there is a large car park in the grounds, the entrance to which is off Forty Hill.
Origin of the name: Fortey (as it was originally spelt) means 'in front of well-watered land' – a reference either to the Turkey Brook or to the Lee Marshes.
Area: 262 acres (106 hectares) including 120 acres leased for farming.
Owned and maintained by: London Borough of Enfield.

The central feature of the present park remains the original Jacobean mansion, built in 1629 for Sir Nicholas Raynton, a wealthy haberdasher and later Lord Mayor of London. In spite of its acknowledged architectural importance and the obvious influence of Inigo Jones in the ornate brick archway leading to the stable courtyard, Forty Hall's original architect is not known with any certainty.

Both the mansion and the surrounding estate were purchased by the Enfield Urban District Council in 1951. The hall was used to house an exhibition of local history from 1955 until the early 1960s, when the house and outbuildings underwent extensive restoration and development. The hall itself was reopened to the public as a museum in 1966 and is well worth a tour for its elaborate plasterwork alone, for although these intricate interior designs date back to the seventeenth and eighteenth centuries, they have survived in remarkably good condition. The conversion of the outbuildings was completed in 1969 and these now house an exhibition gallery, banqueting suite and a friendly café (open 11–6.30 Tue–Sun & 11.30–6.30 Mon; Easter to September only). The Hall itself opens 10–5 Tue–Sun in winter, and from Easter to 30 September, 10–6 at weekends; 10–8 Tue–Fri.

Undoubtedly the most notable of the park's trees – just to the east of the mansion and rather dwarfing it – is a huge spreading cedar of Lebanon which is thought to have been planted in the late seventeenth century. Equally venerable, in its own way, is a large evergreen magnolia, *Magnolia grandiflora*, which climbs the mansion's south wall and which is known, from a lead label attached to the wall behind it, to have been planted in 1852.

Further along, through an opening in the tall red-brick garden wall, is the old kitchen garden, now planted with a great variety of roses, both traditional and modern in origin, along with azaleas, camellias and a wide range of rhododendrons. On a quiet day, the wooden benches here provide a pleasant place from which to appreciate the garden's peaceful seclusion. Pass through another opening in the high wall and you are on a fenced path that leads away from the mansion. Skirting open farmland, this path gives one the sense of being in true countryside, while still within view of the city skyline to the south. Right in the southern corner of the property is another wedge of woodland that also forms part of the park. Turning left here through horse chestnut and hornbeam, the path emerges to leave the estate near the junction of Forty Hill and Clay Hill.

If instead you should explore the grounds to the north of the mansion, across the lake you will notice a double avenue of limes, originally planted in the eighteenth century, apparently to lend a sense of formality to the mansion's northern vista. Walk down between these and you come to Turkey Brook. (In wet weather, you may need your wellies for this bit.) Turning left along the brook, the path arrives at a delightful long three-acre lake. A few years ago this hidden woodland lake was dredged and refilled after being almost completely dried up for several years – a restoration project for which the council received a national conservation award in 1983. The lake had previously been fed by the Turkey Brook until its bank was eroded to such an extent that water no longer flowed through it.

The brook itself is lined with a good variety of trees: alder, elm (though many have also been lost through Dutch elm disease), hornbeam, horse chestnut, holly, sycamore and several oaks which could well be descendants of those which once formed the Great Forest of Middlesex. Continuing along this brookside path, one comes out at the entrance to Whitewebbs Park and Golf Course – a walk which I can recommend. To return to Forty Hill, one need only turn left on to the Gough Park path which follows the old course of the New River. (A comprehensive footpath map, produced by the Enfield Preservation Society, is on sale in the entrance hall of Forty Hall.)

Fryent Country Park

Fryent Way, NW9

How to get there: by tube to Wembley Park station on the Jubilee and Metropolitan lines, or to Kingsbury station on the Jubilee Line. By bus: 719.
Origin of the name: derived originally from Freryn Court, meaning 'Friars' court' or 'manor', in reference to the Priory of St John of Jerusalem.
Area: 252 acres (102 hectares).
Owned and maintained by: London Borough of Brent.

The woodland, hedgerows and farmland here rise above the surrounding houses to two hills – the wooded Barn Hill to the west, and to the north-east the more open Gotfords Hill. In spite of the surrounding suburban housing, the variety of vegetation, the hedgerows and the elevation all contribute to an atmosphere of true countryside. In fact, right up until 1967 the land to the north of Barn Hill and east of Fryent Way was grazed by cattle, the traditional small fields being divided by thick old hedgerows, many of which are still intact today and which are known to date at least to 1597 and possibly as far back as the thirteenth century. The view from Gotfords Hill is regarded as one of the best in north-west London, especially to the west over Harrow, and from Barn Hill it is easy to see the Telecom Tower to the south-east and, on a clear day, beyond, to the BBC transmitter at Crystal Palace.

Apart from these views, perhaps the most interesting area here is the fifty acres or so of mature woodland in the south-western corner, on and around Barn Hill itself. At the crown of the hill are oak, lime, horse chestnut and beech scattered around the shores of an old pond. The pond itself is not of natural origin; though no one has managed to trace any record of when it was dug, maps and other records suggest a date about the end of the eighteenth century. It may have been a cattle pond, an old gravel pit or perhaps part of earlier ornamental landscaping. The slopes of the hill are mostly regenerating oak with hawthorn and blackthorn scrub descending north to mature oak, hornbeam, ash, beech and sweet chestnut, and westward to an area of young oaks regenerating on the site of an old golf course which fell into disuse here in the 1920s.

The whole area is noted for its varied wildlife, especially for the surprising number of bird species that have been spotted here – at least fifty-one in all. In fact, the Barn Hill area has, along with the nearby Welsh Harp Park, been for some time of special interest to naturalists and is rated as having one of the highest densities of birds for any comparable farmland in Britain. The ancient boundary ditches and hedgerows are of particular interest in this regard because of the habitats they provide for various animals, birds and plants. Among the more attractive of the wildflowers to be found here are great stands of the pinkish-purple flowered rosebay willowherb, ragged robin, foxglove, red campion, flag iris and broom.

It is quite possible that the previously mentioned Barn Hill pond was dug by the famous landscape architect Humphry Repton, for Repton is known to have been employed here between 1792 and 1793 by Richard Page, who then owned this large agricultural estate. This old estate is in fact the origin of Wembley Park which has since largely been built over – Barn Hill being one of the few fragments of this to have remained undeveloped. Repton's original design is known to have included the planting of beech trees and the building of a prospect tower by the pond on the hilltop – a tower which, since it was never completed, later came to be known as 'Page's Folly'.

Most of the estate became a private golf course in the 1890s but fell into disuse during the First World War. By the 1920s, however, much of the park was being developed for housing, with Wembley Urban District Council purchasing the forty-four-acre Barn Hill as an open space in 1927. The preservation of the farmland to the east of Fryent Way was then ensured in 1938 when Middlesex County Council purchased this and leased it to a local farmer. Unfortunately, with the change in 1968 from dairy to arable farming, many of the all-important hedgerows were then destroyed. Brent Council has since taken measures to ensure that the land is now more sympathetically managed and has even been actively encouraging conservation work.

In order to foster appreciation of the hill's wildlife, the Brent Leisure Services Department has designed two nature trails starting out from the car park off Fryent Way – one one-and-a-half-hour, two-mile trail and a shorter version of one mile, taking three-quarters of an hour. A guide booklet, *Barn Hill/Fryent Way Nature Trail,* is on sale from local libraries and from the Leisure Services Department, Recreation Division, Brent House, High Road, Wembley, Middlesex, HA9 6SX (01-903 1400 ext. 529).

Fulham Palace Grounds and Bishop's Park

Bishop's Avenue, SW6

How to get there: by tube to Putney Bridge station on the District Line. By bus: 14, 22, 30, 39, 74, 80, 85, 93, 220 or 264.
Origin of the name: both names refer to the palace in which, up until 1973, the Bishops of London lived. The name Fulham means 'Fulla's riverside pasture'.
Area: 41 acres (17 hectares) of which 14 acres (6 hectares) form the present Palace Grounds.
Owned and maintained by: London Borough of Hammersmith and Fulham.

Though it is known that the Manor of Fulham was granted to the Bishop of London in the early eighth century, it is not known when the first Bishop's Palace was built here. Parts of the present building date from the end of the fifteenth century, though even these are known to have replaced a much earlier construction.

Both the modern Bishop's Park and Fulham Palace Grounds were part of the original Bishop's estate, a large part of which was until recently enclosed by an old defensive moat. This original enclosed area included also the present allotment gardens known as the Warren – an area once used as the Bishop's private game reserve.

The gardens of Fulham Palace have been renowned in horticultural circles for more than four centuries, largely as a result of the keen gardening interests of several of the long line of Bishops who have lived here. Probably the most famous of these was Bishop Grindal who planted Britain's first tamarisk tree here in 1582 and who used to send Queen Elizabeth I regular presents of the best fruit from his garden, including bunches of grapes. Many of the historic trees have since died, though a beautiful old cedar of Lebanon and a black walnut have survived along with more recent plantings of magnolia and maple.

Part of the palace's former kitchen garden has been laid out as an educational botanic garden bordered in the old style with miniature hedges and planted with various economic plants, particularly those of the grass, rose, parsley and cabbage families. Here too are collections of heathers and bulbous plants plus a newly formed woodland garden.

Before leaving the Palace Grounds, mention should be made of a special adventure playground situated near the gatehouse and designed for use by handicapped children – one of five such playgrounds in London run by the Handicapped Adventure

Playground Association (HAPA). (For further details telephone 01-731 2753.)

On passing through the gates, one is immediately in what is now referred to as Bishop's Park – a curious 'h'-shaped property which fits snugly round both the Palace Grounds and the Warren allotment gardens. Here, the most attractive features are the long riverside path bordered with mature London planes, offering attractive sylvan views along the Thames, and a compact area of ornamental gardens in front of the Pryor's Bank, near Putney Bridge.

Before being laid out as a public park, this land too was part of the Bishop of London's property – in this case as the demesne lands of the Manor of Fulham. Its acquisition for public recreation was rather piecemeal. The first stage, which included the stretch of riverside land between Pryor's Bank and Bishop's Park Road, along with that strip running from here out to Fulham Palace Road, was acquired in the 1880s and, following the building of the present river wall, was opened in December 1893.

Next to be opened, in 1900, was the old Pryor's Bank garden by All Saint's Church, and then a further stretch of riverside meadow, at the north-western end, was incorporated in 1903, thereby extending the park up to the boundary of Fulham Football Ground. Here, a children's play area and paddling pool have been provided, along with a small aviary and cafeteria.

Walking away from the river, past the bowling green, football pitches and tennis courts, one comes to what is now known as the Moat Garden, so named because it has been formed over a section of the former mile-long palace moat. This section, which is now devoted mostly to a large adventure playground, is the most recent of the Bishop's Park extensions – opened in July 1924.

Finally, then, almost fifty years later, Fulham Palace Grounds itself was thrown open for public enjoyment in June 1974.

Golders Hill Park

The Park, NW11

Map: see Hampstead Heath, page 139.
How to get there: by tube to Golders Green station on the Northern Line. By bus: 2B, 13, 28, 210, 245, 260 or 268.
Origin of the name: the hill is named after the Godyere family.
Area: 36 acres (15 hectares).
Owned and maintained by: London Residuary Body.

Though easily overlooked as merely a western extension of Hampstead Heath, Golders Hill has altogether a different character and history from its wilder, unenclosed neighbour. The park was originally created in the 1760s as a private estate for the entrepreneur and aspiring politician Charles Dingley, and later landscaped under the advice of Humphry Repton for a subsequent owner, John Coore.

In June 1898, the whole estate was almost lost to the speculative builder, but for a group of local residents led by Samuel Figgis and Thomas Barratt, author of *The Annals of Hampstead*. A few days before the property was due to go up for auction, the committee set up a guarantee fund, enabling them to bid collectively for the estate up to an agreed sum. On the day, however, the speculators bid more strongly than expected and soon passed the anticipated £35,000 limit. The estate would almost certainly have been lost then, had it not been for Thomas Barratt who, on a bold impulse, continued bidding on his own account, finally securing the estate when it was knocked down to him at £38,500.

The public fund-raising appeal which followed not only succeeded in repaying Mr Barratt and the other guarantors within a month, but even resulted in the committee having several thousand pounds to spare. In response to the extent of local enthusiasm Golders Hill Park was, within six months of the auction, thrown open to the public in December 1898.

Although the Victorian mansion was destroyed by a parachute mine in 1941, the original walled garden, just north of the Lily Pond, has survived. This is perhaps the most beautiful and restful spot in the whole park, with a good range of flowering plants (including two large *Magnolia soulangiana*) arranged around a central fountain and pergola. Adjoining this is a greenhouse display open to the public on weekends, 2–4 p.m.

Extending westward is a short woodland garden walk which wends its way between rhododendron bushes towards the tennis courts and the larger tree-lined Swan Pond, situated at the wilder, more wooded end of the park, not far from the children's zoo. This modest collection of animals includes such exotic and domestic birds as the South American rhea, guinea fowl, crane, turkey, hen, pheasant and white peafowl, and not far from these is the ever-popular deer enclosure. For the tree-lover, Golders Hill Park has a surprising range of specimen trees, including the black mulberrry, dawn redwood, ginkgo, weeping ash, swamp cypress, Glastonbury thorn, Judas tree, handkerchief tree and corkscrew willow.

Among the park's other attractions are the summer band concerts, a fenced-off toddlers' area (by the deer enclosure) and a recommended self-service cafeteria (open March to October) serving salads, teas, gateaux, coffee and home-made ice cream. Disabled drivers may drive right up to the café, although, because of limited space, staff assistance should be sought.

One could hardly visit the park without making at least a short foray on to the Heath itself, and in particular a visit to the unexpectedly secluded little garden nearby, known simply as 'The Hill'. In 1775 these peaceful two and a half acres were the subject of the riot of Hampstead Heath when they were taken from the common by an actress known as Mrs Lessingham. In spite of both physical and verbal protests, the actress won the subsequent legal dispute and went on to build herself a new house here, Heath Lodge. Over the two centuries that followed, history turned full circle: the house has been pulled down and the surviving garden, complete with its grand pergola walkway, has since been returned to the public through its purchase by the London County Council in 1959. Access to the garden is just off Inverforth Close.

Green Park

Constitution Hill, SW1

How to get there: by tube to Green Park station on the Piccadilly, Victoria and Bakerloo lines. By bus: 9, 14, 19, 22, 25, 38 or 55.
Origin of the name: apparently a rather unimaginative reference to the greenness of the grass.
Area: 53 acres (21 hectares).
Owned by: the Crown.
Maintained by: Department of the Environment.

This is the plainest of the royal parks – a triangular stretch of undulating grassland and trees, providing a pleasantly verdant link from St James's Park, via Hyde Park, to Kensington Gardens. Though in spring the grass is colourfully sprinkled with daffodils and crocuses, the park has no formal flower gardens as such. Nor is there any lake or stream; the Tyburn stream, which did once flow through here on its way from Hampstead to the Thames, has since been diverted beneath the park through underground sewer pipes.

It is perhaps the park's general lack of ornamental features and its small size that make it seem, by comparison with its royal neighbours, so quiet and undiscovered. The park is, however, graced with a good number and variety of trees, including the more common lime, London plane and hawthorn, but also some exceptionally fine specimens of black poplar, black Italian poplar, silver maple and silver lime.

Green Park – or at least thirty-six acres of it – was first enclosed as a royal park by Charles II soon after he came to the throne in 1660. He regarded it then as part of his plans for the improvement of neighbouring St James's Park; in fact, up until the eighteenth century, this went by the name of Upper St James's Park. Two of Charles II's first additions were an ice-house and a snow-house – deep pits packed with the winter's ice and snow – for keeping his wine and other drinks cool during the summer. These features remained here in the centre of the park until the early nineteenth century.

Considering Green Park's apparent plainness, it has been the scene of plenty of dramatic incidents including many duels, three attempts on Queen Victoria's life and several spectacular celebrations, the grandest of which must surely have been the Temple of Peace firework display, marking the end of the War of the Austrian Succession. On 27 April 1749 the park was set up for what was described at the time as the grandest and biggest firework show the world had ever seen, with over 30,000 fireworks, including 10,650 skyrockets each weighing between four ounces and six pounds. To introduce the show, Handel had been specially commissioned to compose a grand military overture, the orchestra for which included 100 cannons.

Unfortunately, on the night, the huge Doric Temple of Peace caught fire shortly after the thunderous overture was performed, and everyone fled in confusion from the great store of gunpowder, so bringing the £90,000 celebrations to an expensively premature close.

Along slightly less spectacular lines, Green Park has also been a very popular venue for an unusual variety of balloon ascents, ranging from the man who made an ascent mounted on a horse, to the intrepid Mrs Graham who had a habit of dropping live monkeys attached to model parachutes from her balloon. Needless to say, not all these ascents ended happily – some, for example, wound up smashing into the houses on the downwind side of the park.

The park is remarkably free of the statues generally found in royal parks, but the name Queen's Walk along the eastern boundary recalls how Queen Caroline, wife of King George II, ordered a private walk here for the royal family 'to divert themselves in the spring'. Charles II is commemorated in the naming of Constitution Hill, said to be so named because the king chose to take his exercise here, among his subjects. Queen Victoria's reign is celebrated by the imposing black and gold ornamental gates at the eastern end of Constitution Hill, which were apparently erected to draw attention to the Victoria Memorial in front of Buckingham Palace.

Greenwich Park

Croom's Hill, SE10

How to get there: by boat from Charing Cross Pier, or from the Tower of London. By train to Maze Hill station. By bus: 53, 108B, 177, 180 or 402.
Origin of the name: the name Greenwich, meaning 'green harbour' or 'port', dates back at least to the tenth century.
Area: 200 acres (81 hectares).
Owned by: the Crown.
Maintained by: Department of the Environment.

Greenwich Park began its existence as such in 1433, when Henry VI's uncle and adviser, Humphrey, Duke of Gloucester, was granted royal permission to enclose 200 acres of Blackheath to form a private park – thereby making this the first of England's royal parks to be enclosed.

Much of the park's present appearance, however, dates from over two hundred years later, when Charles II invited the French landscape architect André Le Nôtre (the designer of Versailles) to redesign the estate in a semi-formal style. Le Nôtre's fascination for geometrical formality is evident in many of the straight paths and avenues today, notably Blackheath Avenue leading up from the south to the Old Royal Observatory, and several of the park's oldest trees are also known to date from this time. Plans for the park's focal point – the Royal Observatory – did not follow until over a decade later, when the King commissioned Sir Christopher Wren to design a suitable building for the newly appointed Astronomer Royal, the Reverend John Flamsteed. This he designed (as Wren himself put it) 'for the Observator's habitation and a little for Pompe'.

Perhaps the most appropriate – and surely the most relaxing and picturesque – way to arrive at Greenwich Park is via the Thames. Boats leave every half hour from Charing Cross Pier and stop at the Tower of London en route, with an informative running commentary on the outward journey. Approaching the park by this historic route, it is easy to see the attraction that Greenwich once held for royalty, and to appreciate the importance of the odd-looking red time-ball suspended on the top of Flamsteed House. This ball was once used for signalling the Port of London's time-check for setting ships' chronometers and is still hauled daily up the turret mast to fall at precisely 1 p.m.

On alighting from the boat – before entering the park – one passes two exhibits that are particularly worth visiting – the fifty-three-foot *Gypsy Moth IV* in which Sir Francis Chichester sailed single-handed around the world in 1967 and, rather dwarfing it, the famous nineteenth-century tea- and wool-clipper, the *Cutty Sark*.

Entering the park itself, through St Mary's Gate, one comes first to a small scented herb garden on the right (at its best in June and July). Ahead, the grassland rises steeply up to the old Flamsteed House, which today houses a famous and comprehensive museum of astronomical and chronological instruments. It was here that the basic principles of modern astronomy and navigation were first developed and this spot (marked by a stone-set strip of brass) has remained ever since the base for the world's system of time zones (hence Greenwich Mean Time) and also the reference point for the world's system of longitude, marking the zero degree meridian which divides the eastern and western hemispheres. This all forms part of the National Maritime Museum – the largest and most comprehensive museum of its kind in the world – the major part of which is housed at the foot of this hill, in Queen's House.

From outside Flamsteed House, by the statue of General Wolfe, is perhaps the best view of the park, looking out over the Thames, the Queen's House and the Royal Naval College below. The statue commemorates Wolfe's victory at Quebec in 1759 in acquiring Canada for Britain. Also at this, the higher, end of the park – not far from the statue – is the historic Queen's Oak, around which King Henry VIII and Anne Boleyn are said to have danced. The tree died in about 1878 and is now no more than a twenty-foot stump. Inside it is a cavity, six feet in diameter, in which Queen Elizabeth I is said to have frequently taken refreshments. At one time it had a door and window cut in the trunk, a paved floor and seating for fifteen people.

A good number of the park's older trees still survive, notably many beautiful gnarled and twisted sweet chestnuts, some of which were planted as far back as 1633. There are several old cypress trees and particularly fine specimens of paper birch, prickly castor-oil tree and the country's stoutest known specimen of *Euodia hupehensis*. The park's excellent variety of trees also includes several Indian bean trees, tulip tree, single-leaved ash, Chinese yellow wood, pride of India, red oak and foxglove tree.

A survey carried out here at the beginning of the century listed over 250 wild plants and eighty-one species of birds of which thirty-four were known to have bred in the park. No doubt the number of wild plants has since diminished, as have the bird numbers; a 1975 survey lists only sixty-one species of wild birds, of which thirty-two were known to breed here.

The best nature reserve here is known appropriately as the Wilderness – an area of some thirteen acres in the south-eastern corner. Though closed to the public and hard to find, let alone see into, this enclosure is of interest in supporting the park's thirty fallow deer. Greenwich Park's venison-raising tradition began at least as early as 1510 and appears to have continued here even when the park was sold to a speculator in 1653, at which time the herd numbered ninety-six. Today, to keep the animals healthy, their blood lines are occasionally crossed by the transfer of deer between here and the royal parks at Bushy and Richmond.

Close by is the islanded ornamental lake (with twenty species of waterfowl), some attractive flower gardens and, to the west, near the Ranger's House, a magnificent rose garden.

The Ranger's House itself was, as its name suggests, once the official residence of the rangers of Greenwich Park. It was converted by the Greater London Council to an art gallery in 1974 and today houses the Suffolk Collection (open daily, with no admission charge). For further details, telephone 01-853 0035.

For further details on the Maritime Museum, telephone 01-858 4422 ext. 221.

Gunnersbury Park

Popes Lane, W5

How to get there: by train to Gunnersbury station. By tube to Acton Town station on the Piccadilly and District Lines. By bus: E3. Free car park.
Origin of the name: Gunnersbury means 'Gunnhild's manor', though it is not clear who Gunnhild was.
Area: 186 acres (75 hectares).
Owned and administered by: London Boroughs of Hounslow and Ealing.

Though perhaps better known for its excellent museum of local history than for its grounds, Gunnersbury Park itself offers many attractive features – reminders of the historic improvements that Princess Amelia and later the Rothschild family once made to their private estate.

My favourite spot here is an area easily missed: the woodland shore of the Potomac Fishing Pond at the south-western corner of the grounds. Here the wildness of the woodland and the quiet intent of the anglers seem somehow to enable one to overlook the constant roar of the M4 motorway passing almost overhead. This corner of the park, purchased by Lionel de Rothschild in 1861, was originally a large pit used for digging pottery clay which was later flooded to create the present ornamental lake. The 'folly' tower on the lake bank, forming part of the boat house, appears to have been converted from the old pottery kiln.

The Round Pond near the museum is another attractive area, with its ducks and Canada geese. There are boats for hire here and, across the lake, a rather grand and elegant building called simply 'The Temple' – one of the places where Princess Amelia used to sip tea or dine with guests. This classical structure is thought to have been built in the 1760s as an ornamental dairy and is the only one of Princess Amelia's garden pavilions still to survive. The Round Pond is believed to have been landscaped for the previous owner of the estate, Mr Furness, by the renowned architect and designer William Kent. There are some lovely trees in this part of the estate, including tulip trees, Indian bean and a very large beech tree near the café (open daily from April to August and at weekends throughout the year).

Nothing now remains of the third pond, Horseshoe Pond, the clay lining of which was damaged by bombs during the last world war. What remained of the old pond had then to be filled in for financial reasons.

If you should feel that the noise from the M4 motorway or the overhead roar from air traffic in and out of Heathrow detracts from the atmosphere of the place, consider that matters could well have been a lot worse, for some sixty years ago Gunnersbury Park itself came very close to being the site of an airport. In 1923 the Civil Aviation Board judged Gunnersbury Park to be one of the best of twelve possible sites for a London airstrip, considering that it was only thirty minutes by road to Charing Cross and that only the trees and pond needed to be removed. However, a campaign began the following year to buy the park as a public recreation ground and by Christmas of 1925 it had been saved through its purchase from the Rothschilds by Ealing and Acton Borough Councils with substantial financial help from Middlesex County Council.

At a gathering of several thousand people, Gunnersbury Park was formally opened to the public by Neville Chamberlain, the then Minister of Health, on 21 May 1926. The former Rothschild house was opened three years later as a museum, which is now devoted to illustrating how both the wealthy and ordinary people of the area once lived. The pride of the museum's collection is its horse carriages – said to be one of the best-preserved collections of such carriages in this country – and its archaeological collection, which is said to be one of the finest of its kind in Greater London.

The museum (which is accessible to wheelchairs) is open every afternoon except Good Friday, Christmas Eve, Christmas Day and Boxing Day (free admission; telephone 01-992 1612 for further details). The park itself has extensive sports facilities, including thirty-six football pitches, two miniature golf courses, two bowling greens, two putting courses and a riding school. Provision is also made here for tennis, netball, rugby, lacrosse, cricket and hockey.

Hainault Forest
Romford Road, Chigwell

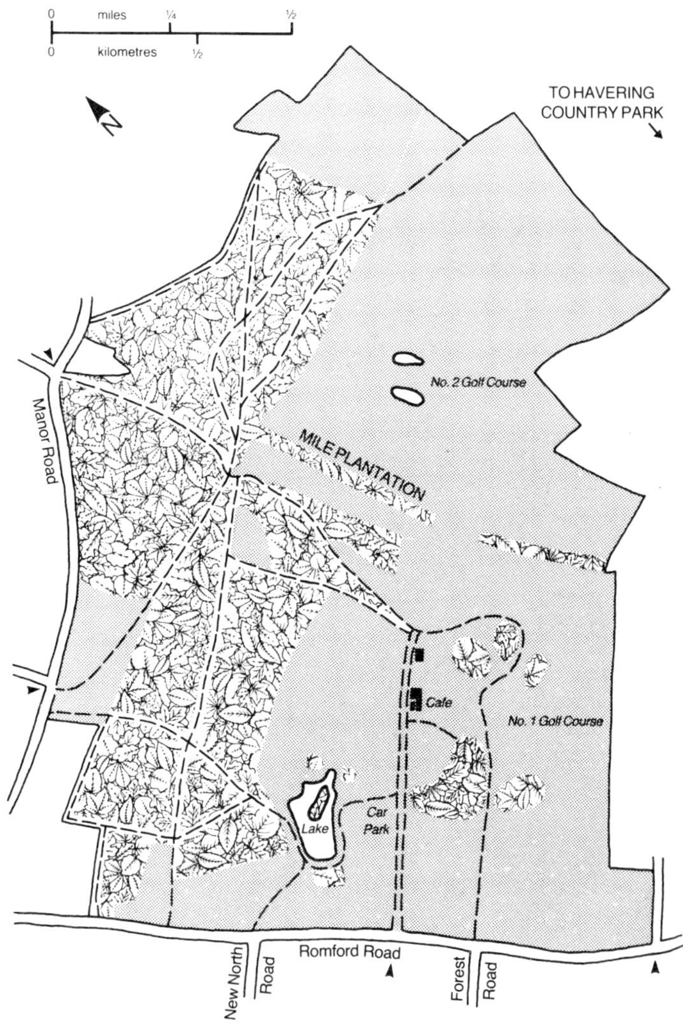

How to get there: by tube to Hainault station on the Central Line and then bus 247 (not Sundays) or 150. By bus: 62, 247 (not Sundays) or 150.
Origin of the name: 'wood belonging to a religious community', in reference to the fact that almost all of the original Hainault Forest once belonged to the Abbey of Barking.
Area: 1132 acres (458 hectares) of which 230 acres (93 hectares) is used for agricultural purposes.
Owned by: Essex County Council and the London Boroughs of Redbridge and Havering.
Maintained by: London Borough of Redbridge.

This, like Epping and Hatfield Forests, is one of the surviving fragments of the great Royal Forest of Essex, which at one time covered almost the whole of that county. Though a forest by name, a large proportion of this – even in very early times – was so termed only because it was subject to forest laws, for though wooded in parts, it was interspersed with areas of heath, marshland and grassy plains. For centuries this huge hunting ground had been 'especiallie and above theire other fforests, prized and esteemed by the King's Maiestie and his noble progenitors the Kings and Quenes of this Realme of England, . . . for his and theire own pleasure, disport and recreation'.

These royal hunting interests had for centuries served effectively to preserve the forest intact but, following the reign of Charles II – the last monarch to hunt here – enclosures and deer stealing in the forest were soon on the increase.

The greatest blow came in the form of the Hainault Forest Disafforestation Act of 1851. As a direct consequence of this Act – all in the space of six short weeks – the greater part of the magnificent timber for which Hainault Forest was once celebrated was felled, and the stumps grubbed up and dragged out by steam tackle in order to convert the old forest into poor grade agricultural land.

The forest would no doubt have been completely destroyed, had it not been for a Mr E. North Buxton, a verderer of Epping Forest who, seeing the potential recreational value of what remained, petitioned the Corporation of the City of London and the London County Council for its acquisition as a public open space. Buxton's task was not an easy one but he soon gained the backing of the Commons and Footpaths Preservation Society, the Kyrle Society, the Metropolitan Public Gardens Association and the National Trust and, by January 1903, 803 acres had been purchased by the London County Council. In a complete reversal of policy, the work of replanting the forest began and by July

1906 Hainault Forest was opened to the public as an open space for ever.

In spite of the 1851 Act, a sizeable tract of the original oak, beech and hornbeam woodland did survive and a number of the original pollarded hornbeams can still be seen today. These pollarded trees are a remnant of the days when – from Norman times up until a century ago – the forest was systematically managed to provide wood for building and fuel. Trees were cut every fifteen years and allowed to resprout to produce a new crop of poles. Unlike the similar system of coppicing (as was used, for example, in Ruislip Woods), pollarding involved cutting the trunks at about seven feet above ground level in order to ensure that the new growth would be out of reach of foraging deer and cattle. In the past century many of these pollarded hornbeams, having been left to grow unchecked, have assumed some quite distorted and fascinating shapes.

The woodland floor and herb-rich meadow clearings are equally interesting with lesser celandine, forget-me-not, stitchwort, wood sorrel, dog violet, bluebell, rosebay willowherb, bugle, foxglove, ox-eye daisy and white bryony. Some of the forest clearings are managed specifically to encourage the growth of wildflowers through periodic flailing rather than mowing, and many of these glades make pleasantly secluded picnic areas. Both grey squirrels and rabbits are common and foxes, badgers, voles, moles, stoats and shrews are around. Nightingales have recently returned and woodpeckers can frequently be heard drumming their beaks on the trees.

Apart from the woodland attractions for walking and horse riding, there are two well-used eighteen-hole golf courses, a number of football pitches and an artificial lake popular with anglers. There is a licensed restaurant (open all year) and a refreshment kiosk serving light refreshments (Easter to October) on the Foxburrows Farm Road, near the car parks. Unisex toilets accessible to the disabled are situated nearby.

Hall Place

Bourne Road, Bexley

How to get there: by train to Bexley station – then about three-quarters of a mile. By bus: 89, 132, 400, 401, 421, 492, 725 or 726.
Origin of the name: the mansion derives its name from its being the local manor house, or hall.
Area: 146 acres (59 hectares).
Owned and maintained by: London Borough of Bexley.

The sixteen-acre cluster of gardens surrounding the historic Hall Place provides the highlight of the mansion grounds, described by the national judges of 1983's 'London in Bloom' competition as being 'amongst the finest in England'. The judges, in awarding Bexley the top trophy in the contest, added that these gardens 'are extensive, imaginative and in the different features within the boundary of the park attain a complete spectrum of the very best examples of art and finesse in gardening.'

Perhaps the most striking of these features is the topiary – a collection of individual yew bushes pruned and trained to form various geometric shapes and animal sculptures. There are at Hall Place over forty examples of this Roman gardening art, including an intriguing row of figures representing the ten Queen's Beasts (the heraldic figures from the Royal Coats of Arms) planted here for the Queen's Coronation in 1953. The figures here represented are: the Lion of England, the Griffin of Edward III (a griffin has a lion's body with an eagle's beak and wings), the Falcon of the Plantagenets, the Black Bull of Clarence, the White Lion of Mortimer, the Yale of Beaufort (a yale is said to look like a horse with tusks, horns and an elephant's tail), the White Greyhound of Richmond, the Red Dragon of Wales, the Unicorn of Scotland and the White Horse of Hanover.

Adjacent to this is the rose garden which has likewise been planted in the traditional Elizabethan style, with over 4000 roses representing a wide range of varieties – the aim being to foster public interest in rose growing and to help local residents discover how new varieties fare locally.

Also adjacent to the topiary is a rectangular enclosed garden with a colourful display of bedding plants, surrounded on three sides by a buttressed yew hedge. And then, next to this, a herb garden, designed especially for the blind, with a variety of both common and rare herbs labelled on knee-high posts in braille.

Nearest the A2 motorway – and adjacent to the herb garden –

is a sunken garden, originally a pond since drained and planted with peat-loving plants such as azaleas, dwarf rhododendrons and dwarf conifers.

The river Cray here marks the southern boundary of the main gardens, though the grounds in fact extend beyond the river with many attractive groups of shrubs and a particularly beautiful rock and water garden constructed from local Kentish ragstone. These, and the adjacent white, pink and mauve heather garden, are at their best in May.

Also worth seeing in April and May is the spring garden – some three or four acres of daffodils and narcissi spreading around a range of flowering cherries and crab apples.

All these horticultural features provide a fitting setting for Hall Place itself – a sixteenth-century rubble-masonry mansion with a seventeenth-century red-brick extension. Though the present house dates back to about 1540, there have been earlier houses on this site as far back as 1241. The most recent occupant, Lady Limerick, sold the mansion and sixty-two-acre estate to Bexley Borough Council in 1935. (Some eighty acres were added to the property in 1946.) Today it is the headquarters of Bexley's Libraries and Museums Department, housing regular art, craft and historical exhibitions.

During the war, when the mansion and part of the grounds were used by the United States Army in connection with their top secret 'Ultra' code-breaking project, Hall Place suffered badly from neglect. Extensive renovation to the gardens was necessary before they were opened to the public by the Duchess of Kent in 1952. (The mansion was officially opened in May 1969.)

By the main Bourne Road entrance there is ample free car parking, a café which opens most weekends, and – on the site of the former kitchen garden and orchard – a conservatory and four-acre municipal nursery. Shrubs and trees for the whole borough and the bedding plants for the Hall Place grounds are grown here, while the conservatory itself houses a wide range of flowering plants, including orchids and various tropical plants. This is open to the public every day (though closed for lunch 12.30–1.30) and is well worth a visit, even in the winter months.

Ham Common

Ham Gate Avenue, Richmond

How to get there: by bus: 65 or 71.
Origin of the name: from the name of the village, which means 'land in a river-bend' (referring to the course of the Thames at this point).
Area: 126 acres (51 hectares).
Owned and maintained by: London Borough of Richmond upon Thames.

Ham Common is large enough to be a significant open space in its own right, but more so because it adjoins the 2500-acre Richmond Park to the east, and – via the pedestrian south avenue – Ham House Grounds to the north. It consists essentially of two sections, each with a quite different character. To the west of the main Richmond to Kingston road, the common has the atmosphere of a village green, frequently with games of football and cricket in progress, while around the common's small pond people sit enjoying the water lilies or feeding the ducks.

In contrast to this, the wilder eastern section, straddling Ham Gate Avenue, is much larger and more wooded – with oak, silver birch and an undergrowth of bracken and hawthorn; in spring there are bluebells, cuckoo pints, greater stitchwort and dog violets. Though parts of the common can be hard going in wet weather due to the effects of horse riding, the riders do on the whole keep to the marked bridleway. Perhaps the best-drained and most pleasant footpath is the one which runs close to, and parallel with, Church Road – this being generally secluded enough to allow one the sense of being in rural woodland and an opportunity to appreciate the woodland birds.

The history of any common has as much to do with the temperament of the local lord of the manor as anything else. Since the lords here – the Dysarts – were always more or less at war with the local vestry, it is not surprising that the struggle to preserve the common for the use of the public has been a protracted and difficult one. The Dysarts were frequently on the look-out for ways to increase their power and property, even to the extent of making the rather absurd claim that waste land they rented on an annual basis from the vestry had always been their own private property.

In view of the threat to the common, it might have been prudent for the Local Board to register the land under the new Metropolitan Commons Act of 1866, but the Dysarts went practically unchallenged until January 1891, when the steward of the Dysart estate erected several public notices around the common fields: 'This Land is private and all Persons found trespassing or committing damage thereon are hereby warned that they are liable to be ejected and will be prosecuted with the utmost rigour of the Law.'

This public proclamation finally provoked a local reaction. At a public meeting on the common called by a local butler, Edward Nicholas Radford, the assembled crowd of between 1500 and 2000 voted unanimously that if the notice boards were not voluntarily removed within a fortnight, they would be cut down. The fortnight passed and the Dysarts did nothing, so, to the delight of the assembled villagers, each of the signs was duly sawn off.

By the time the four men involved were brought to court, local people had already raised a substantial defence fund, and when the case was heard on 22 October, the court jury were able to declare Edward Radford, George Hall, Shadrach Hopkins and William Piggott 'not guilty'. The defendants had become village heroes; returning from Richmond to Ham, the four men were greeted with cheers and shouts and the waving of aprons, evergreen branches and anything else that happened to be handy when the carriage passed by. The commoners' first battle with the Dysarts had been won.

Ham Common was still by no means secure. For the next five years Lord Dysart continued to attempt to take the common as his private property, until 1896 when he introduced a private Bill in Parliament concerning the common. Under the innocent title of the Petersham and Ham Lands and Footpaths Bill, Lord Dysart was in fact offering this common land back to the public in *exchange* for taking other stretches of common land. Fortunately, the Commons, Open Spaces and Footpaths Preservation Society noticed that this was in fact a Private Inclosure Bill under another name, and with their strong opposition it was finally thrown out by Parliament by a majority of 144. As part of a campaign to preserve the panoramic view from Richmond Hill of the Thames and its valley, another more honourable bill – the Richmond Hill, Petersham, and Ham Act – was finally passed in 1902 and Ham Common was at last protected for public enjoyment.

Ham House Grounds

Ham Street, Richmond

How to get there: by train to Richmond station, then bus 65 or 71. By tube to Richmond station on the District Line, then bus 65 or 71. By bus: 65 or 71 to the Fox and Duck Inn, Petersham.
Origin of the name: the name Ham dates at least from 1150 and means 'land in a river-bend' (referring to the course of the Thames at this point).
Area: 21 acres (8½ hectares).
Owned by: the National Trust.
Maintained by: Department of the Environment. (The house and its contents are cared for by the Victoria and Albert Museum.)

Although Ham House was built originally in 1610 for Sir Thomas Vavasour, Knight Marshal to James I, its present appearance dates from about sixty years later when the building was enlarged by the Duke and Duchess of Lauderdale. The splendour of the estate at this point is well recorded by the diarist John Evelyn who visited in 1678:

> After dinner I walked to Ham to see the House and Garden of the Duke of Lauderdale, which is indeed inferior to few of the best Villas in Italy itself; the House furnished like a great Prince's; the Parterres, Flower Gardens, Orangeries, Groves, Avenues, Courts, Statues, Perspectives, Fountains, Aviaries, & all this at the banks of the Sweetest River in the World, must needs be surprising.

Remarkably, the house still contains almost all its original furnishings and with the recent restoration of the gardens to their seventeenth-century design, Ham House can now truly claim to portray more aspects of seventeenth-century life than any other house in the country.

Entering the grounds of Ham House from the river side, one passes through the original gateway into a walled forecourt, along three sides of which are placed thirty-eight busts portraying Charles I and II along with various Roman emperors and Classical ladies. Though those busts set into the garden walls remain in their original positions, the sixteen sculptures set into the north wall of the house were not transferred to their present locations until about 1800.

To the right of the house and through a small courtyard is the original kitchen garden laid out now with richly scented roses in a delightful range of colours. And, overlooking this, the former orangery, the eastern end of which now serves as a tea room. Two trees of particular interest here are a low-spreading specimen of the Christ's thorn tree and, at the other end of the orangery, a particularly fine example of the Judas tree – an unusual ornamental tree which in late spring produces pea-like rose-pink flowers.

Leaving this enclosure, one enters the main south front garden which, like the cherry garden to the east of the house, was restored between 1976 and 1979 by the National Trust as a contribution to European Heritage Year. With the help of surviving garden plans, this part of the grounds has been reconstructed in the seventeenth-century style, with eight grass squares divided by wide gravel paths, providing the foreground for a *patte d'oie* (or goose-foot-styled) 'Wilderness'. A popular garden feature of the period, this wilderness is laid out with hornbeam hedges, punctuated by field maples, to form an area of grassy walks and secluded 'rooms'. To complete the scene, reproductions of the original garden furniture have been commissioned and arranged here to conform with the appearance of the garden as portrayed in seventeenth-century illustrations.

Likewise, to the east of the house, the old cherry garden has been returned to its former design with meticulously cared for plantings of cotton lavender within a box-edged parterre, surrounded in turn by yew hedges and arbours of hornbeam. Both within this garden and along the south-side terrace the rich herbal scents of sage, rosemary and lavender are in the air – evoking visions of how life might have been when the Lauderdales were in residence.

Connecting the estate with Petersham Road to the east and to the south with Ham Common , two half-mile-long avenues have survived to provide an appropriately rural pedestrian approach to the house from the landward side. Of the two Thames-side access points, the one by the car park at the end of Ham Street is the easiest to find.

Although the grounds are open daily free of charge, the house opens only in the afternoons Tuesday to Sunday (a small admission charge is made). Wheelchair access to the house and grounds is reasonable and there is a wheelchair-accessible loo. Telephone 01-940 1950 for further details.

Ham Riverside Lands

Riverside Drive, Richmond

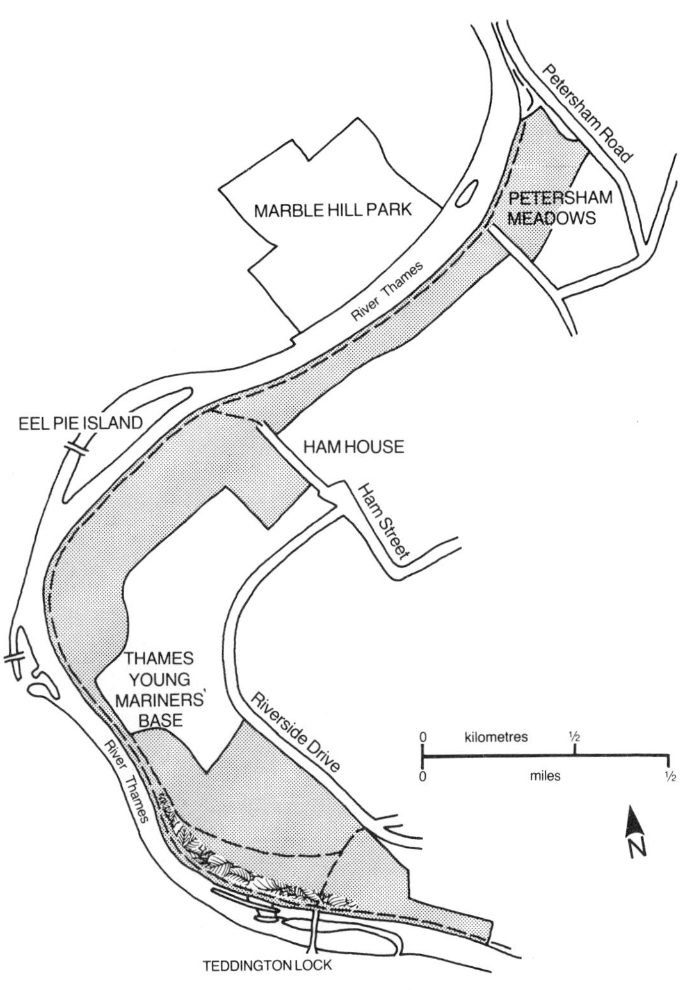

How to get there: by train to Richmond station and follow the towpath from the end of Water Lane. By tube to Richmond station on the District Line. By bus: routes 65 and 71 give access to both ends of the Lands.
Origin of the name: the place name Ham comes from an Old English word meaning 'land in a river-bend' (referring to the course of the Thames at this point).
Area: about 200 acres (80 hectares).
Owned and maintained by: London Borough of Richmond upon Thames.

This two-and-three-quarter-mile strip of flattish meadow land, wending along the eastern bank of the Thames from Petersham Meadows to just past Teddington Weir, provides one of the wildest and most pleasant stretches of Thames riverside walking within Greater London.

The riverbank's varied ecological habitat supports an unusually wide range of wildflowers including the more common rosebay willowherb, yarrow, broom, nettle, shepherd's purse, coltsfoot, hedge mustard, dead nettle, mallow and chickweed – even wild hops and chives. And there is a surprising range of trees – elder, sycamore, hawthorn, horse chestnut, elm, ash, willow and oak. In all, over 200 species of plants have been recorded here and at least fifty-two species of birds. And the range of butterflies known to be either breeding or visiting runs to an exceptional twenty-one species – a range which is due in part to the varied flora but probably also to the lack of insecticides used here. Not surprising then that this – one of London's few surviving natural riverbanks – should long have been of interest to naturalists, attracting botanists from the Royal Botanic Gardens at Kew and entomologists from the British Museum of Natural History.

It is not only naturalists who are drawn here, for Ham Riverside Lands is popular also with anglers, cyclists and horse riders, as well as with those just out for a riverside stroll or picnic.

The riverside path – which for the most part follows the old Thames towpath – offers good views across the river of Marble Hill Park and House, and of Eel Pie Island (named, incidentally, after a one-time local delicacy), passing the entrance to the Thames Young Mariners' Base (a good place to look out for herons and cormorants) and Teddington Lock. This lock marks the tidal limit of the Thames estuary; a stone pillar on the bank nearby marks the boundary between the jurisdiction of the Thames Water Authority upstream and the Port of London Authority downstream.

The weir, first built in 1811 and since reconstructed several times, is raised and lowered at high and low tide to maintain a constant water level upstream. There are here three locks ranging from the 650-foot Barge Lock, through the original Launch Lock, to the forty-nine-and-a-half-foot Skiff Lock – affectionately known as 'the coffin' because of its small size and shape.

From 1904 the land was excavated for gravel by the Ham River Grit Co. Ltd, with the resulting pits being infilled mostly with blitz debris from the Second World War. In fact, one local gardener, while digging a hole to plant a tree nearby, recently came across the roof of a double-decker bus.

While the gravel digging was still in progress, evidence here of a much earlier period was found in the form of flint implements, indicating prehistoric settlement, and an iron-age fort is said to have been situated in the area now occupied by the Young Mariners' Base.

In more recent times, though, from the seventeenth century to the end of the nineteenth, Ham Lands belonged to the Earls of Dysart – the same family who so unscrupulously managed Ham Common . A pay gate across the towpath opposite Eel Pie Island provided the Earl with the opportunity to levy a charge in 1770 of threepence on each towing horse passing along this section of the river.

Today, the use of the path is, of course, free of charge. And since Ham Riverside Lands practically joins Richmond Park at the northern end, via Richmond Gate, it offers opportunities for a number of quite rural circular walks of varying lengths, returning to the riverside either via Ham Gate, Ham Common and Teddington Lock, or via Kingston Gate and Kings Road to the towpath near Canbury Gardens.

Hampstead Heath

Spaniards Road, NW3

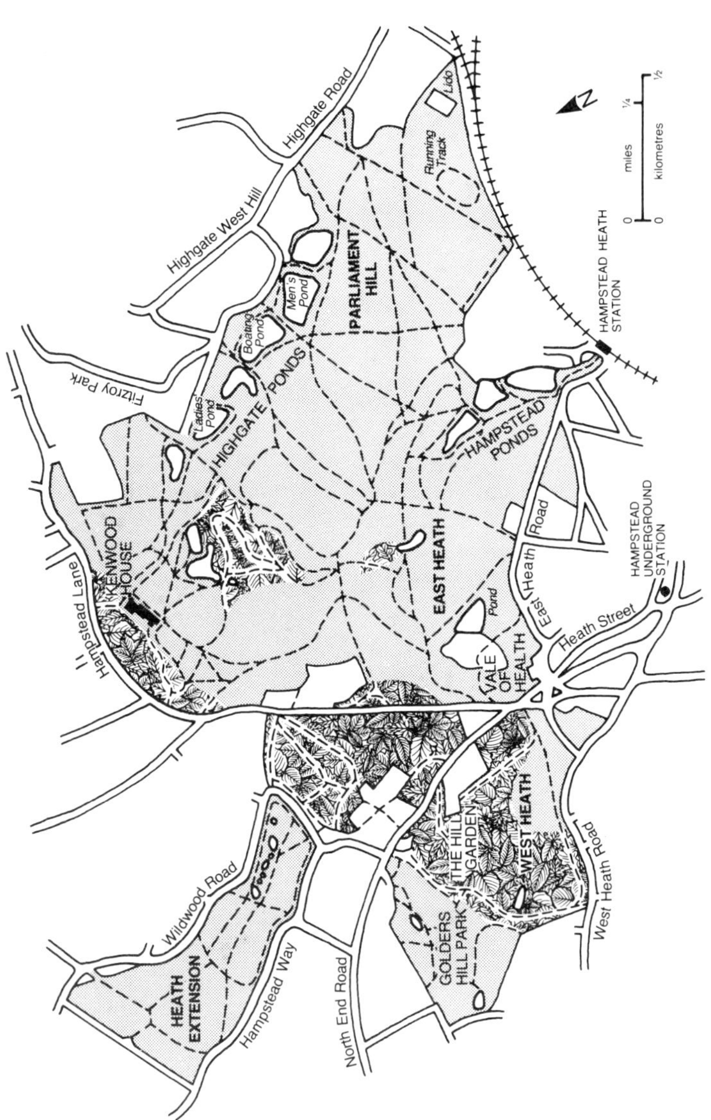

How to get there: by train to Hampstead Heath station. By tube to Hampstead on the Northern Line. By bus: 3, 210, 214 or 268.
Origin of the name: meaning 'heathland by a homestead' or 'dwelling-place'.
Area: 789 acres (319 hectares) including Golders Hill and Kenwood.
Owned and maintained by: London Residuary Body.

Hampstead Heath is one of London's most remarkable open spaces. Here, just four miles from the city centre, is over a square mile of rolling woodland and meadows forming a rural scene of such unspoilt natural beauty as to have inspired Keats, Coleridge and Constable.

From the Iveagh Bequest art gallery and summer lakeside concerts of Kenwood to the 'secret' Hill garden and deer of Golders Hill – from the breezy city panorama from Parliament Hill to the secluded bathing lakes and bird sanctuaries of Highgate Ponds – Hampstead Heath is surely a place one can never tire of.

To the naturalist, the heath has for centuries held a special appeal; in fact, its flora is now said to be among the best documented of any equivalent area in the world. The heath's ecological importance was acknowledged as far back as 1597, with numerous references to it being made by the renowned herbalist, John Gerard, in his *Herball, or General Historie of Plantes*, and today parts of the heath enjoy the protection of having been declared Sites of Special Scientific Interest (SSSI).

In spite of the overall loss in wildlife that one would expect for the heath over that period, there are still some eighty-three species of birds, including the lesser spotted woodpecker, tawny owl, kestrel, great crested grebe and heron. Rabbits are still numerous and foxes not uncommon. Of the heath's trees perhaps the wild service tree is the most interesting – this being one of Britain's rarest native trees, and one whose presence is frequently regarded as proof of the antiquity of the woodland in which it is found.

Considerable thought is nowadays given to how best to manage the heath so as to maintain its ecological diversity. To attract butterflies to breed, buckthorn is planted and some nettlebeds left to grow unchecked. Selected dead trees are left standing to provide nesting sites for the three species of woodpecker, and meadow flowers are both sown and encouraged to grow, through cutting some of the meadows on an annual basis.

The work of wildlife conservation is just one aspect of the long and eventful struggle to preserve the character of Hampstead Heath – a struggle which at times, in the eyes of some commentators, verged on guerilla warfare.

Although the heath had steadily been shrinking with the eighteenth-century expansion of Hampstead, it was not until 1829 that Hampstead's 'Guerilla War' began in earnest. As common land of the Manor of Hampstead, the heath, though subject to the traditional rights of local commoners, was the property of the lord of the manor – in this case, Sir Thomas Maryon Wilson. In 1829 Sir Thomas lodged the first of a series of Bills in the House of Lords in an attempt to give himself permission to build over and around the heath. Fortunately this Bill was defeated, but Sir Thomas was a stubborn man and it was only through the concerted opposition of a number of tireless campaigners – notably a local banker, John Gurney Hoare – that every one of the fifteen such Bills to be lodged over the next forty years by Sir Thomas was also defeated. Each new protest by the people of Hampstead only served to harden Sir Thomas's resolve, so that the long struggle only found its resolution with the old man's death in 1869.

Fortunately for us, Sir Thomas's brother and heir, Sir John, was a more amiable and conciliatory character and in 1871 the first 220 acres of the present heath were purchased from him by the Metropolitan Board of Works – on condition that 'the Board shall for ever keep the Heath open, unenclosed and unbuilt on'.

The battle for the heath was, however, by no means yet over, for it was to be another hundred years before the whole of the heath as we know it today could finally be protected for public enjoyment. Parliament Hill was added in 1889, Golders Hill Park in 1898, the Heath Extension (to the north) in 1907 and Kenwood between 1924 and 1928; this was followed by a number of smaller acquisitions such as the Pitt House garden in 1954, the Elms garden in 1959 and the Hill garden in 1960.

It is ironic that this struggle has not only been with the speculative builder but also with the 'beautifier'. In 1853, C. R. Cockerell drew up plans to create a 'Hampstead New Park' along the lines of Nash's Regent's Park. Then again in 1871, after the Metropolitan Board of Works finally gained jurisdiction over the heath, a letter appeared in *The Times* urging the board to 'improve' the heath along the lines of Hampton Court or Kew Gardens. Such pleas and attempts to formalize and 'tidy up' the heath's wildness persisted until it finally became clear that to effectively preserve such a large and beautiful landscape an independent conservation body was needed, and in 1897 the Hampstead Heath Protection Society (now the Heath and Old

Hampstead Society) was formed 'for the protection of Hampstead Heath and the preservation of its natural beauties'.

And so the struggles go on, for there are still those who, unmoved by the wild natural beauty of the heath, would like to see it built over.

Hampton Court Park

Hampton Court Road, East Molesey

Map: see Bushy park, page 77.
How to get there: by train to Hampton Court station. By bus: 111, 131, 216, 267, 461, 713, 715, 716, 718 or 726.
Origin of the name: Hampton means 'farm in a river-bend', referring to the pronounced loop here in the course of the river Thames.
Area: 693 acres (281 hectares).
Owned by: the Crown.
Maintained by: Department of the Environment.

Most of the 700,000 visitors to Hampton Court each year come to view the impressive one-time home of Cardinal Wolsey – Hampton Court Palace – and frequently overlook both the great range of ornamental gardens surrounding the palace and the deer park which stretches east to the Thames.

The Hampton Court gardens have, over the past four and a half centuries, undergone many changes under the various monarchs who have lived here. Most of what survives today dates from the late seventeenth century (the reign of William III and Mary II) and is an example of the formal, architectural style which was predominant until the landscape gardening revolution of the early eighteenth century.

The first feature to catch one's attention on looking at a map of the park, or indeed from the roof of the palace, is the enormous radiating *patte d'oie*, or goose-foot, design formed by three broad avenues of conically pruned yews leading from the palace beyond the Little (semicircular) Canal to avenues of limes. The 'middle toe' of the design is formed by the Long Water, a perfectly rectangular formal lake or canal extending for three-quarters of a mile through the deer park almost to the Thames.

Without a doubt, the most famous and most frequently visited feature of the gardens is the triangular yew and privet maze to the north of the palace near Lion Gate. Originally clipped from hedges of hornbeam, this was planted in 1714 for Queen Anne and has since become what is reputed to be the most famous maze in the world with over 500,000 users a year, attempting to lose and find themselves along its half mile of paths.

Close by is the Laburnum Walk – not to be missed in May or June when its cascades of yellow flowers catch the light to form an airy and golden tunnel. To the west of the maze, in the seven-acre Tilt Yard Gardens, there is a fine display of roses –

many of them examples of older, more traditional varieties. The garden's name refers to a pastime once enjoyed here by Henry VIII – a hazardous sport called jousting, in which the participants, wearing their full battle armour, would ride against each other with levelled lances.

Continuing on round to the south of the palace, by the river, are several other garden features of particular interest, notably the world-famous Great Vine brought here as a cutting from a Black Hamburg vine at Valentines Park, East London, in 1768. Today, the Great Vine produces 500 or 600 bunches of grapes each year, in some years amounting to over 700 pounds of fruit! At the end of August or the beginning of September, the grapes are usually on sale to the public.

Then, too, there are the ancient and colourful pond gardens with their miniature box bushes and vast array of bright flowerbeds (at their best from spring to autumn), a re-created Tudor-style knot garden (with tulips, hyacinths and daffodils), Queen Anne's orangery and the privy garden (designed originally for the private use of the various royals who once lived here). This last, with its combination of flowers, statues and fountains, is considered to show formal gardening at its very best. Alongside, dividing this garden from the Thames, is the famous Tijou's Screen – twelve wrought-iron panels created in the late seventeenth century by the master smith Jean Tijou.

Venturing further east through the gateway one emerges into the vast deer park, where one can escape the palace crowds, often encountering only sheep gathered in the shade of trees or some of the park's 200 fallow deer grazing.

To explore further this sense of wildness and space, cross Hampton Court Road to enter neighbouring Bushy Park with its magnificent Waterhouse Woodland Garden.

Happy Valley Park

Coulsdon Road, Coulsdon

How to get there: by train to Coulsdon South station. By bus: 4, 190, 405, 409, 411, 411A, 414 or 419.
Origin of the name: from the pleasant valley which forms the greater part of the park.
Area: 250 acres (101 hectares).
Owned and maintained by: London Borough of Croydon.

Happy Valley Park, together with the adjoining Farthing Down and Coulsdon Common, stretches in a three-mile arc from near Coulsdon South railway station to Kenley Aerodrome, covering around 500 acres of public land. This delightfully unspoilt belt of countryside provides a popular venue for walkers and wildlife enthusiasts alike, proving popular also with picnickers and with those just wishing to enjoy the park's long and beautifully rural views. Both ends of the valley are supplied with marked nature trails which provide circular links with the adjoining commons. Guides to these two trails (which can be purchased from the Welcome Tea Rooms at the southern end of Farthing Down) help the walker to identify the more common plants, birds, animals and insects to be found here.

The Happy Valley is one of a number of dry valleys which cut into the north-facing slope of the North Downs and which are thought to have been formed following the last Ice Age as a product of erosion from the vast snow-melt. The variety of soil types and of habitats – woods, woodland belts and open pasture – have together contributed towards the valley's rich and varied wildlife. The flora of the western end of the valley – the Devilsden Wood area – is especially rich, as is illustrated by a survey carried out in the late 1950s in which a total of 279 plant species (many of them rare) were recorded here. It is this rich and varied wildlife which has earned the Devilsden Wood end of the park the designation of Site of Special Scientific Interest (SSSI).

The land was purchased as a park in several stages in 1937 and 1938 under the Metropolitan Green Belt Scheme, thereby providing a strategic bridge between the two Coulsdon commons at either end of it, already acquired through the foresight of the Corporation of the City of London in 1883.

The land was at first largely leased for farming, but with the destruction of the rabbit population through myxomatosis in the 1950s, scrub began to take over many acres of the valley, smothering as it did so the rich variety of chalkland wildflowers.

In order to check this reversion to woodland and maintain the floral diversity of the grassland, the council decided to keep to a selective scrub clearance programme, which has led to the return of much of the beautiful and interesting wild flora. Of these wildflowers, perhaps the most spectacular are the wild orchids – the bee orchid, common spotted orchid, scented orchid, pyramidal orchid, man orchid and common twayblade. Plentiful also are the more common wildflower favourites – violets, primroses and cowslips.

The valley is rich also in butterflies; in summer one can see the chalk hill blue, common blue, orange tip, small copper, speckled wood, large white, peacock, red admiral, small tortoiseshell and the yellow brimstone. And of course there are many bird species – green and great spotted woodpeckers, nuthatch, treecreeper, linnet, bullfinch, yellow-hammer, dunnock, tawny owl, redwing, fieldfare and jay, to name just a few, and all the common mammals including the fox and badger.

Car parking is provided at both ends of the park: on Fox Lane and Ditches Lane. Refreshments and toilets are situated at the western end of Devilsden Wood, on Farthing Down.

Havering Country Park

Orange Tree Hill, Havering-atte-Bower

How to get there: by train to Romford station, then by bus. By tube to Elm Park on the District Line, and then bus 165. By bus: 165 or 294.
Origin of the name: from the neighbouring village of Havering-atte-Bower, meaning 'place of the people of Haefer, near a royal residence'.
Area: 168 acres (68 hectares).
Owned and maintained by: London Borough of Havering.

For years, Havering Park has been a naturalist's paradise, well suited for bird watching and for the study of local flora and fauna. The predominantly oak and birch woodland is interspersed with gently sloping meadows, ideal for picnicking, while the park's three miles of waymarked bridlepaths provide popular riding routes linking the wood with nearby Hainault Forest. Likewise, for the walker there are many footpaths both within the park itself and along the Havering Ridge, west to Hainault Forest or east (via a short stretch of road) to Bedfords Park.

For the most part the tree cover consists of oak, birch, sycamore, hawthorn and pine, with a mature avenue of Wellingtonias running east–west across the northern end of the park, and an undergrowth dominated by blackberry, holly, wild rose and elder interspersed in places with nettle, willowherb and bracken. Management of the wood has involved some tree planting to screen the park from adjacent building development, the removal of dead and diseased trees and the regular thinning of sycamores which would otherwise preclude the growth of the park's native and more ecologically-significant trees. The park's facilities include provision for car parking and, for the moment, temporary toilets on the park's south-western corner.

Like Epping and Hainault Forests, Havering Country Park was originally part of the great Royal Hunting Forest of Essex. In the late 1920s the site of the present park was subdivided into large plots for smallholdings and weekend use by Londoners in search of a break from city life. These modern Arcadians built themselves modest huts here, frequently bringing building materials to their new plots in motorcycle sidecars, and planting flowers, ornamental and fruit trees nearby, to create their own temporary retreats from the smoky East End. A newspaper advertisement from 1937 typifies the scene at the time: 'Ideal Week-End Holidays – Plot 60ft. by 78ft., freehold; fenced; Hut 6ft. × 5ft., tent (sleep 2); lav.; £30 cash or terms; Beautiful scenery.'

By the end of the Second World War these weekend retreats began to be used on a more permanent basis, but with green belt planning restrictions it was not possible for the plotholders to make improvements either to their simple structures or to the amenities. As London expanded to meet, and later to engulf, Havering, so the innocence of the once rural retreat was gradually lost to opportunistic traders and others with little apparent sympathy for homesteading.

In 1961 Essex County Council decided to clear the area – a decision adhered to by the Greater London Council when it took power in 1965. A public inquiry followed in 1971 to hear the various arguments for and against the compulsory purchase of individual plots as part of a scheme to replan the whole area as a regional Country Park, and in October 1979, with the first phase of restoration completed, Havering Country Park was formally opened to the public.

Hayes Common

Croydon Road, Bromley

How to get there: by train to Hayes station. By bus: 146 (except Sundays), 353 and 357 all stop in the middle of the common.
Origin of the name: the name Hayes can be traced back as far as 1177, when it was spelt Hesa from the Old English *hoese*, meaning 'a settlement in open land overgrown with shrubs and rough bushes'.
Area: 207 acres (84 hectares).
Owned and maintained by: London Borough of Bromley.

For those familiar only with London's more open, grassy commons, like those at Wandsworth, Clapham and Tooting, Hayes Common comes as a surprise: it is almost entirely wooded. At the western end oak predominates with an undergrowth of holly, blackberry, gorse and rhododendron. Moving eastward, this undergrowth becomes generally less dense, consisting mostly of bracken, while at the very eastern end the oak gives way to silver birch. There is, however, a square-shaped green at the top of Station Hill and this is conveniently supplied with attractive rustic benches, a drinking fountain (out of order!) and two oak trees – one of which was planted to commemorate the death of Sir Winston Churchill in 1965. For the horse rider, a good network of bridlepaths has been provided and railed to protect the interests both of pedestrians and wildlife.

From the common's southernmost corner, it is a short and worthwhile walk (along Heathfield Road) to Keston Common – one of the best areas of relict heathland in the whole of Greater London.

Across Croydon Road at the western end is West Wickham Common, which is similarly wooded and generally indistinguishable from the larger Hayes Common. The history of these two commons is closely interrelated. West Wickham Common was the waste land of the old Manor of West Wickham and Hayes Common the waste of the Manor of Baston. When, in the 1860s, the Lord of both manors, Sir John Lennard, began selling off plots of West Wickham Common as sites for villas, there was a good deal of concern that Hayes Common would before long succumb to the same fate. It was this fear which led a large body of commoners, in 1868, to organize their opposition to the enclosure of Hayes Common – a movement which was to lead to Hayes Common becoming the first common in England and Wales to be given legal protection against enclosures under the new Metropolitan Commons Act of 1866.

Like commons elsewhere in Britain, Hayes Common had for centuries been a place where local people had the right to graze their cows and sheep and to collect firewood, and by the early nineteenth century it also became the regular site of the *Hays Fair*. A poster for the one held in 1804 lists some of the amusements of the day:

> A Match at Grimace or Grinning through a Horse Collar.
> A Match at eating Hot Hasty Pudding, by Boys.
> A Match at drinking Hot Tea, by Elderly Ladies.
> An Ass Race. . . with various other amusements.

A cautionary note adds: 'No Ladies permitted to enter the Prize Lists who may appear to have drank too freely of Strong Waters.'

In 1828, there is a record of the day when two men and a horse descended by balloon on to the common. With so much going on, it is perhaps not surprising that, with the opening of the railway to Hayes in 1882, the common was to become a popular place for Londoners on day excursions.

When, in 1869, legal protection was finally given to Hayes Common, the Act passed to confirm its new status arranged for management by a board of conservators (in the same way as Wimbledon, Mitcham and the Chislehurst Commons are administered). In 1954, however, this responsibility passed to Bromley Council, though Hayes Village Association, among others, has continued to take a keen interest.

High Elms Estate

High Elms Road, Orpington

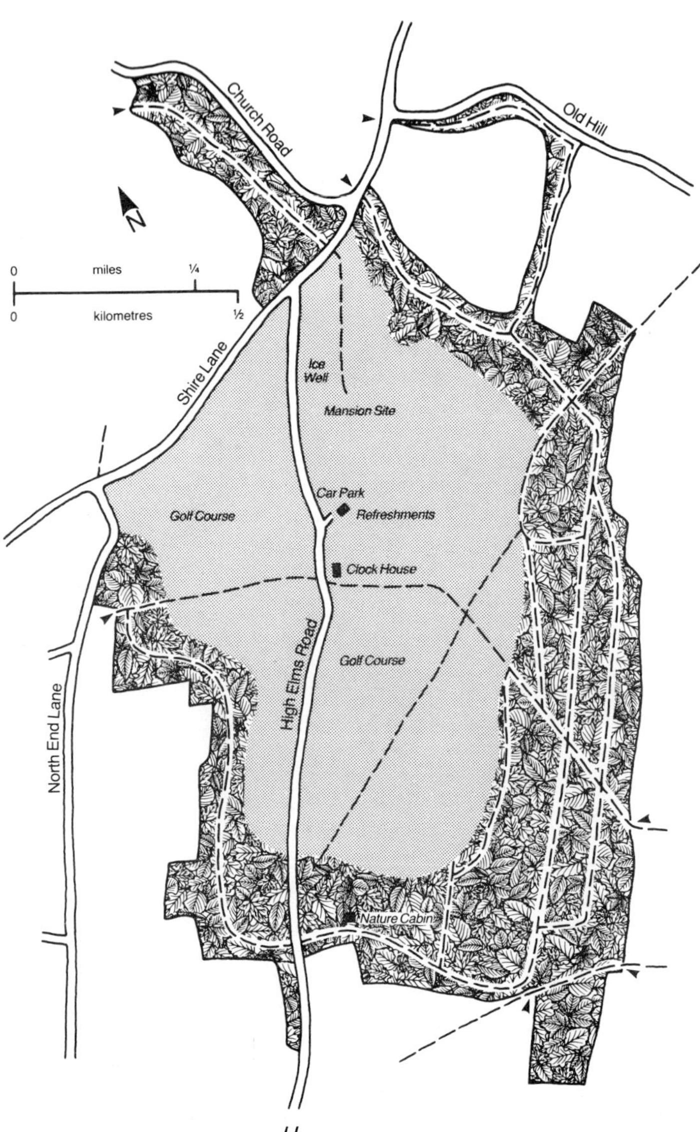

How to get there: by bus – the 858 Green Line goes through the estate. Otherwise take a bus to Farnborough and walk down Church Road. By car – there is parking and access from High Elms Road.
Origin of the name: presumably from the large elms on the estate, several of which have had to be felled because of Dutch elm disease.
Area: 353 acres (143 hectares). Besides this public area, the property includes a further 605 acres of agricultural land.
Owned and maintained by: London Borough of Bromley. (Environment Bromley maintains the Wash House picnic site and the old ice-well.)

A part of the green belt country, High Elms Estate consists of a 150-acre golf course surrounded on three sides by an area of rich and varied woodland. On the estate, more than 550 plant species have been recorded, over 400 different moths and butterflies and over sixty kinds of birds. It is not surprising, therefore, that most of the woodland has been designated as one of London's Sites of Special Scientific Interest (SSSI).

Although the estate does still produce some timber both for sale and for use on this and other council properties, the priority of the present management is to foster the estate's wildlife, hence selective clearing, thinning and coppicing are all practised here, and dead wood is racked into piles to provide cover for small mammals. Apart from the oak and beech one might expect to find, there are plantations of Scots pine and European larch planted shortly after the war by the Forestry Commission, and a rich variety of specimen trees too, including the tulip tree and strawberry tree, plus several kinds of cedar, spruce and fir. In places, the woodland floor has a dense cover of wild privet, first introduced here as cover for game birds, and in spring both wild violets and wood anemones are plentiful.

The history of the land can be traced back to the time when it was part of the huge estates given by William the Conqueror to his brother, Bishop Odo of Bayeux, for his help at the Battle of Hastings. The early history of the land is as farmland for the rearing of sheep and later dairy cattle, pigs and poultry, the estate taking on much of its present appearance under the influence of the third baronet of the Lubbock family, John William Lubbock, who lived here from 1840. He was responsible for the planting of specimen trees and the laying out of a former race course on the estate. Sir John was perhaps best known for his study of the tides, which earned him a Royal Society Medal, and for his book, *Theory of the Tides* (1830).

The best-known owner of the estate was, however, the *fourth* baronet, Sir John Lubbock (they all had the same name), to whom we owe the introduction of August Bank Holiday (once popularly referred to as 'St Lubbock's Day') and several Acts of Parliament for the protection of wild birds, open spaces, ancient buildings and the provision of public libraries. In the scientific world he served as president of twenty learned societies, was author of many scientific books, and gave public support to his friend and neighbour, Charles Darwin, in the controversy surrounding his publication of *Origin of Species*. On being made a peer in 1900, the baron's interest in the Avebury stone circles (which he saved from building development in 1871) led him to choose the title Lord Avebury.

Although the old mansion burned down in 1967, many reminders of the old estate are still here, including an interesting ice-well to the left of the driveway. This still survives in good condition and, though usually kept locked, is easily appreciated from above ground. (It is occasionally opened to the public, as advertised by the entrance and elsewhere.) It is thought to date from about 1850 and, like similar wells found elsewhere, was once used for the refrigeration of food and drinks.

Although High Elms Clock House, in the estate on High Elms Road, is private property, you can catch a glimpse of the old clock tower once used to signal the working hours to the estate workers, and perhaps spot one of the few surviving horse-gins – a kind of horse-powered water-pump. Further on again (over North End Lane) is the site of the mansion's old washhouse, now a public picnic site.

Also interesting are the estate's two 'dene holes', or chalk wells, one of which, in Cuckoo Wood, has been found to be twenty feet deep and twenty-five feet wide at the base where it opens out into three chambers. Although there are other similar holes elsewhere in Kent and Essex, nobody is sure what they are or how they came to be there. The prevailing theory is that this one was used as a source of chalk for liming the soil nearby.

One of the best ways to enjoy the estate is to take the three-and-a-quarter-mile circular walk through the woodland belt which borders the golf course. Throughout the woods there is a plentiful supply of rustic benches and many excellent spots to stop and enjoy a woodland picnic. On High Elms Road there is a café and restaurant open to the public, and there are toilets in Church Road, accessible to wheelchairs. Information and a few exhibits on the estate and its wildlife can be found at the small Nature Cabin (open Sundays 2.00–4.00 p.m.); this is signposted from the car park in High Elms Road.

Highbury Fields

Highbury Place, N5

How to get there: by tube to Highbury & Islington station on the Victoria Line. By bus: 4, 19, 30, 43, 104, 236, 271, 279 or 279A.
Origin of the name: Highbury means 'high manor', from the fact that it stands on higher ground than either Canonbury or Barnsbury.
Area: 29 acres (12 hectares).
Owned and maintained by: London Borough of Islington.

A little over a century ago this whole area consisted of open fields and fertile dairy pasture. Not only did the fields then supply milk for the city, but they were also a favourite place for Londoners to visit to taste warm milk straight from the cow, and to eat cakes dipped in cream and other dairy delicacies. Earlier still, in 1666, this was one of the areas to which thousands of refugees from London's Great Fire fled to set up camp. Evelyn's diary of 5 September describes how these:

> poore inhabitants were dispersed . . . several miles in circle, some under tents, some under miserable huts and hovels, many without a rag, or any necessary utensils, bed or board, who from delicatenesse, riches, and early accommodations in stately and well-furnished houses, were now reduced to extremest misery and poverty . . . [Throughout the area were some] 200,000 people of all ranks and degrees, dispersed and lying along by their heapes of what they could save from the fire, deploring their losses, and though ready to perish for hunger and destitution, yet not asking one penny for relief.

Today, Highbury Fields consists of a gently sloping stretch of grassland bordered and crossed by avenues of London planes, rising to one of the highest points in this part of London at 144 feet above sea level. At the lower, southern end is an enclosed swimming pool, with a statue nearby commemorating the ninety-eight Islingtonians killed during the South African War of 1889–1902, while at the northern end are two large grassy children's areas, a two o'clock club, café and tennis courts.

As a public open space, the fields were acquired by the Metropolitan Board of Works from the descendants of John Dawes, a wealthy stockbroker and resident of the old Highbury Manor House, and declared open to the public 'henceforth and for ever' on 24 December 1885.

At the time, the motivation for acquiring such public open land was primarily one of concern for public health – a fact which is evident from an article about the fields published at the time in the *Islington Gazette*. In support of the case for purchasing such land, the paper states 'that such open spaces tended more to promote the health and pleasure of the people than any sanitary precautions, and moreover, it had a tendency to reduce sickness, and thereby diminish the number of sick poor in the parish infirmary.'

Though there is no sign of it now, there used to be an old stone-covered spring here and lead conduits which in the fifteenth century supplied water from here right down as far as Moorgate, thus giving the park its earlier name of Conduit Field. This water supply was part of a scheme by Sir William Eastfield, Lord Mayor in 1438, for 'water to be conveyed from Highberry, in pipes of lead, to the parish of St Giles without Cripplesgate, where the inhabitants of those parts incastellated the same in sufficient cisternes.'

Earlier still, during Wat Tyler's peasant revolt of 1381, Highbury Fields was the site of a 20,000-strong popular rebellion against the imposition of a poll tax, led by Jack Straw, which, after burning and destroying the priory in St John's Street, came here to destroy also the prior's country-house – Highbury House. Hence the one-time name of the Manor House – Jack Straw's Castle – the same name given to the well-known pub by Hampstead Heath.

From the northern end of Highbury Fields it is just over half a mile's walk to Clissold Park, via Highbury Park, turning right into Kelross Road which leads then into Kelross Passage and Collins Road.

Highgate Wood and Queen's Wood

Muswell Hill Road, N10

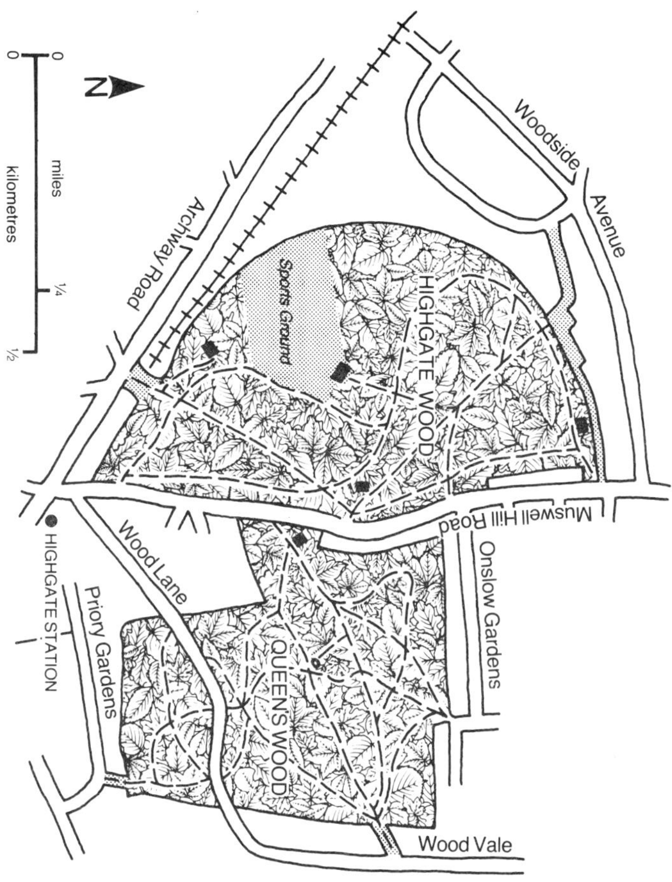

How to get there: by tube to Highgate station on the Northern Line. By bus: 43, 104, 134 or 263.
Origin of the names: the name Highgate refers to an early toll gate set up by the Bishop of London on the Great North Road at one of the highest places in the old County of Middlesex. Queen's Wood was so named in honour of Queen Victoria's Diamond Jubilee in 1897.
Area: 122 acres (49 hectares) total, of which Highgate Wood covers 70 acres (28 hectares).
Owned and maintained by: the Corporation of the City of London (Highgate Wood) and the London Borough of Haringey (Queen's Wood).

Between them, these woods offer a delightful escape from their urban surroundings. The better-known Highgate Wood to the west of Muswell Hill Road, stretches over more or less flat land opening out into a nine-acre meadow, most of which serves as cricket and football pitches. The wood has something of a city park atmosphere with its narrow asphalt footpaths, wooden benches and even a children's playground. Indeed, Highgate Wood – with a woodland floor which in places will support no more than grass – has lost much of its once celebrated wildness. None the less, there are still quite a number of birds here, sixty-three species of which were spotted between 1967 and 1978, and foxes are well established. Here, too, are foxgloves, wood anemones, wood violets and lesser stitchwort, along with a good range of butterflies including the speckled wood, the holly blue and the painted lady. Oak and hornbeam are the dominant trees, with silver birch, beech, willow, mountain ash and elder, hazel and holly. In late summer one can find ripe blackberries.

On the other side of Muswell Hill Road, Queen's Wood has quite a different character; the ground is frequently steep, with an undergrowth which is so much more dense than that of Highgate Wood that it attracts more than twice the number of ground-feeding birds. The vegetation of the two woods is different for perhaps two reasons: one, the slope of the woodland here allows more light into the understorey and, two, the soil is less easily compacted because it is less well used – for Queen's Wood is frequently deserted but for the occasional jogger or dog walker. It is a pleasure on entering the wood to hear the sound of traffic recede as one walks down the winding tarmac paths, perhaps stopping at a wooden bench to listen to the birds or to enjoy the filtered light through the leaves above. At the heart of the wood it is a surprise to come across a children's paddling pool and some picnic tables nearby.

Both Queen's Wood and Highgate Wood are remnants of the Great Forest of Middlesex with parts, at least, showing signs of their ancient origins. Wild service tree is present, as is the indigenous bluebell (as opposed to the more common hybrid). Coppicing appears to have been practised in Queen's Wood from at least the sixteenth century, when it contributed to the supply of wood to London and probably the fuel for Hornsey and Finchley as well, while bracken from here would have been collected for the bedding of animals.

Excavations in the north of Highgate Wood have uncovered early Roman pottery from about AD 60, and a similar site is thought to exist at the southern end. Later, from around the time of the Norman Conquest, this wood formed (along with Cherry Tree Wood) a part of the Bishop of London's hunting park. Later still, in the nineteenth century, it became known as Gravel Pit Wood in reference to the gravel extracted from the north-west corner, where some signs of the old pits can still be seen.

Highgate Wood was saved from building development in 1885, when the Ecclesiastical Commissioners presented the land to the Corporation of the City of London who formally opened it to the public in October 1886. The Lord Mayor then pledged its use in perpetuity as an open space – a fact which it is hoped will be remembered by the Department of Transport as it considers cutting into it with its present plans for an Archway Road motorway.

In the same year there was talk also of saving Queen's Wood, though nothing was done until 1895, when the Ecclesiastical Commissioners were just about to sell it off as building sites. The announcement of these plans led to the immediate setting up of a campaign to purchase the wood in celebration of Queen Victoria's Diamond Jubilee in 1897. Hitherto, it had been known as Churchyard Bottom Wood – a name which is thought to refer to a pit on the western edge of the wood where some of the victims of the Great Plague were buried in 1665 – but with this purchase it was suggested that it be renamed either Queen's or Victoria Wood.

With almost one-quarter of its purchase price having been raised from private donations, Queen's Wood was finally opened 'for the free use of the public for ever' on 23 July 1898.

The appeal of the two woods has recently been extended by the opening of the Parkland Walk – a walk along a disused railway line that now links Finsbury Park with Alexandra Park via Queen's and Highgate Woods – and this is certainly worth exploring as part of a visit to the woods themselves.

Holland Park

Kensington High Street, W8

How to get there: by tube to Holland Park station on the Central Line. By bus: 9, 27, 28, 31, 33, 49 or 73.
Origin of the name: named after the home of the earls of Holland, Holland House, part of which still stands in the park.
Area: 54 acres (22 hectares).
Owned and administered by: Royal Borough of Kensington & Chelsea.

Although only just over half the size of St James's Park, Holland Park has the largest area of woodland in central London and a bird life to rival any equivalent area of countryside well outside the city.

Add to this the spectacular Dutch Garden and what has remained of the historic architecture, and Holland Park must surely be one of London's most beautiful parks.

Entering by the main ornamental gates on Kensington High Street, the avenue brings one to what today survives of Holland House – a manor house originally built for Sir Walter Cope in 1605. Its present name, however, dates from its next owner, Sir Henry Rich, first Earl of Holland who, after vacillating between his support for the Cavaliers and Roundheads, was executed by the Roundheads in 1649. The house survived with various additions and alterations until the Second World War when the main part of it was bombed and destroyed. When the London County Council bought Holland estate from the Earl of Ilchester in 1952, they began to restore the ground storey, the arcades of the central portion and the east wing. This east wing was opened as part of the new King George VI Memorial Youth Hostel in 1959, and the central section was opened in 1964 as an open-air theatre where each summer dance, opera, ethnic music, jazz and theatre events are held.

Adjoining the house is one of the park's most celebrated features – the Dutch Garden, with its brilliant display of tulips and other flowers, bordered in formal geometrical parterre style with miniature box hedges. The modern layout conforms largely to its original design of 1812 for the third Lord Holland, Henry Richard Fox, by Buonaiuti, his librarian and 'factotum'. Its original name – the Portuguese Garden – was changed during the last century when Portugal fell out of favour with England.

Between the Dutch Garden and the orangery is the tranquil Iris Garden, formed around an elegant fountain and pool, and said to be the place where Lady Holland raised the country's first dahlias (though it has since been established that the precise site lies a few yards away on the terrace just north of the Belvedere Restaurant). In the corner of this is a circular brick building with a conical tiled roof; this dates also from the eighteenth century and is thought to have been the old ice-house, the restoration of which won the council a European Heritage Year Award in 1975. Just behind this is a delightful little café (open February to December) with some outdoor seating beneath two magnificent spreading horse chestnut trees.

On the opposite side of the Iris Garden is the old orangery, built by the fourth and last Lord Holland in 1850 and now providing an appropriate venue for the various small art exhibitions which are frequently on display here. The adjoining Belvedere Restaurant (telephone 01-602 1238) was originally the granary of the stables, which the last Lord Holland converted to a garden ballroom in about 1849.

To the north is the Yucca Lawn, whose almost tropical atmosphere is created by its spear-leaved Mexican yucca and unexpected range of exotic birds including the South American rhea (of the emu family), African guinea-fowl, and those most spectacular of birds – peacocks. And just to the east of the Yucca Lawn is the Rose Walk, which leads up to a statue of the third Lord Holland, Henry Richard Fox, and which contains some of the Caroline Testout roses planted here by Lady Ilchester in 1894.

Now you are in 'The Wildernesse' – an area of natural beauty unrivalled in London's West End. To retain a rural atmosphere, several of the paths have purposely been left unmade and you will notice dead trees that have not been felled because the rotting wood not only provides a more natural appearance, but attracts a much greater variety of wildlife. The park's unusually rich bird life has already been mentioned, but in the woodland alone thirty-one species of birds were seen during 1976, including the tawny owl and great spotted woodpecker. There are ash trees, birch, elm, oak, plane and sycamore trees with two named avenues – one of limes planted by Lady Holland in 1876 (with many of the original limes still surviving), and one of horse chestnuts – especially worth seeing in May when their flowers are out. In spring the woodland floor is particularly attractive with the flowers of bluebells, crocuses, daffodils, rhododendrons and azaleas.

Unisex toilets for the disabled are 200 yards from the Abbotsbury Road car park.

Horniman Gardens

London Road, SE23

How to get there: by train to Forest Hill station. By bus: P4, 12, 63, 176 or 185.
Origin of the name: after F. J. Horniman, MP, who established the gardens and the adjoining museum in the late nineteenth century.
Area: 26 acres (10 hectares).
Owned and maintained by: Inner London Education Authority.

Horniman Gardens is full of variety and interest, from the secluded water garden and large formal sunken garden at the southern end of the park to the extensive views and miniature zoo not far from the Horniman Drive entrance. Apart from facilities for tennis and putting, the park has also no less than three nature trails and, in the south-eastern corner, one of London's finest anthropological museums.

For all this we are indebted to Frederick John Horniman, MP, a Victorian tea magnate and collector who, in 1901, donated both the park and museum to the London County Council for the enjoyment of the public 'for ever'. Horniman began collecting for his museum in about 1860, travelling twice round the world, via Egypt, India, Sri Lanka, Burma, China, Japan, Canada and the United States, gathering articles as he went that would illustrate either the natural history, the arts or the handicrafts of the countries he visited.

Initially this collection was assembled in his own home, steadily filling one room after another until he was forced to give up his whole house and move to nearby Surrey Mount. By 1890, the new museum had grown so popular that he decided to allow free public access to his collection on a regular basis three days a week, and then in 1895 to open also the adjoining grounds to form the nucleus of the present park.

When, in January 1901, Horniman handed over his whole property along with the anthropological collection to the London County Council, his remarkable generosity could only be compared with that of the governors of Dulwich College (who donated the land for Dulwich Park), of Sir Sydney Waterlow (who donated Waterlow Park) and of Sir Spencer Maryon-Wilson (donor of Maryon Park).

Apart from the park's more formal areas, the grounds here consist largely of grassy slopes descending steeply to the south and west from the commanding summit some 300 feet above the

Thames to the embankment of the dismantled Victoria to Crystal Palace railway. Occasionally on a very clear day it is possible to see, almost exactly due west, the towers of Windsor Castle. Throughout the park is an unusually wide range of interesting trees and shrubs including – to name just a few – a dawn redwood, ginkgo, deodar cedar, swamp cypress, western hemlock, spindle tree, snake bark maple, corkscrew willow, tulip tree and Indian bean.

This horticultural diversity, and the addition in 1973 of the western strip of railway land, lend the gardens to use for nature study, for which three walks have been designed – the Railway Trail, the Dutch Barn Trail and the shorter Coach House Trail. Copies of the two guide leaflets covering these trails are available both from the park manager's office and from the Horniman Museum (open weekdays 10.30 a.m. to 6.00 p.m. and Sundays 2.00–6.00 p.m.; telephone 01-699 2339 for further details).

The Dutch Barn, after which one of the trails is named, was originally brought here from Holland by Mr Horniman and serves each summer now to house free art and craft exhibitions. Down the hill from this is one of the park's most distinctive features: a formal flower garden enclosed by brick rose bowers. But, without a doubt, my favourite spot is the secluded water garden by the tennis courts – definitely worth a visit if you are looking for somewhere quiet and soothing.

Across London Road to the south, the park continues, taking in the triangle of land enclosed between Sydenham Hill and Sydenham Rise. This includes the park's refreshment kiosk (which, during summer school holidays, serves teas and snacks) and a second paddling pool. Just a few hundred yards further south and one arrives at the entrance to Cox's Walk and thence the ancient Sydenham Hill Wood – a remnant of the Great North Wood which once covered this entire area.

Horsenden Hill

Horsenden Lane, Greenford

How to get there: by train to Greenford station and take the path alongside Greenford Golf Course from Rockware Avenue. By tube to Perivale or Greenford stations on the Central Line, or to Sudbury Town on the Piccadilly Line. By bus: 187 (except Sundays) or 92.
Origin of the name: it has been debated whether Horsenden originally meant 'the hill belonging to Horsa', or 'a hill where horses are kept'.
Area: 236 acres (95 hectares) of which about one-third is occupied by Horsenden Hill Golf Course and playing fields.
Owned and maintained by: London Borough of Ealing.

From several finds of flints, the history of the hill can be traced right back to the late Neolithic period, i.e. the latter part of the Stone Age. Sherds of pottery found here appear to date from the late Bronze Age through to the Iron Age, and considerable surface evidence survives of an ancient hill fortification in the form of complex ditch and bank defences near the summit of the hill.

A local architect claims that there is evidence also that the hill had an ancient mystical significance, perhaps similar in prehistoric times to Stonehenge or Glastonbury. He has mapped out more than thirty ley-lines radiating out from Horsenden Hill like spokes of a wheel, connecting old church sites, and suggesting similarities with other such centres as St Michael's Mount in Cornwall.

In more recent times this area was in use as farmland. Many of the ancient hedges to the west of Horsenden Lane still survive in good condition and are once again being 'laid' (i.e. partly cut and pleached) in traditional style to provide a better habitat for wildlife. Though a proportion of this western part is now used as playing fields, the whole area is still remarkably attractive for walking. The hedges break up what might otherwise be a rather bleak stretch of grassland into a series of meadows which offer a sense of discovery as one emerges from one field into the next through gaps in the hedgerows. If you enjoy sloe gin, jam or wine, you may be tempted in late autumn to collect the fruit here, but please bear in mind that these berries are an important food source for many winter birds.

On the east side of Horsenden Lane the hill itself rises up to 279 feet (85 metres) above sea level – the highest spot in the borough. From the grassy plateau there is an impressive panoramic view over five or six counties, across a sea of bright tiled roofs, factories and offices – a view relieved by the occasional line of trees and the fields to the west. On a clear day, Box Hill can be seen to the south, the Chiltern Hills to the west, Stanmore Common to the north and Hampstead Heath and St Paul's Cathedral to the east. Descending from the summit to the north is a welcome patch of ancient woodland (often used as a woodland film set for television and cinema) well supplied with hornbeams and mature oaks, with some specimens of wild service tree, wild cherry and, in spring, a sprinkling of bluebells. To the north-east from the summit is Horsenden Hill's attractive nine-hole golf course, leading on eastward to Sudbury Golf Course.

During the First World War there used to be a horse-drawn anti-aircraft gun stationed on the hill, the horses for which were kept in a large Victorian hay barn which was subsequently demolished when the land was opened as a public park in 1933.

Around the time of the purchase of Horsenden Hill by Ealing, Wembley and Middlesex councils, the old lane which divides the property was under threat of widening, but the anticipated destruction of hedgerows and the dangers of a high-speed road led to the lane's rural character being preserved. Parallel to this runs a narrow asphalt footpath to the east of the old lane-side elm and hawthorn hedge. This and the regenerating woodland on the other side of the path further contribute to the hill's refreshingly rural atmosphere, as does the Paddington Arm of the Grand Union Canal, which runs along the park's south-western boundary. Following the opening of the canal in 1801, it carried locally-produced hay to London's stables, returning with manure for the fields. During the Second World War the fields were again brought under cultivation to produce potatoes and wheat, and just recently haymaking has been reintroduced to foster the growth of meadow wildflowers, such as ragged robin, buttercups, bird's-foot trefoil and knapweed. The hill's wildlife also includes rabbits, foxes, kestrels, over twenty-five species of butterflies and many other wildflowers, notably the not-too-common dyer's greenweed.

Horsenden Hill's fauna and flora benefit also from the proximity of one of Britain's oldest nature reserves – Perivale Wood Nature Reserve – situated to the south, just across the Grand Union Canal. Though privately owned and generally accessible only to members of the Selbourne Society, the general public are admitted on the first Sunday in May each year to see the magnificent display of bluebells.

On Horsenden Hill itself, the council has been very active recently in encouraging wildlife both by the hedge-laying and haycutting already mentioned, and also by reintroducing the traditional scheme of woodland management called coppicing. The council has also laid out an excellent two-and-three-quarter-mile waymarked nature trail, and a guide booklet – *Horsenden Hill Countryside Walk* – is available from them.

Hounslow Heath

Staines Road, Hounslow

How to get there: by tube to Hounslow West station on the Piccadilly Line, then about a mile's walk. By bus: 116, 117, 120, 237 or 257.
Origin of the name: spelt Hundeslawe in the thirteenth century, meaning 'Hund's mound or tumulus'.
Area: 204 acres (83 hectares), excluding the golf course.
Owned and maintained by: London Borough of Hounslow.

Though now a mere fragment of its former 4293 acres, Hounslow Heath is still large and wild enough to be a significant reserve for wildlife. Most of the land is flat, open grassland with patches of gorse, broom, blackberry and hawthorn, clumps of the less-common dwarf gorse, heather and petty whin, and elsewhere small areas of young oak woodland.

The heath is intersected by footpaths and marked bridleways, and is provided with benches and picnic areas. Dog walking and blackberry picking continue to be two of the heath's major attractions, but its value for the study and appreciation of wildlife is becoming better known since it has been declared by the Nature Conservancy Council a Site of Special Scientific Interest (SSSI). The banks of the river Crane are of particular interest, since they are among the few such remaining natural riverbanks in London. Indeed, Hounslow Council has recently designed a nature trail which follows this section of the river, starting from the golf course car park at Baber Bridge on Staines Road, continuing to the Feltham goods yard and then back to the car park.

The heath is of particular importance to six species of bird, namely the short-eared owl, the skylark, stonechat, whitethroat, meadow pipit and reed bunting, but at least twenty-eight bird species are known to breed here and some seventy-three species have been sighted. Hounslow Heath also has a particularly high butterfly population, since many of the plants on which they feed and breed are present. Though the fox population fell dramatically in 1976 when they were driven out by gypsy travellers, they have since recovered, so that now at least three families are breeding and others have been seen hunting.

Over the centuries, the heath has seen a good deal of activity, partly because it was on the main route between London and the West Country. The frequency of passing stage coaches and the isolated nature of the heath made this an ideal hideout for footpads and highwaymen – so much so that during the eighteenth century Hounslow Heath became one of the most dangerous open spaces in all of London.

For the same reason the heath was, as far back as 1215, also of strategic importance to the army and in fact continued to be used occasionally by the military right up until the end of the First World War. Perhaps the most significant event on the heath during that time was in 1784 when Major General William Roy of the Royal Engineers began the triangulation measurements which were to become the basis of the entire series of Ordnance Survey maps. The first five-mile measurement was made with a series of glass rods and then remeasured eight years later to check for accuracy. Remarkably, the discrepancy between these measurements was a mere two and three-quarter inches.

The heath again attained notoriety when it was used in 1909 and 1910 for some of the first aeroplane flights, and again in 1919 when Hounslow Heath became the site of the country's first civil airport and departure point for the world's first scheduled air service.

Before the heath became a public open space it was used for large-scale gravel extraction, and was finally purchased by the Greater London Council in 1979, two years after Hounslow Council laid out the present golf course.

Hyde Park

Bayswater Road, W2

How to get there: by tube to Marble Arch on the Central Line, or to Hyde Park Corner on the Piccadilly Line. By bus: 2, 2B, 6, 7, 8, 9, 12, 14, 15, 16, 16A, 19, 22, 23, 25, 30, 36, 36B, 38, 52, 52A, 55, 73, 74, 88, 137 or 500.
Origin of the name: from the sub-manor of Hyde – a name derived from a 'hide of land', i.e. an area of approximately 120 acres.
Area: 344 acres (139 hectares).
Owned by: the Crown.
Maintained by: Department of the Environment.

Both Hyde Park and neighbouring Kensington Gardens were acquired originally from the Abbot of Westminster in 1536 by King Henry VIII as part of the King's plans to extend his private hunting estate from his palace at Westminster out to Hampstead Heath. The new park was then promptly fenced off from the public, with the proclamation that:

> As the King's Most Royal Majesty is desirous to have the games of hare, partridge, pheasant and heron preserved, in and about the honour of his palace of Westminster, for his own disport and pastime, no person, on the pain of imprisonment of their bodies, and further punishment at his Majesty's will and pleasure, is to presume to hunt or hawk [here].

And so Hyde Park and Kensington Gardens remained as private hunting grounds, until King Charles I declared them open to the citizens of London more than a century later.

It is remarkable that such a large stretch of open land – 619 acres in all – should still survive intact today so close to such prestigious areas as Knightsbridge and Mayfair. That is not to say that there have been no attempts to sell it; there have. In 1652, the Commonwealth government decided to dispose of the whole estate 'for ready money', in three lots for a total of £17,068 2s 8d. Fortunately, when in 1660 Charles II was restored to the throne he immediately reclaimed the land and opened it once more to the public without charge.

Hyde Park has since been the scene of a colourful variety of exhibitions and demonstrations, the most spectacular of which was the Great Exhibition of arts and sciences held here in 1851. This was staged in an enormous eighteen-acre 'greenhouse' –

Prince Albert's Crystal Palace – which was erected specially for the purpose between Rotten Row and South Carriage Drive and later moved to Sydenham, where sadly it was destroyed by fire in 1936.

Perhaps the most historic political meeting here would have been the riotous demonstration in 1866 of the Reform League – an event which was to lead to the creation of the present Speaker's Corner at the north-eastern end of the park near Marble Arch. The riot began when the demonstrators (campaigning for electoral reform) were refused entry to the park by an army of 1700 police, and it was after this that it occurred to the authorities that it might be more prudent in relation to political meetings to take a less defensive stance. Though perhaps few people nowadays take the tradition very seriously, the custom of free speech has continued here (particularly on Sundays) ever since. Nearby, in sobering contrast, is the site of what was once – in less tolerant days – the largest gallows in London (the notorious Tyburn Tree) where dissenters and thieves were hanged, up to two dozen at a time.

The park's real centrepiece, though, is the Serpentine – a thirty-two-acre lake along the southern side of the park, which, along with the nine-acre Long Water, forms part of the improvements that George II's wife, Queen Caroline, made to Hyde Park and Kensington Gardens in the early eighteenth century. It is incidentally also to Queen Caroline that the present distinction between Hyde Park and Kensington Gardens can be attributed, for it was at her suggestion that 200 acres of the original hunting estate were taken as an extension to the grounds of Kensington Palace. The path to the south of the Serpentine, known as Rotten Row, is the creation of her husband and appears to have originally been very poorly surfaced, for royal carriages frequently overturned here, upending all the occupants. This, however, is not the origin of the name, which is in fact a popular corruption of *Route du Roi* – the 'King's Way'. This is one of the places in Hyde Park (along with West and North Carriage Drive) where horse riding is still permitted. Elsewhere across the park's vast acres there is also provision for bowling, putting, fishing (with permits only), boating, swimming, football and band concerts.

Although largely flat grassland, Hyde Park has a good range of mature trees, some of them particularly noteworthy, including what is believed to be the country's tallest manna ash and, near Hyde Park Corner, a good specimen of yellowwood – a tree which is fairly scarce in Britain. There are also particularly fine specimens of Caucasian wingnut (by Rotten Row), Chinese varnish tree and Chinese evergreen magnolia (both by the park nursery), Indian bean tree and red oak.

Of the royal parks, only in Richmond Park have more bird species been recorded. In 1975, ninety-six species (excluding introduced birds) were sighted in Hyde Park and Kensington Gardens, of which thirty-three are thought to have bred here. And with the recent creation of a kingfisher bank by the London Wildlife Trust and Royal Parks Department, these birds will soon be added to the list.

Access in Hyde Park for the disabled is generally good, with wheelchair-accessible toilets at the northern end of the park, one at Marble Arch and one at Lancaster Gate station. There is easy access, too, to the Serpentine rowing boats and canoes on the north side of the lake, to the Lido on the south side and to the Dell self-service restaurant at the eastern end. The main restaurant by the Serpentine Bridge also has flat access.

Joyden's Wood

Vicarage Road, Bexley

How to get there: by train to Bexley station. By bus: 400, 401 or 421.
Origin of the name: connected in the sixteenth century with the family of William Jordayne of Dartford.
Area: 319 acres (129 hectares) including Gattons Plantation.
Owned and maintained by: Forestry Commission.

Bounded on the west by agricultural land, on the south by Chalk Wood and elsewhere by residential development, Joyden's Wood covers an expanse of undulating land, rising from one hundred feet at the north-western corner to 250 feet in the south and east. The whole wood, while managed by the Forestry Commission primarily to produce marketable timber, is also open to the general public for recreation.

The main timber crop here is Corsican pine, followed by beech and other broad-leaved trees, with a natural undergrowth of bracken, blackberry, bluebells, foxgloves, rosebay willowherb and even some heather. Throughout the wood there is a good network of paths, those to the west being allocated for horse riding, while those on the eastern side are reserved for walkers. Perhaps surprisingly there are several features of historical interest within the wood, notably an ancient earthen bank running in two sections more or less north–south and known as *Faesten Dic* (meaning 'strong or fortress dyke'). All evidence points to it having been a defensive ditch and dyke constructed probably between the fifth and ninth centuries AD and most likely connected with the fighting recorded in the *Anglo-Saxon Chronicle* as the Battle of Crecganford (Crayford) in AD 457. From the excavation of a hard path on the eastern side of the dyke it seems that the earthworks were intended to be patrolled against invaders from the Cray valley.

Less conspicuous in and around the wood are a number of 'dene holes' – or at least collapsed remains of them. These are funnel-shaped holes, often with shafts opening into interconnecting chambers below. For a time it was thought that they were used as underground dwellings but it now seems clear that these were pits used for excavating chalk or marl for spreading on nearby farmland to render the soil more alkaline.

At the south-eastern corner of the wood various Roman remains have been excavated, notably those of a pottery kiln along with pottery sherds, coins and tools.

Until the wood was acquired by the Forestry Commission in 1956, it formed part of the Mount Mascal estate and was managed for shooting, the rights of which continued to be let right up until 1965. What had been a mature crop of Corsican and Scots pine, beech, oak, sycamore, sweet chestnut and hornbeam had already been felled at the end of the Second World War, so that apart from the occasional old coppiced sweet chestnut or oak and a natural regrowth of birch, most of the present trees have been planted since 1956 by the Forestry Commission. About half the present crop is Corisican pine, about one-quarter beech, the rest being mainly European, Japanese and hybrid larch, western hemlock, red and common oak, Norway maple, sycamore and lime. The most mature trees are at the northern end, planted in 1957, and the youngest were planted at the southern end in 1970.

Throughout the wood are a number of painted posts – some white topped, the others light-green topped. These mark two circular nature trails, one starting at the Summerhouse Drive entrance (between houses number 176 and 178) and the other starting from the private access road (turning off Vicarage Road by The Rising Sun). The track for this trail starts about half a mile up the access road on the left, just before the Mount Mascal Stables.

Although the Forestry Commission has, since 1972, made provision here for recreation, the public are asked to be considerate about not leaving litter and, most importantly, to take precautions against starting fires. The wide fire engine access paths and water tanks within the wood serve as a reminder that much of the wood has at one time suffered from accidental fires, frequently through public ignorance of the dangers.

Kennington Park

Kennington Park Road, SE11

How to get there: by tube to Oval station on the Northern Line. By bus: 3, 36, 36A, 36B, 95, 109, 133, 155, 159, 172 or 185.
Origin of the name: originally Kennington Common, from the Manor of Kennington, meaning 'farm or estate associated with Coena'.
Area: 37 acres (15 hectares).
Owned and maintained by: London Borough of Lambeth.

As common land, the tenants of Kennington Manor had the right to graze their cattle and horses here each summer until the common became a public park in 1854. In 1833, some 400 to 500 tenants could still claim this right, but as with other London commons, Kennington was already being monopolized by dairy herds belonging to the local milkman. By 1849, industry too had arrived and the waste products of a vitriol factory on the east side were being emptied into the surrounding ditch, mixing with what was already a 'black offensive muddy liquid, receiving constant contributions from numerous unmentionable conveniences attached to a line of low cottage erections'. The common was also by this time the cemetery of all the dead puppies and kittens of the vicinity, whose 'decaying carcases [could] be seen floating on the surface of their watery graves, in all the green and purple tints of putrefaction'.

The common had long been used for recreation, attracting 'idle youths occupied in low gambling' and 'numerous parties playing at cricket obstruct[ing] the paths in all directions' from whom the passer-by risked 'having an eye knocked out or a nose broken'. It was the scene also of a number of gruesome executions such as that of several officers of the Manchester Regiment who failed in their attempt of 1745 to regain the throne of England for the Jacobites. For high treason they were hung for three minutes, then cut down, stripped, beheaded and disembowelled, then their hearts and entrails were publicly burnt by the executioner.

Kennington Common also served as a kind of Speaker's Corner, popular with preachers such as the eighteenth-century Whitefield, who preached here to congregations of up to 40,000 people, and Father Mathew, a celebrated Irish temperance advocate who claimed during his career to have made over one million converts.

Following the Reform Act of 1832, when Lambeth was given

parliamentary borough status, Kennington Common became the scene of the nomination of the borough's first parliamentary candidates. There was a powerful working-class movement, the Chartists, who were not content with the new Act and who sought to impose six electoral reforms as part of the National, or People's, Charter. The most important of these was the demand for universal suffrage, for at that stage neither the working classes nor women had any right to vote. Out of this movement came Kennington Common's most famous political meeting which, it was said, evoked 'a feeling of terror throughout the Metropolis'. On 10 April 1848, 25,000 delegates and supporters of the Charter met on the common to march to Parliament to present a 'monster petition' (said to have had six million signatures) but were successfully prevented from doing so by a firm police confrontation, backed up by 170,000 special constables and thousands of discreetly stationed soldiers.

It has been suggested that the 1851 revival of plans to turn Kennington Common into a public park (and hence a more respectable and orderly place) was largely inspired by this dangerous event. In any case, it was just a few years after this that Kennington Common was opened as a public park.

In all, the formation of the park seems over the years to have been a great improvement for, apart from the addition of railings, there are now flower gardens, drinking fountains, a swimming pool, adventure and children's playgrounds, synthetic sports pitch, one o'clock club, café, toilets, tennis courts and skateboard park. And not only have the common's facilities multiplied in that time, but since its opening in March 1854, Kennington Park has almost doubled in size.

One of the most innovative of recent developments here is the provision of a special adventure playground on Bolton Crescent, run by HAPA (the Handicapped Adventure Playground Association) for disabled children along with their non-handicapped brothers, sisters and friends. The playground – called the Charlie Chaplin Playground – caters for around 400 children every week and is staffed by experienced playleaders. (Closed Sundays and Bank Holidays; telephone 01-735 1819 for further details.)

But by far my favourite part of the park is the enclosed Old English garden, which offers such a quiet and graceful seclusion that many casual passers-by never suspect its existence. There are plenty of benches in here, each privately nestled within a semicircular hedge. And just outside the enclosure is a quaintly fenced-in Tea Lawn and Refreshment House. Otherwise, in spite of a good number of mature trees, the park is rather open and not sufficiently well shielded from the considerable traffic noise from

Camberwell New Road and Kennington Park Road (formerly the ancient Roman road, Stane Street).

Before leaving the old common, mention should also be made of the nearby Oval Cricket Ground, which was formed from a market garden soon after Kennington Common became a park. The Prince Consort was concerned that, with the creation of the park, the local inhabitants were losing their old cricket ground, so he suggested that this site could be leased for that purpose by the Duchy of Cornwall, thus leading to the formation of the Surrey County Cricket Club.

Kensington Gardens

Bayswater Road, W2

How to get there: by tube to Queensway or Lancaster Gate, both on the Central Line. By bus: 9, 12, 33, 49, 52, 52A, 73 or 88.
Origin of the name: from the surrounding district of Kensington, whose name means 'the farm or estate of Cynesige'.
Area: 275 acres (111 hectares).
Owned by: the Crown.
Maintained by: Department of the Environment.

To many visitors, Kensington Gardens appears to be an integral part of Hyde Park, as indeed it was until 1690 when William III bought what is now Kensington Palace. In fact though, the atmosphere of Kensington Gardens is altogether different from that of its more informal neighbour – more sedate and secluded – due no doubt in part to its royal associations, but also to the absence of public meetings and road traffic.

Kensington Gardens as we know it today is largely the creation of Queen Caroline of Ansbach, wife of King George II. It was she who decided to take over such a large tract of Hyde Park to further extend the grounds of Kensington Palace, and it is to her that we owe the existence of the Serpentine in Hyde Park and both the Long Water and Round Pond here. Queen Caroline's alterations were ambitious and expensive, but the King agreed to them since she was paying for them. . . or so he thought. When Queen Caroline died, the King discovered that she had secretly spent over £20,000 of the royal funds on her private projects.

It was not until after Queen Caroline's death that Kensington Gardens was opened to the public, but then only at weekends and to those in formal dress; soldiers, sailors and servants were, for example, excluded. Over the years the gardens grew less exclusive until Queen Victoria opened both the gardens and the palace (including the room in which she was born) to the general public. Today, part of Kensington Palace is still open (but not on Sunday mornings), though much still remains private as a kind of royal lodging house for members and relations of the royal family.

Two features of the modern gardens pre-date Queen Caroline – the orangery and the sunken garden near the palace – both improvements designed for Queen Anne. Although Queen Anne did make some (unsuccessful) attempts to grow oranges here, she is said to have used the orangery more as a venue for her summer supper parties and for taking tea; today it houses a collection of royal vases and statues. The sunken Dutch garden in front of the palace, which consists of a lovely rectangular pond bordered with flowerbeds and enclosed by a tunnel of pleached limes, is well worth a glimpse through one of the gaps in the hedge.

Around the gardens are a number of statues and monuments commemorating such diverse folk as Queen Victoria, Prince Albert and Peter Pan. The impressive, if somewhat grandiose, rocket-like monument opposite the Royal Albert Hall is the Albert Memorial, built in 1872 to honour the Prince Consort and his Great Exhibition of arts and sciences held in Hyde Park in 1851. The book in his hand is a copy of the Exhibition Catalogue and the figures around him represent the extent of the Prince's interests. The four corner pedestals represent Engineering, Agriculture, Manufacture and Commerce, while at the foot of the steps four continents – Africa, Europe, Asia and America – are shown.

Running along the south side of this is one of the world's first illuminated highways, South Carriage Drive, created by order of King William III as a link between Kensington and St James's Palace.

There are quite a few ancient trees in the park, including one sweet chestnut said to date back to 1700. Kensington Gardens has also Britain's tallest recorded hawthorn and Montpelier maple, and a single-leaved ash with the greatest recorded girth. Here also are particularly fine specimens of swamp white oak, red oak, bay, field maple and silver lime.

It is interesting to note that between 1925 and 1975 the number of bird species here has significantly increased and now includes the great crested grebe and little grebe. The closure of the Long Water to boating has been one factor in encouraging some of the shyer birds like herons, and the Parks Division has recently been providing nest boxes for tawny owls to replace the serious loss of nesting sites due to Dutch elm disease.

For refreshments, there is a tea kiosk at the north-western end of the park near Black Lion Gate, and the much larger Serpentine Restaurants by the Serpentine Bridge. Almost opposite here is an earlier refreshments house which now houses the Serpentine Gallery where art exhibitions and concerts are held.

There are wheelchair-accessible loos between the Serpentine Gallery and the Albert Memorial.

Kenwood

Hampstead Lane, NW3

Map: see Hampstead Heath, page 139.
How to get there: by bus: 210 (which stops at both Archway and Golders Green underground stations). Car parking facilities by the house.
Origin of the name: spelt Caenwood in the sixteenth century, its origin is unclear, though it may be based on the Anglo-Norman-French word for oak – *keyne*.
Area: 120 acres (49 hectares).
Owned by: English Heritage.
Maintained by: London Residuary Body.

Though in one sense part of Hampstead Heath, Kenwood has a character and history all of its own. It was, like Golders Hill Park, originally landscaped as a private estate in the eighteenth century by Humphry Repton. The mansion itself was built in about 1700, though substantially altered by Robert Adam in 1764 for William Murray, the first Earl of Mansfield – a man described as having been 'without question the greatest judge of the eighteenth century'. We owe to him the modern conception of copyright and a significant judgement on the legality and morality of slavery. When a black slave claimed his freedom here under English law, Lord Mansfield is reputed to have said:

> *Fiat justitia ruat coelum;* let justice be done whatever be the consequence . . . The state of slavery . . . is so odious, that nothing can be suffered to support it, but positive law. Whatever inconveniences, therefore, may follow from the decision, I cannot say this case is allowed or approved by the law of England; and therefore the black must be discharged.

Among the alterations Mansfield commissioned Adam to make to the mansion were the addition of a third storey and the creation of what is regarded as one of the finest Adam rooms in existence – the library. By this time, a large part of the old wood, after which the estate is named, had already been felled to make way for farmland and this the first Earl set about having landscaped, with two ornamental lakes, along with the well-known dummy bridge, in the 'natural' landscape style of 'Capability' Brown. This work was then continued by Humphry Repton for the second Earl – the serpentine drives, the arrangement of lawns and the flower garden adjoining the house all being characteristic of his work.

When, in 1914, it was learned that the sixth Earl of Mansfield had decided to sell the entire estate for building development, a Kenwood Preservation Appeal fund was set up, finally enabling the purchase in 1922 of 100 acres at the southern end of the estate and in 1923 a further thirty-two acres of woodland along with the two lakes. All the original Adam furniture had already been sold off by auction and plans were now afoot for dividing the remaining land into building plots. The Preservation Council had by this time come to the end of its resources, but fortunately Kenwood House and its immediate grounds were rescued by a wealthy businessman and public benefactor, Edward Cecil Guinness, the first Earl of Iveagh. He refurbished the house and installed his own valuable collection of paintings with the intention of leaving to the nation a fine and complete example of an eighteenth-century country gentleman's house. Lord Iveagh died just one year before the Georgian mansion was opened to the public in 1928.

The Iveagh Bequest museum is now open to the public every day except Good Friday, Christmas Eve and Christmas Day. (Telephone 01-348 1286/7 for further details. Refreshments available in the Coach House and Old Kitchen Restaurant.) Particularly worth seeing are the Adam library and paintings including Rembrandt's *Self Portrait, The Guitar Player* by Vermeer and *Lady Howe* by Gainsborough.

The woodland to the south of the mansion has been declared a Site of Special Scientific Interest (SSSI) and is thought to be a surviving fragment of the ancient Forest of Middlesex; as such it has probably remained under continuous tree cover since prehistoric times, though it would no doubt have been managed during that time to produce wood. In summer the Kenwood lakes here provide an enchanting setting for evening orchestral concerts.

Unisex toilets for the disabled are situated at the Coach House Restaurant, 150 yards from the car park. The house itself is also wheelchair-accessible.

Kew Gardens

Kew Road, Richmond

How to get there: by riverboat from Westminster Pier by Westminster Bridge. (April to October only. Though picturesque, can be very slow if the tide is against you.) By train to Kew Gardens station. By tube to Kew Gardens station on the District Line. By bus: 27, 65 or (on Sundays) 7.
Origin of the name: derived from the Old English *kai hoh*, meaning 'a neck or spur of land by a landing place'.
Area: 300 acres (121 hectares).
Owned by: the Crown
Administered by: Trustees of the Royal Botanic Gardens, Kew.

Contrary to popular belief, the primary function of the Royal Botanic Gardens, Kew, is not to serve as a public park, but rather as a centre for scientific research. Indeed, for over a hundred years now, Kew Gardens has acted as a major centre for the world-wide identification and distribution of plant material. Yet, while maintaining the honour of being one of the world's most highly esteemed research and educational establishments, the beauty of its gardens continues to attract over one million visitors a year, many of whom have no specialist botanical interest.

The gardens have been created essentially from two independently designed estates, one the country residence of George II and Queen Caroline, and the other the residence of their son Frederick, Prince of Wales, and his wife Augusta. Thus, the laying out of the western, or river side of the present gardens was the work of Lancelot 'Capability' Brown who created, for example, the original lake and the dell now planted with rhododendrons. The eastern, or Kew Road side is largely the work of Sir William Chambers, who designed much of the garden architecture including the orangery, the ruined arch, several temples and the famous ten-storey 'Chinese' pagoda.

It was not until the 1770s, under George III, that the two properties were amalgamated into a botanic garden, though some ten years earlier, Princess Augusta had already planted the first small nine-acre botanic garden, south of the orangery. Following a period of decline in the early nineteenth century, the gardens were taken over by the state in 1841.

At whatever season you visit Kew, there is always something to see. The scale of the gardens and the sheer variety of plants (over 50,000 species) is such that one can easily spend a whole day exploring the greenhouses, walks, garden pavilions and museums. The best place to start a tour is at the orangery bookshop at the northern end near the Main Gates where one can view the orientation exhibits and pick up one of the Botanic Garden's excellent guide booklets.

Kew Gardens is especially beautiful in spring when the daffodils, crocuses, tulips and bluebells (especially in the grounds of Queen Charlotte's Cottage) are in bloom, along with magnolias, azaleas, rhododendrons, flowering cherries and apples. But even in the coldest months there is still the Heath Garden near the pagoda, a range of winter-flowering cherries and, in the north-eastern corner, the Alpine House, while the ferns, cacti and palms are worth seeing at any time of year.

Planted in groves around the grounds are fascinating collections of related trees each labelled according to its species and country of origin. Such collections include for example an astonishing range of ash trees and hollies, plus large groups of oak, beech, birch, alder, poplar, willow and walnut. But my favourite trees at Kew are the mulberries and weeping beeches.

The famous greenhouses contain wonderful collections of arum lilies, ferns, orchids, aquatic plants, cacti, mountain plants, palms and tropical water lilies, while in the Australian and Temperate Houses most of the plants are arranged geographically, representing Africa, Asia, America, Australasia and Europe. In the centre of the main block is probably the world's largest greenhouse plant – a Chilean wine palm raised from seed at Kew in 1846.

Down by the river, behind Kew Palace, is the small self-contained Queen's Garden, named after HM Queen Elizabeth II, who opened it in May 1969. Here only herbs and flowers known to have been popular in the seventeenth century have been planted, along with such period features as a formal parterre, pleached alley, sunken garden and gazebo.

Wheelchair access within the gardens is generally good and both a refreshment pavilion (open April to October only) and refreshment kiosk (open all year) are provided. The gardens open daily (except Christmas and New Year's Day) from 10.00 a.m., closing (depending on the season) between 4.00 p.m. and 8.00 p.m. The entrance fee, though now raised from the traditional 'one penny', is still nominal. (For further details telephone 01-940 1171.) No dogs allowed.

King's Wood

Kingswood Way, South Croydon

How to get there: by train to West Croydon or East Croydon stations, then bus 403 or 483. Get off at Hillsmead Way, and follow this, forking right along Hazelwood Grove. To the right of the green, take the footpath into King's Wood. By bus: 403 or 483.
Origin of the name: from the fact that the woodland once belonged to the King family, mentioned in local records in 1332.
Area: 147 acres (60 hectares).
Owned and maintained by: London Borough of Croydon.

The most unusual feature of this oak woodland is the fact that it is divided by a network of wide and perfectly straight paths into a number of equal squares, the sides of which are each exactly one furlong, or 220 yards, in length. This grid of paths was originally laid out as rides for game shooting, in which each section of woodland would be systematically worked by beaters to drive the game towards the marksmen.

A network of irregular lineal earthworks run across the paths at intervals and are thought to be remnants of ancient field boundaries. In 1955 and 1959 the excavations of an archaeologist turned up a number of ancient remains confirming a Romano-British settlement on the northern boundary, about a hundred yards from Kingswood Way. It seems that there was a small farmstead here about 2000 years ago, and pottery finds indicate that the area was occupied from about AD 50 to 150. The archaeologist also counted forty-six 'dene holes', that is, underground pits in which a central shaft usually opens out into several separate chambers, thought to have been used for the extraction of chalk for marling agricultural land. Excavation of one of these revealed pottery remains from the Iron Age.

King's Wood is predominantly oak woodland, with sweet chestnut, silver birch and hazel and an undergrowth of bracken and blackberry, nettles, sycamore, elder and, in May, carpets of bluebells. Much of the wood was cleared of its best timber by the army during the Second World War, though this is now regenerating with birch and hazel. King's Wood supports a good variety of wildlife including, according to a recent survey, forty-nine species of birds, which include all three British woodpeckers – the green, greater and lesser spotted.

There are rustic-style seats in the wood, though for toilets or shelter one needs to take a half-mile walk along Kingswood Way to Selsdon Wood – a National Trust bird sanctuary.

Avery Hill Winter Garden: the Greek goddess Galatea
by Leopoldo Ansiglioni

Bishop's Park (*see* Fulham Palace Grounds):
looking towards Putney Bridge

Bostall Woods

Crystal Palace Park

Danson Park: the Old English Garden

Hainault Forest: pollarded hornbeam

Hall Place

Highbury Fields

The Hill Garden (*see* Golders Hill Park)

Hyde Park: the Serpentine

Kew Gardens: the Temperate House

Norwood Grove (*see* Streatham Common)

Osterley Park: the Temple of Pan

Regent's Park

Trent Park

Wanstead Flats (*see* Epping Forest): the commoners' cattle still roam

Ladywell Fields

Ladywell Road, SE13

How to get there: by train to Catford, Catford Bridge or Ladywell stations. By bus: 75, 106B, 122, 124, 124A, 141, 185 or 261.
Origin of the name: from the well which once existed near the church of St Mary the Virgin, and which is thought to have been named after Our Lady by the faithful.
Area: 51 acres (21 hectares).
Owned and maintained by: London Borough of Lewisham.

This park was once part of the Manor of Lewisham and, as such, features as the 'thirty acres of meadow there' in the Domesday Book of 1086. It consists of a series of streamside meadows, stretching for almost a mile along the banks of the river Ravensbourne from Catford Bridge to Ladywell railway station. Its name, as mentioned above, derives from the old medicinal well of that name, which was said to have been 'of the same quality as those at Tunbridge'. The site of this, though now covered over by the present Ladywell Road Bridge, was not far from the western bank of the railway. A woman apparently stayed here to serve the water gratis to the parish inhabitants; indeed, according to one theory it is to her, rather than to Our Lady by the faithful, that the name Ladywell refers.

The first forty-six acres of the present park were purchased in 1889, though considerable improvement works were necessary before the land could be made suitable for recreation – mostly because the area is so prone to flooding. Part of the problem is due to the huge watershed of the Ravensbourne above Ladywell Bridge, estimated to be 30,000 acres, or nearly forty-seven square miles. Alterations involved the straightening and enlarging of the channel while adding weirs to prevent the bed from drying up in the summer. In spite of these improvements, there was more serious flooding in 1968, necessitating the deepening of the river and the building of new anti-flood walls.

The Ravensbourne is definitely the fields' most attractive and central feature, helping to give this strip of land its rural and secluded atmosphere. This, along with the railway, not only provides the park's physical boundary but also succeeds in softening the visual impact of the harsh industrial and administrative buildings by the hospital.

A walk along the riverbank provides some interesting glimpses of nature, so it is pleasing to note that the parks department has a policy here of leaving some stretches of the bankside vegetation to grow wild in order both to encourage a diversity of wildflowers and to attract birds. At the southernmost end of the fields, between the railway embankment and the river, the council has even set aside a bird sanctuary area. There is here a good variety too of the more common trees, including ash, black poplar, London plane, sycamore, weeping willow, oak, lime, horse chestnut, Lombardy poplar and even a weeping ash.

The range of facilities here includes the provision of seats along some sections of the river, hard tennis courts and children's playground, bowling green, keep-fit trail, football pitches and, opposite the well-used running track, a refreshment kiosk.

Also worth visiting – at the northern end, across the footbridge – is the pleasant disused cemetery by the Lewisham Parish Church, with its pretty little rose garden among several old yew trees. And a little further afield, Hilly Fields, Blythe Hill Fields and Lewisham Park are all less than a quarter of a mile's walk away.

Lee Valley Park

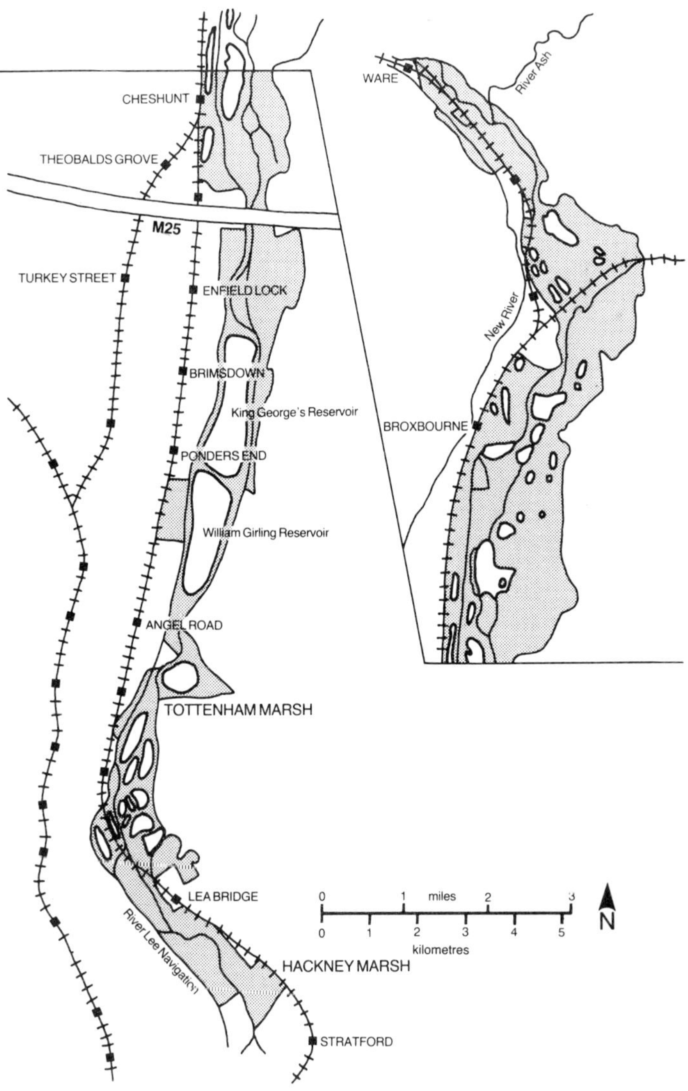

How to get there: By train from Liverpool Street to any of the stations between Tottenham Hale and either Ware or Roydon. By tube to Tottenham Hale or Blackhorse Road stations on the Victoria Line.
Origin of the name: of Celtic origin, the name of the river – spelt either Lee or Lea – may mean either 'bright one' or 'dedicated to Lugus'.
Area: approximately 10,000 acres (4050 hectares) most of which lies outside Greater London. The park extends for a distance of some 23 miles, from London's East End to Ware in Hertfordshire.
Owned by: various public bodies, including the Lee Valley Regional Park Authority who own or control about twenty-seven per cent of the total.
Administered by: the Lee Valley Regional Park Authority, comprising twenty-eight members representing the local authorities within whose boundaries the park falls.

The area was first established as a park in 1967, and yet even now, some two decades later, few Londoners know of its existence. True, most of the park and many of its facilities lie outside the city boundary, but even south of Waltham Cross there are miles of pleasant walking (much of it accessible to wheelchairs), with opportunities for fishing, bird watching, plant spotting, horse riding, sailing and even ice skating (at the Lee Valley Ice Centre in Lea Bridge Road – telephone 01-533 3151).

Although a canalside footpath follows the entire length of the park right out to Ware, even the eleven miles or so which lie within Greater London are well worth exploring, from Enfield Lock to Hackney Marsh, and even on then through Victoria Park to Mile End Park. Rather surprisingly, the most pleasant stretch of this lies close to the heart of London, by the Walthamstow and Hackney Marshes, and the disused Hackney filter beds which have evolved to produce a series of attractive wetland habitats with reedswamp, marsh and willow woodland. Further north, amid pylons and factories, one comes across sheep and cattle grazing on the steep reservoir embankments, hovering kestrels, plenty of gulls and the occasional geese. Plenty of wild plants too: hawthorn, willow, elder and alder, comfrey, bittersweet, wild hops, stinging nettles, dead nettles, rosebay willowherb, mallow and so on. In places the towpath is solidly packed with anglers, each with their tray of writhing maggots and an impressive array of equipment.

Walthamstow Marshes, apart from being one of the most rural spots along the entire London end of the walk, has also a remarkable flora. One ecologist identified an astonishing 340 species of plants, including plant hybrids found nowhere else in Great Britain. And the Walthamstow reservoirs, a little to the north, are of such importance to a great variety of birds, many of which use the reservoirs as a resting place on their migratory route through Britain, that they have been designated a Site of Special Scientific Interest (SSSI). In spite of the marsh's ecological significance, the LVR Park Authority drew up plans to extract gravel from here, though fortunately the Greater London Council's Minerals Sub-Committee, realizing the site's wildlife value, managed to stop them. The LVR Park Authority then tried to launch the same scheme under the guise of excavating a sailing lake, but thanks to the Save the Marshes Campaign, these plans have now also been shelved and the site is likely now also to be registered as an SSSI.

The canal, called the River Lea Navigation, is still used by narrow boats and cruisers and most of the original towpath is still open – in fact, it is this that forms the footpath that runs the length of the park. The Lee has been an important waterway since at least AD 896 when the Danes sailed up from the Thames to establish their fort at Ware. Later, during the Great Plague, when many outsiders were understandably reluctant to enter London, the watermen of Ware maintained the flow of essential supplies into the City, for which they were rewarded with being granted the freedom of the Port of London – a right which they still enjoy today.

To extend the canalside walk through to Victoria Park, cross diagonally through Mabley Green and take the 'Red Path' walkway, turning right at Eastway and right again under the motorway. It is also quite easy to reach Springfield Park from the towpath near Springfield Marina, or to take the narrow walk from the towpath through North Mill Fields.

For further information contact the Lee Valley Regional Park Authority, PO Box 88, Enfield, Middlesex (Lea Valley 717711).

Lesnes Abbey Woods

Abbey Road, Belvedere

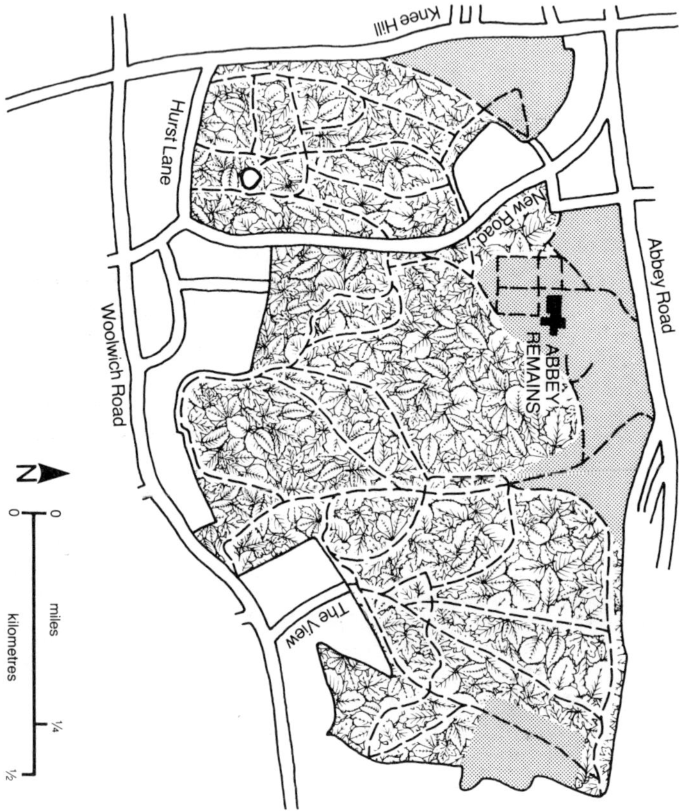

How to get there: by train to Abbey Woods station. By bus: 177, 178, 180, 269 or 272.
Origin of the name: woodland belonging to Lessness, or Lesnes, Abbey. The name Lesnes means 'meadow promontory' in reference to the land here projecting into the Erith Marshes.
Area: 215 acres (87 hectares).
Owned and maintained by: London Borough of Bexley.

For most people the two greatest attractions of the woods are the ruins of the twelfth-century Lesnes Abbey and the *twenty acres* of wild daffodils – a sight which is said to be unsurpassed in the south of England.

Just south of the abbey ruins, the woodland floor rises steeply in a thick springtime carpet of yellow and orange daffodil blooms, with wild violets, wood anemones and bluebells. In early April these woods are worth a visit for this sight alone. Further south and to both the east and west the woodland continues rolling over north–south ridges and valleys sometimes rising as much as one hundred feet in one hundred yards. This steep and varied terrain provides an excellent site for one of London's permanent orienteering courses, used for a new sport described as being like car rallying without the car, or as competitive navigation on foot. (The object of the sport is to find one's way between a given series of numbered posts, thirty-eight of which are placed throughout the woods and over Knee Hill in Bostall Heath and Woods.)

There is also a good number of easier well-defined paths throughout what was once predominantly chestnut coppice interspersed with oak, but which is now predominantly oak and birch woodland interspersed with wild cherry and sweet chestnut.

Near the centre of the woods is an area of national importance for geological research scheduled as a Site of Special Scientific Interest (SSSI). This area is very rich in fossils which are here more plentiful and better preserved than anywhere in the Blackheath Beds. Permission to dig or sift for such fossils can be obtained only from the park manager.

Near the south-western corner is the woodland's only pond, delightfully lined with rhododendrons and well enough fenced in with iron railings to provide a small refuge for the wildlife with which the woods abound.

The ruins of Lesnes Abbey itself are at the northern end of Abbey Road. Most of the walls are now no more than knee-high but enough still remains to get a clear idea of most of the original lay-out. Nearest the café was the nave of the old church with its north and south aisles leading to the central tower, the presbytery and high altar ahead and, to the sides, the north and south transepts. The lower parts of the four massive scalloped piers which once supported the central tower are still in fair condition.

The sole surviving doorway was the western entrance to the cloister, and to the north of this, the refectory and kitchens, the long narrow dormitory and finally, at the northern end, the reredorter (toilets). Several details are labelled on site and in the café a map of the ruins and an artist's impression of the original abbey are on display. (Excavated material from the abbey can be seen at Hall Place Museum, Plumstead Museum, Victoria and Albert Museum and St John's Church, Erith.)

Lesnes Abbey was founded in 1178 by Richard de Luci, royal deputy to Henry II, probably as an act of penance for his close involvement in the murder of Thomas à Becket in Canterbury Cathedral eight years earlier. The abbey was one of the first monasteries in England to be suppressed, being dissolved by Cardinal Wolsey under papal licence in 1524. The abbey's income was subsequently used to set up Christ's College, Cambridge.

Over the centuries much of the stone was removed for local farm buildings and roads until the abbey and woods were purchased from Christ's Hospital, London, by the London County Council in 1930 to form part of the permanent green belt around London. The Woolwich Antiquarian Society first excavated the site from 1909 to 1913, during which time the stone de Luci effigy (now in the Victoria and Albert Museum) was unearthed in the Lady Chapel.

The grounds were laid out as a park and opened in 1931 with further excavation and repair of the abbey by the council from 1939 until the 1950s.

Apart from the maps and artist's impression of the abbey on display at the café, there is a brief history and a small fossil display from the woods, donated to the parks office by the Tertiary Research Group. Orienteering maps are available from the park office adjoining the café.

The immediate abbey grounds are wheelchair-accessible, as is a 'daffodil walk' at the foot of the woods. There is a wheelchair-accessible toilet behind the café.

Maryon Park and Maryon Wilson Park

Thorntree Road, SE7

How to get there: by train to Charlton or Woolwich Dockyard stations. By bus: 51, 53, 54, 96, 161, 177 or 180.
Origin of the name: after the landowners, Sir Spencer Maryon Maryon-Wilson (who donated Maryon Park) and his son Sir Spencer Pocklington Maryon-Wilson (who donated Maryon Wilson Park).
Area: 62 acres (25 hectares) total, of which Maryon Wilson Park covers 32 acres (13 hectares).
Owned and maintained by: London Borough of Greenwich.

Nestled beneath steep wooded banks which rise up both to the south and west, Maryon Park enjoys an atmosphere of seclusion which ranks it among the most beautiful of London's small parks. The land was presented as a gift to the public by the Lord of the Manor of Charlton, Sir Spencer Maryon Maryon-Wilson, in 1891 (and then extended in 1909).

At the northern end is Cox's Mount, a large mound covered with rambling paths leading up to a grassy summit with views out over the Thames and the recently constructed Thames Flood Barrier. The mound acquired its name from a Mr Cox of Charlton Terrace who rented the knoll from the lord of the manor in 1838, and who planted poplars here, building a large summerhouse (long since demolished) in the centre for entertaining friends. Because of its height, the mount was also once used as a site for one of a series of semaphore stations which transmitted messages between the Channel coast and the city; and in the 1850s it was used by the Admiralty to adjust ships' compasses.

In the eighteenth century this land was known as Charlton Sandpits, for it was once the source of much of the sand used for sprinkling on parlour floors before carpets came into fashion. And when the park was being laid out in the 1890s workmen here discovered the foundation of an old brick kiln at the base of Cox's Mount – evidence of the red-brick manufacture which once flourished here.

This is a park in which to explore or just to sit and listen to the birds. At the north-western end there are tennis courts and a hard-surfaced children's playground, and during the summer months the café, overlooking a display of formal flowerbeds by the Maryon Road entrance, serves refreshments.

Across Thorntree Road is another park donated to the public by the same family – Maryon Wilson Park. The land was originally offered as a gift in 1912, but with the intervention of the First World War the site was used at first as allotments, and not laid out as a park until the war was over. Maryon Wilson Park was formally 'dedicated to the public for ever' in July 1926.

The park's steeply undulating ground helps it to avoid the neat and sterile formality of many other small parks, with patches here of nettle, gorse and blackberry all getting a chance to lend their wildness to the scene. Even the meandering brook has managed to escape the culverting that is so common elsewhere in London. This is a place for wildlife, with plenty of squirrels, birds and butterflies and, at the northern end, a children's zoo.

Excavations of the area have unearthed many pieces of almost perfectly preserved pottery dating back to Roman times, and in Hanging Wood, of which both these parks once formed a part, was a fortified camp, probably used by the early Britons and Romans. This wood was also one of the local hiding places for highwaymen who roamed Shooters Hill and Blackheath. There are records of several of their robberies from around the eighteenth century, including one amusing one where two highwaymen were pursued by the entire garrison of Woolwich, finally to be caught near here when they 'imitated the example of hunted foxes' and disappeared underground down an old drain.

Both parks form important links in the Green Chain, which provides a green connecting walkway between the Thames Flood Barrier and Cator Park, New Beckenham.

Mitcham Common

Croydon Road, Mitcham

How to get there: by train to Mitcham Junction. By bus: 64, 118, 127, 127A or 234.
Origin of the name: the name Mitcham is derived from the Old English words *micel ham*, meaning 'large village'.
Area: 455 acres (184 hectares), including Mill Green.
Owned by: Mitcham Common Board of Conservators.
Managed by: the Board, with the London Borough of Merton acting as agents. (The 15-acre Mill Green is managed by the London Borough of Sutton.)

Mitcham Common is all that remains today of what was once more than 900 acres of common pasture that spread into Beddington, Wallington and Croydon. The reasons why it survived at all are interesting.

First, the soil here in the Middle Ages was not considered fertile enough to be worth seriously cultivating and hence there was then no great temptation to enclose it. Secondly, the parish was fortunate enough to be divided between four manors, the boundaries of which were uncertain, so that no one lord of the manor was able to control the whole common. This rivalry among the lords gave the parishioners the upper hand, so that even as early as 1240, the parishioners of Mitcham were able successfully to defend their rights of common in court against one of the lords, the Prior of Merton. And thirdly, with the help of the Commons Preservation Society and the Corporation of the City of London, the survival of the common can be attributed to the tenacity of a good number of local individuals, probably the best known of whom would be George Parker Bidder, QC, in memory of whom a rough-hewn granite memorial was erected on the common in 1896.

Of course the battles to preserve the common were not *always* won – most of the houses along the northern and eastern boundaries have been built on what was previously common land, as have the railways. Other conspicuous encroachments include the Mill House near the centre of the common, which was originally a hollow-post grain mill, and the factory on East Commonside – a site taken originally for a workhouse founded here under old Poor Law in 1781.

Although Mitcham Common seems today rather rough and unkempt, it was once considered by many as 'one of the most picturesquely rugged pieces of country in the neighbourhood of

London'. The loss of topsoil through the cutting of turf, the frequently rough terrain created by gravel digging, and the once indiscriminate tipping here of household refuse have all led to the common's deterioration. The present management, however, is taking a more enlightened view of the land's ecological potential and is managing it now more with wildlife and natural beauty in mind. Such management involves occasional mowing to control the rougher grasses, periodic cutting back of scrub and weeding out of sycamore and Robinia seedlings, while planting thousands of trees more appropriate to the type of soil found here.

In spite of its earlier poor management, it is perhaps surprising that Mitcham Common can still boast a much richer range of flora and butterflies than, say, Wimbledon Common. Twenty-one species of butterflies have been identified here, particularly common being the tortoiseshell, peacock, cabbage white, small heath and red admiral. As part of the management policy, patches of nettles are left to serve as a food plant for the Vanessid butterflies. Likewise there has been some thought of nurturing the brimstone population by introducing one of its food plants.

Some of the more interesting plants to be found here include dropwort, petty whin, heather and, as well as common gorse, the relatively rare dwarf gorse. Hemlock is widespread, as are several attractive garden escapees such as the star of Bethlehem, golden rod and sunflower.

Most of the birds here are garden species, though kestrels do visit and both barn and tawny owls nest. Seven Island Pond (north of the golf course) has its occasional swan, coot, moorhen and tufted duck, and usually mallard. And winter migrants such as fieldfares, redwings and lapwings come to the common to feed. Local fauna includes also the more common mammals – hedgehogs, bats, foxes, various kinds of mice, shrews, voles and rabbits.

Though still marshy in places, particularly during wet weather, Mitcham Common is much better drained now than it once was. Of the many ponds that were created from gravel digging, most were filled in between the wars, and only three now remain – the Seven Island Pond already mentioned, One Island Pond and Arthur's Pond.

Just east of Seven Island Pond is an excellent elevated point from which to view the common and surrounding land. This large earth mound is known as the Arena, and was originally constructed as such by the Croydon Corporation in the 1950s. However, its initial contours appeared so unnatural, making it seem like a military fortification, that in 1969 the mound was recontoured to its present, more natural downland shape.

But by far the common's largest and possibly its most attractive feature is its public golf course. It is perhaps ironic that back in 1891 such a battle was fought over its formation for, since it has been the only part of the common to receive continuous maintenance, its varied habitats now support a wonderful variety of wildflowers. One can find here, for example, tormentil, eyebright, coltsfoot, purple sandwort, harebell, heather, adder's-tongue fern, spiny restharrow and even orchids and several rare hybrid violets.

Monken Hadley Common

Hadley Wood Road, Barnet

How to get there: by tube to Cockfosters on the Piccadilly Line. By bus: 263 to the western end of the common; 298 for the eastern end. Approaching from the eastern end, take Chalk Lane which leads into Games Road by the Cock Inn; continue through the white wooden gate to enter the common.
Origin of the name: 'common wood in heathland, held by monks'. (The manor was once held by the monks of Walden Abbey in Essex.)
Area: 190 acres (77 hectares).
Owned by: the Churchwardens of Monken Hadley Church, in trust for the commoners.
Administered by: the Curators of Monken Hadley Common.

This large wedge of woodland was originally part of the royal forest of Enfield Chase which, at the end of the eighteenth century and the beginning of the nineteenth, largely succumbed to the rash of Enclosure Acts. The introduction to the 1777 'Act for dividing the Chase of Enfield' explains: 'the said Chase, in its present state, yields very little profit or advantage either to the King's Majesty or to the said Freeholders and Copyholders or their Tenants, in comparison of what it might do if the same was divided and improved.' With the passing of this Act, the chase was then divided up and distributed between the Crown as owner and those from the four bordering parishes whose inhabitants had been entitled to rights of common. Thus, those parts of the chase allotted to South Mimms, Enfield and Edmonton were enclosed and divided between the commoners, while the commoners of Hadley alone decided to retain collective control of their land, leaving it open for common grazing.

These old common rights still exist today on the same basis as they did then – a commoner being defined as an owner or tenant of a house existing within the parish in the year 1777 and paying in that year a Land Tax of at least ten pounds per annum. These grazing rights are distributed among the commoners as 213 stints – each stint representing the right to graze one animal at any time between 1 May and 31 October. Likewise, it is only these Hadley commoners who are permitted to ride here. The trustees have the legal right to impound and sell any animal found straying or grazing on the common illegally.

The common, which extends for some one and three-quarter miles from Monken Hadley to Cockfosters, is still mostly wooded, largely with huge old oak trees and hornbeams, with some beech and ash, and an abundant undergrowth of holly and blackberry. One of the loveliest parts is towards the eastern end of the property where, fed by the Monken Mead brook, there is an attractive venue for fishing – the Beech Hill lake. (Fishing by permit only.) For a longer walk, it is certainly worth crossing east over Cockfosters Road to explore the much larger Trent Park – another remnant of the old Enfield Chase.

Unlike most urban commons, the ownership and management responsibility for Monken Hadley Common does not lie with the local authority. Back in 1777 it was arranged that the freehold of the common should be vested in the Churchwardens of Monken Hadley Church in perpetuity upon trust for the freeholders and copyholders of the parish. There were occasional problems with this, such as what to do with the compensation paid by the Great Northern Railway Company when they acquired a strip of the common for the laying of their northern main line. This was, however, easily solved by the lawyers claiming most of the money in costs. Less easily solved was the situation which arose in 1978 when the new rector found he had no churchwardens. With the increasing recreational use of the common and more frequent disputes over boundaries, volunteers for the post were getting hard to find. The difficulty was finally overcome by setting up a separate management committee which selects curators from interesting local people, independent of their status within the church.

Morden Hall Park and Ravensbury Park

Morden Road, Morden

How to get there: by train to Morden Road station. By tube to Morden station on the Northern Line. By bus: 80, 93, 118, 154, 156, 157, 164 or 293.
Origin of the names: Morden comes from Mordune, meaning 'hill by marshland', in reference to the slight elevation between Beverley Brook and the Wandle. The name Ravensbury is derived from Raf's bury, meaning 'Ralph's manor'.
Area: though the Morden Hall property officially covers 124 acres (50 hectares), not all of this is open to the public. Ravensbury Park is 17 acres (7 hectares).
Owned and administered by: the National Trust (Morden Hall Park) and the London Borough of Merton (Ravensbury Park).

Practically joined to each other, and linked by a pleasant riverside path, these two parks are laid out along the banks of the river Wandle – a feature which provides both a common focal point and a common thread of history.

Enclosed behind high brick walls, Morden Hall Park consists of pleasant, lush meadows, with attractive avenues and groups of trees, of which perhaps the weeping beech at the southern end is the most striking and unusual. In a winter morning mist, when its leaves have fallen, it can assume quite an eerie form. The Wandle flows swiftly through the park in a number of channels running beneath overhanging trees and providing a reminder of the old industries once associated with the river. Likewise, it is easy here to imagine the deer, sheep and cattle that roamed in the park even up until quite recent times. It is unfortunate that the heart of the property is fenced off with a high and ugly mesh of barbed wire, thus enclosing the old Morden Hall and Morden Cottage which are presently leased by the National Trust to Merton Borough Council for housing some of its administrative offices.

To the south, just across Morden Road, Ravensbury Park seems by comparison more intimate and secluded, with its own grassy playground, seats and picnic area, all within what in fact is an island in the Wandle. The most attractive access to this is via a narrow path leading from Morden Road, along the northern bank of the Wandle – and this is accessible to wheelchairs.

The historical link that these two parks share is in the industries that sprang up in association with the river. Morden Hall and Ravensbury Bridge were both sites of snuff mills where tobacco leaves and stems, having been first kiln dried, would be fed into a large shallow bowl turned by waterwheel. Inside the bowl would run a stone wheel which ground the leaves to a fine powder, which was then sifted, weighed and packed for sale. This business prospered at both sites from the mid-eighteenth century up until the turn of the nineteenth century, by which time the use of snuff was already giving way to the habit and fashion of smoking.

The two mills at Ravensbury Bridge – by the junction of Morden and Wandle roads – went then from snuff to tobacco manufacture and became known as the home of 'Mitcham Shag' tobacco (once very popular in the Midlands and south of England) before finally closing down in 1925. Also at Ravensbury (at a site now covered by a municipal housing estate) a calico bleaching and printing business flourished from about 1700 until the 1860s, when the local industry could no longer compete with the new mills in Lancashire.

At Morden Hall there were also two snuff mills, both of which were leased by the lords of the manor, the Garths, to various millers. When the Hatfeild family of Taddy & Co. took the mills over in 1831 they did such good business that they were eventually not only able to buy Morden Cottage and the mills outright, but also much of the land in Morden previously owned by the Garths, thus finally displacing that family as lords of the manor of Morden.

During the First World War, just before the snuff business finally collapsed, Mr Gilliat Hatfeild (the last lord of the manor of Morden) offered Morden Hall to the governors of the London Hospital for use as a convalescent home for military patients. And in 1940, when he died, Mr Hatfeild generously bequeathed both Morden Hall and its grounds to the National Trust, who have maintained most of it as a public park ever since.

Ravensbury Park, on the other hand, originally formed part of the grounds of the old Ravensbury manor house, only a few hidden fragments of which now remain. The park itself was purchased for public recreation in 1930.

Osterley Park

Jersey Road, Islesworth

How to get there: by tube to Osterley station on the Piccadilly Line. By bus: 91 or 704.
Origin of the name: Osterley means 'a wood near an enclosure for sheep'.
Area: 140 acres (57 hectares).
Owned by: the National Trust. (The adjoining farmland is still privately owned by the Earl of Jersey.)
Maintained by: Department of the Environment (the park) and the Victoria and Albert Museum (the house).

From Jersey Road, the long driveway up to the park and house leads through open farmland along a delightful shady avenue of mature horse chestnuts, limes, oaks, maples, sweet chestnuts and beeches – finally arriving at the car park and lakes, which mark the beginning of the main part of the park. From here, the park's focal point, Osterley House, comes suddenly into view across an expanse of neatly-kept lawn, amid groups of majestic old trees.

Although this old four-towered mansion dates from the time of the park's enclosure in the latter part of the sixteenth century, its present fame and appearance are due more to the considerable alterations made to it between 1760 and 1780 by the famous architect Robert Adam.

Osterley House was built originally for the founder of the Royal Exchange, Sir Thomas Gresham, who was said to be the richest merchant of his time. Other famous residents here were Nicholas Barbon who, after the Great Fire of London, instituted fire insurance in England, and later Francis Child, founder of Child's Bank, often described as 'the father of banking'.

It was his son (also called Francis) who initiated the great changes at Osterley which transformed the old Tudor house into what is now frequently described as a 'monument of eighteenth-century classicism'. The house is remarkable in that not only does it survive in something like its eighteenth-century state, but it also has much of its eighteenth-century décor, including some fine carpets and tapestries, as well as all the furniture that was designed during that period for each of the principal rooms.

The setting for the house is an expanse of almost perfectly flat parkland, relieved by the generous planting of trees and an assortment of garden buildings. The most striking of these trees are the magnificent group of dark spreading cedars between the house and the lake. These may well now be over two centuries old, for they are thought to have been planted to celebrate the birth of Lady Sarah Sophia Fane in 1785.

Just nearby, within a protective enclosure of iron railings by the lake, is an ancient cork oak tree – one of the very few in London – the same species of tree from which commercial cork is harvested in Spain and Portugal. A little further to the west, also by the lake, a large earth mound (with a few yew and cherry trees growing on it) covers the site of the old ice-house, in which ice cut from the lake in winter was stored for keeping food and drinks cold in the summer.

The woodland strip which runs along the western end of the park is a wonderful sight in spring, when its rich carpet of bluebells is in flower. All around the park there is a remarkable variety of specimen trees, including ashleaf maple and this country's tallest recorded examples of Hungarian oak and shellbark hickory. There are good specimens, too, of wild service tree, silver and Montpelier maples, Caucasian lime, sweetgum, many other types of oak (including Mirkbeck's, Turner's, daimyo, red and pin oaks), golden poplar and black Italian poplar. It is perhaps this range of mature trees which makes Osterley Park itself so especially worth visiting. This and the variety of birds that the park attracts. In 1975, for example, eighty-two species were spotted here, of which forty-six were known to have bred in the park. There are great crested grebes, kestrels, corn buntings – all of which breed here – and kingfishers, which have been known to nest.

Continuing the walk around the western wooded end of the park, one arrives eventually at the charming little Doric Temple – the Temple of Pan – said to have been built by John James of Greenwich in 1720, though modern experts believe it more likely to be the work of Sir William Chambers. A little further on, facing the garden temple, is the semicircular Garden House, designed by Adam in about 1775 and then, behind this, the old kitchen garden.

This brings us to the back of the stable block, which may well have been the original manorial dwelling. Here refreshments are served in the summer months (except Mondays).

Walking on to the north-eastern end of the park, along the shoreline of the second lake, provides one with some lovely long views over closely cropped grass, back towards the mansion. Ahead, the three lakes stretch into the distance beyond the present public park boundaries, under the M4 motorway. These lakes were originally formed by damming the small stream, and then enlarged in the eighteenth century from what were previously described as 'faire ponds'.

The park and house were given to the National Trust by the ninth and present Earl of Jersey in 1949. Osterley House is open to the public in the afternoons on Thursdays, Fridays, Saturdays and Bank Holidays. Closed Good Friday, Christmas Eve, Christmas Day, Boxing Day and New Year's Eve. The grounds are open free throughout the year. (Telephone 01-560 3918 for further details.)

Oxleas Woodlands

Rochester Way, SE9

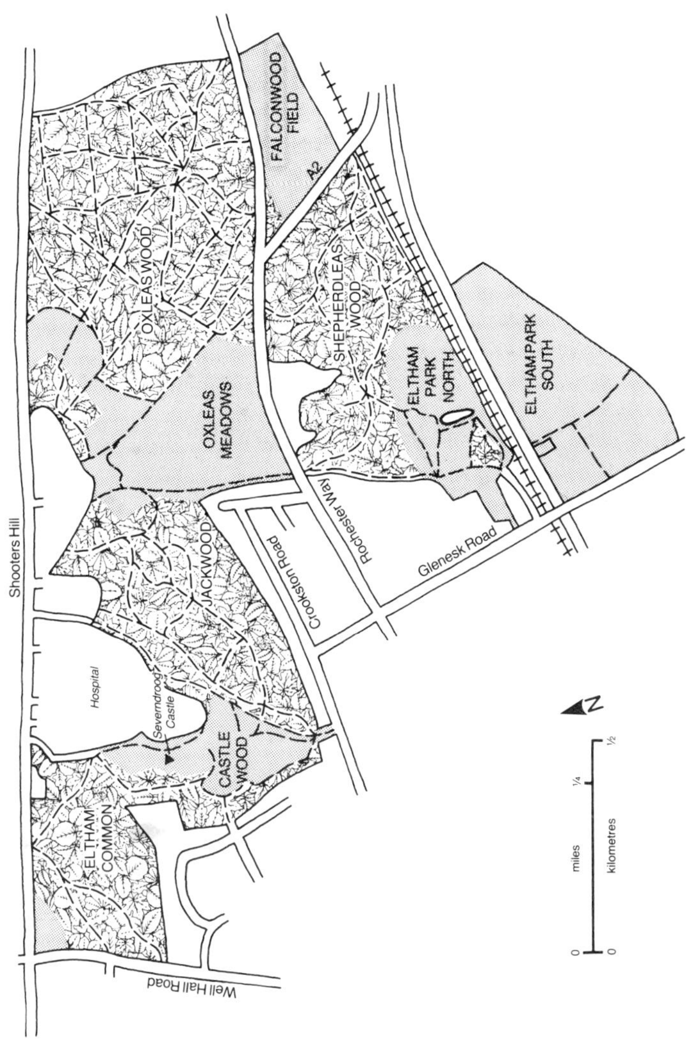

How to get there: by train to Eltham Park or Falconwood stations. By bus: 89, 122, 160, 160A, 161, 291 or 402.
Origin of the name: meaning 'wood, or clearing in a wood, frequented by oxen'.
Area: 375 acres (152 hectares) total.
Owned and maintained by: London Borough of Greenwich.

Appropriately dubbed in the 1920s the 'Hampstead Heath of the South', this is one of the largest areas of woodland in south-east London. As a chain of adjoining open spaces covering almost 400 acres, it forms the heart of a much larger belt of parkland – known as the Green Chain – which extends for some fifteen miles from the Thames Barrier and Thamesmead through to Cator Park, New Beckenham.

The first step to acquire this cluster of open land was taken in 1902, with the purchase of Eltham Park South – an area of open grassland, serving now mostly as playing fields. Then came the beautiful, steeply terraced Castle Wood and Jackwood, both opened in 1925 with the help of public-spirited individuals and such bodies as the Metropolitan Public Gardens Association and the Poulter Trust. The 'castle', from which the wood takes its name, is in fact a three-cornered crenellated tower, erected here in 1784 as a memorial to Sir William James of Eltham Park. Severndroog Castle, as the tower is known, was built 'to commemorate that gallant officer's achievements in the East Indies during his command of the Company's Marine Forces in those Seas. And in a particular manner to record the Conquest of the Castle of Severndroog off the Coast of Malabar which fell to his superior valour and able conduct on the 2nd Day of April 1755.' The fortress of Janjeera Soowurndroog (an island south of Bombay) had been the hideout of some 1000 pirates, the capture of whom meant the freeing of the Malabar Coast trading routes.

Though now no longer used, the castle has at various times served as a viewing point, a museum, a summerhouse and, during the Second World War, a look-out post. Below, the view to the south is extensive – over a fine rose garden, towards Eltham – while a walk to the east brings one to the rhododendrons and ornate garden walls of Jackwood.

Eltham Park North was, in 1929, the next to be acquired. It was purchased largely as a way of preserving the ancient Long Pond which forms such an attractive feature of the park today. With its weeping willows and swamp cypress, bullrush and reed mace, this small pond attracts the usual mallard ducks, along with a pair of moorhens which nest here every year.

In the meantime, Eltham Common, though still owned by the

War Office, had also been opened to the public. The manorial rights had been purchased by the War Office back in 1812, but by the early 1900s they tried claiming to have absolute rights over the land, with the right to enclose the common and build on it – an attempt which was effectively foiled by the Commons Preservation Society's solicitor, Mr Birkett, in 1908. This attractive area of oak woodland did not finally come under undisputed public control until its purchase by the London County Council in 1938.

The most significant purchase of all, though, and the one which united all the others, was that of Oxleas and Shepherdleas Woods in 1934. These are both surviving fragments of ancient woodland – i.e. woodland whose origins can be traced right back to the end of the last Ice Age. Such woodlands, which invariably have a great diversity of wildlife, are fast becoming rare in Britain and this is one of the few to have survived within London. Beneath oak, ash, sweet chestnut, hornbeam, birch, alder and field maple are shrubs of guelder rose, holly, wayfaring tree, dogwood, blackthorn and hazel. Across the woodland floor tangles of blackberry sprawl, with honeysuckle and wild rose, and such pretty woodland flowers as bluebells, wood anemone, wood avens, lesser celandine, stitchwort, wood sage and wood sorrel, yellow archangel, enchanter's nightshade, common cow-wheat and the unusual Forster's wood rush. There are, in all, at least thirty species of trees and shrubs including the less common wild cherry and butcher's broom, and more specimens of the rare wild service tree than can be found in any other wood in north-west Kent.

Besides the trees, there are at least another one hundred flowering plants, over 210 species of fungi (including several rare species), over one hundred species of butterflies and moths (some of these also rare) and just under 200 species of beetles. The area is particularly rich in breeding birds, and has all the species one generally associates with natural woodlands far outside such built-up areas, including all three British species of woodpecker, the tree creeper, wood warbler and even the shy woodcock.

One of the reasons for this immense richness is the fact that for centuries these woods have been managed as 'coppice-with-standards' – a management regime that was practised here right up until the Second World War and which has recently been reinstated by the Greater London Council. Coppicing involves cutting certain trees (usually hazel, sweet chestnut and hornbeam) at ground level, on a rotational basis, allowing the stumps to resprout to produce a new crop of poles, while the standards (usually oak) are left to grow to maturity. This periodic opening of the woodland canopy, and the sunlight that it permits to reach the woodland floor, is of particular value in sustaining a wide variety of wildlife species.

In recognition of the unique nature of the woodland, 180 acres were designated under Section 28 of the Wildlife and Countryside Act in November 1984 as a Site of Special Scientific Interest (SSSI).

What with the protection given to it by the Green Chain planning policy and this recent SSSI designation, it might seem that the woodland's future is now quite secure, but alas no. The Department of Transport has every intention, at the time of writing, of building a four-lane highway (as part of the East London River Crossing) right through the middle of it.

Parkland Walk

N4

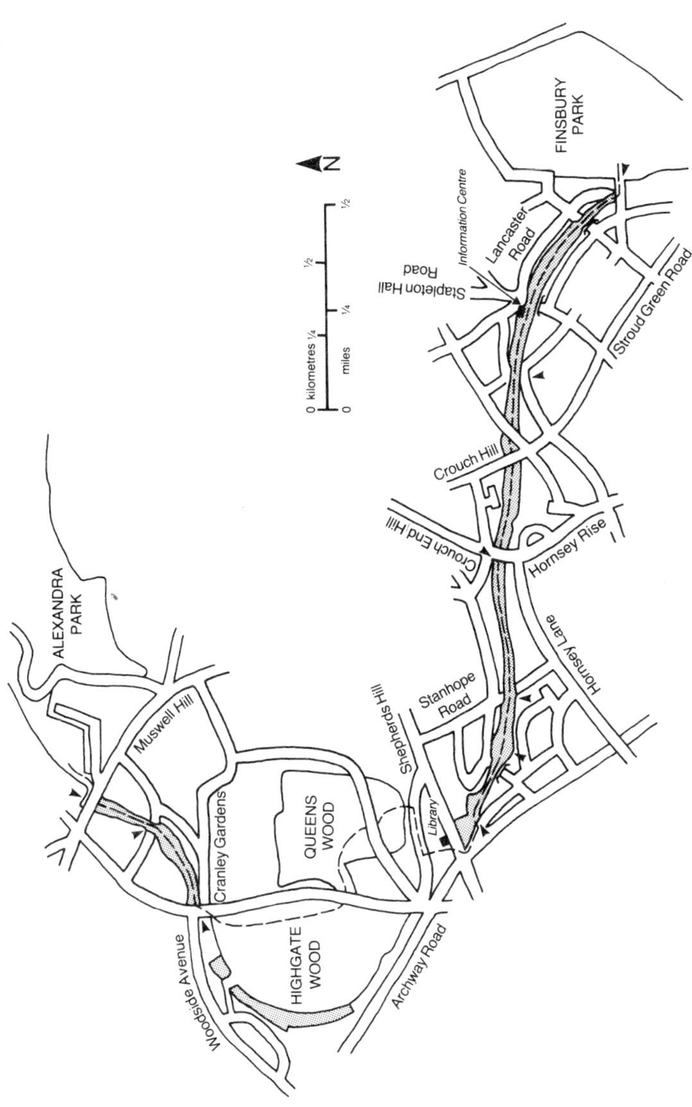

How to get there: by train to Finsbury Park or Alexandra Palace (previously called Wood Green) stations. By tube to Finsbury Park on the Victoria and Piccadilly Lines. By bus: 4, 19, 29, 106, 210, 221, 230, 236, 253, 259, 279, 279A, W2, W3 or W7. (To return to Finsbury Park from Alexandra Palace, take the W3 bus or the train from Alexandra Palace station.)
Origin of the name: from the park's linear nature.
Area: 24 acres (10 hectares).
Owned and maintained by: London Borough of Haringey.

The Parkland Walk is a meandering strip of open land running north-west from Finsbury Park, along the old Finsbury Park to Highgate railway line and then north-east along the short branch line to Alexandra Palace. This refreshingly rural strip of land not only provides the route for one of London's most remarkable urban countryside walks, but also serves as an important local nature reserve. Here thirty-two per cent of Britain's breeding butterfly species can be found and fifty-two species of birds, of which twenty-four are known to breed along the walk. Here also are at least 233 different kinds of flowering plants, including such rarities as hare's foot clover, Hungarian spurge and nettle-leaved bellflower.

Such corridors of natural surroundings not only provide vital links for wildlife between many of London's larger parks, but also offer unique opportunities for the walker. By following the Parkland Walk footpath, it is possible to take a four-mile stroll all the way from Finsbury Park via Queen's and Highgate Woods to Alexandra Palace Park, using no more than 400 yards of road.

The old Highgate railway line was first opened as part of the route to Edgware in 1867, and the branch to Alexandra Palace in 1873 (to coincide with the formal opening of the palace). In the early 1900s, when Muswell Hill was developing as a suburb, the palace branch line was well used by freight trains carrying building materials but, in spite of later attempts to modernize the line, demand soon fell and on 3 July 1954 the last passenger train ran. The Finsbury Park to Highgate section, on the other hand, continued to be used for the transfer of Northern Line tube carriages from Drayton Park right up until 29 September 1970, and by the end of 1971 the tracks had been completely removed.

Haringey Council originally had plans for house building along part of the southern section of the walk, though strong public opposition led to a public inquiry in 1978 which ruled against building development, in favour of preserving the natural character and amenity value of the area.

Starting from the Finsbury Park end, access is via the

footbridge by Oxford Road. The first point of interest is the Station House Information Centre off to the right and down the steps from the path, at 73c Stapleton Hall Road (telephone 01-341 3582). Here, exhibits both about the history and natural history of the park are on display, with photos, large-scale historical maps and a selection of informative leaflets.

Returning to the path, one passes between the platforms of the old Crouch End station, eventually reaching the tunnel under Shepherds Hill. Here the walk temporarily leaves the old railway and turns left up on to Holmesdale Road, right into Archway Road and right again into Shepherds Hill. Turn left immediately before the library, along a rough track down to Priory Gardens and then right for 250 yards to an alleyway on the left between the houses, which takes you then into Queen's Wood.

From the other side of Queen's Wood one can walk across Muswell Hill Road through to the northern corner of Highgate Wood, and from here (at the corner of Cranley Gardens and Muswell Hill Road) the final Alexandra Palace leg of the walk is accessible.

Although much of this connecting walk through Queen's and Highgate Woods is unsuitable for wheelchairs, the two railway sections (even if a little rough in places) are accessible. In particular I would recommend to wheelchair users this northern Alexandra Palace branch, both because of the ease of access and because of the impressive views it offers over the roof tops of Hornsey.

Peckham Rye Common and Peckham Rye Park

Peckham Rye, SE15

How to get there: by train to Peckham Rye station, just under half a mile from the common. By bus: 12, 37, 63, 78, 184 or P3.
Origin of the name: Peckham means 'village by a hill', referring to the site of the old village, a little west of Telegraph Hill. Rye comes from the Old English word for a small stream; thus Peckham Rye means 'the district of Peckham by a stream'.
Area: 113 acres (46 hectares).
Owned and maintained by: London Borough of Southwark.

Do not let the dullness and lack of trees on the common lead you to overlook the beauty and seclusion of Peckham Rye Park. This has all the features one looks for in a park – a thoughtful blend of the wild and the cultivated, of open grass and woodland, a stream-fed lake and children's playgrounds. My favourite spot is the enclosed Old English garden which, with its many benches, is such a pleasant and quiet place for outdoor reading. If you prefer the more formal style of floral designs, then in summer visit the beautiful flowerbeds at the north-western end of the park.

The common dates back at least to the fourteenth century and was once well-wooded and considerably larger than it is now. Evidence suggests that it once extended as far west as Goose Green. Parishioners here were more alert, though, to defending the common from encroachments than in many parts of London, for there are records of their protests in the vestry minutes from as far back as 1766 and 1789. The parishioners had very little power actually to protect the common but, with the arrival on to the common of thirty-two vans of 'Wombwell's Wild Beast Show' in 1864, the local inhabitants decided to protest. The parishioners wanted to find some way of protecting the common in particular from building development, but when the subject was brought up in Parliament, the lord of the manor claimed that since there were no longer any copyholders in the manor, he therefore had absolute rights and could do what he liked. The locals were, however, able to prove otherwise and by 1868 the rights of the lord of the manor, whatever they were, were bought by the Camberwell Vestry, who in turn sold the common in 1882 to the Metropolitan Board of Works, thus protecting it for public use for ever.

But with a scarcity of local public open space, Peckham Rye Common was soon being so well used by south Londoners in general that for many months of the year the grass was entirely worn away. It was this over-use of the common that led to the idea of an extension on to what was then the adjoining Homestall Farm. A committee was formed and campaigned for some years to acquire this extension, which is now known as Peckham Rye Park. Substantial donations towards the cost of the forty-nine-acre park were collected from the Camberwell Vestry, the London County Council and the Charity Commissioners, with smaller donations from the Lambeth Vestry, St Mary's Church in Newington and St George the Martyr Church in Southwark. Finally, after laying-out work, Peckham Rye Park was opened to the public on Whit Monday, 1894.

Facilities for the common and park now include a bowling green, several football and cricket pitches, tennis courts, putting green, refreshment kiosk, a conventional children's playground, an adventure playground and a swimming pool.

From here it is just over a quarter of a mile's walk down Homestall Road (named after the old farm) to enjoy the roses of Brenchley Gardens and the views from One Tree Hill.

Petts Wood

Orpington Road, Chislehurst

How to get there: by train to Petts Wood station, then a half-mile walk via the subway under the railway from Hazelmere Road. By bus: 61 or 161 to St Paul's Cray Common; the path heading south through the common leads into Petts Wood.
Origin of the name: named after the Pett family of shipbuilders, who are believed to have owned the wood in the sixteenth century.
Area: 135 acres (55 hectares) of which 47 acres (19 hectares) are technically regarded as part of the Hawkwood Estate.
Owned by: the National Trust
Administered by: the Petts Wood Management Committee. Funds come from National Trust subscriptions, with grants from the London Borough of Bromley and Petts Wood Residents' Association.

This predominantly silver birch, oak and chestnut woodland is made all the more attractive by the woods which surround it – St Paul's Cray Common to the north and, north again of this, the newly-opened Scadbury Park.

The undergrowth of Petts Wood is more or less open, with blackberry and bracken frequently giving way to a carpet of lesser celandine, wood anemone, wood sorrel, common dog violet and – especially in the western Edlmann Wood – bluebells. Rhododendrons form dense clumps in places and there is the occasional rowan, elder, pine and the odd patch of rosebay willowherb, with any number of grey squirrels and a good population of birds.

The wood is provided with the occasional simple wooden bench and criss-crossed with a good number of walking tracks and a broad bridlepath which passes close by the two stone memorials that tell the history of the wood's conservation. These two monoliths refer to the fact that Petts Wood consists technically of two properties – Willett Wood to the east and Edlmann Wood (a part of the Hawkwood Estate) to the west. Each has its distinct history.

Willett Wood was purchased in 1927 as a memorial to the work of William Willett, who pioneered daylight saving – an idea originally intended to give people the chance to enjoy their summer evenings, but first introduced to save fuel during the First World War. Willett's campaign for British Summer Time began long before this and sadly he had to face a good deal of criticism – even ridicule – without ever seeing his idea accepted. He died in 1915, a year before its introduction.

In 1925, the year daylight saving began on a permanent basis, Petts Wood was on the market and about to be sold for building development. The Early Closing Association were considering what might be a suitable memorial to William Willett and his energetic campaign, when they heard of the appeal already underway by Chislehurst residents to save the wood. Since Mr Willett had, himself, been a resident of Chislehurst and it is said that it was while riding in these woods that he first conceived the idea of daylight saving, the association decided to launch an appeal to buy Petts Wood and name it after him.

After over a year of campaigning for funds, eighty-eight acres of the wood were purchased and ceremoniously opened in May 1927, with the unveiling of the two-and-a-half-ton granite Willett memorial sundial, which still stands at the northern end of the wood in a rather secluded spot not far east of the central bridleway.

The Willett memorial campaign had, however, been unable to raise enough funds to purchase the whole of Petts Wood, so, in 1927, Francis Edlmann moved to protect the remaining forty-seven acres by purchasing this as an extension to his Hawkwood Estate.

It had seemed to all concerned that the battle to save Petts Wood was at last over, but in 1950, when Colonel Edlmann died, his executors tried to sell the entire estate to builders and appealed against planning restrictions designed to stop them from doing so. The strength of local opposition, however, led to their appeal being dismissed by the Minister of Housing.

At this point Francesca and Robert Hall, who were keen local conservationists, were so impressed by the peace and beauty of 'Bluebell Wood' that they decided to save the Hawkwood Estate by buying it and handing it over to the National Trust as a gift. At the opening ceremony, in April 1958, the second granite monolith – the Edlmann memorial stone – was unveiled, marking the end of the thirty-year conservation struggle. This still stands, a few yards west of the bridleway.

Plumstead Common

Plumstead Common Road, SE18

How to get there: by train to Plumstead station, then half a mile walk. By bus: 51, 53 or 291.
Origin of the name: meaning 'place of plums'.
Area: 104 acres (42 hectares).
Owned and maintained by: London Borough of Greenwich.

This is one of the most attractive and interesting commons in south London, stretching for one and a half miles from St Margaret's Grove in the west to Wickham Lane in the east. The terrain varies from flat grassland to steeply undulating woodland, including one surprising ravine. This ravine, known as the Slade, is perhaps the most beautiful part, with its steep slopes descending to a small lake by the end of Roydene Road. The vegetation has changed a good deal over the centuries through heavy military use, but patches of gorse still remain, with areas of oak, silver birch and the occasional London plane. The whole common is intersected by roads, one of which – Old Mill Road – commemorates an eighteenth-century windmill which once overlooked the common. In 1848 this was converted into the present Old Mill pub, which stands on the corner of Inverary Place. To the east, the common merges into Bostall Heath and Woods and then on to Lesnes Abbey Woods, to create a three-mile chain of almost 500 acres of open land.

In the early nineteenth century, commons all over London were being gradually eroded as chunks were steadily nibbled from their borders for sale by the lords of the manors, and Plumstead Common was no exception. As the rate and size of enclosures here increased in the mid-1800s, so too did the strength of local opposition, until it became quite clear that Queen's College, Oxford, as lords of the manor, intended by degrees to sell the entire common. Up until that time, the respectable image of the college had protected it from anything stronger than verbal protest.

In 1866, however, a group of well-known Plumstead residents – John Warrick, Julian Goldsmid, William Dawson and Joseph Jacobs – filed a court action against the Provost and scholars of Queen's College, Oxford, for the illegal sale of parts of their common land. In spite of an appeal by the college, the commoners finally won the case in 1871 and the college was ordered to pay the costs and to return all parts of the common that it had taken since the proceedings began.

Not only did this decision mark a victory for the commoners of Plumstead, but the legal points on which the case was won subsequently helped in the saving of commons elsewhere.

Things might have rested there had not the War Office decided earlier in the same year that they had the right to exercise their troops on the common in training for the Franco–German War. First they destroyed the gorse and blackberry, and before long every blade of grass had disappeared too, changing what was once a beautiful common into a barren desert.

By 1876, the wrath of the commoners could no longer be contained and a movement, led by John de Morgan, began a campaign of civil disobedience to reclaim lost common land. The movement grew rapidly until there were as many as 10,000 people meeting on the common to pull out and burn fences around all the recent and not-so-recent enclosures.

It was not long, however, before John de Morgan and some of his followers were charged with riotous assembly and disturbing the public peace. Although de Morgan's followers were acquitted, he himself was sentenced to two months in gaol. To the inhabitants of Plumstead this could only raise de Morgan from being their hero to being their martyr.

After only seventeen days in gaol, de Morgan was mysteriously released by order of the Home Secretary and told (according to de Morgan) that his sentence had been a wrong one. His release could hardly have been more appropriately timed as far as the people of Plumstead were concerned, for it was on 5 November, the anniversary of Guy Fawkes' Gunpowder Plot. Preparations were already underway for a celebration on the common, but de Morgan's release added a new enthusiasm to the occasion! At Beresford Square, a crowd of around 20,000 people had gathered to cheer and welcome de Morgan as he told them that this was a victory for the commoners of Plumstead against 'the strongest Conservative government the country has ever seen' and that he had now returned to resume his battle against 'the land thieves of Plumstead'.

Before the march on to the common began, de Morgan sought an assurance from the crowd that they were going to hold a peaceful demonstration and then he climbed aboard the 'conquering hero's triumphal' carriage to set off as part of the torch-lit procession which marched to a plateau on the western side of the Slade. Here, in front of a crowd that had by now swelled to 30,000, the appropriate effigies were ceremoniously sacrificed at the funeral pyre, putting the symbolic seal of victory on de Morgan's campaign.

Thankfully, within a year the Metropolitan Board of Works had decided to buy the common along with Bostall Heath, thereby protecting them at last from building speculators. Today, the common is owned by Greenwich Borough Council and provides several recreational facilities including a neatly-hedged bowling green, hard tennis courts, adventure and children's playgrounds, and, at the eastern end, a new fitness trail.

Primrose Hill

Primrose Hill Road, NW3

How to get there: by tube to Camden Town or Chalk Farm stations on the Northern Line, or Swiss Cottage or St John's Wood stations on the Jubilee Line. Although Camden Town is the furthest station from Primrose Hill (a little under one mile), a walk along the Regent's Canal towpath from the access on Chalk Farm Road makes a pleasant approach. By bus: 74.
Origin of the name: thought to be a reference to the primroses which once grew here. The name dates back at least as far as 1586.
Area: 62 acres (25 hectares).
Owned by: the Crown.
Maintained by: Department of the Environment.

Primrose Hill forms a northern extension of Regent's Park. The hill was, like Regent's Park, once a part of Henry VIII's hunting forest of Marylebone Park and was added to Regent's Park in 1841, when the Crown exchanged some of their land at Windsor with Eton College, who had previously owned the hill. This, incidentally, was the same year in which the decision was taken to form Victoria Park – the first 'people's park' in London – at the eastern end of the Regent's Canal.

At 216 feet above sea level, the view from the summit of this conical hill is impressive. Looking south over central London, it is easy to see the dome of St Paul's Cathedral, Telecom Tower (once the tallest building in England) and the towers of Westminster Cathedral and Westminster Abbey. In fact, virtually the whole of central London forms part of the panorama, along with most of Regent's Park and London Zoo. Unfortunately, both the original panorama indicators here have been stolen, presumably by over-zealous souvenir hunters.

The elevation of the hill above what was otherwise flat farmland resulted in Primrose Hill once being a favourite spot for duels and other acts of revenge. In fact, it was once said to be haunted by the ghost of Sir Edmondsbury Godfrey, who was mysteriously murdered in October 1678; his body was found in a ditch at the foot of the hill. The superstition led to an old rhyme:

> Godfrey walks up hill after he was dead;
> [St] Denis walks down hill carrying his head.

Today, the hill has more cheerful associations, especially for kite-flying enthusiasts and in winter for tobogganing and even (though doubtlessly unofficially) for skiing.

The hill does not offer the usual flowerbeds that one might associate with a central park, but consists instead largely of open grassland, with rows and clusters of mature trees. It unfortunately lost a good deal of its former charm during the Second World War, when the land was cleared for allotments, though there have been attempts to improve it since. In 1981 the London Wildlife Trust requested permission to plant a primrose here to mark its inauguration in May of that year. The refusal by the Department of the Environment led to some amusing if embarrassing press notices, with such headlines as: 'Primroses are banned from Primrose Hill.' Apparently, though, the DOE has since taken up the idea of primrose planting itself, but it is sad to find a public body so wary of the planting of appropriate trees and flowers in London's parks, especially considering the current climate of severe cuts in public spending. After all, commemorative planting here does have its precedent. Shakespeare's Oak was planted in 1864 to celebrate the 300th anniversary of the playwright's birth, though the original tree has since died and been replaced.

From Primrose Hill, it is worth exploring local sections of the Regent's Canal towpath, either west to Little Venice, or east to Camden Town. And, of course, there is Regent's Park itself and London Zoo.

Ravenscourt Park

Paddenswick Road, W6

How to get there: by tube to Ravenscourt Park station (closed on Sundays) on the District Line. By bus: 27, 88, 91, 260, 266, 267 or 290.
Origin of the name: the manor's original name was Palyngewyk – meaning 'Paelli's outlying farm' – which was corrupted to Paddingswick in the sixteenth century, and then changed to Ravenscourt when Thomas Corbett acquired the property in 1746, probably from his coat of arms which depicted a black raven on a white background.
Area: 34 acres (14 hectares).
Owned and maintained by: London Borough of Hammersmith and Fulham.

At first glance from the park's southern entrance, there is little, except perhaps for the flowering cherry avenue, to suggest the former grandeur of what was once the grounds of Ravenscourt House. But a brief look at the history of the estate attunes us to some of the park's more hidden beauty.

Ravenscourt Park had taken on much of its present form by 1750, by which time the long avenue leading from King Street to the site of the old mansion was already well established. An advertisement from a 1754 newspaper describes the estate as it was auctioned after the death of Thomas Corbett, Secretary to the Admiralty, as 'consisting of a capital mansion-house, out-houses, gardens, lands, farms and messuages, thereunto belonging and adjoining . . . the situation of which is admirable, the house in the finest repair, and improved with every conveniency that can be desired; the lands of the rich and fertile soil, the gardens elegantly laid out, and the whole calculated to give delight.' Under a later owner – in fact, the estate's last major private owner, George Scott (who bought the property in 1812) – the grounds were then further beautified to the designs of the landscape architect Humphry Repton.

Although Ravenscourt House itself was unfortunately destroyed in 1941 by enemy action (it stood originally on the lawn on the east side of the lake), the stables still remain, today housing the popular Ravenscourt tea house (open 11 a.m.–dusk, serving salads and soups, pizzas and quiches and much more besides). The bowling green nearby dates back at least to the 1750s and the beautiful lake here is thought to have once formed part of the moat around the old house. This area is attractively shielded from traffic noise and the railway by a curving bed of shrubs and trees. There are gracefully shaped flowerbeds here too and the lake's island is thick with birdlife.

There are far more trees distributed across this, the northern end of the park and the undulating ground here provides a welcome contrast to the flat grassland towards the railway. Apart from the lake area and tea house, another important attraction here is the enclosed Old English scented garden, laid out for the blind in the park's north-eastern corner, with crazy-paved pathways and wooden benches arranged around a central fish pond. Some of the benches have attractive wooden shelters to provide for the vicissitudes of the English weather.

It is fortunate that the grounds survived London's rapid building development towards the end of the last century, for even as far back as 1839 there were proposals to build villas along the line of the present avenue, with parts of the park destined to be let off for detached villas, for which it was regarded as 'particularly adapted from its secluded situation and proximity to London'.

Just before the grounds became a public park in 1888, the London and South Western Railway Company took a strip of land at the southern end of the property for the building of their Kensington to Richmond line which was opened in 1869. The Metropolitan Board of Works purchased the grounds in 1887, with half the cost being met by the Vestry of Hammersmith, and then Ravenscourt Park was formally opened to the public on 19 May 1888.

Apart from the facilities already mentioned, the park also has hard tennis courts, football pitches, a putting green, summer theatre (telephone 01-741 3696 for events), a children's playground and paddling pool, a one o'clock club for under-fives, and an adventure playground for under-sixteens.

Regent's Park

Prince Albert Road, NW1

How to get there: by tube to Regent's Park station on the Bakerloo Line or Baker Street on the Circle, Metropolitan, Bakerloo and Jubilee lines. By bus: 3, 18, 27, 30, 53, 137 or 176.
Origin of the name: in honour of the Prince of Wales, later George IV, who ruled as Prince Regent from 1811 to 1820.
Area: 472 acres (191 hectares), *including* Primrose Hill.
Owned by: the Crown.
Maintained by: Department of the Environment.

Regent's Park originally entered royal ownership at the Dissolution of the Monasteries, when Henry VIII had the land enclosed as another of his private hunting grounds, namely Marylebone Park. And so the land remained in royal hands until the execution of Charles I when the park fell to Oliver Cromwell, who promptly proceeded to sell leases on the property to pay off his enormous war debts. The park's hitherto wild character then underwent a most drastic change, with most of its original 16,297 trees being felled for sale, for the new landholders, knowing that their tenure could hardly be secure, were anxious to recoup their outlay as swiftly as possible.

In 1660, with the restoration to the throne of Charles II, the King had on his hands what might have seemed a thorny problem – the question of land tenure. This was effectively dealt with by the execution of the chief landholder, and apparently ignoring the claims of the other tenants. The King then proceeded to sell new leases on the same land for pastoral use. Indeed, right up until the formation of Regent's Park proper, this land remained one of London's most important sources of hay and dairy produce.

The site returned to parkland with the advent of the Prince Regent who commissioned his favourite architect, John Nash, to come up with a grand design for a neo-Classical or Palladian development of the entire area. The present boating lake, Regent's Canal and the grand encircling terraces are all part of Nash's final design, as is the focal point of the park: the Inner Circle. This last now encloses the lovely Queen Mary's Gardens (named after the consort of George V) which is definitely one of the best rose gardens in the British Isles (best seen from June to September). Nearby are several noteworthy trees, including the pillar apple and manna ash which are regarded as among the finest British specimens of their species, and likewise specimens of red maple, small-leaved lime and Oregon ash by the boating lake. Other trees to look out for in the park are Lobel's maple, Himalayan tree-cotoneaster, bay, Caucasian elm and weeping willow.

My favourite corner of the park is a spot so hard to find that it is sometimes called the secret garden. It is just off the Inner Circle near St John's Lodge. You will recognize it (if you find it) by an unusually graceful statue of a shepherd girl with a young goat, dedicated 'to all protectors of the defenceless'. Somehow here it seems possible to merge with the magic of this garden and leave the city far behind.

The Inner Circle also encloses the Open Air Theatre, the Rose Garden Restaurant and a beautiful lake, which is one of the original features of the old Royal Botanical Society's gardens. The theatre, whose first play was staged in 1932, presents mostly Shakespeare. (Wheelchair-accessible loos are situated near the corner of Broad Walk and Chester Road.)

For such an urban setting, Regent's Park has quite a varied bird life and although this can no doubt mainly be attributed to the variety of habitats here, it is said that London Zoo by the canal also contributes, since many birds drop in to steal the animals' food. Indeed, in 1977, eighty-seven species of wild birds were sighted within the park, of which thirty-six, including kestrels, herons and great crested grebes, were known to be breeding here. Complementing this is the official collection of introduced waterfowl which includes twenty-four types of duck and eight kinds of geese.

One particularly interesting new wildlife development is the recent attempt to reintroduce the native red squirrel (now rare throughout the British Isles). This experimental scheme involves teaching the native squirrels to operate 'weight selective food hoppers' which are accessible to the red squirrels, but which are automatically closed by the weight of their ubiquitous competitors, the much heavier grey squirrels.

The park may not have become all that Nash promised – it cost his client four times the original estimate and the building development provided only a third of the income Nash promised – but it did in other respects prove to be an extremely successful venture in town planning. As Crabb Robinson, the diarist, wrote in 1872: 'This enclosure, with the New Street leading to it from Carlton House, will give a sort of glory to the Regent's government, which will be more felt by remote posterity than the victories of Trafalgar and Waterloo, glorious as these are.'

Richmond Park

Richmond

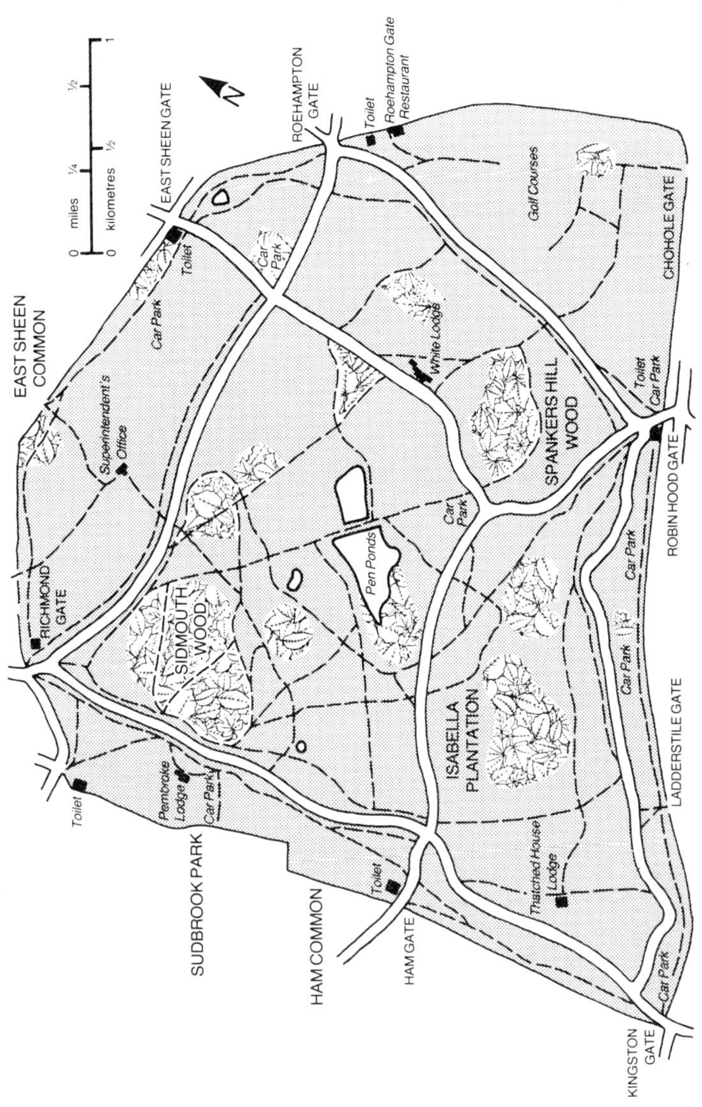

How to get there: by tube to Richmond station on the District Line and then either a one-mile walk or take the 65 or 71 bus. By train either to Richmond station as above or to North Sheen station and walk half a mile to Kings Ride Gate. By bus: 65, 71, 72, 85, 710, 714, 715, 718 or 730. There are nine car parks within the park; for Isabella Plantation the nearest one is halfway between Ladderstile Gate and Robin Hood Gate.
Origin of the name: originally 'New Park', its modern name has been transferred from King Henry VII's earldom, Richmond in Yorkshire.
Area: 2358 acres (955 hectares).
Owned by: the Crown.
Maintained by: Department of the Environment.

Richmond Park is spectacular for its size alone, being by far the largest of London's ten royal parks, and having a perimeter of over eight miles. The park consists mostly of undulating high grassland and bracken, scattered with an estimated 200,000 trees, many of them ancient descendants of those that once formed part of the Great North Wood.

The park's best-known attraction is its 400 dappled fallow and 300 red deer which, contrary to popular opinion, are not stocked here as a tourist attraction, but rather to provide venison for the royal table and for various VIPs. Although the deer can seem surprisingly tame, the public are warned to leave them alone at all times, particularly during the mating season (October and November). And if driving within the park, take special care, bearing in mind that thirty to thirty-five deer are killed by traffic each year, many of them while being chased by dogs.

Other popular features of the park are the Pembroke tea house and gardens at the western end, not far from Richmond Gate, and the Pen Ponds at the centre of the park (fishing by permit only). Just to the east of these ponds is one of the park's few buildings, the White Lodge, built for George II and Queen Caroline in 1727 originally as a hunting-box and now housing the Royal Ballet School. Other features within the park include seven and a half miles of riding tracks, two golf courses, a playground (by Ham Gate) and a second restaurant (by Roehampton Gate).

My favourite spot here is, without a doubt, the forty-two-acre Isabella Plantation – a woodland garden – which, though especially worth seeing in late April and early May, is well worth a visit at any time of year. Its pride is the azaleas and great variety of rhododendrons, but there is a tremendous variety of other shrubs and trees, such as a pocket handkerchief tree, strawberry tree, tulip tree, dawn redwood and roble beech. The numbers at the foot of these trees refer to information in an HMSO publication, *Isabella Plantation*, which contains a self-guided tour. (Copies of this are available from Richmond Public Library at Little Green.) As you will notice, the birdlife here is remarkably rich – in fact this little woodland garden contributes significantly towards the high total of bird species that can be spotted within the park, 103 species of which were recorded in 1975. The Isabella Plantation gardens are largely the inspiration of one man, George Thomson, superintendent of Richmond Park from 1951 to 1971, after whom one of the plantation's three ponds is fittingly named.

The history of the park itself goes back much further. The whole area was enclosed by Charles I as a private hunting ground in 1637. He took, or forced the purchase of, much of the land from the existing landowners, consistently ignoring both the opposition of the landowners and the counsel of his advisers. It is an irony that Charles's obstinacy and greed should have resulted in the creation of what today is one of the finest nature reserves in southern England.

King Charles's solution to this opposition to his 'New Park' was to begin building a wall round the proposed park, so cutting landowners off from their own land and thereby encouraging them to see the wisdom of selling it to him; those who would not sell simply had their land taken from them. Such undiplomatic tactics led eventually to Charles losing his throne and later his head. To be fair, the King finally bowed to public pressure over access and later provided both a good number of gates and several stepladders against the walls so that poor people could continue to collect firewood.

Those who followed Charles were not so generous. The worst offender was perhaps Princess Amelia who closed the park to the public soon after taking up her appointment as ranger in 1751, admitting only her personal friends and those few issued with special permits. Local indignation appears to have been first expressed when the Richmond Anglican minister, the Rev. Thomas Wakefield, along with members of his congregation, tore down a section of the park wall, pouring triumphantly through the breach.

What appears to have had a more lasting effect on the matter was a court action brought in 1758 by a Richmond brewer, John Lewis, against the gatekeeper, Martha Gray, for assault. (She had given him a slight shove in the chest to prevent him entering the gate.) The judge, Sir Matthew Forster, who confirmed the survival of pedestrian rights, ordered that the illegally-removed ladder-stiles be returned. The princess angrily complied, but made sure that the ladders were so awkward to use that only the most agile of folk could climb them. Lewis persisted and applied to the court once again, leading the judge to order the stiles to be constructed so that even children and old people could use them.

Now that the public once again had free access, the Princess lost interest and went to live at Gunnersbury. Meanwhile John Lewis, who later fell into great poverty partly because of legal expenses incurred during the fight, became a local folk hero.

Ruislip Woods and Reservoir

Reservoir Road, Ruislip

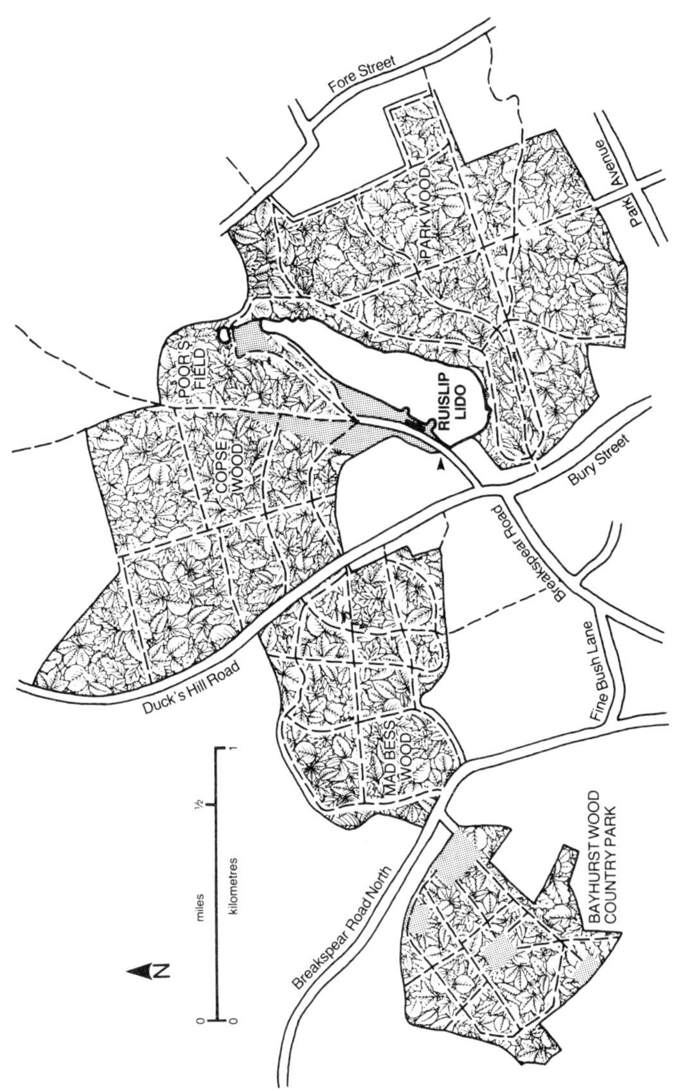

How to get there: by tube to Ruislip station on the Piccadilly or Metropolitan Lines and then bus 114 (on summer Sundays, also E2).
Origin of the name: Ruislip means 'rushy leap', in reference to a crossing point on the river Pinn which in the eleventh century or earlier was negotiable only by agile travellers.
Area: 662 acres (268 hectares).
Owned and maintained by: London Borough of Hillingdon.

Together with the neighbouring Bayhurst Wood Country Park, this cluster of oak, birch and hornbeam woods extends to over 750 acres of public open land, at the heart of which nestles an attractive forty-acre lake with its own sandy beach. The lake's enchantingly natural setting, with shady woodland descending right to the water's edge, quite belies its artificial origins, and yet artificial it is. The Lido, as it is more popularly known, was originally created in the early nineteenth century to supply water to the Grand Union Canal, but serves now more recreational interests such as sailing, boating, water-skiing, windsurfing, fishing and swimming.

The first steps to form the new reservoir were taken in 1804 when a small stream was dammed by Dell Farm Road. Flooding the valley involved submerging at the northern end a whole hamlet of cottages, the residents of which must have received little by way of compensation, since it was apparently necessary to call out soldiers from Windsor barracks to keep the unfortunate householders 'in order'. By 1816 Ruislip Reservoir and the feeder canal was in use, but by the middle of the century it had already fallen into decline, due to the extension of the much larger Welsh Harp Reservoir at Hendon.

It was not until almost one hundred years later that the Lido and foreshore were developed for recreational use. Apart from the water sports already mentioned, Ruislip Lido is equipped with lawn deckchairs for sunbathing, a crazy-golf course, a twelve-gauge miniature railway, children's paddling area, two cafés and a delightful one-and-three-quarter-mile waterside woodland walk. The miniature railway, which is one of the very few twelve-gauge railways in the country, normally operates every weekend and public holiday from Good Friday to the end of October and daily throughout July, August and the school holidays. The present five-eighths-of-a-mile loop at the south-eastern corner of the Lido is in the process of undergoing a major extension which eventually will reach around the northern end of the reservoir through to the main gate area in Reservoir Road.

This whole reservoir area is fenced off from the surrounding woodland, with a small admission charge payable at weekends from April to September, weekdays July to September (all other times free). Hours from 8 a.m. to 5 p.m. in winter; 9 or 10 a.m. – 8 or 9 p.m. in summer, depending on the weather.

Beyond the Lido enclosure – and freely open at all times of year – are the woods: Park Wood, Copse Wood, Poor's Field and Mad Bess Wood. The names themselves tell something of their history. The name Park Wood is thought to date from Saxon times, when the wood was enclosed for game hunting; Copse Wood refers to the wood's historic coppice management; Poor's Field was an area once reserved as grazing land for the poor of Ruislip, and is frequently now known also as Ruislip Common. But as for the name Mad Bess Wood, though it is known to date at least from 1769, no one knows its origin for sure. Among the theories is the assertion that Mad Bess was a demented old woman who once lived in the wood, or that the name refers to Queen Elizabeth I's having ridden here. Some believe Mad Bess was Dick Turpin's horse gone crazy after his master's execution, while others will tell either of the gamekeeper's wife murdering offending poachers or the wife of the wood's owner attacking lumberjacks sent by the King to requisition timber from the wood for building warships.

Throughout these woods is a good network of bridlepaths and footpaths and an abundance of wildlife. In fact, Ruislip Woods is one of Greater London's key ecological sites, being regarded as almost certainly Britain's best surviving example of a coppiced hornbeam wood. Most parts of the woods are believed to have been under more or less continuous tree cover since the end of the last Ice Age – a fact which, along with its coppice management, has greatly contributed to the area's ecological significance. Up until 1981, about 450 species of fungi alone had been identified here, and in Copse Wood a count of beetle species in 1980 recorded 159 different kinds. There are at least forty-one kinds of trees and shrubs, 228 other flowering plants and forty-four bird species. In recognition of this rich natural diversity – especially with regard to the fungi – the whole area has been accorded by the Nature Conservancy Council the protective designation of Site of Special Scientific Interest (SSSI).

It is easy now to take such woods for granted, yet with the arrival of the underground line and the building of Ruislip railway station in 1904, almost the whole of this area was threatened with suburban development. Plans had already been drawn up for building four and a half houses to the acre throughout Park Wood, and in Copse Wood, 'the most suitable in every respect for the larger class of house', three to the acre, when the First World War interrupted the developers' plans. By then, so much disquiet was being expressed by the Ruislip Residents' Association over the loss of the woods that the tide had turned. Park Woods was then formally opened to the public in July 1932, and Mad Bess Wood along with what still remained of Copse Wood was added in 1936.

To the casual visitor the coppiced hornbeams may well be the most interesting feature of the woods, but look out also for patches of foxgloves, wood anemones and bluebells on the woodland floor where this system of coppicing has been reintroduced. You may even hear or see the recently returned nightingales and wood warblers. Another tree to look out for is the rather rare wild service tree, a feature of ancient woodland such as this, and here not uncommon.

Ruskin Park

Denmark Hill, SE5

How to get there: by train to Denmark Hill station. By bus: P4, 40, 68, 176, 184 or 185.
Origin of the name: after John Ruskin, who lived nearby from 1823 to 1871.
Area: 36 acres (14 hectares).
Owned and maintained by: London Borough of Lambeth.

For its size, Ruskin Park is one of the most pleasant parks in south London. Not only is it aesthetically beautiful, but it succeeds also in providing a good range of amenities.

The park's central features are its traditional wooden bandstand encircled by graceful silver maples and the old pond, whose origins date back to the days when this land formed part of the private grounds of Dane House. Judging by an early photograph, it has since been considerably improved and today the water's edge is attractively planted with a sugar maple, corkscrew willow and, more recently, a young ginkgo or maidenhair tree. Benches here provide a place from which to admire the curving lakeside flowerbed with its giant rhubarb and the island's lone willow dipping its leaves in the water.

Around the park is an unusually rich variety of well-chosen trees, including the magnificent Indian bean tree and the Caucasian wingnut with its improbable-looking long catkins carrying their winged seeds. There are cedar, beech and Judas trees too at this, the eastern, more ornamental end of the park, while bordering the western end is a long line of ash with large horse chestnuts, limes, oak and even a tulip tree.

In 1904 this land was up for sale for development as a housing estate and it is largely due to the campaign of one man – a local resident named Frank Trier – that these plans were abandoned in favour of creating the present park.

The contract for the preliminary development of what was to be the Sanders' estate had already been signed when Mr Trier moved to set up the Ruskin Park Purchase Committee. His campaign drew strong public support and soon had the backing of both the Commons and Footpaths Preservation Society and the Metropolitan Public Gardens Association. Many local people made private donations towards the campaign, as did the London County Council and the borough councils of Camberwell, Southwark and Lambeth. With these funds, the first twenty-four acres of the present park were purchased in January

1906 and formally opened to the public on 2 February 1907.

John Ruskin (author of *Modern Painters* and *The Stones of Venice*), who had lived most of his life nearby at Denmark Hill, had died just a few years earlier and it was thought that if the park were named after him, donations towards its purchase might come from 'admirers of the great man of letters'.

Shortly after the opening of the park, building development was again about to get underway – this time on a block of land adjoining the south-western end of Ruskin Park. Again Mr Trier helped to form a committee, which succeeded in purchasing this land too for use as playing fields, thereby forming a twelve-acre extension, which was formally opened to the public on 19 February 1910.

Today, Ruskin Park caters for many tastes, with its children's play area, one o'clock club, cricket and football pitches, and – bordered on one side by a brick pergola covered in wisteria and roses – a beautifully-kept bowling green. This last feature, enclosed by sculpted yew hedges providing buttresses of privacy between the green's wooden benches, occupies the site of one of the former kitchen gardens. Other facilities within the park include netball and tennis courts, a café, toilets and shelter.

This last – the wisteria-covered shelter – is formed from the brick and wooden portico of one of the houses that used to stand here. Another relic from the park's past is the base of a terracotta sundial, situated near the staff yard, by the Ferndale Road/ Denmark Hill corner. This, with its Tudor rose designs, once bore an inscription commemorating the fact that here stood the house where Mendelssohn wrote *The Spring Song*.

St James's Park

The Mall, SW1

How to get there: by tube to St James's Park or Westminster stations on the Circle and District lines, or to Charing Cross on the Northern, Bakerloo and Jubilee lines. By bus: any route that stops at Trafalgar Square or Parliament Square.
Origin of the name: after the leper hospital, which was dedicated to St James.
Area: 93 acres (38 hectares).
Owned by: the Crown.
Maintained by: Department of the Environment.

Both St James's Park and St James's Palace were named after a hospice founded here in the thirteenth century to accommodate 'fourteen poor leprous maidens'. Like all the hospitals of its time, this was a religious foundation; hence its dedication to one of the saints.

Henry VIII liked the site of the hospital and its view so much that he dispatched the occupants, had the building pulled down and arranged to have a home built for himself in its place. St James's Park came about when the King then acquired and drained the surrounding marshy fields as an adjoining garden and deer nursery.

The park's present appearance dates from over a century later when Charles II – inspired during his exile abroad by the formal gardens of Versailles – had a number of major improvements made. The most important of these was the creation of his Dutch Canal – a rectangular lake like the one at Hampton Court, and typical of the period. The present lake, though now very different in shape, has retained a trace of this original design in the straight contours of its northern bank.

Apart from exercising his famous spaniels in the park, King Charles enjoyed two of his other interests here, both of which are commemorated by modern features within the park: Birdcage Walk along the southern boundary and, by the northern boundary, The Mall. The name Birdcage Walk refers to a long row of aviaries once laid out roughly along the site of the present walk for the King's entertainment, while The Mall refers to the once-fashionable croquet-like game of Palle Maille, which the King used to enjoy playing just nearby.

Another century passed and that famous landscape architect 'Capability' Brown was here remodelling the park; though the most important changes of all were made by John Nash at the direction of George IV in 1829. It was Nash who introduced the informal 'natural' look to the present spanner-shaped lake, and he who introduced curved paths and groups of trees to replace the previous rigid formality of straight avenues.

It is today these informal curves that make St James's such an attractive park; these, and the fact that St James's is so central – just over a hundred yards from Trafalgar Square. And what a welcome haven it is from the speeding taxis and cars, especially on a Sunday when The Mall itself is also closed to traffic.

Nash's lake is the park's central feature, with its wildlife and beautiful views, particularly east towards Whitehall. This lake is fed from an artesian well on Duck Island, via a pumping station which also feeds both the Long Water in Kensington Gardens and the Serpentine in Hyde Park.

Duck Island is also the base for a 1000-strong bird colony tended by two full-time ornithologists. The park's first bird collection was that of King James I who kept such 'outlandish fowl' as cassowaries and cormorants. Later, Charles II added exotic geese, ducks and two pelicans from the Russian ambassador. Though the cassowaries have since disappeared, the tradition of the other royal birds has remained, the diversity of their countries of origin leading one writer to refer to the lake here as a 'Feathered United Nations'. On the whole, harmony here has prevailed, the greatest exception perhaps being with the recent strange behaviour of two of the park's pelicans. At first, one of them picked off a feral pigeon from the water's edge, drowned it and swallowed it whole. Then it took a duckling. And finally the two pelicans took a brood of rather valuable snow geese goslings. The offending pelicans have since been removed to London Zoo and replaced by two specimens with more conservative tastes.

Apart from these introduced birds, St James's and Green Park together see about forty-five species of birds, of which around half are known to breed here. Of the park's trees, perhaps the most attractive are the weeping willows along the banks of the lake, the old London planes, some figs and a particularly fine honey locust tree – best seen in autumn when the leaves turn a rich, attractive gold.

As with all the royal parks, St James's had long been open to the public subject to the generosity or otherwise of the ruling monarch. Charles II, for example, in his reign, welcomed as many of his citizens as cared to enter, but later, in Queen Victoria's time, soldiers and other lowly members of the public were excluded. It was with regard to St James's Park that Sir Robert Walpole gave his famous reply to Queen Caroline's question about what it would cost to limit the park's use to the royal family. Walpole's witty response was enough to deter her: 'Only three Crowns, Madam.'

The public are today well catered for with the provision at the western end of a children's playground and, at the eastern end, a bandstand (used in summer lunchtimes for brass and military band concerts), with the Cake House nearby serving light refreshments. There is a wheelchair-accessible loo in the park by The Mall, opposite Marlborough Road.

Scadbury Park

Perry Street, Chislehurst

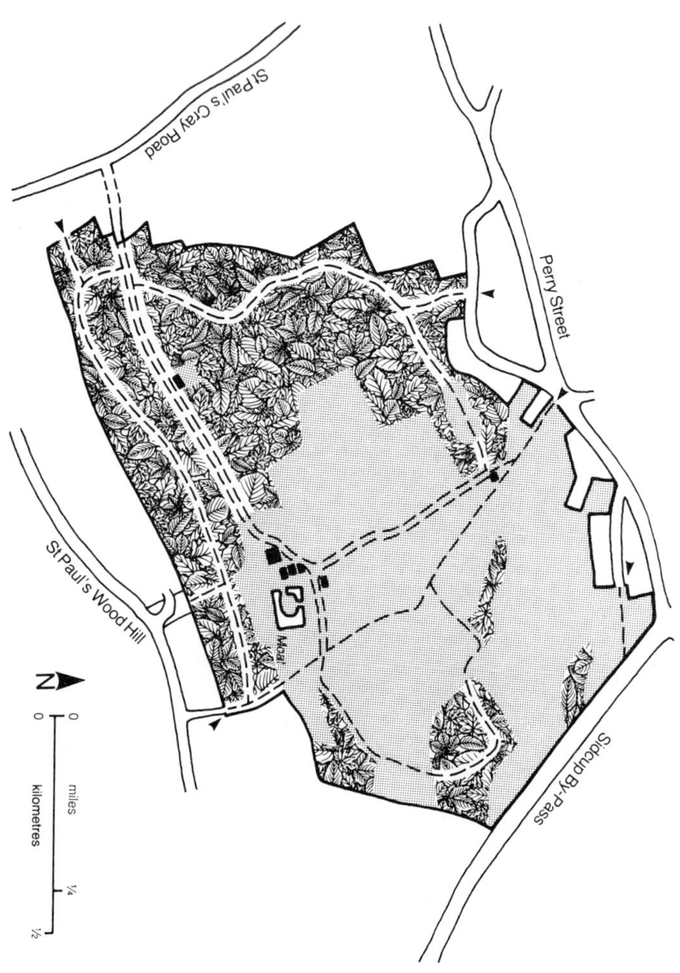

How to get there: by bus: 161, 228, 725 or 726 to the Perry Street entrance opposite Beaverwood Road; 61 or 161 for the St Paul's Cray Road entrance; or 229 or 299 for the Midfield Way entrance.
Origin of the name: Scadbury means 'fortification used by criminals or thieves', possibly in reference to the use of the moated site in Saxon times.
Area: about 290 acres (117 hectares), of which some 110 acres (45 hectares) is let as farmland.
Owned and maintained by: London Borough of Bromley.

Opened on 30 April 1985, this new park provides a valuable extension to the already large open space formed by Chislehurst and St Paul's Cray commons, Petts Wood and Hawkwood. Together, this cluster of public open land now covers almost 800 acres, of which well over half is woodland.

From a wildlife point of view, the park presents a range of habitats rarely found in Greater London, or even in south-east England. Because the land has never been subjected to intensive farm management, Scadbury Park has survived as an example of Kentish countryside as it used to be. Many of the original hedgerows can still be seen criss-crossing the fields, as can various scattered copses, old meadows, ponds and streams.

The woodland, which is mostly at the south-western end of the estate, is rich in its variety of ages and species of trees, ranging from massive oaks (some of which have been estimated to be 400 years old) to patches of young sycamore and silver birch recolonizing previously cleared areas. Some of these older oaks appear from their arrangement to form ancient field boundaries, while elsewhere are geans, or wild cherries, yews, cedars and pines with a spring carpet of bluebells to rival those of the so-called Bluebell Wood nearby (in Petts Wood). And in addition to tawny owls and nuthatches, all three British woodpeckers are present.

To foster appreciation of the estate's wildlife, the council has, with the help of various voluntary bodies, cleared a two-and-a-quarter-mile circular woodland walk. This, for the most part, follows close to the park's perimeter, passing two or three of the park's nine ponds which together provide important sanctuaries for various amphibians such as the rare great crested newt. The trail then passes through an area of farmland, part of which was planted as an orchard until the 1960s. Though most of the old fruit trees have since been cleared, the trail does pass a few of the surviving apple trees. Access on the farmland is limited to footpaths only and it is, of course, important to keep dogs under control. Also by the trail is a picnic site area, which is situated between the Perry Street and Old Perry Street entrances.

One other area without public access is the site of the former medieval Manor House and moat. This is presently on a five-year lease to the Orpington and District Archaeological Society, while they carry out a detailed archaeological excavation – a project which is sure to result in some fascinating finds.

For centuries, Scadbury Park was one of the most important stately homes in England, owned first by the de Scathebury family and later by the Walsinghams. It extended once to over 1000 acres of farmland and royal hunting forest, around a medieval moated manor, complete with drawbridge. Though the manor was torn down 250 years ago, the moat and the roof of the great hall have survived. This roof was reconstructed out of historical interest from (what is believed to be) its original timbers by Major Hugh Marsham-Townshend in 1921 in a truncated version of the original building.

The best-known of Scadbury Park's residents were Viscount Sydney of the Townshend family (after whom Australia's largest city is named) and Thomas Walsingham, who is depicted on the Chislehurst village sign on Chislehurst Common. The village sign depicts the occasion on which he was knighted by Queen Elizabeth I at Scadbury on 20 or 21 July 1597. Queen Elizabeth's visit to Scadbury Park was likewise commemorated by her planting of several trees here, including some fig trees by the ancient archway leading to the moat and manor house, and attempts have been made to attribute the planting of some of the oldest of the park's oak and beech trees to her.

Selsdon Wood

Old Farleigh Road, South Croydon

How to get there: by bus: 354, 355 and 357 all turn round at the end of Court Wood Lane.
Origin of the name: spelled Selesdune in around AD 880, meaning 'Seli's hill'.
Area: 199 acres (81 hectares).
Owned by: the National Trust.
Maintained by: London Borough of Croydon.

This delightfully wooded nature reserve, which alone stands undeveloped in the midst of what is now a large housing estate, was saved only through the foresight of a good number of people back in 1923. Towards the end of that year, an appeal for funds to purchase the land as a bird sanctuary was launched by the Croydon Natural History and Scientific Society and some members of the Surrey Garden Village Trust. Over the next ten years the purchase of the whole 199-acre wood was made possible by private donations from *over 10,000* people, along with contributions from such organizations as the Royal Society for the Protection of Birds, the Metropolitan Public Gardens Association and the Commons, Open Spaces and Footpaths Preservation Society. Selsdon Wood was then formally opened to the public as a nature reserve by the Lord Mayor of London on 5 June 1936.

Although most of the reserve is covered with oak woodland, there are also about fifty acres of grassland in the form of tranquil meadows clustered mostly in the wood's western corner. During the Second World War, these fields were cultivated by Italian prisoners of war, though now their function is more recreational, with a number of benches supplied from which to enjoy the view, either into the wood itself, or out over the housing estate to which the wood now provides such an inspiring contrast.

Selsdon Wood is full of paths leading through a great variety of plantations and coppices, each with a different name and character. The area near the centre of the wood, known as Steven's Larch, was planted with larch seedlings about ninety years ago, though since felled for pit-props during the last world war, and subsequently – like several other areas of the woods – replanted. The reserve as a whole is known to support at least 177 different flowering plants and ferns, thirty-one types of fungi, sixty-two species of birds (most of which are known to be breeding here) and no less than 242 types of moths and butterflies. There are various kinds of mice, voles, bats, rats and shrews to be found here, plus several other larger mammals including foxes and the diminutive Chinese muntjac deer. To protect the reserve's wildlife, signs at the wood's entrance ask that dogs be kept under control, for as many as 1000 dogs a week are brought here in the spring and summer months alone and even the odd one running wild can create a major disturbance for wildlife. Some days, though, you may meet only the occasional orange-robed Buddhist monk from the nearby Thames Buddha Vihara temple, or an interested naturalist come to study some aspect of the wood's rich flora and fauna.

Management of the reserve today includes the planting of thousands of trees, while selecting small areas for coppicing – a traditional practice which, if properly carried out, enhances the wood's range of wildlife. The cut timber is then used for fencing and the like in other parks managed by the London Borough of Croydon. The council has also fenced off three small areas of the wood in order to protect the undergrowth, regenerating tree seedlings and nesting animals and creating special sanctuaries for wildlife.

The reserve's main entrance is from Old Farleigh Road, where toilets and a car park have been provided. Apart from two other smaller entrances in that road, there is one at the end of Court Wood Lane and one at the northern Linton Glade corner.

From Selsdon Wood, there is a very pleasant walk, starting from the western corner of the wood, following Kingswood Way for three-quarters of a mile, to arrive at King's Wood. Alternatively, from the northern corner of Selsdon Wood, one can follow the bridlepath marked 'To Selsdon Park Road', to arrive at Littleheath Wood – also a walk of around half a mile.

Southwark Park

Southwark Park Road, SE16

How to get there: by train to South Bermondsey station. By tube to Surrey Docks station on the East London Line. By bus: 1, 47, 70, 188, 208 or P5.
Origin of the name: the park was intended primarily for the inhabitants of the old parliamentary borough of Southwark, whose name means 'defensive work of the men of Surrey'.
Area: 63 acres (25 hectares).
Owned and maintained by: London Borough of Southwark.

Southwark Park's focal features are its bowling green and ornamental lake with semicircular rose garden. Here, arching round the rosebeds, is a row of well-used wooden benches pleasantly sheltered from the wind, catching the southern sun. At the centre of the garden are the remains of an old sundial, usually surrounded by dozens of expectant pigeons. The concrete-sided lake, which provides the foreground for the view, is not in fact a part of the park's original design and was only added later at some expense. An old lake-side noticeboard depicts and names the more common waterfowl here: Muscovy duck, moorhen, tufted duck, mallard and pintail.

In the northern end of the park is that hallmark of all the old London parks: mature avenues of London plane trees. Here and there in the spring there are small clumps of purple and yellow crocuses, a few primroses and later daffodils.

Opened in 1869, Southwark Park was London's first municipal park (though the site for Finsbury Park had in fact been *chosen* nineteen years previously). Up until that time, this land was being used as market gardens, as was most of the land in the district – which perhaps explains why so many people at the time regarded the park's acquisition as extravagant and unnecessary.

The area had also long been a popular place for taverns, tea houses, gardens and open-air entertainment, and several names of those old establishments survive today in local street names. St Helena Road to the south of the park, for example, is named after the St Helena Tavern and Tea Gardens, Jamaica Road after Jamaica House and Tea Gardens; likewise Cherry Garden Street and Blue Anchor Lane. In spite of the area's popularity, the region had one major drawback: on either side of the road were such deep ditches of muddy water that on dark nights the route was a hazard for drunken parties as they returned home. It became almost a regular event for their carts to career off the road, upending all the passengers into the ditch.

The Metropolitan Board of Works began negotiations to obtain permission from Parliament to acquire the land for the park in 1864. Most of the land was purchased the following year from the Lord of the Manor of Rotherhithe, Constable of the Tower of London, Sir William Maynard Gomm, after whom Gomm Road on the eastern side of the park is named.

Originally the intention was to sell part of this land then for building plots but, as with both Finsbury and Victoria Parks, the extent of public opposition to these plans led the board to abandon the idea.

The roads that had previously crossed the land were first broken up and turned into tar-paved footpaths, leaving only the road known today as Park Approach. At the north-western corner of the park was a district known as Seven Islands, which consisted of several tidal ditches and the large Mill Pond, all of which were filled in when the park was formed. (Not long before the inhabitants of the area had relied on these dirty ditches for their water supply.) When the laying-out and fencing work was completed, the park was formally opened to the public on 19 June 1869.

The park's facilities today include football pitches, tennis courts, an open-air swimming pool, bowling green, cricket pitch, a large hard-surfaced children's playground and, at the northern end, an adventure playground. At the southern end is the new Southwark Park sports complex with Astroturf pitch, 'Tartan' athletic track and field events area. By the pool is the Café Gallery, with regular and often interesting free exhibitions put on by the Bermondsey Artists Group.

Springfield Park

Springfield, E5

How to get there: by train to Clapton or Stoke Newington stations. By bus: 253.
Origin of the name: from the Georgian Springfield House, from whose grounds the park is formed.
Area: 38 acres (15 hectares).
Owned and maintained by: London Borough of Hackney.

From the main Clapton Common road, this beautiful park is quite hidden behind the Webb and Fawcett estates, only coming into view after a short walk down either Springfield or Spring Hill. Once inside the park, the view opens out to the north over the Springfield Marina and the Warwick and Maynard reservoirs, and east over the river Lee and Walthamstow Marshes. At once one is impressed by the absence of traffic noise and the sense of rural space conveyed by the park's expansive view and its steep rolling contours.

At the top, southern, corner stands the original Georgian Springfield House – serving now as a centre for the park's administration and housing a small café along with toilets (wheelchair-accessible). Adjacent is another of the park's central features: an ornamental pond, complete with weeping willows, and fenced off with low iron railings to protect both the fish and waterfowl. Just below the pond is the park's attractive bowling green, and beyond this again – in the extreme south-eastern corner of the park down by the river – is a well-hidden children's playground.

There is a refreshing variety of colour in the seasonally planted flowerbeds, and in the shrubs and trees scattered around the park. Apart from the more common horse chestnut, oak, ash, beech, rowan, hawthorn, lime, London plane and sycamore, there are specimens of holm oak, cedar, copper beech, pine, even a tulip tree and, by the house, a specimen of the curious foxglove tree which produces erect purple flowers each May before the leaves appear. Also to be enjoyed here in spring are the bluebells, daffodils, rhododendrons, laburnums, flowering cherries and lilacs. Just where the lawn drops away steeply down to the river is an attractive row of wooden benches each partly enclosed and sheltered from the wind by a low yew hedge.

In all, the park has the elegance of some private country estate, which indeed it once was – for the immediate neighbourhood was not developed for housing until between 1877 and 1888. In fact, the Springfield estate survived intact as a private open space right up until 1902 when it too went up for sale as building land. The land was finally saved largely through the efforts of the Springfield Park Acquisition Committee – a group of local gentlemen who entered into a contract with the owner of the estate to prevent it being sold by public auction in May 1904. With a deposit of £1000, the committee secured an option to purchase the estate from Mr T.K. Bros, and proceeded to campaign for funds both from private individuals and from various public bodies.

At this point, the London County Council took over responsibility for the park's acquisition and it was they who finally opened Springfield Park to the public on 5 August 1905. Apart from Springfield House, there were two other large residences on the estate, known as Springhill House and The Chestnuts, but both of these had to be demolished due to their more or less dilapidated condition, while Spring Lane – a public road which ran through the estate – was re-routed along the riverside. Modern facilities include (apart from the café, playground and bowling green already mentioned) an all-weather football pitch, tennis and netball courts, cricket, hockey and rounders pitches, open-air theatre and one o'clock club.

The towpath at the foot of the park provides an attractive link with various parts of the Lee Valley Park and, via the Robin Hood, the Anchor and Hope and the King's Head public houses, to the northern corner of North Mill Fields.

Stanmore Common

Warren Lane, Stanmore

How to get there: by tube to Stanmore station on the Jubilee Line, then a one-mile walk via Kerry Avenue, Stanmore Country Park and Dennis Lane, or by 142 or 709 bus from the station.
Origin of the name: Stanmore means 'stony pool', probably in reference to one of the ponds which still exist in the area.
Area: Stanmore and Little Commons together cover 128 acres (52 hectares).
Owned and maintained by: London Borough of Harrow.

Stanmore Common is almost entirely wooded, steeply undulating, with several streams and boggy ponds. Over the past fifty years or more, the common has changed considerably from open heathland studded with gorse bushes, to a fairly dense woodland of birch, beech and oak, with bracken and blackberry undergrowth. Some areas of heathland and sphagnum bog have remained, as has the tremendous range of fungi for which the common is well known among naturalists. In fact, the wildlife of the common has been admired now for over a century and the area is still regarded as having one of the richest and most varied floras of anywhere in the London area. At least 270 species of fungi alone have been identified here – a fact which has contributed to this site (like neighbouring Harrow Weald Common and Bentley Priory Park) having been declared by the Nature Conservancy Council a Site of Special Scientific Interest.

Stanmore and Little Commons are all that have survived of the common fields of Great Stanmore, 216 acres of which were enclosed in 1813 under The Great Stanmore Lands to Enclose Act and shared among the wealthiest of the local landowners. Up until that time, the extent of these common fields had remained virtually unchanged since Domesday, for just over 700 years.

The traditional rights enjoyed here by the copyhold tenants of the manor included the grazing of cattle and the taking of 'furzes, heath, gravel and such like things growing and being upon the said commons or wastes for their fuel and other necessary use'. This gravel digging, both by the parishioners and by the local authorities, has left the common today with an often irregular surface and, at the south-eastern corner, with several ponds. There is, however, one feature of Stanmore Common whose origin I have been so far unable to ascertain – a curious ancient circular mound created near the centre of the common, apparently known today as 'Pillow Mound'.

Stanmore Common appears to be used now primarily for horse riding, though a few local people also exercise their dogs here. Perhaps better known is Little Common by the Vine Inn on Wood Lane, with its beautiful tree-lined village pond, thought by many to have been the 'mere' after which Stanmore takes its name. As recently as 1914, it was ordered that this common should 'be left uninclosed for the accommodation of the neighbouring inhabitants to dry their clothes'.

Stanmore Common is just one of a cluster of attractive and interesting open spaces here – Bentley Priory Park, Harrow Weald Common and Stanmore Country Park – which together provide several opportunities for circular walks. Access to Bentley Priory from Stanmore Common is via Priory Drive and along the public footpath. To Stanmore Country Park, the easiest access is still from about halfway down Dennis Lane; the Harrow Weald Common adjoins Common Road about half a mile from Stanmore Common.

Streatham Common, The Rookery and Norwood Grove

Covington Way, SW16

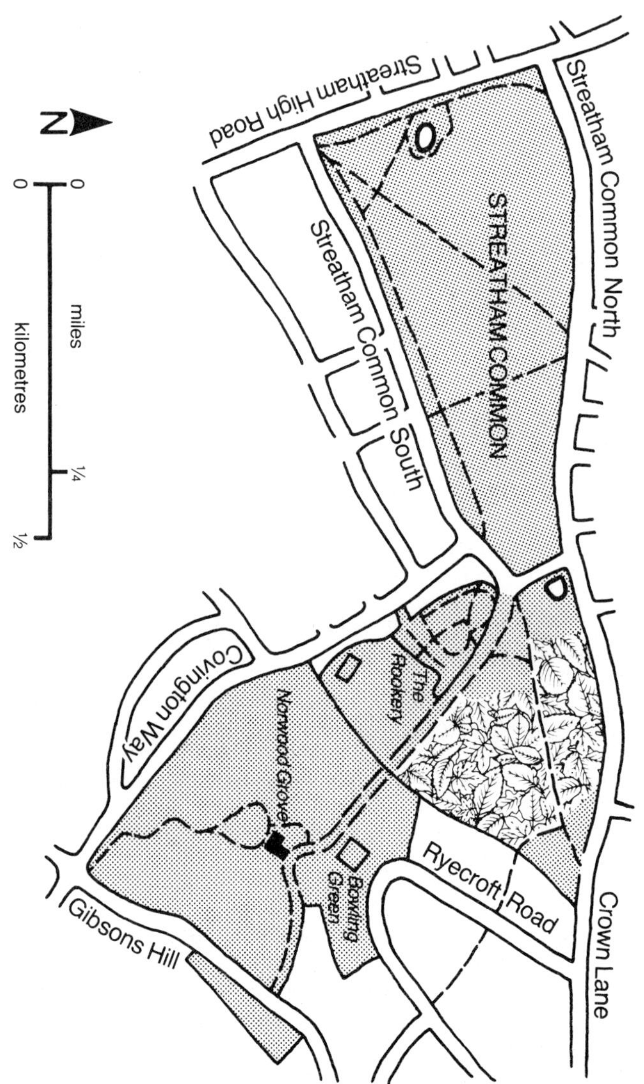

How to get there: by train to Streatham station. By bus: 50, 60, 109, 118, 130, 137, 159 or 249.
Origin of the name: Streatham means 'village by a (Roman) road', referring to what is now Streatham High Road. The name Norwood refers to the fact that this was once part of the Great North Wood.
Area: Streatham Common and The Rookery cover 60 acres (24 hectares); Norwood Grove extends to 34 acres (14 hectares).
Owned and maintained by: London Borough of Lambeth (Streatham Common and The Rookery) and London Borough of Croydon (Norwood Grove).

From Streatham High Road, this common appears to be simply an open grassy slope dotted with a few deciduous trees; and yet up at the eastern end the property is beautifully wooded and secluded, with two charming old gardens which, though once private estates, are now open to the public. These estates – The Rookery and Norwood Grove – were both once an integral part of Streatham Common and so have to some extent a shared history.

The modern Streatham Common is but a fragment of what was referred to in the Domesday Book (1086) as Lime Common, which at that time extended from Norwood to Tulse Hill. Protection finally came to it in 1888, when the Metropolitan Board of Works purchased the land from the then lords of the manor, the Ecclesiastical Commissioners, for the sum of £5 – a telling contrast to the £18,000 paid for Clapham Common eleven years earlier

Although Streatham Common does not seem to have suffered from the same nineteenth-century spate of enclosures as most other London commons, there have been the usual battles here between commoners and the lords of the manor. One of these took place in 1794, when the Duke of Bedford, who had until then always let the poor people cut gorse for firewood, arranged to sell off the fuel for £80. The locals were so incensed that they met on the common and decided to make their protest by preventing the sale and setting the gorse on fire. Then, in the same year, the Duke tried further to erode the rights of the poor by enclosing the area that they used for feeding their cattle. This time the response was more restrained; by the same evening 'a hackney coach drove to the spot, when six men, draped in black and crapes over their faces, got out of the carriage, cut down the paled enclosure, returned into the coach, and drove off.' Without such active protests it is doubtful whether the common would have survived today.

Saving The Rookery and Norwood Grove was a different story.

For these we are indebted to Mr Stenton Covington of Gibson's Hill, after whom the adjacent Covington Way is named. When the Rookery came on to the open market for redevelopment in 1910, Mr Covington formed a preservation committee which succeeded in raising half the purchase price of the estate (the other half was met by the London County Council and Wandsworth Borough Council). The Rookery was then purchased by the LCC in 1912 and, after the demolition of the eighteenth-century mansion, the grounds were opened to the public on 23 July 1913. Likewise, when Norwood Grove was threatened with redevelopment in 1924, Mr Covington re-formed his committee and campaigned for funds for its preservation. The Grove was then opened to the public on 16 November 1926.

The Rookery used to be known as Streatham Wells or Wells House after the once famous medicinal springs here, and one of these three wells (dating from 1659) still remains in good condition in the Old English Garden. The popularity of Streatham spa water is recorded in an early eighteenth-century advertisement:

> The true Streatham waters, fresh every morning, only at Child's Coffee House, in St Paul's Churchyard; Nando's Coffee House, near Temple Bar; the Garter Coffee House, behind the Royal Exchange; the Salmon; and at the Two Black Boys in Stock's Market. Whoever buys it at any other place will be imposed upon.
>
> N.B. – All gentlemen and ladies may find good entertainment at the Wells aforesaid, by Thomas Lambert.

The Rookery has been laid out now as a terraced lawn sloping away to some large old cedars, with winding paths leading to secluded wooden benches, rock and water gardens, flowering shrubberies and finally down to the park's most famous feature: the White Garden – a novel collection of plants all of which bear white flowers. Perhaps the most beautiful part of The Rookery is the Old English garden itself, with rose pergolas, flagged walks, an ornamental pool with fountain, and seasonally planted flowerbeds. This immaculately kept garden is in fact the former kitchen garden, probably from the days when the estate belonged to the wealthy city merchant James Coster, who lived here in the early nineteenth century.

The magic of The Rookery and Norwood Grove gardens lies in their unexpectedness, for not only is it a surprise to pass through the railings and screen of trees at the top of the common to find oneself in The Rookery, overlooking formal terraced gardens, but it is even more serendipitous to come across Norwood Grove. Follow the path leading away from the common, along the top boundary of The Rookery, past the Lodge, to the rather inconspicuous entrance on the right by the old Norwood Grove mansion. In late summer, the dahlias near the greenhouses are in flower, and look out for the old mulberry tree to the east of the house by the ancient cedars. The Mansion (known locally as The White House), stuccoed with a bow in the middle of the façade, dates from the early nineteenth century and is now a listed building. This was once the home of Arthur Anderson, joint founder of the Peninsular and Oriental Steam Navigation Co., and of members of the Nettlefold family, founders of Nettlefolds Ltd, brass founders and general ironmongers.

Here, at Norwood Grove, is an attractive bowling green (on the uphill side of the house), while the common itself offers children's playgrounds and horse-riding paths, and includes an attractive café near the corner of Covington Way and Streatham Common South (open, weather permitting, every day from 10 a.m. to 6 p.m.; closed in winter).

Sydenham Hill Wood and Cox's Walk

Sydenham Hill, SE26

How to get there: by train to Forest Hill or Sydenham Hill stations. By bus: 12, 176, 185 or P4 for the northern access or 63 for the Crescent Wood Road or Sydenham Hill access.
Origin of the name: Sydenham is the modern spelling of what in 1206 was known as Chipeham, meaning 'cippa's village'. Cox's Walk is named after either Francis Cox who, in the mid-eighteenth century, was proprietor of the Green Man, or possibly after David Cox, the painter, who lived near Dulwich Ponds.
Area: Sydenham Hill Wood – 27 acres (11 hectares); Cox's Walk – 3 acres (2 hectares).
Owned by: London Borough of Southwark.
Maintained by: the London Wildlife Trust, under a twenty-five-year lease from the council in the case of the wood. The council itself maintains Cox's Walk.

For the most part, this oak and hornbeam woodland is a remnant of the ancient Great North Wood which once covered much of south-east London and north Kent, and as such it dates back some 10,000 years to the last Ice Age. Not only is this ancient lineage of historical interest, it also governs the great diversity of wildlife to be found here – a diversity which is literally impossible to re-create, thus making the wood one of London's key ecological sites. Here one can find lesser celandine, Forster's woodrush, native Solomon's seal, butcher's broom and Midland hawthorn; in fact the site is known to support, in all, at least 138 species of plants, including fifty-two kinds of trees. Here too are a number of interesting birds, including all three British woodpeckers, tawny owls and the brilliantly-coloured (and rather rare) golden oriole – just some of the fifty-three species of birds found in the wood, of which thirty-one are known to breed here.

Through the middle of the wood runs a disused railway cutting which once carried the old Crystal Palace High Level Railway – a route first used in 1865, the last train running in 1954. The old footbridge at the northern end still survives, as does the boarded-up tunnel at the southern end, where the track continued under Crescent Wood Road to a point close to the site of the Dulwich Upper Wood ecological park in Farquhar Road.

Along the southern and eastern edges of the wood there are signs of the Victorian houses which once occupied these fringes of the wood, but which were demolished in the 1960s. Here, for example, are rhododendrons, cherry laurels, cedar of Lebanon and even a monkey puzzle tree, along with flora typical of areas recently recolonized by wild plants, such as sycamore, birch, buddleia and blackberry. Here, too, in the south-eastern corner of the wood, is a disused tennis lawn and, near the centre of the wood, an imitation Gothic ruin, or folly.

To maintain and improve the wood's wildlife, the London Wildlife Trust undertakes frequent management work, including the cutting back of rhododendrons and sycamores to favour the growth of native species, and the excavation in 1984 of a new pond (not far from the Gothic ruin). The pond is designed to create a habitat for frogs, newts, dragonflies, pond skaters and water birds.

By far the most beautiful access to the wood is via Cox's Walk from the corner of Dulwich Common and Lordship Lane, though Cox's Walk is also accessible from Sydenham Hill and there is a third point of access to the wood via Crescent Wood Road.

With such widespread destruction elsewhere of Britain's ancient woodlands in recent years – over fifty per cent of which have been lost since 1947 – the part that the Wildlife Trust plays in managing the wood is to be commended. This wood is, however, now sadly also under threat, this time from Southwark Borough Council, which has immediate plans to build houses over one-third of it. Although strong local protest and the results of a recent planning inquiry seem so far to have temporarily averted the threat, the council has not yet committed itself to the wood's preservation.

Syon Park

London Road, Brentford

How to get there: to Brent Lea Gate by tube to Gunnersbury station on the District Line, then bus 237 or 267. By train to Syon Lane or Brentford stations, then half a mile walk; or to Kew Bridge station, then bus 237 or 267.
Origin of the name: after the monastery of the Holy Saviour and St Brigid of Zion, founded by Henry V in 1415.
Area: about 208 acres (84 hectares).
Owned by: the Duke of Northumberland.
Administered: in part by the Gardening Centre Ltd.

Unlike most of the parks in this book, Syon Park is privately owned and entrance fees are charged to most of the park's many attractions. The most spectacular and unusual feature here is the London Butterfly House – believed to be the largest live butterfly 'safari' in the world. Opened in July 1981, this tropical greenhouse is alive with the rich and spectacular colours of free-flying butterflies from all over the world, ranging from the common peacock and comma to the poisonous golden birdwing and African citrus swallowtail. Though this display is open throughout the year, the best time to visit is in summer (telephone 01-560 7272 for details).

Then there is Syon Park's Motor Museum which, with its collection of over ninety cars, ranging from the earliest 1895 Wolseley to vehicles of the present day, houses what is in fact the world's largest collection of historic British cars. (For further details, telephone 01-560 1378.)

And, finally, there is the renowned formal landscaped gardens laid out in the style of 'Capability' Brown, with the old crenellated mansion, the Great Conservatory and Syon Park Garden Centre.

Gardening on this estate dates back to the fifteenth century when the Bridgettine Order laid out thirty acres of orchards and gardens, following which Henry VIII suppressed the monastery in response to an allegation, 'certefyinge the Incontynensye of the Nunnes of Syon with the Friores'.

In the sixteenth century Dr William Turner, author of *Names of Herbes* (1548) and known as the 'Father of English Botany', established England's first botanical garden here. Two of England's first mulberry trees were planted at Syon House during this period and these still survive and bear good fruit. Sadly, though, little else of this historic garden now remains.

The present layout of the park dates for the most part from the period between 1767 and 1773, when the first Duke of Northumberland commissioned Lancelot 'Capability' Brown to landscape the grounds. Both the park's lakes, many of the present trees – cedars, limes, oaks, chestnuts and beeches – and the statue of Flora (the goddess of flowers atop her fifty-five-foot Doric column) date from this period. (To be exact, the present statue of Flora is in fact a fibre-glass replacement for the original which was toppled by a gale a few years ago.)

The gardens, which were first opened to the public in 1837, are still an excellent place to see fine specimen trees, including Britain's tallest known native sessile oak, a hybrid catalpa, sweet gum and Caucasian elm. The gardens have long been famous also for their swamp cypress trees and a rare specimen of Afghan ash. Here, too, are good examples of Turkish hazel, cork oak and such rarities as swamp oak and horned maples. Just outside the formal garden, down by the river, is an area particularly rich in wildlife, and home of several rare snails, along what is one of London's few remaining stretches of Thames riverside marshes, now officially recognized as being a Site of Special Scientific Interest (SSSI).

Overlooking, and forming an impressive centrepiece to, the gardens is the striking and well-proportioned Great Conservatory with its large glazed dome, built in the 1820s by Charles Fowler for the third Duke of Northumberland. It is the only conservatory of its type and size in the world and was used as a model for the Crystal Palace built for the Great Exhibition of 1851. Today it houses an aviary and aquarium, in addition to a good many tropical plants.

In a separate enclosure by the house is the park's famous six-acre rose garden, one of the few such gardens in Britain, with more than 8000 roses (best seen between June and September). Syon House itself dates from the mid-sixteenth century, though the interior was reconstructed for the first Duke of Northumberland by the Adam brothers in the eighteenth century. The house contains much fine period furniture and is open during limited hours to the public (closed in winter).

Considering the great number and variety of attractions here, it really is quite surprising that Syon Park is not better known. For more details about the house, the formal gardens and Great Conservatory telephone 01-560 0881/3, and for the Syon Park Garden Centre telephone 01-568 0134/5. For wheelchair-users, ramps are provided for the conservatory and there are wheelchair-accessible toilets. A café and free car park are provided within the grounds.

Tooting Commons

Tooting Bec Road, SW16

How to get there: by train to Balham, Streatham or Streatham Hill stations. By tube to Balham on the Northern Line. By bus: 49 or 249.
Origin of the name: Tooting means 'people of Tota'. In the Middle Ages there were two manors here: Upper Tooting or Tooting Bec, held by the abbey of St Mary of Bec-Hellouin of Normandy, and Lower Tooting or Tooting Graveney, held by Richard de Gravenel. Hence the name of the two commons.
Area: 220 acres (89 hectares) in total.
Owned and maintained by: London Borough of Wandsworth.

In spite of the way in which these commons are now cut up by railways and roads, they are still regarded by many as the fineest of any in south London. The land is mostly open grassland, with small copses, thickets of gorse, overgrown marshes and two lakes. These lakes at the southern end are old gravel pits from the days when the inhabitants of the two manors had common rights here to dig gravel, turf and loam – rights which included also the grazing of sheep, pigs, cattle and horses, and the cutting of gorse, fern and heath. Since then most of the woodland, including a great many elm trees, has given way to open close-cropped grassland, partly in order to provide for the present sports facilities and partly as a result of the epidemic of Dutch elm disease. In spite of the common's open grassy appearance, there are several beautiful patches of mature oak woodland, which together form an enjoyable one-and-a-half-mile circular walk, if one goes along either side of the main railway.

Between the two lakes runs Doctor Johnson Avenue, named after Dr Samuel Johnson of English dictionary fame, who often visited the Thrales at what is now called Streatham Park, at the southern end of the common. It is from the car park near here that the Tooting Common nature trail begins (guide booklets available from local libraries). This hour-and-a-half trail takes in Streatham Woods east of the railway, Bedford Hill Woods north of Bedford Hill and the larger of the two lakes, before returning again to the car park.

The Tooting commons have dwindled considerably over the centuries – at one time they stretched as far as Streatham Common – and there would no doubt have been nothing left at all had it not been for local vigilance and hard-won legal battles.

In 1569 one-fifth of the two commons was taken by Robert

Lenesey, as a result of which it was officially ordered that 'hereafter he do it not'. Later, a church and school in Church Lane not only claimed part of the commons, but those who helped with the building of them were given portions of the commons as payment. Likewise, the present district of Streatham Park was taken from the common by Mr Thrale with the express permission of the Duke of Bedford. With the increasing demand for building land, legislation was passed in 1851 denying the lord of the manor of Tooting Graveney the right to take any more of the common land, but even with this the struggle was not over.

When the manor was put up for auction in 1861, the local people collectively agreed not to bid against one of the would-be purchasers, Mr Thompson, since it was well known that he was opposed to further enclosure of the commons. But after he succeeded in buying the manor and some house property for the low price of £3285, his resolve evaporated with the realization that some of the land was worth £1000 an acre as building sites. The inhabitants of the manor were furious and each time he erected fences to enclose parts of the common, they would pull them down again. And so the battle dragged on for several years, until 1870 when Mr Betts, a local butcher, succeeded in securing a court injunction to uphold common rights.

Five years later, the Metropolitan Board of Works bought the two commons in a final effort to save the land for public recreation. It is interesting to contrast the price of £17,771 that they paid to the lords of the manors for the two commons with the payment by which the de Gravenel family once held the entire Tooting Graveney manor – the payment of one rose yearly at the feast of St John the Baptist.

Strolling around the commons, you are likely to spot many birds, including jays, nuthatches, tits, wrens, robins, spotted flycatchers, goldcrests, woodpigeons and dunnocks. Around the lakes, there are the usual white-beaked coots, red-beaked moorhens, Canada geese and mallards. There are plenty of grey squirrels both on the ground and in the trees – some of them quite tame – and, in spite of the loss of trees already mentioned, there is still a good variety, with more being planted. There are avenues of horse chestnut and rows of hornbeams, planes and limes along with Turkey oaks, red oaks and many magnificent specimens of the common, or pedunculate, oak, silver birch, ash, both common and copper beeches, black and Lombardy poplars, black and honey locust trees and many others.

Apart from tennis courts and football pitches, there is a putting green, open-air swimming pool and athletics track, a café (near the Hillbury Road/Bedford Hill corner) and a playground.

Trent Park

Cockfosters Road, Barnet

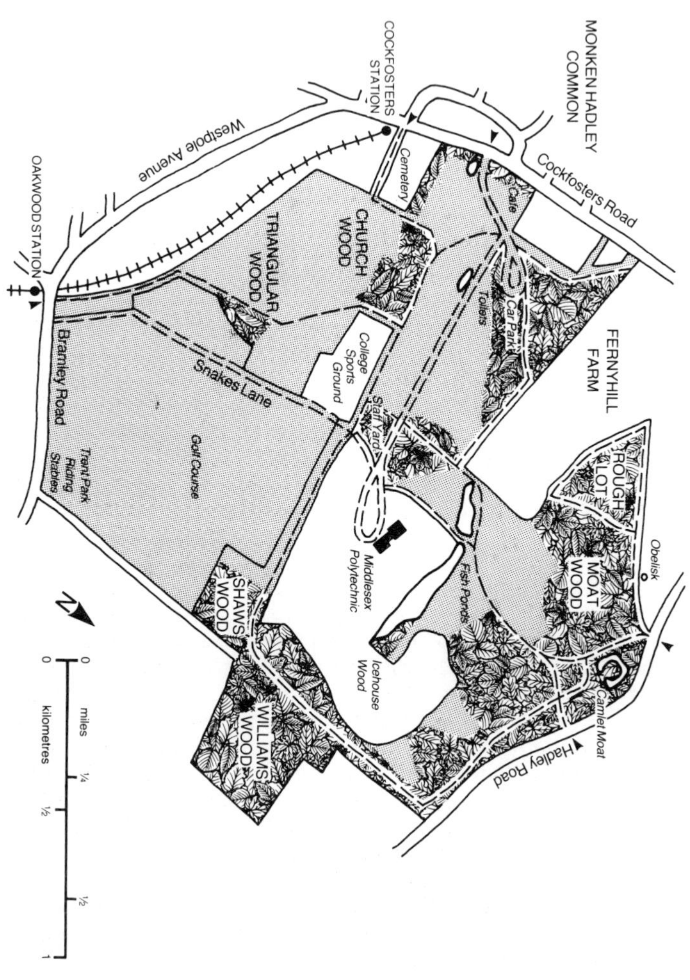

How to get there: by tube to Oakwood or Cockfosters on the Piccadilly Line. By bus: 107 or 121 to Oakwood station, or 298 to Cockfosters Gate. There are two free car parks – one off Cockfosters Road and one off Hadley Road.
Origin of the name: named after Trent, or Trento, in Italy.
Area: 413 acres (167 hectares).
Owned and maintained by: London Borough of Enfield.

Trent Park, like Monken Hadley Common, once formed part of the great royal hunting forest of Enfield Chase and much of the park's 250 acres of woodland is a remnant of this.

Trent Park's first recorded inhabitant appears to have been Humphrey de Bohun, later Earl of Hereford. We know that in 1347 he was given permission by Edward III to fortify his manor house and it seems this refers to the digging of the ancient Camlet Moat which can still be seen in the woods just west of the Hadley Road car park. Excavations on the island, where the manor house once stood, have uncovered a whole dungeon with a chain attached to the wall and several fifteenth-century coins.

The park's present name and much of its modern appearance date from the late eighteenth century when George III granted a crown lease on 385 acres to his physician, Richard Jebb, for saving the life of the King's brother, the Duke of Gloucester. Out of respect for the royal family, Sir Richard named his new estate after Trent, or Trento, in northern Italy – the place where the Duke had made his recovery. It was Jebb who had the nucleus of the present mansion built and he who is said to have employed Humphry Repton, the landscape architect, to dam the brook below the house, creating the two lakes which form the centrepiece of the present park. It was Repton who planted many of the exotic trees and created the great lawn below the house.

Subsequent residents, especially John Cummings, Robert Bevan and Sir Philip Sassoon, continued to develop the estate. Among Sassoon's more important alterations were the addition of the orangery, swimming pool and terrace – all within the present college grounds – and the Japanese garden to the north of the lake which is presently being restored. Sir Philip also introduced the park's first daffodils and a formidable collection of waterfowl, including penguins, flamingos, black-necked swans and seventy species of duck and geese.

At the beginning of the Second World War, the estate was requisitioned and used for the interrogation of prisoners of war, and in 1947 it was taken over by the Ministry of Education as an emergency training college for teachers. Five years later, the land was bought by Middlesex County Council and opened as a public park by the Greater London Council in 1973. The mansion and 200 acres of adjoining land are also owned by the London Borough of Enfield and used by Middlesex Polytechnic.

Of the park's three main entrances, the original approach to the mansion through Cockfosters Gate is the most imposing. From here one can follow the double avenue of limes (planted by Robert Bevan in 1837) and turn left before entering the polytechnic grounds, or veer left past the car park and follow the path leading through Oak Wood. Both routes will bring you to the lakes and can be the start of a three-mile circular walk around the central part of the park.

Trent Park is a pleasant mixture of meadows and woodland, with such suggestive names as Rough Lot, Moat Wood, Camlet Hill and Ride Wood. The bluebells and daffodils are magnificent in spring and there are all the common deciduous trees – oak, beech, sycamore, silver birch, ash, elm, horse chestnut, sweet chestnut, hawthorn and elder, even hornbeam and wild cherry. Along the park's eastern boundary a bridlepath has been provided and this connects with the Trent Park Riding Stables on Bramley Road. In season, fishing is permitted from the north bank of the lakes – day tickets from the park manager's office.

Trent Park also offers considerable scope for walking and bird spotting, for the park does have a good range of habitats and is managed with wildlife in mind. (Some coppicing is practised here, sycamore is removed and replaced by native trees and dead wood is generally left in place to rot.)

Perhaps, though, Trent Park's best-known attraction is its Woodland Trail for the Blind. This is the brainchild of a local blind resident, Ron Stevenson, and a former park manager, George Matthews, and consists of a three-quarter-mile trail with an ankle-high log tapping-rail laid out through the area known as Church Wood. At intervals along the trail are groups of logs sunk into the ground, each signalling the existence of a braille information post nearby. At the top of each of these posts (vandals notwithstanding) is a horizontal copper plaque informing the reader of a seat behind, or of the bark of a tree to be felt and so on. For many blind people this offers a new sense of freedom: to enter an area of woodland alone while their guide dog runs free. The trail starts by Cockfosters Gate; for first-time users it is a good idea to contact the park manager on 01-449 8706.

For refreshments, visit the friendly café near the Cockfosters Gate car park, open every day from about 10 a.m. to 5 p.m. (or later in the summer). There are small art exhibitions on display here each Sunday, and wheelchair-accessible toilets nearby (and likewise twenty-five yards from the Hadley Road entrance).

Valentines Park

Cranbrook Road, Ilford

How to get there: by train to Ilford station. By tube to Gants Hill station on the Central Line. By bus: 66A, 123, 129, 139, 144, 145, 148, 150, 167, 179 or 247.
Origin of the name: from the former occupants of the estate, the Valentine family, whose name occurs in documents dated 1665 and 1684.
Area: 136 acres (55 hectares).
Owned and maintained by: London Borough of Redbridge.

This, along with Wanstead Park, is one of Redbridge's most attractive parks. The central feature is the canal-like Long Pond, in front of the old Valentines mansion, which flows south into a particularly beautiful ornamental lake with wooded island and shoreline, which in turn flows via a channel to the park's boating lake. To the east of the ornamental pond is a gently undulating stretch of ground with winding pathways and an inspiring variety of trees, including many evergreen species, hundreds of rhododendrons and a very fine cedar.

By the old Valentines mansion is a charming walled floral garden, with each of the beds bordered in the old style with low box hedges. A magical atmosphere is conveyed to it by the ducks calling from below, and the alluring birdsong from the unseen aviary behind the garden's upper wall. Below the garden, on the shore of the Long Pond, is a rock-work grotto – one of the surviving eighteenth-century features of the old estate. Heading south from here, past the tree-lined lake, one passes an old wishing well and then, following the stream, comes to one of the remaining above-ground sections of the Cran Brook. At the western end of the boating lake is an imposing clock tower, presented in the year that the park was opened – 1899 – by the chairman of Ilford's Parks Committee, W.P. Griggs.

Considering that many of the most attractive features of the original estate have been preserved, there is a surprising number of sports facilities available here. Valentines Park includes no less than four bowling greens and thirty-two tennis courts, with a miniature golf course, putting green, provision for football, cricket and hockey, and an open-air swimming pool. Toilets accessible to the disabled are situated adjacent to Valentines mansion and near the café by the boating lake.

The mansion itself, at the north-western end of the park, is believed to have been originally built in 1696–7 by James

Chadwick, though largely reconstructed by Robert Surman and Sir Charles Raymond in the eighteenth century. After 1907, it was used by various clubs and, during the First World War, housed Belgian refugees; today it provides offices for the borough's Housing Department. Just nearby is the site of Valentines' once famous black Hamburgh vine, originally planted as a cutting by Sir Charles Raymond in 1758. Although the vine was exceptionally large – producing about two hundredweight of grapes every year – its fame now attaches to the enormous Hampton Court vine, which is said to be the most famous in the world and which was taken as a cutting from here in 1768. Unfortunately, though, its Valentines parent was not so long-lived and has been dead and gone for over a century.

The southern part of what is now Valentines Park was declared officially open to the public 'for ever' on 16 September 1899 under the rather unimaginative name of Central Park. The grand opening, attended by an estimated 10,000 people, was preceded by a twelve-carriage procession, led by mounted police, the town band and the fire brigades and engines from Ilford, Wanstead, Barking, East Ham, Romford, Leyton and Leytonstone. Unfortunately, the opening itself turned out to be something of a shambles, particularly as regards the band who insisted on playing off-cue, first drowning out the town clerk's opening speech with 'Rule Britannia', and then, when the chairman of the council declared the park open, failing to strike up 'God Save the Queen' – they were off getting their refreshments. The VIPs did their best to improvise and went on with their speeches, but, just as Councillor Weedon was in full flow, the band returned and drowned him out too with the long-awaited national anthem. The official party stood up with red faces, looking very much embarrassed, and the band enthusiastically went into the second verse. And so Ilford's first park was formally opened.

At this point Central Park extended to just forty-seven acres, all of which had been purchased from Sarah Ingleby, whose son, Holcombe Ingleby, went on to donate the American Gardens. With further purchases, the park was gradually extended to its present size, and renamed in the early 1900s.

Victoria Park

Victoria Park Road, E9

How to get there: by train to Cambridge Heath station. By tube to Mile End station on the Central, District and Metropolitan Lines. By bus: 6 or 277.
Origin of the name: named after Queen Victoria who was petitioned in 1840 as to the need for the park.
Area: 218 acres (88 hectares).
Owned and maintained by: London Borough of Tower Hamlets.

Victoria Park was the first of London's public parks to be created for the people rather than for royalty. As such, it provided the precedent for what was to become one of the largest urban public park systems in the world.

The need for such a park in this part of London was particularly acute in the early nineteenth century; appalling sanitation and air pollution in the East End had made it a breeding ground for some of the worst infectious diseases then sweeping through London. To create a park would, it was argued, not only have the effect of diluting the polluted air, but would also ease the shocking disparity between the living conditions in the West End and here.

Since there was as yet no London-wide governing body, the only way such a park could be created was by petitioning the Queen and the national government for a special Act of Parliament. In 1840 Mr George Frederick Young, MP, drew up an elaborate petition which, within a few weeks, was signed by 30,000 inhabitants of Tower Hamlets and presented to Queen Victoria by the Marquis of Normanby.

To appease those who begrudged the expense of a non-profit enterprise, it was suggested that the purchase price of the park be raised by selling York House, in Stable Yard, St James's (later renamed Lancaster House) and that the perimeter of the new park could be let off as building sites for large upper-class housing. The Queen approved and so too did Parliament.

It is significant that this particular site was chosen, since part of the land had been a popular meeting place for demonstrations by radicals and Chartists, in much the same way as Kennington Common in south London. No doubt, a similar theory prevailed here – that by enclosing the land as a public park it could be more effectively policed and such uprisings prevented. In spite of this, in 1848, only three years after Victoria Park was unofficially opened, a 'monster meeting and demonstration' was called to support the third presentation of the Charter – a petition of six million signatures demanding electoral reform, in particular with the plea to extend the vote to the working classes. The nature and size of the police presence was, however, sufficient to prevent the collective presentation of the petition, for stationed within the park were 1600 foot police (500 of them armed with cutlasses), 100 mounted police, 500 recalled police pensioners and a large detachment of the 1st Life Guards cavalry armed with sabres.

After this confrontation, the Chartists were less active, but the park remained a forum for political and religious debate, attracting such speakers as Henry Hyndman, Bernard Shaw and William Morris. Some of the political awakening of the East End associated with the park is portrayed in a nineteenth-century song:

The Park is called the People's Park
And all the walks are theirs,
And strolling through the flowery paths
They breathe exotic airs,
South Kensington, let it remain
Among the Upper Ten
The East London, with useful things,
Be left with working men.

The rich should ponder on the fact
'Tis labour has built up
A mountain of prodigious wealth
And filled the golden cup.
And surely workers who have toiled
Are worthy to behold
Some portion of the treasures won
And ribs of shining gold.

The designer of the park, James Pennethorne (protégé of John Nash and later designer of Battersea Park) was distinctly unenthusiastic about the choice of site, which he described as 'dead flat, without variations of any kind, except excavations for clay and gravel'. These excavations had left the land lower than its surrounding canal banks and the soil was poor. Nearly 40,000 trees and shrubs needed to be planted and in the following years the old bathing lakes and ornamental boating lake were added, though plans to encourage the building of large houses around the park in order to earn high ground rents did not materialize and the building plots had to be quietly sold off.

Victoria Park is pleasantly nestled in the junction of two canals – the Hertford Union and the Regent's Canal – linking this with

Mile End Park to the south and Lee Valley Park to the east and making it possible to walk from Mile End to Waltham Abbey on the edge of Greater London almost entirely without using roads.

Though two of the original bathing lakes at the eastern end of the park have recently been filled in to make way for a new children's playground, the large ornamental lake near the canal junction survives, as does the smaller islanded lake by the Victoria Fountain and a shallow concrete-sided lake to the east of the new playground. The Victoria Drinking Fountain, a palatial octagonal 'Gothic' structure near the centre of the park, was a personal gift from Angela Georgina Burdett-Coutts, an extremely wealthy philanthropist who frequently sought rather grand and ostentatious solutions to poverty and oppression. She was an unusual woman for her time, for when she married at the age of sixty-six, her husband had to change his name to hers. Respect for her was such that she became the first woman to be honoured with a peerage through her own achievements and not those of her husband.

Most restful is that part of the park which lies to the east of the fountain. Here, the smaller lake, with its wilderness island of hawthorn, lime and blackberry, seems comparatively undiscovered, while further east again is perhaps the park's most attractive, and certainly its most secluded, feature – the Old English flower garden. Here the wooden benches carry inscriptions providing fitting memorials to the peace others have sought and found here.

Not far away is a one o'clock club and bowling green, just two of the many facilities provided, which include an open-air swimming pool, an open-air theatre, putting green, facilities for fishing (16 June to 14 March), football, cricket, hockey, netball and tennis. There are two cafés – one by the main ornamental lake (open throughout the year) and one by the cricket pavilion (open April to September), and the park's toilets are wheelchair-accessible.

Victoria Park is interesting also for its good range of trees, for of the park's 4000 trees and shrubs, several are regarded as being among the finest British examples of their species. Such trees include Caucasian lime, Chinese privet, willow-leaved pear, Kentucky coffee tree, euodia, several kinds of maple (Italian, Oregon and ashleaf), ash (manna, narrowleaf and white) and a good specimen of the rather rare white mulberry.

Wandsworth Common

Bolingbroke Grove, SW11

How to get there: by train to Wandsworth Common station. By bus: 19, 49, 189 or 249.
Origin of the name: Wandsworth means 'Waendel's enclosure'.
Area: 175 acres (71 hectares).
Owned and maintained by: London Borough of Wandsworth.

Wandsworth Common is generally flat grassland with a slight incline to the south-west, cut into a total of ten separate pieces by several roads and two railway cuttings. Though the common is used primarily for sport, particularly football, cricket, tennis, bowling, putting, fishing and archery, it is also locally popular as a pleasant walking route. Parts of the common also provide some points of interest for the naturalist; there are over fifty different kinds of trees and shrubs and at least thirty bird species.

One area of particular interest is that known as The Scope, in the south-western corner of the common. Here the council has adopted a minimal management policy – that is, a policy sensitive to wildlife – which has attracted a good number of butterflies and birds, and permitted the growth of over twenty different species of grasses. The gorse here, with its beautiful yellow flowers in spring, is a traditional inhabitant of the common, though the small pond is new, having been dug with the help of the British Trust for Conservation Volunteers (BTCV) in 1980 to provide a suitable habitat for frogs, other amphibians and aquatic plants. The name of this area is derived from a gigantic telescope – at that time the largest in the world – which was constructed here by the Rev. John Craig in 1852.

The Central Pond across Trinity Road over by the railway cutting supports a wide variety of plants and animals. There are the usual waterfowl – Canada geese, mallard, coot, moorhen, plus the tufted duck and diver which nest on the island along with the common brown rat. Information boards near the bridge depict the pond's various waterplants and other animals.

As the principal tract of waste land of the large Manor of Battersea and Wandsworth, this common once extended as far as Clapham to the east and Wimbledon to the west, but it has since suffered from encroachments probably more than any other common in London. Obvious enclosures include the Wandsworth Prison, the Royal Victoria Patriotic Building, the Emanuel School and Spencer Park School. In fact, between 1794 and 1866 there were no less than fifty-three enclosures, of areas varying in size from a quarter to ninety-six acres.

Even prior to this period, though, encroachments had already become such a serious threat that Garratt Lane residents decided to form a kind of club in about 1760 to combat the problem. After each general election, local people elected the president of this association, who came to be known as the 'Mayor of Garratt'. The Garratt elections became so popular and entertaining that they often attracted up to 100,000 people, blocking all the roads within a mile's radius of Wandsworth. But by 1796 the elections had been banned, leaving the common vulnerable once again to the threat of encroachment. In fact, by the time a body of conservators succeeded in acquiring the land from Earl Spencer, the Lord of the Manor, in 1871, the spate of enclosures which had followed the banning of the elections was well on the way to swallowing up the entire common.

The common had by then fallen into a 'disgraceful and neglected' condition, and when its management was passed over to the Metropolitan Board of Works in 1887, it was described as being 'bare, muddy and sloppy after a little rain, undrained, and almost devoid of trees or seats'. It was covered with 'huge gravel-pits, many of them full of stagnant water, which, in addition to being very offensive, constituted a positive source of danger owing to their great depth and want of protection'. Needless to say, public ownership and management has meant that these problems have since been dealt with.

Two features of the common which bear individual mention are what now remains of the old windmill and Neal's Farm. This windmill was used for pumping water into a lake belonging to Lord Spencer, called the Black Sea. The site of Lord Spencer's lake has since been covered over by the building of Spencer Park, while of the old windmill only the base now remains by Windmill Road as a supplementary listed building.

Neal's Farm continued in production right up to the early 1900s; in fact, even as recently as the Second World War, a piggery operated here, while parts of the common itself were cultivated for food. The present café/restaurant, staff yard and toilets are all a part of this old farm complex.

Play facilities for children are based near Chivalry Road and include the Lady Allen Playground, provided by the Handicapped Adventure Playground Association (HAPA), specifically for handicapped children and their sisters, brothers and friends. (Telephone 01-228 0278.) And there is a nature study centre by Dorlcote Road, open occasional afternoons (with wheelchair access), offering a basic introduction to the common's wildlife and its conservation. (Telephone 01-785 9916 for details.)

Wanstead Park

Warren Road, E11

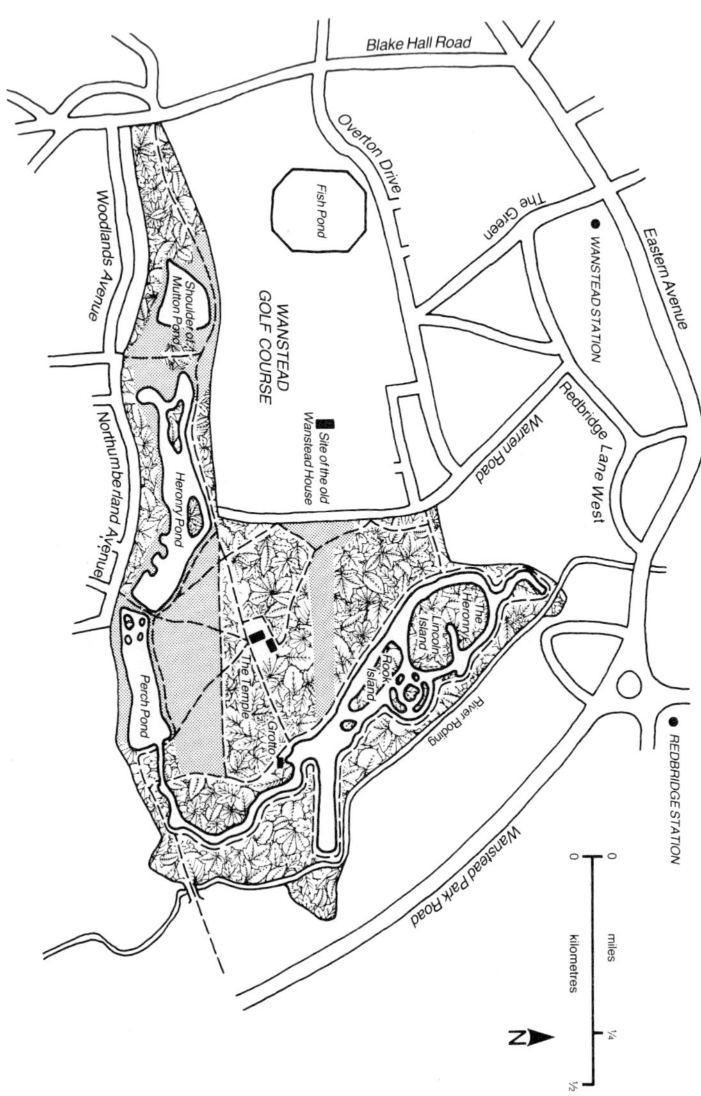

How to get there: by tube – the easiest access is from Wanstead station on the Central Line, using the entrance in Warren Road, just past the golf course. By bus: 101 or 162.
Origin of the name: the name Wanstead dates back at least to 1050 and means 'place by a hillock'.
Area: 184 acres (74 hectares).
Owned and maintained by: Corporation of the City of London.

Considering how close to central London it is, Wanstead Park is surprisingly well wooded and wild, with about half the park's total area covered with oak and sycamore, with some elm, silver birch and beech and an undergrowth of gorse, broom, blackberry, holly, rhododendron and hawthorn. Extending along the southern and eastern boundaries is a one-and-a-half-mile chain of lakes – Shoulder of Mutton Pond, Heronry Pond, Perch Pond and Ornamental Water – together covering just over thirty-four of the park's 184 acres. The remaining area of rough grassland provides a contrasting sense of space, but rarely do the surrounding houses impose on the rural scene, even in winter after the woodland leaves have fallen.

The whole area is well managed from an ecological point of view. Dangerous trees are felled and left to rot on the woodland floor, thereby attracting a richer variety of fauna and flora. Natural regeneration is encouraged rather than relying on replacement planting, and this appears to be just as effective, partly because such self-seeded trees are less prone to vandalism. The bird life is remarkable, with 122 species having been spotted in and around the park, of which almost fifty are known to be breeding here.

Although the original Wanstead House was demolished in the 1820s (its site is on the neighbouring Wanstead Golf Course), two of the original garden houses survive from the mid-eighteenth century when Wanstead Park was still a private estate. One, called simply The Temple, with its Classical portico, is situated centrally within the park, west of the keeper's house. The other is what now remains of an old grotto, due east of here, by the shore of the Ornamental Water. This once had a fine stained-glass window lighting a large room, the roof of which was embedded with shells, pebbles, stalactites, crystals and mirrors, and the floor composed of a mosaic of deer bones. It was at one time regarded as finer than Alexander Pope's famous grotto at Twickenham, but was unfortunately largely destroyed by fire in 1884 and today only a small part of the façade remains.

Though the history of the land can be traced back to the existence of a Roman villa here in around AD 100, the park itself was not enclosed until 1545. Just four years earlier, the previous owner, Sir Giles Heron, had his estate here seized by the Crown and was beheaded at Tyburn for refusing to acknowledge King Henry VIII as head of the Church of England. Likewise in 1661, the estate was again forfeited, this time from Sir Henry Mildmay, Master of the King's Jewel House, for acting as one of the judges in the trial of Charles I. Sir Henry was sentenced to life imprisonment and to being drawn annually on a hurdle to the gallows at Tyburn and back to the Tower, though, on appeal, his sentence was later changed to deportation. In fact, the Crown appears to have had some kind of interest in the estate for over two centuries, with Mary Tudor visiting in 1553, Elizabeth I visiting on several occasions, James I using the house as a royal palace, Charles I living here in 1636 to escape the plague in London, and George III visiting with Queen Caroline in 1764.

Wanstead Park began to take on the beginnings of its present form under Sir Josiah Child, whose wealth was acquired through the East India trade, largely by ruthless exploitation of his position as chairman of the British East India Company. John Evelyn, the diarist, wrote following his visit to Child's estate in 1683: 'I went to see Sir Josiah Child's prodigious cost in planting walnut trees about his seate, and making fish-ponds, many miles in circuit, in Epping Forest, in a barren spot, as oftentimes these suddainly moneyed men for the most part seate themselves.'

It was, however, Sir Josiah's son, Sir Richard Child, later Earl Tylney, who in 1715 commissioned Colin Campbell to design a palatial new mansion here which was intended to be to east London what Hampton Court was to the west. Though definitely of grand proportions and design, the final mansion was a good deal more modest, covering an area of 260 feet by eighty feet, and adorned by a portico with six Corinthian columns, in a style comparable to that of Kensington Palace. Meanwhile, under the influence of Jean Rocque and possibly of 'Capability' Brown, the park itself achieved the distinction of being described at that time as one of the finest examples of the English Landscape Movement of the eighteenth century.

It was during this period, too, that Wanstead Park became an important centre for astronomical research, attracting such scholars as Sir Isaac Newton, who arranged for the building here of what was then the largest telescope in the world (125 foot long), and the Rev. James Bradley, later the Astronomer Royal, whose observations here led to two great discoveries – the aberration of light and the nutation, or oscillation, of the earth.

This was the peak of the estate's development. The property's demise came soon after Catherine Tylney-Long, who had just inherited the estate, married the nephew of the Duke of Wellington, William Wellesley Pole. Within ten years, from being the richest heiress in England (outside the royal family), Catherine and her husband were a quarter of a million pounds in debt and the house contents, including furniture and art treasures, had to be sold, with the mansion being demolished and sold for building stone in 1824.

Following the Epping Forest Act, 1878, the mansionless park was acquired by the Corporation of the City of London, as part of the action they took in saving the whole of what remained of Epping Forest. Wanstead Park was then formally opened to the public by the Chairman of the Epping Forest Committee, Mr Deputy Hora, on 1 August 1882.

Waterlow Park

Highgate High Street, N6

How to get there: by tube to Archway station on the Northern Line, and then a half-mile walk up Highgate Hill. By bus: 143, 210 or 271.
Origin of the name: in honour of Sir Sydney Waterlow who donated his entire estate here for use as a public park in 1889.
Area: 26 acres (10 hectares).
Owned and maintained by: London Borough of Camden.

In November 1889, Sir Sydney Waterlow wrote to Lord Rosebery, the first chairman of the London County Council, the following letter:

> My Dear Lord Rosebery,
> ... Commencing the work of my life as a London apprentice to the mechanical trade, I was, during the whole seven years of my apprenticeship, constantly associated with men of the weekly-wage class, working shoulder to shoulder by their side. Later on, as a large employer of labour, and in many various other ways, I have seen much of this class and of the poorer people of London, both individually and collectively. The experience thus gained has from year to year led me more clearly to the conviction that one of the best methods for improving and elevating the social and physical condition of the working classes of this great Metropolis is to provide them with decent, well-ventilated homes on self-supporting principles, and to secure for them an increased number of public parks, recreation-grounds, and open spaces ... Therefore, to assist in providing large 'gardens for the gardenless', and as an expression of attachment to the great city in which I have worked for fifty-three years, I desire to present to the Council, as a free gift, my entire interest in [my] estate at Highgate ...

Laying out a park costs money and, although the grounds of the estate were already well timbered with oaks, old cedars of Lebanon and many other well-grown trees and shrubs, plus one and a half acres of spring-fed ornamental water, Sir Sydney had the foresight to include a further gift of £6000 in cash to be used either to defray these expenses or to buy the freehold interest of an adjoining two-and-three-quarter-acre block of leasehold land.

Sir Sydney Waterlow was a printer and Lord Mayor of London

in 1872, and lived for many years just nearby, at Fairseat House. His statue now stands at the northern end of the park, a little south of the Highgate High Street entrance.

Waterlow Park is surely one of the most beautiful parks in London, boasting a rich wildlife for its small size, and although this is partly due to the famous and wild Highgate Cemetery across Swain's Lane (formerly Swines Lane) and to the south, it is due also to the wonderfully rich variety of trees here. There are copper beeches, golden catalpas, silver limes, tulip trees, maidenhair trees, yews, wingnut and Indian bean trees, to name just a few. Apart from the usual pigeons, thrushes, blackbirds, very tame and fat grey squirrels and a great variety of waterfowl, both kestrels and foxes have been seen here. There is, at the eastern end of the park, an aviary with finches and parakeets, and a scented garden by Lauderdale House designed specifically for blind people. Lauderdale House itself, which dates from the late sixteenth century, now houses a restaurant and café.

The whole park is laid out on an undulating hillside with extensive shrubberies, rockeries and colourful flower borders. Especially beautiful in spring is the display of daffodils, crocuses and snowdrops on the grassy slopes above the three-level lake. Though the maintenance of the park has suffered in recent years because of staff cut-backs, with good management this could mean more areas within the park serving as nature sanctuaries, thereby enhancing the park's already rich bird population.

The undulating nature of the land has precluded much provision for sports, though there are tennis courts and a putting green. This rolling lie of the land makes it heavy going for wheelchairs, but it does lend a welcome element of surprise and discovery to a walk along the park's many winding paths.

Welsh Harp Park

Birchen Grove, NW9

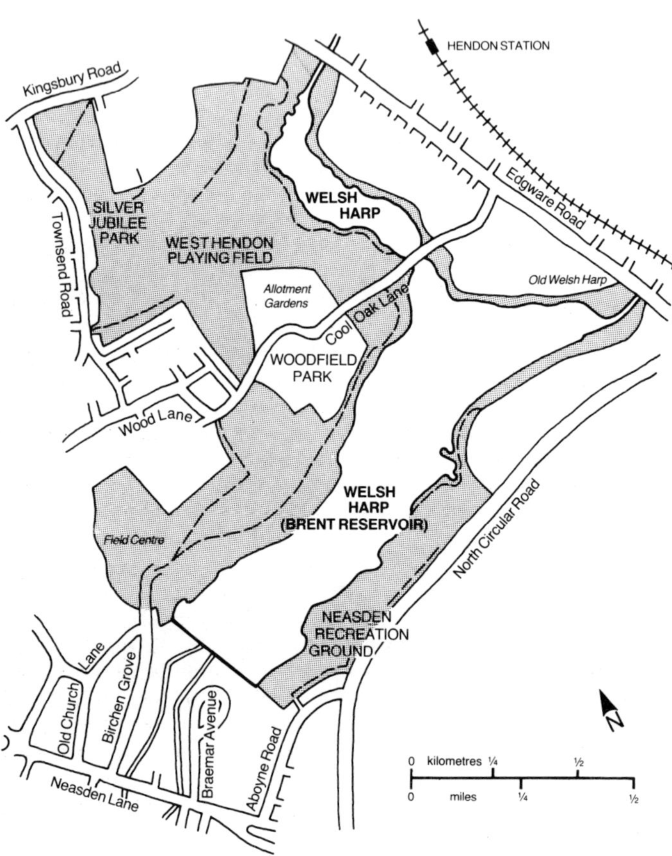

How to get there: by tube to Neasden station on the Jubilee Line. By bus to Neasden Lane on the 52, 182, 245, 297, or 719 and then walk along Birchen Grove.
Origin of the name: the reservoir is named after the once-famous Welsh Harp public house which stood on Edgware Road, just north of the Brent River Bridge. The modern Welsh Harp is also known as the Brent, or Kingsbury, Reservoir.
Area: 343 acres (139 hectares).
Owned and administered by: the British Waterways Board, the London Boroughs of Barnet and Brent. Administrative guidance is provided by the Welsh Harp Joint Consultative Committee.

This large reservoir and its surrounding recreational land have only recently been promoted collectively as a park and yet this area has for over a century offered attractive opportunities for waterside walking and nature study. Today, the park's main attractions are sailing (the Welsh Harp Sailing Association holds the lease) and bird watching. In fact, the Welsh Harp area can now boast of having the best-documented bird life in urban Britain. At the western end of the park, Brent Council have set up a nature study centre for the use of schools in their borough – the Welsh Harp Day Field Centre (Birchen Grove) – which appears to be both popular and well used. Britain's first artificial bat cave was opened here in 1986. The hibernaculum, where bats can roost during their winter hibernation, can house several hundred of them.

Although the number of species of breeding birds here has dropped from seventy-two to forty-seven over the past century, the habitat remains important enough to earn the reservoir and its marshland shore the designation of Site of Special Scientific Interest (SSSI). It has been known in some years to support a third of the total of Britain's over-wintering smew – a kind of rare duck which spends its summer breeding in the Arctic. There are dozens of nesting great crested grebes here too; in fact, in all, it is possible to spot up to 145 different bird species, many of these being migrants stopping off to rest and feed on their travels north through Britain in the spring or back south in the autumn. The area is also remarkably rich in flora, especially wetland plants; in fact, some of the plants in the Alexandra Park nature reserve were taken from here during conservation work to create a more open habitat for wildfowl at the Welsh Harp. Providing for the wildlife here forms an important part of the reservoir's management, including such work as the provision of nesting rafts for the terns. The credit for much of this conservation work lies with various voluntary groups.

The Welsh Harp Reservoir was originally constructed in response to the increased demand for water to feed London's canal system, following the opening of the Regent's Canal in August 1820. Although the reservoir's first stage was completed in 1835, with a small extension being made in 1837, it is a subsequent addition that is commemorated by the short metal posts along the shores of the reservoir today, each marked with the Prince of Wales's feathers and the date 1854.

The Brent Reservoir still forms part of the British Waterways system, feeding the Grand Union Canal and providing water for sale to various factories. Nowadays, water enters the canal feeder from a tunnel in the dam, in which automatic sluices and large black syphons have been incorporated in order to prevent the recurrence of the disastrous accident of 1842, when the dam was breached and several people and livestock were drowned.

Back in the days of the Old Welsh Harp Inn, after which the reservoir was popularly named, the lake was just one of many famous attractions of the area, which at one time included a large concert hall, horse racing, boxing matches, pigeon and duck shooting contests and, in winter, ice skating on the reservoir. The Welsh Harp's former popularity is commemorated in at least four music-hall songs, including the following, entitled 'The Jolliest Place That's Out':

Now if you want a change, I'll tell you what to do,
Just take a 'bus from Turnham's, and bid London Smoke adieu,
On the pleasures of a rural spot – I have a word to say,
Where anyone who's fond of fun, can spend a jolly day.

Warner's Welsh Harp! – Have you ever been there?
Picnics, such tricks! ev'ry day are seen there,
You couldn't find its equal if you walked for miles about,
There's no mistake about it – it's the Jolliest Place That's Out.

Whitewebbs Park

Clay Hill, Enfield

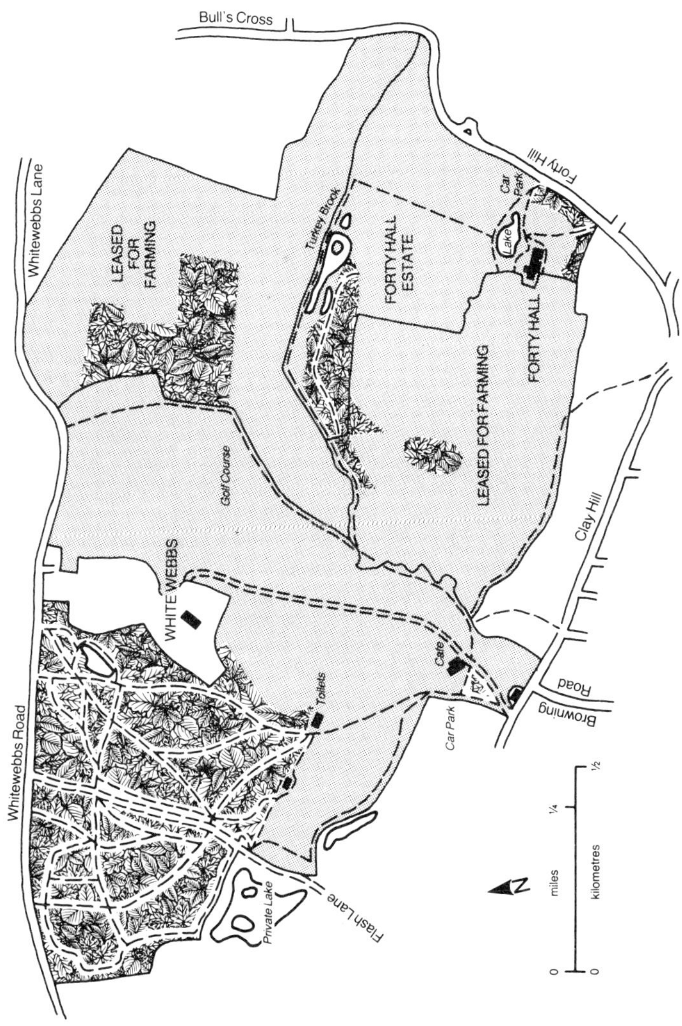

How to get there: by train to Gordon Hill station. By bus – to Lancaster Road on the W8, 191 (except Sundays) or 231, then walk north along Browning Road. The park's main entrance is to the left of the Rose and Crown.
Origin of the name: the name can be traced back to 1543 when it was spelt White Webbes, though its origin is unknown.
Area: 232 acres (94 hectares) of which 100 acres (40 hectares) is occupied by the Whitewebbs Golf Course.
Owned and maintained by: London Borough of Enfield. (The local branch of the Royal Society for the Protection of Birds, RSPB, maintains the Nature Trail.)

Apart from the eighteen-hole golf course, this park is almost entirely wooded, predominantly with oak and hornbeam – some of them coppiced – but also with alder and elder, beech, birch, ash, sycamore, horse chestnut and hawthorn. There are dozens of attractive wildflowers such as lady's smock, lesser celandine, wild strawberry, dog violet and wood anemone, with at least forty species of birds and a number of common butterflies, such as the peacock, red admiral, large white and orange tip. There is a wide range too of mammals, including the more common grey squirrels, rabbits, moles, voles, shrews and pipistrelle bats, but also the small and rather shy Chinese muntjac deer (first introduced into England in 1900). The area known here as Whitewebbs Woods was, until 1803, still common land, having originally been part of Enfield's share of the large royal hunting forest of Enfield Chase. The chase was divided up in 1777 and distributed between the Crown as owner and the four bordering parishes – South Mimms, Enfield, Hadley and Edmonton – whose inhabitants had traditionally been entitled to rights of common. In 1803, Enfield's portion was enclosed and divided among the local people, this wood being the share given to Dr Wilkinson of Whitewebbs House, who subsequently incorporated the land into his existing estate.

Whitewebbs House, which still stands near the centre of the park, was built by Dr Abraham Wilkinson in 1791 and now houses an old people's home. From the southern car park, it stands out as a bright white mansion among the trees to the north. The house was greatly enlarged in the mid-nineteenth century and altered again in the 1870s to the design of Charles Stuart Robertson.

The original Whitewebbs House, which lay further to the north across Whitewebbs Lane, was lived in during Queen Elizabeth's reign by Dr Huicke, physician to Henry VIII, Edward VI and Queen Elizabeth. When, in 1605, the Guy Fawkes

Gunpower Plot was discovered, the inhabitants of this house were implicated and one of them – Anne Vaux (under the false name of Mrs Measey) – was subsequently arrested and imprisoned in the Tower.

An interesting and recent development in the park is the laying out by the Edmonton/Enfield Group of the Royal Society for the Protection of Birds of a waymarked, one-and-a-third-mile nature trail. The trail, which takes about two hours to complete, starts from either the southern car park by the Golf House, or from the northern car park by North Lodge in Whitewebbs Lane, with attractive maps positioned at both ends. Trail guide booklets are on sale both at the Forty Hall Museum (see under Forty Hall Estate) and at the golf professionals' shop at the southern end of the park.

Following the western boundary of the park, this trail skirts past two private neighbouring lakes, one of which – Wildwood Lake – was created originally as a duck decoy to cater for shooting interests. Just nearby are the remains of an old cottage, once owned by the former New River Company and demolished in 1942. Many of the trees and shrubs from the old garden still grow here, including lilac-flowered rhododendrons, privet, yew and mock orange.

The park's own lake is situated north of Whitewebbs House, near the North Lodge Gate. Known today as the Fish Pond, this small but attractive lake is stocked with tench, but attracts also plenty of waterfowl, including various ducks and black-headed gulls. The lake, with its water lilies and weeping willow, is fed by a natural spring which emerges from an old brick conduit house once associated with the original Whitewebbs House of Dr Huicke's time. Near the lake are also some interesting conifers, such as Wellingtonia, a line of cypress trees, Douglas firs and Norway spruce.

For refreshments there is a café next to the southern car park, which is open both to park golfers and the general public. (Opens 7 a.m. on Tuesdays, Saturdays and Sundays, otherwise at 8.15 a.m., and closes at 5 p.m.) Besides a golf course, there is provision here also for cricket and football, and pleasant public footpaths through to Hilly Fields Park and to the Forty Hall Estate. Copies of a local footpath map are available from Forty Hall Museum.

Wimbledon Common and Putney Heath

SW19 and SW15

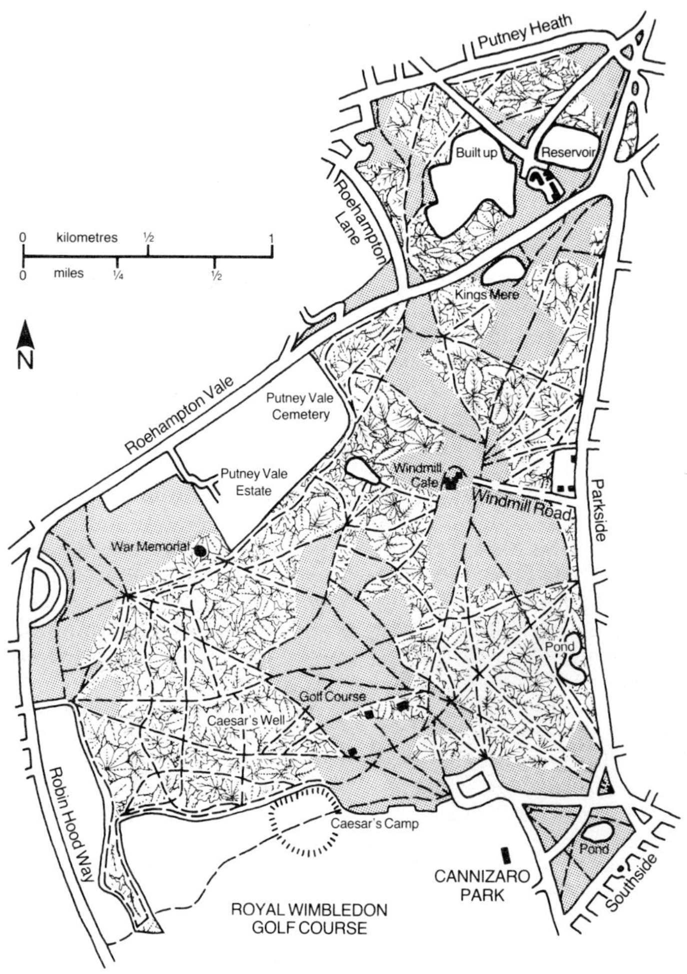

How to get there: By train to Wimbledon station, then bus 80 or 93. By tube to Wimbledon station on the District Line, then bus 80 or 93.
Origin of the names: the modern name Wimbledon is derived from the tenth-century spelling Wunemannedun, meaning 'Wynnman's hill'. Putney means 'Putta's quay or landing place'.
Area: 1060 acres (429 hectares).
Owned and administered by: the Conservators of Wimbledon and Putney Commons.

Along with Richmond Park to the west, this forms by far the largest stretch of open space in London. Even on its own it is (apart from Epping Forest, which lies mostly outside Greater London) London's largest common.

Mostly rough undulating grassland, broken into informal meadows by patches of oak and birch woodland, a large part of the common has been designated a Site of Special Scientific Interest (SSSI). Of particular interest to the ecologist are the relict heathland and – an unusual habitat for London – sphagnum bogs. There are pretty patches of heather, gorse, dwarf gorse, broom and needle whin, along with a great variety of other wildflowers, many of them rare. At least eighty-six species of birds can be seen, of which half breed here. There are badgers (at least fifty individuals), foxes and any number of rabbits.

For centuries, Wimbledon Common and Putney Heath have provided grazing land, timber and gravel for the tenants of the manor, but in the eighteenth century, as the feudal manorial system began falling into decay, the lord of the manor behaved more and more as if the commons were his own unencumbered private property. He established a brickyard here, producing 20,000 tiles per week, sold large amounts of gravel, and felled and sold off practically all the mature trees, many of which had for centuries been carefully managed in order to provide a regular supply of winter fuel for the local inhabitants. All this appears to have gone on more or less unchallenged until 1864.

In that year the Lord of the Manor, Lord Spencer, promoted a private Act of Parliament to extinguish local commoners' rights altogether, to enclose about two-thirds of the common as a public park and to sell off the remainder as building plots. This caused a furore on the part of the commoners, leading to a long and successful campaign, led by a wealthy commoner and fellow Member of Parliament, Henry (later Sir Henry) Peek.

Finally, in 1871, Wimbledon and Putney Commons came under the protection of an Act of Parliament and passed into the care of a body of eight conservators, five of whom were (and still are) elected by local residents and three by Ministers of the Crown. Funds for the maintenance of the commons are raised in an unusual, but seemingly fair, way. Rates are levied on local residents who live within three-quarters of a mile of the commons, the amount varying according to how close to them they live.

Probably the common's most interesting landmark today is the old Wimbledon Windmill – England's only surviving example of a hollow-post flour mill, inside which, on the first floor, is an excellent little museum depicting the history of windmilling in England (open Saturday and Sunday 2–5 p.m. from Easter to the end of October. Telephone 01-788 7655). The mill was built in 1817 by Charles March, a Roehampton carpenter, and ceased to be used in 1860, when the lower floors were converted to form six cottages. It was here in the Mill House, in 1908, that Lord Baden-Powell wrote parts of his famous handbook *Scouting for Boys*. Just next door to the mill is a car park and café serving light refreshments.

Perhaps the common's next best known feature is an iron-age hill fort on the southern boundary of the common, known as Caesar's Camp, though the site has in fact no connection with Julius Caesar and was not given this name until the early nineteenth century. From pottery excavated here in 1937 it is thought to date from somewhere between the fifth and third century BC. Unfortunately, the ancient earthwork is not very conspicuous since the landowner, John Erle-Drax, MP, did his best to destroy it in 1875 in revenge for being restrained from making a broad metalled road across the common.

A little to the north of this is Caesar's Well – again nothing to do with Caesar. Although largely filled in for safety's sake, it is still clearly marked at the surface by a granite stone circle engraved with the letters 'H.W. PEEK MP 1872', marking Sir Henry's triumph in saving the commons the previous year.

For anyone interested in golf, there is certainly no shortage of opportunity, with three clubs all operating either on or adjacent to the common, and for the equestrian there are plenty of well-kept horse-riding routes. But the greatest attraction of all must surely be the absence of traffic noise, and the feeling of being able to hear the wind in the trees and the common's rich birdsong.

Appendix of Local Parks & Woodlands

The parks discussed in this appendix are a selection of London's smaller parks or those likely to be of more local interest. Since it is anticipated that this section will be of most use for local historical reference, details such as bus routes and lengthy descriptions are not given. For the most part these parks are administered and owned by the local councils and, with the notable exception of the Tradescant Gardens by Lambeth Palace, all are over two acres (or about one hectare) in area.

Abney Park Cemetery

Stoke Newington High Street, N16 *(32 acres)*

The park's name commemorates the family of Sir Thomas Abney who held the manor of Stoke Newington in the early eighteenth century. Abney Park was originally laid out as a cemetery between 1839 and 1843 in the grounds of Abney House and part of the garden of Fleetwood House. Though a few burials into existing family graves do still take place, the park functions now very much as a public open space and as a wildlife reserve.

Among the various memorials – including those of William Booth, founder of the Salvation Army, and Isaac Watts, the poet and theologian – are huge horse chestnut trees, sycamore and willow, with ivy, cow parsley and bluebells below. In spite of busy roads on three sides, the heart of this walled-in natural wilderness offers a surprisingly peaceful seclusion.

Acton Park

The Vale, W3 *(27 acres)*

Purchased from the Goldsmiths' Company and the Ecclesiastical Commissioners in 1888 and opened to the public later in the same year. A windmill stood at what is now the north-western corner of the bowling green.

Addington Park

Kent Gate Way, Croydon *(24½ acres)*

The park and the adjoining privately owned golf course were both once part of Addington Palace grounds, landscaped by Lancelot 'Capability' Brown in 1781.

The original palace, dating from about 1780, can be seen to the west from the tennis court area.

Archbishop's Park

Lambeth Palace Road, SE1 *(10 acres)*

The park forms part of the grounds of Lambeth Palace which, since the beginning of the thirteenth century, has been the official London residence of the Archbishops of Canterbury. Its history as a public park began when Archbishop Archibald Campbell Tait (appointed 1869) opened part of the palace grounds to the local poor so that 'scores of pale children' could play often in the fresh air. The permanent and unrestricted opening of the park for 'the use and enjoyment of the People of London' did not, however, take place until its formal opening by Archbishop Benson in 1901.

Though some of the park's original features have since disappeared – a pond with rustic bridge and a red granite drinking fountain – there are some attractive lawns and flowerbeds surrounded by a surprisingly rich variety of trees and shrubs.

Of special interest nearby is the recently opened Tradescant Museum of Garden History housed in the church of St Mary-at-Lambeth, also in Lambeth Palace Road.

Arnos Park

Arnos Road, N11 *(44 acres)*

In Tudor times this area was managed as coppice woodland, supplying firewood, charcoal, and bark for tanning. Arnos Park was purchased from Lord Inverforth in 1928 just before the building boom which resulted from the arrival of the Piccadilly Underground Line – the viaduct which carries the tracks across the park's western corner being built in about 1930.

Avenue House Grounds

East End Road, N3 *(16 acres)*

Originally laid out by Henry Stephens in the 1880s, Avenue House and grounds were donated by him to the people of Finchley in 1918 and opened to the public as a park in 1928. 'Inky' Stephens – as he was more popularly known – was the son of Dr Henry Stephens, the originator of Stephens Ink. In order to continue research into methods of improving the firm's products he established a laboratory here shortly after his move to Avenue House in 1874. This still exists, along with its original equipment, on the first floor.

In the grounds is an unusually wide range of trees, including several that are quite rare. There are, in all, over one hundred species of woody plants including specimens of weeping beech, Himalayan lilac, eagle-claw maple, one-leaved ash and black mulberry. A guide booklet listing these trees is available from the Avenue House reception desk and from the local library.

Barham Park

Harrow Road, Wembley *(25 acres)*

This was originally the grounds of Barham House, home of the managing director of the Express Dairy Co., Titus Barham, who left his mansion and grounds to the borough on his death in August 1937. His father, George Barham, was the founder of the company and in 1904 became the first dairyman ever to be knighted.

Barking Park

Longbridge Road, Barking *(74 acres)*

Opened in 1898, Barking Park has been described as probably the finest municipal park in east London. The central feature is a ¾-mile long boating lake, fed by the Loxford Water, a tributary of the Roding, and an indoor bowls centre – opened October 1970 – for the use of club members. There is also a public outdoor bowling green, open-air swimming pool and miniature railway, with pleasant flower gardens and avenues of trees.

Beaulieu Heights

South Norwood Hill, SE25 *(17½ acres)*

The name Beaulieu means, appropriately, 'beautiful place'. This fine oak wood covers the eastern slope of South Norwood Hill, on the top of which is sited a television mast. The area appears on Rocque's map of 1762 as being wooded, lending credence to the oft-made assertion that this is a survival of the Great North Wood.

Bethnal Green Gardens

Cambridge Heath Road, E2 *(12 acres)*

This is one of the few remaining pieces of the common waste lands of the Manor of Stebonheath, or Stepney. To protect the land from being built over, a group of people purchased fifteen and a half acres from the Lady of the Manor, Philadelphia, Lady Wentworth, in 1667 and arranged for the profits from the use of the land to go to local poor families – hence the old name for the gardens: Bethnal Green Poor's Lands.

The first such annual distribution of income was in 1685 when twelve chaldrons of coals and £12 in cash was equally divided among twenty-four poor families of the hamlet of Bethnal Green and £9.10s in coal and cash to a another nineteen poor families.

As the value of building land rose in the 1880s, the then trustees favoured selling the land for building development and investing the proceeds, seeing that this would bring in a larger income. Both the London County Council and the Metropolitan Public Gardens Association vigorously opposed the scheme, partly because the original trust-deed had expressly prohibited the erection of new buildings.

What at that time had consisted of a rather neglected orchard, paddock, kitchen garden and pleasure grounds, was then purchased by the London County Council and laid out as public gardens. These were formally opened to the public on Whit Monday, 1895.

Big Wood

Bigwood Road, NW11 *(18 acres)*

The name seems a little out of place now, but even as recently as 1894 the wood covered about eighty acres. It is a remnant of the Middlesex oak forest.

Biggin Wood

Covington Way, SW16 *(13½ acres)*

Biggin Wood is one of London's few remnants of the ancient Great North Wood; as such it provides a small bird sanctuary in an otherwise built-up area.

Blythe Hill Fields

Codrington Hill, SE6 *(18 acres)*

Before its purchase by the London County Council in 1935, Blythe Hill Fields was largely rough farmland belonging to Brockley Farm. Today, the steep grassy hill offers commanding views from almost 200 feet above sea level across to Telecom Tower in the north, east over the Ravensbourne valley to Shooter's Hill and south to the high ground of Surrey.

Boston Manor Park

Boston Manor Road, Brentford *(34 acres)*

Until its acquisition by the Brentford District Council in 1924, the manor house and park had been continuously owned by the Clitherow family for almost 300 years. James Clitherow, who acquired the property soon after a fire destroyed part of the house in 1670, was a London merchant and son of Sir Christopher Clitherow, Lord Mayor of London in 1635.

The grounds, which are now part of the much larger Brent River Park, are beautifully laid out with formal flowerbeds, a small ornamental lake and many mature trees, including one particularly magnificent old cedar.

The house itself (originally built in 1622 for Lady Mary Reade) is open to the public free of charge on Saturday afternoons from the end of May to the end of September. Telephone 01–570 7728 for details.

Brenchley Gardens

Brenchley Gardens, SE23 *(6½ acres)*

Just across the road from One Tree Hill, along part of the dismantled Nunhead to Crystal Palace railway, is an attractive double terrace of rose gardens. The gardens, like the street, are named after William Brenchley, one-time vestryman and Mayor of Camberwell. There is a story that the London County Council would not approve the name since the alderman was still alive, to which the borough council replied that in that case they would name it instead after Brenchley in Kent.

Bretons Outdoor Recreation Centre

Rainham Road, Rainham *(184 acres)*

Named after the Breton family who lived in Hornchurch from the twelfth to the fourteenth century. Up until its recent development as a recreational area, Bretons Farm was used for sewage disposal. Today, it is being developed for various sports, including sailing, BMX racing, archery, angling, horse-riding, rugby and football.

Brook Green

Brook Green, W6 *(4½ acres)*

The green, which is named after a brook now running entirely underground, is in two parts: a triangle to the west of Shepherds Bush Road and a long narrow wedge to the east. As former wasteland of

Fulham Manor, Brook Green entered public ownership when the Metropolitan Board of Works bought it from the Lords of the Manor, the Ecclesiastical Commissioners, in 1881. The green remained in safe custody until the early 1930s when Hammersmith Council announced plans to build their new Town Hall right in the centre of it. This, however, led to such vociferous protest from local residents that in 1935 the council was forced to abandon the idea.

Brookmill Park

Brookmill Road, SE8 *(6½ acres)*

In the 1840s this land was occupied by a reservoir about five times the size of the present pond, surrounded by an area of grass and trees. As the local population increased, the water supply gradually became inadequate and by 1900 the reservoir had fallen into disuse. A small area of land had been used as a public park as far back as 1880 and this was extended in the 1920s by infilling part of the reservoir and again after adjacent housing on Brookmill Road was destroyed in 1944 by a German V-2 rocket. The 'new' park was opened in 1953 and named Ravensbourne Park after the river which flows along the north-eastern boundary. This opening is commemorated by the Coronation Gates at the park's entrance off Brookmill Road which have the date incorporated into the design. In more recent years the name has been changed to Brookmill Park.

Broomfield Park

Broomfield Lane, N13 *(54 acres)*

Opened on 25 April 1903, Broomfield Park was Southgate's first public park. In it stands Broomfield House, the ownership of which can be traced back as far as 1566. Since council ownership, the house has been used by Southgate County School, as a shelter for Belgian war refugees, as a children's clinic and, until a recent fire, as a local museum.

Apart from a range of sporting facilities, there is a 400-square-yard herbaceous border – said to be one of the longest in north London – and a scented garden laid out especially for the blind. Nearby is a small aviary, a pergola walk and three attractive ornamental lakes, the lowest of which was, up until 1913, used for public bathing.

Bruce Castle Park

Lordship Lane, N17 *(21 acres)*

The name refers to the castellated mansion of Robert the Bruce, one of several members of the Scottish royal family who once owned the property. After over two hundred years as the manor house of Tottenham, Bruce Castle was purchased in 1827 by the family of Sir Rowland Hill, the postal reformer, for use as an experimental school.

In 1891 the property was acquired by the local authority and on 13 August the following year Tottenham's first public park was formally opened to the public. Bruce Castle itself was opened in 1906 as a museum which today houses a collection of material on all aspects of the history of the British Post Office from the sixteenth century to the present day.

Bunhill Fields

City Road, EC2 *(4 acres)*

Although the name almost certainly derives from 'bone hill', its exact origin is obscure since its use pre-dates the transfer here of burial remains from St Paul's Charnel House in 1549.

Up until 1854 more than 120,000 bodies were buried here, particularly those of Nonconformists and liberal humanists, since this was the only place in London where burials could take place without the ministration of an Anglican clergyman.

Following bomb damage during the Second World War, the northern section was cleared of monuments and laid out as a public garden, while the southern end has retained many of the more important graves. Among these are the tombs of the poet-painter William Blake; author of *Pilgrim's Progress*, John Bunyan; the anti-slavery philanthropist Thomas Fowell Buxton; author of *Robinson Crusoe*, Daniel Defoe; and founder of the Society of Friends, George Fox.

Camberwell Green

Camberwell Road, SE5 *(2½ acres)*

This is the old village green of Camberwell, site of a once famous annual fair held originally in observance of the Feast of the Dedication of the Church of St Giles. In the early eighteenth century the fair, which dated from at least as far back as 1279, was curtailed from its original three-week-long celebration to just three days, and in August 1855 the 'rare doings at Camberwell' were finally suppressed.

Soon after the last Camberwell Fair local people began to raise funds to purchase the rights to their green from the lord of the manor in order to protect it as an open space, and in April 1859 Camberwell Green was formally reopened to the public.

Camley Street Natural Park

Camley Street, NW1 *(2½ acres)*

Sandwiched between gas holders and the Regent's Canal, within a few yards of King's Cross and St Pancras stations, is one of London's new wildlife parks. The land, which for many years had been used as a rubbish dump, was about to be converted into a lorry park when, in 1981, the London Wildlife Trust began its campaign to rescue the site to form an ecological park. The site has particular value for this purpose because it is situated along one of London's most effective wildlife corridors – the Regent's Canal.

The park, with its large pond, reed beds, marsh, meadow and scrub, forms a wildlife refuge of special value for education. A visitor centre and classroom with wheelchair access have been provided and these are open all week for the use of schools and other visitors (telephone 01-833 2311 for details).

Cannon Hill Common

Cannon Hill Lane, SW20 *(53 acres)*

The modern name is misleading for this is not a common in the original sense of the word, but rather a part of the old Canon Hill Estate. Before the mansion was built this had for centuries been a farm, probably having been originally developed by the canons of Merton Priory. In the 1850s it was the home of the Victorian millionaire Richard Thornton, one of the wealthiest and most influential members of Lloyd's marine insurance corporation.

At the time of writing the London Wildlife Trust is hoping to set up a nature reserve on part of the 'common'.

The Canons

Madeira Road, Mitcham *(6 acres)*

These are the grounds of what was at one time the manor house of Mitcham – the 'Canons', a much altered but still interesting mansion of the Restoration period. The name is thought either to be derived from the canons of Bayeux, supposed owners of the manor in the eleventh century, or, more likely, from the canons regular of the Augustinian priory of St Mary Overie at Southwark – owners of the manor of Mitcham in the Middle Ages.

Within the grounds is what is thought to be the oldest surviving complete building in Mitcham: the original dovecote, believed to have been built in 1511. Other historic survivals in the vicinity of the house include one of the original 'stew ponds' (near the dovecote) used during the Middle Ages to provide fresh carp for the inhabitants of the estate, and an obelisk on the corner of Madeira Road and Cricket Green. The obelisk was erected in 1822 in gratitude to God for the appearance of a spring during the extreme drought of 1821 and 1822. Unfortunately, though, the water supply failed (or so it is said) soon after the monument was erected.

Since the purchase of the house and estate for the public in 1939, the grounds have undergone a good deal of improvement and restoration to something like their late seventeenth-century appearance.

Canons Park

Whitchurch Lane, Edgware *(49 acres)*

The park's name refers to its ownership in the fourteenth century by the canons of St Bartholomew, Smithfield. In the early eighteenth century, the property was developed as a family estate by the first Duke of Chandos, who is commemorated by the names of a nearby street and recreation ground. The splendour of the house and grounds at this time so impressed Daniel Defoe that he wrote in 1724: 'In a word, no nobleman in England, and very few in Europe, lives in greater splendour, or maintains a grandeur and magnificence, equal to the Duke of Chandos.' The Duke's extravagance even ran to the expense of maintaining an orchestra to play in his private chapel and entertain while he and his family dined.

The King George V Memorial Garden here was laid out on the site of an old walled-in kitchen garden and opened to the public by the Bishop of Willesden in 1937.

Cator Park

Aldersmead Road, Beckenham *(17 acres)*

The park is named after the Cator family who, up until the early 1930s, owned and controlled the property, providing it primarily for the private use of those residents of their estate who paid an annual subscription fee. The grounds were originally laid out for this purpose between 1885 and 1889 and hence were already well matured as a park – with facilities for cricket, football, tennis and bowling – when the council decided to purchase it in 1931. Cator Park was formally opened to the public by Sir Lawrence Chubb in April 1932.

Central Park

Rancliffe Road, E6 *(25 acres)*

The park was formed from the grounds of the early eighteenth-century mansion, Rancliffe House, which, though demolished in 1908, is commemorated by the road of that name on the south side of the park. The grounds were acquired in 1898, with later purchases extending the park to its present size.

Central Park

Rainham Road North, Dagenham *(133 acres)*

Largely flat grassland with a good range of sporting facilities, Central Park was formed from Eastbrook Farm and opened to the public in 1932.

Charlton Park

Charlton Park Road, SE7 *(43 acres)*

Charlton Park was part of the estate attached to Charlton House, once owned by Sir Adam Newton and more recently by the Maryon-Wilson family. Both the house and estate were purchased by Greenwich Borough Council in 1926 with a little over half the grounds being subsequently developed for housing. The remaining forty-three acres were laid out mostly as playing fields and opened as a public park in July 1929.

The original house built for Sir Adam in 1612 still stands and is today regarded as one of the best examples of Jacobean architecture in the country and the finest in London. Although traditionally attributed to

Inigo Jones, it is now thought to have been designed by a less well-known architect, John Thorpe. Charlton House is now used as a community centre and library.

Cheam Park

Cheam Park Way, Sutton *(67 acres)*

Just inside the boundary of Greater London, adjoining Nonsuch Park, are the former grounds of Cheam Park House, once owned by Mrs Bethel. The council acquired the property in 1937, but the house was unfortunately completely destroyed by a flying bomb in 1944. In its early days the park's greenhouses contained such tropical novelties as bananas, though these have sadly since succumbed to spending cuts. Modern-day attractions include a long avenue of mature beeches and an unusually good variety of specimen trees, including a healthy black mulberry and a number of commemorative trees.

Cherry Tree Wood

Brompton Grove, N2 *(13½ acres)*

The history of this remnant of ancient woodland can be traced perhaps as far back as the time of the Norman Conquest or even earlier, when the western half of Hornsey was used by the Bishop of London as a hunting park; Cherry Tree Wood, or Dirthouse Wood as it used to be known, is one of the few surviving fragments of this.

Some of the old hornbeams are presently being recoppiced and oaks replanted in an effort to assist regeneration in the southern part of the wood.

Chinbrook Meadows

Mayeswood Road, SE12 *(31 acres)*

The name is derived from the central feature of the meadows: the stream commonly known as the river Quaggy but sometimes referred to as the Kyd Brook or Chinbrook.

Chinbrook Meadows was originally simply an eight-acre children's playground on the edge of the Grove Park housing estate. This was opened by a former Lord Mayor of London, Sir J. E. Kynaston Studd, on the inauguration of the estate in 1929 and later extended with the help of the London County Council by the purchase of a further twenty-three acres which were opened to the public in June 1937.

Chislehurst Common

Centre Common Road, Chislehurst *(90 acres)*

The common is aptly described by its name which derives from the Anglo-Saxon *Ceosol Hyrst*, meaning 'a wood on gravel'. The common's wooded character is, however, relatively recent, having resulted largely from the natural recolonization of an area which up until a century or so ago was rather sparsely timbered.

With such heavy public use it is not surprising that the woodland flora has suffered in recent decades but there are still several attractive patches of gorse, willowherb and harebell and several interesting breeding birds including the great spotted woodpecker, spotted flycatcher and long-tailed tit.

One of the common's most interesting historic features is the old cockpit, the site of which is clearly marked by a stone set in the ground near Watt's Lane due south of the war memorial. The cockpit is one of the very few in this country to have survived in perfect condition. Also of historic interest is the attractive old village sign, a few yards to the east of the war memorial, depicting the knighting of Thomas Walsingham by Queen Elizabeth I at Scadbury on 20 (or 21) July 1597.

The common suffered from much the same problem of encroachments as elsewhere with, at times, quite spirited protests from the local commoners, including such acts of civil disobedience as the pulling out by night of offending fences. Legislative protection came with the Metropolitan Commons (Chislehurst and St Paul's Cray) Supplemental Act, 1888, in which the present system of management – by an elected board of conservators – was constituted.

Church House and Library Gardens

High Street, Bromley *(17 acres)*

Together these form what today is one of the borough's most beautiful parks. In spite of its name, Church House Gardens has no connection with the vicarage. It was planted and landscaped by a Mr Abel Moysey before its purchase by Bromley Town Council in 1926 and connected with the existing upper level Library Gardens before being opened to the public in July 1927.

Clapton Common

Clapton Common, E5 *(7½ acres)*

Clapton Common was described in the 1890s as a place where, in the early morning 'before chimneys and factories poison the air with their smoke, it is possible to sniff the ozone of the pure sea-breeze'. Earlier still, before houses were built to the north-east, the view over the Lea valley from 'the heights of the mellow, old-fashioned suburb of Clapton' was described as being 'not inferior in its way to that of classic Richmond Hill itself'.

Clapton and Stoke Newington commons are Hackney's only true commons, the rest being lammas lands, that is land which was common only for part of the year.

Coldfall Wood

Creighton Avenue, N10 *(34 acres)*

Though little now remains of what could be called primary woodland –

that is, woodland that has been continuously present since prehistoric times – evidence of the wood's antiquity can be seen in the presence of a few specimens of Midland hawthorn (as opposed to the common hawthorn) and of a large clump of wild service tree (opposite the end of Beech Drive).

Perhaps as recently as 1930, when Coldfall Wood was purchased by Hornsey Council for public recreation, the hornbeams were still being coppiced and the oaks grown as standards; in fact, evidence of this system of management can still be seen in the forms of some of the older trees. Unfortunately, though, through subsequent lack of management, the wood now has practically no undergrowth and such a lack in the range of ages of the trees that the future of this surviving fragment of the ancient Forest of Middlesex is endangered.

Coram's Fields

Guildford Street, WC1 *(9 acres)*

Named after Thomas Coram who founded 'The Hospital for the Maintenance and Education of Exposed and Deserted Young Children', otherwise known as the Foundling Hospital. Though the hospital – built here in 1747 – has long since moved into the country, this part of the original grounds has been preserved.

Adults are not admitted unless accompanied by a child.

Crane Park

Ellerman Avenue, Twickenham *(66 acres)*

Almost two miles long, this delightful riverside park contains within it a four-and-a-half-acre nature reserve, Crane Island, and – about halfway between Chertsey and Hounslow Roads – an exceedingly well preserved example of an old shot tower.

The banks of the river Crane had long been an important site for the production of gunpowder; in fact it is nearby that England's first gunpowder is reputed to have been made. Of the gunpowder mills which operated here between 1768 and 1927, this tapering brick tower with conical roof is all that survives. It apparently dates from the late eighteenth century and was still being used right up until the early 1920s. Lead shot was manufactured here through a process of dropping the molten metal from a height into water, effectively and immediately 'freezing' the droplets of lead into the spherical shapes which they had assumed during their fall.

It is curious that a process such as this, requiring the use of fire, should have been sited so near stored gunpowder, for explosions in these riverside mills were not uncommon and frequently quite violent – some being felt as 'earthquakes' as far away as the City.

Richmond and Twickenham Friends of the Earth currently have plans to convert the tower into an educational nature centre and are meanwhile active in the development and management of the adjacent island reserve.

Cranford Park

Cranford Lane, Hayes *(148 acres)*

Just south of the M4 motorway, not far from the surviving stable or barn block, is the site of the old Cranford House which, up until the end of the last century, was the seat of the Berkeleys. This early Georgian mansion was demolished at the end of the Second World War, about the time the park came into public ownership.

Today, most of the park is flat, treeless grassland offering only good views of air traffic and fumes from Heathrow Airport just yards away. There are, however, two small but attractive areas of woodland – one near the motorway and the other along the park's eastern boundary on the banks of the river Crane.

The straight section of the river to the east of the stables originally formed part of an ornamental canal in the formal rectangular style of the lake at Hampton Court. At the northern end of this (across the M4) are the remains of an old moat marking the site of Cranford Moat House, occupied in the seventeenth century by the rectors of nearby St Dunstan's and pulled down in 1780. The charming old church itself – approached through a lych-gate by the stable block – dates from the fifteenth and seventeenth centuries and is the old parish church of Cranford.

Croham Hurst

Croham Manor Road, South Croydon *(85 acres)*

Along the infertile pebbly ridge of this wooded hill, stunted silver birch and Scots pine predominate with patches of ling heather, sheep's sorrel and wavy heath grass, giving way on the lower more fertile slopes to large oak and beech trees with great expanses of bracken. The wood appears to be of ancient origin with a correspondingly wide range of flora and fauna, including such uncommon plants as butcher's broom and Solomon's seal.

Five mesolithic, or middle stone-age, hut circles and a bronze-age round barrow have been found. In 1968, when the Croydon Natural History and Scientific Society excavated two of these hut sites on the eastern side of the northern ridge-clearing, they were found to have had a central hole for a roof support post and, it is thought, low turf walls. The bronze-age tumulus – a circular mound about eighteen inches high and forty feet across – is to be found in the next clearing to the south along the ridge; a plaque set in the ground clearly marks its site.

When, at the turn of the century, there was talk of the Hurst being subdivided for house building, local opposition was so strong and united that all the working men of Croydon are reputed to have sworn an oath not to lay a brick on it and, in 1899, 7502 signatures were collected petitioning for it to be preserved for 'the use of the people for ever'. Croham Hurst was finally purchased by the council in 1901 and some years ago received the protective designation of Site of Special Scientific Interest (SSSI).

Dagnam Park

Dagnam Park Drive, Romford *(147 acres)*

This park is particularly attractive in the spring when the bluebells, celandine and wood anemone are in flower in Hatter's and Fir Wood. Most of the grounds were originally part of the Dagnam estate, former home of the Wrights who lived here from 1600 to 1750, and later of the Neaves. At the park's northern end, just beyond the scrub-hidden pond, is the site of the original mansion described in 1665 by Pepys as the most noble and pretty house for its size that he had ever seen. Some impression of its former grandeur can be pictured from the fact that it had no less than twenty-four hearths and was built round a courtyard within a square moat.

Also within a moat, at the southern end of the park, was another mansion, probably that of the family of Roger Cockerell who were tenants of the manor during the reign of Henry III, thus making these earthworks now over 700 years old. Cockerell's Moat, which has recently been registered by the Department of the Environment as an Ancient Monument, is still in fairly good condition and is well worth looking out for (just south of the large angling pond). The moat still holds water and has an earth causeway for access from the south, though there are no remains now of the original building.

The park itself was purchased along with the surrounding land by the London County Council for the building (1948–58) of the Harold Hill housing estate.

Downhills Park

Downhills Park Road, N17 *(30 acres)*

Once part of the 290-acre Mount Pleasant estate, the first twenty-six acres of Downhills Park was formally opened to the public in August 1903, the old house having been pulled down by the council soon after the estate was bought in 1902. By the end of the following year, when the district was only just recovering from a serious smallpox epidemic, a campaign was already underway to make a major extension to the park. The strong association in the minds of those at the time between the provision of parks and public health can be seen in the statement of the District's Medical Officer: 'If we take the expense of the treatment of Infectious cases as 1s 3d per head . . . it will be seen that from a pecuniary as well as from a Public Health standpoint, economy is on the side of those who advocate the provision of ample Open Spaces for the people.'

This campaign eventually resulted in a much smaller extension to Downhills Park being informally made in 1906.

Duck Wood

Sheffield Drive, Romford *(20 acres)*

In spite of the wood's name, the long chain of ponds here no longer has much to offer ducks, though with a little attention the ponds could no doubt be returned to something of their former beauty. From a late eighteenth-century map it would appear that the western end of the wood is older than the eastern, though mature hornbeams are found throughout, along with a delightfully rich carpet of bluebells and wood anemones in spring.

Dulwich Upper Wood

Farquhar Road, SE19 *(5 acres)*

Sometimes known also as the Farquhar Road Wood, Dulwich Upper Wood is one of three City Nature Parks maintained by the Ecological Parks Trust. Part of these woods is thought to descend directly from the ancient forest of south-east England and part is the result of the recolonization of neglected gardens in an area bombed during the Second World War.

Farquhar Road itself was constructed in 1870 along with several large Victorian houses along the western edge of the wood. All that remains of these now (they had all gone by 1960) is a series of excavated basement areas and parts of the walls of the old cellars.

To develop the attraction of the area both for recreation and study the trust has, with community support, constructed paths and a tree nursery; in order to attract a greater variety of wildlife some areas have been coppiced and at present a permanent interpretive centre is being built. The site warden may be contacted on 01-761 6230.

Eaglesfield

Eaglesfield Road, SE18 *(9 acres)*

This includes the highest point of Shooter's Hill, which at one time played an important role in the relaying of information to the City. There was a beacon here for that purpose as early as 1570 and at the turn of the eighteenth century a semaphore-like shutter relay station was erected which was later used to signal Wellington's victory at Waterloo in 1815.

Eaglesfield was purchased by the London County Council in 1907 and formally dedicated to the public on 29 February 1908.

Ealing Common

Uxbridge Road, W5 *(47 acres)*

In July 1874, when public concern was growing over the common's future, Ealing Local Board called an inquiry into whether the continuing existence of common rights could still be proven here. In the light of struggles over common rights that went on in other parts of London the Ecclesiastical Commissioners, who owned the land, were unusually generous in admitting these rights of common and in selling their own rights for the nominal sum of £5 – a far cry from the £10,000 paid to Lord Spencer, for example, only three years later for his half of Clapham Common.

For centuries the land had been used as grazing for the villagers' fowl, geese and sheep and as a site for May Day festivals, fairs and donkey races. In fact, one custom continued here as late as 1928 and that was the use of the common by local people to hang out their washing. By that time this was probably unique in a London suburb and, though frowned upon by some, was staunchly defended at the time as a 'picturesque custom'.

East Sheen Common

King's Ride Gate, Richmond *(53 acres)*

This triangle of common land is predominantly oak woodland which, due to the absence of deer grazing, has an undergrowth quite different from that of the adjoining Richmond Park. The land was donated to the National Trust by the East Sheen Common Preservation Society in 1908 and is managed by the London Borough of Richmond upon Thames.

Eelbrook Common

Musgrave Crescent, SW6 *(14 acres)*

Although there were indeed once eels to be found in the ditch which at one time surrounded much of the common, the common's name appears to have had a different derivation. In 1410 the name was spelt Hillebrook, later Helbrook, Hillbrook, Ellbrook and finally – in the nineteenth century – Eelbrook, suggesting that the historic brook was named instead after a nearby hill or hillock.

There are records of the common having been whittled away from as far back as the seventeenth century, but by the 1870s the commoners decided to take the landowners to court – an action which led finally to the commoners' rights being upheld in Parliament in 1872 and again in 1878. One last strip of common land was lost to the building of the District Underground railway line just before Eelbrook Common was acquired by the Metropolitan Board of Works in 1881.

Elmstead Wood

Elmstead Lane, Chislehurst *(61½ acres)*

The history of the wood can be traced back at least to 1320 when Bishop Hamo de Heth 'was necessitated to sell the wood of Elmsted in Bromleigh, which he did for two hundred marcs [£133.33], to pay the debts which his church had incurred, in soliciting the affairs of it at the court of Rome.'

Apparently Elmstead Wood supplied timber for shipbuilding and, in the sixteenth century, timber from here was used for the repair of the Bishop's Palace at Bromley (where part of the Civic Centre now stands). The wood is thought to be one of London's remnants of ancient forest – certainly most of the present wood appears on Rocque's map of 1744 and subsequent maps as being wooded. Today, the dominant trees are oak and sweet chestnut, with hornbeam, silver birch and sycamore.

Elmstead Wood came into public ownership in 1936–7, with part of the purchase price being met by the London County Council.

Elthorne Park

Boston Road, W7 *(48 acres)*

In July 1908 Lord Jersey, the previous owner of the grounds, was first approached to see if he would be prepared to sell the site for use as a recreation ground. So enthusiastic was he for the idea that he opened the grounds unofficially to local children long before its actual sale.

The first part of the park was dedicated to the use of the public for ever in June 1910 by Lord Villiers, with a large extension being later made from a reclaimed rubbish tip.

The whole park now forms an integral part of the 850-acre Brent River Park.

Fairlop Country Park

Forest Road, Ilford *(300 acres)*

This new country park, though still in the process of being developed, is already open to the public. It is situated on the land known as Fairlop Plain, bounded on the north by Forest Road and on the west by the underground Central Line.

For years the plain has been used for sand and gravel extraction and until recently has been the site of one of the borough's main rubbish dumps. During both the First and Second World Wars it was used as an airfield and in the 1930s was even considered as a possible site for a major London airport.

The ambitious plans for the present country park were first announced in the mid-1970s and are only just now coming to fruition. The old eleven-acre sailing lake (originally one of the gravel pits) has recently been extended to thirty-eight acres with provision also made for both fishing and windsurfing. As part of a major landscaping operation 300,000 saplings and shrubs have been planted and an eighteen-hole golf course and par-three course are under construction. Yet to come are bridleways, a nature reserve, children's playground and improved cycle speedway track.

Faraday Garden

Portland Street, SE17 *(3 acres)*

The garden is named after the distinguished scientist and discoverer of electromagnetic induction, Michael Faraday, who was born nearby in 1791. The original one-acre garden was donated by the Ecclesiastical Commissioners and opened to the public in July 1905.

Figges Marsh

Manship Road, Mitcham *(25 acres)*

Figges Marsh is part of the ancient common pasture of the village of Mitcham, though, since manorial boundaries here have always been rather vague, it is unclear to which particular manor the marsh belonged. Most likely Figges Marsh belonged to the manor of Biggin and

Tamworth. Its name derives from a Mr William Figge who lived in Mitcham in the early fourteenth century.

It is described by one local historian as 'flat as a pancake, 26 [sic] acres of dog-fouled turf, surrounded by well-disciplined characterless trees'. The loss of the marsh's character is attributed partly to the abolition of grazing in favour of mowing (which cuts out the variety of wildflowers) and the draining of the old pond at the northern tip of the marsh.

Figges Marsh was acquired by the local council in 1923.

Forster Memorial Park

Whitefoot Lane, SE6 *(43 acres)*

The woodland strip which borders most of the park conveys to the grassland within it the sense of a rural meadow. In spite of the traffic noise from Whitefoot Lane, there are birds here in their hundreds and the park does have some interesting specimen trees such as the maidenhair (or ginkgo) tree and a yellow-leaved cypress.

Lord Forster, a local resident and one-time Governor-General of Australia, made a gift to the public of part of his estate in 1919 as a memorial to his two sons, Alfred Henry and John, who were both killed during the First World War. The park (originally twenty-four acres) was opened to the public in Lord Forster's absence by his daughter, Mrs Lubbock, in 1922 and later extended following a deal between the Forster Estate Company and the London County Council in 1937.

Frank's Park

Parkside Road, Belvedere *(41 acres)*

Named after Frank Beadle, a former council chairman who lived adjacent to the present park at 'The Oaks' in Friday Road and who bequeathed to the urban district council the money for the park's purchase. Much of the park is steeply undulating and wooded predominantly with a range of broad-leaved trees including several handsome old oaks.

Furnivall Gardens

Lower Mall, W6 *(4½ acres)*

The gardens are named after Dr Frederick James Furnivall (1825–1910), known for promoting the sport of rowing and as a scholar of English literature. As part of redevelopment plans following extensive bomb damage to the area during the Second World War, Furnivall Gardens was opened to the public in May 1951.

Garratt Green

Burntwood Lane, SW17 *(8 acres)*

Earl Spencer finally surrendered his ownership rights to the green for £110 in 1899, making this one of the last commons in London to come into public ownership. The green has long had an association with the rowdy elections of the once famous mock Mayor of Garratt, whose function it was to protect local common rights. The election ceremony, which soon became popular elsewhere, was the subject of a farce by Samuel Foote. The last of these Garratt elections took place here in 1796.

Geffrye's Garden

Kingsland Road, E2 *(2 acres)*

Named after Sir Robert Geffrye, Lord Mayor of London in 1686, who bequeathed funds to the Ironmongers' Company for the erection and maintenance of the almshouses here. Proposals in 1908 to develop the site were opposed by the National Trust and the Metropolitan Public Gardens Association, leading the London County Council to purchase the property as a public open space in 1910.

The garden was opened to the public in July 1912, while the almshouses now serve as a museum specializing in exhibits of furniture, plaster casting and ironwork.

Geraldine Mary Harmsworth Park

Lambeth Road, SE1 *(16 acres)*

Originally the site of the third Bethlem Hospital, this land was saved from building development by Viscount Rothermere who purchased the entire estate for the public as a permanent memorial to his mother, the late Geraldine Mary Harmsworth. Lord Rothermere presented the estate to the London County Council in 1926 and it was formally opened as a public park in July 1934. The central part of the former hospital is now occupied by the Imperial War Museum.

Gladstone Park

Dollis Hill Lane, NW2 *(93 acres)*

These are the grounds of the old mansion built at Dollis Hill in 1824. The park's name derives from the time when the Earl of Aberdeen lived here and Mr Gladstone, then the Prime Minister, was a frequent guest of his.

The movement to buy the land as a park, which began in 1898, met with considerable local opposition both because of the expense and because the area was not yet built up. In fact, a newspaper of the time described Dollis Hill Lane as 'a delightfully rural approach to the house' winding 'its way through the greenest of fields, with hedges and blackberry bushes on either side'.

The park was, however, eventually purchased in spite of these objections with the help of private donations and formally opened to the public in May 1901.

Grangewood Park

Grange Road, SE25 *(28 acres)*

This originally was part of the eighty-acre Whitehorse Wood, named after Walter Whitehors, Lord of the Manor in 1368. Though the estate was subdivided for building development in the mid-nineteenth century, thirty acres to the east of Grange Road were left to form a private estate, and it is this which was purchased by the Corporation of Croydon to form the present park in 1900.

The original Grange Wood Mansion was demolished in 1957, but the stables still exist, as do many of the old trees which today attract such a variety of birds and no shortage of very tame squirrels.

Grovelands Park

Park Gate, N21 *(91 acres)*

This is part of what was called Lords Grove and later Winchmore Hill Woods. In Queen Elizabeth I's reign it was owned by Lord Burghley, the Lord High Treasurer, and used then as a coppice wood. Both the park and lake are known to have been landscaped by Humphry Repton during the period when the land was still a private estate.

Despite considerable local opposition, the property was purchased by the Southgate Urban District Council in 1911 and opened as a public park two years later.

Gunnersbury Triangle

Bollo Lane, W4 *(6 acres)*

Enclosed by three railway embankments, this triangle of wild land is one of the few pieces of natural woodland left in this part of west London. Predominantly birch and willow, the woodland supports an interesting variety of birds including the tawny owl, great spotted woodpecker, redpoll and both the willow and sedge warbler, along with several interesting wild plants, a family of foxes and at least 109 species of beetle.

The land was originally enclosed just prior to the opening of the North London and District railways in 1869, being protected from development since then largely by its inaccessibility. When recent plans were unveiled to develop the site for warehouses and factory units, the Chiswick Wildlife Group (a branch of the London Wildlife Trust) stepped in to save the wood as a nature reserve, and since 1984 it has been managed as such by them under licence from the London Borough of Hounslow.

At present there are plans for a field studies hut, nature trail and wildlife pond. Access is via Bollo Lane, opposite Chiswick Park underground station.

Hackney Downs

Downs Road, E5 *(42 acres)*

Like most of the Hackney commons, Hackney Downs was in fact lammas land, that is, land where rights common to the tenants of the manor were enjoyed for only eight months of the year. During the remaining four months – the haying season – the rights belonged exclusively to those individuals who had leased the land from the lord of the manor.

Of the many encroachments from which the Downs has at various times suffered, the most obvious is that of Stormont House School on the north side of Downs Park Road. Such land was often taken without any regard to the rights of existing commoners so that when this enclosure was followed by that of Hackney Downs School (formerly Grocer's School) the extent of public unrest led to local rioting. So persistent was the lord of the manor in disregarding these rights that even after the Metropolitan Board of Works succeeded in taking over the common's management in 1872, the lord's filching of land continued unabated. It was not finally until 1884 that the Board of Works succeeded in assuming full control, thereby enabling the Downs to be protected in perpetuity as a public park.

Hackney Marsh

Homerton Road, E9 *(336 acres)*

As the modern name suggests, these meadows were once marshland, having been first drained in the ninth century by order of King Alfred to hinder the navigation of the Danes along the river Lee. Still earlier it was the site of a Roman stone causeway that probably formed part of the ancient link between London and Essex.

Drainage channels were also cut by the London County Council in the 1890s in order to prevent periodic flooding and again after the Second World War the marsh was further reclaimed by dumping rubble from many of London's bombed sites.

For centuries Hackney Marsh had been lammas land – that is land used for common grazing during the months of August until April – and it was during one of these seasons of common rights that in 1889 a dispute over the right to play football led to the marsh's eventual purchase for that purpose by the London County Council.

The marsh, which nowadays forms just one part of the 10,000-acre Lee Valley Park, has since become a veritable sea of goal posts, providing over one hundred rugby and football pitches which can on a single day be used by as many as 2500 players.

Hanworth Park

Hounslow Road, Feltham *(144 acres)*

This is the site of the old Royal Palace of Hanworth, destroyed by fire in 1797 and replaced in 1802 by the present Hanworth Park House. During the First World War, the house was fitted out by the British Red Cross as a hospital for sick and wounded soldiers and, after being put to a variety of other uses, is now run by the council as an old people's home.

In 1917, following the underground diversion of the historic Longford river, J.A. Whitehead of Whitehead Aircraft Ltd turned the grounds into an airfield and this is how the park continued, under various companies, until the opening of nearby Heathrow Airport at the end of the Second World War. The grounds were purchased as a public park in 1956 and today serve mostly as playing fields.

Harrow Lodge Park

Hornchurch Road, Hornchurch *(129 acres)*

There is a number of attractive trees scattered along this river valley, the west bank of which provides a pleasantly shaded walk. Apart from this and the long eight-and-a-half-acre boating lake, the main attractions are the sporting facilities: bowling, fishing, tennis, indoor swimming and miniature golf. Plans have recently been unveiled for an ambitious £1.75 million sports centre to include badminton courts, multi-purpose sports hall, squash courts, fitness salons and a health studio.

Harrow Weald Common

Common Road, Stanmore *(48 acres)*

Most of the original 1500 acres of common land here was lost under the Enclosure Act of 1803. With apparently no resistance from the villagers – whose rights were simply ignored – the common was divided up between the existing landowners, leaving only the present acreage unenclosed.

When in 1886 the local vestry attempted to complete the deed by selling this last forty-eight acres, the earlier injustices had not been forgotten and the previously apathetic locals acted to contest and finally to defeat the proposal.

Harrow Weald Common came under public control in 1899 and has since been declared by the Nature Conservancy Council a Site of Special Scientific Interest (SSSI). In part the common's attraction and ecological interest is due to its proximity to Stanmore Common and Bentley Priory Park, but significant also is the fact that it is a remnant of the ancient Forest of Middlesex.

Hawkwood Estate

Botany Bay Lane, Chislehurst *(245 acres)*

In order to protect this estate from the speculative builder, it was donated in 1958 by Francesca and Robert Hall to the National Trust. Most of the estate is now either under cultivation by a tenant farmer or in use for horse grazing with public access being limited to only a few footpaths.

The two areas likely to be of interest to the general public are the small Pond Wood near the western end and the much larger Edlmann Memorial Wood which, since it forms part of Petts Wood, is dealt with more fully under that heading. Both woods are particularly attractive in spring when the woodland wildflowers such as bluebells and wood anemones are unusually prolific.

Heathfield

Ballards Way, South Croydon *(18 acres)*

Although open to the public the year round, these gardens still retain the appearance of a private estate. The entrance path descends steeply between mature trees and colourful rhododendron bushes to the old

Heathfield House which, in the early nineteenth century, served as the farmhouse for Stone's Farm. The house underwent its conversion to a country mansion soon after being purchased by the Honourable Henry Goschen, second son of Viscount Goschen, in 1866, and it is thought that the planting of many of the specimen trees from around the world dates from this time.

The gardens to the east of the house, however, date largely from the residence of a more recent owner, Mr Raymond Riesco, who purchased the estate in 1927. It was he who employed a firm of landscape gardeners to lay out the present terraces and rock garden, along with its pool, adjacent to the original approach to the house.

Other attractions here include the circular rose garden, the colourful herbaceous border by the house (at its best in August) and in May the rhododendrons and azaleas.

Highams Park

The Charter Road, Woodford Green *(84 acres total)*

Like Wanstead House, the Manor of Higham belonged during the reign of Henry VIII to Sir Giles Heron. The present manor house (now the central part of Woodford County High School) was built in 1768 for the then Lord of the Manor, Antony Bacon MP, and it was he who first enclosed this part of Epping Forest. In 1794, acting on the advice of the landscape architect Humphry Repton, he went on to form the tree-lined Highams Park lake which today is one of the park's most attractive features.

About three-quarters of the park's total area has since been officially returned to Epping Forest and is hence administered by the City of London. The remaining eastern side (about twenty-four acres) was purchased from Courtenay Warner with the help of local donations in 1890 and is now administered by Waltham Forest Borough Council.

Hilly Fields

Hilly Fields Crescent, SE4 *(45 acres)*

By the 1880s Deptford Common just to the north of Hilly Fields had already disappeared, so when plans were announced to build over this hill too the local people of Lewisham set up a campaign to save the land as a public park. It was argued that nearby Deptford was one of the poorest districts of London with no significant open space apart from Deptford Park.

It was as a direct result of this spirited campaign that Hilly Fields was eventually purchased by the London County Council with substantial donations from a number of sympathetic charities and City companies. Up until that time, part of the site had been used for brickmaking, so this area had first to be levelled and the swampy sections drained, but finally, on 16 May 1896, Hilly Fields was dedicated to the public.

Probably the park's main asset today, apart from its sports facilities, is the good views from its rounded summit some 175 feet above sea level, out to the south over Ladywell and north to the river Thames.

Hilly Fields Park

Phipps Hatch Lane, Enfield *(66 acres)*

Before its acquisition by Enfield Urban District Council in 1911, this attractive property was known as Park Farm and was owned by the Venerable Archdeacon Potter. In spite of some provision for such sports as putting and cricket, Hilly Fields Park is laid out primarily with passive recreation in mind. The park straddles a tributary of Turkey brook, with two asphalted public footpaths crossing it to connect north across Clay Hill to Whitewebbs Park and thence on to the Forty Hall Estate, where a local footpath map is available.

Hornchurch Country Park

Ingrebourne Valley, Hornchurch *(160 acres)*

This is part of the former Hornchurch airfield and is now being developed as a country park. The plan is to include large areas of woodland, a network of footpaths and bridleways, picnic areas, a car park and some open grassed areas for informal games.

Hornfair Park

Charlton Park Lane, SE7 *(26 acres)*

Hornfair Park was originally acquired in 1935 under the name of Charlton Playing Fields and renamed in October 1948. Its present name derives from an annual fair held nearby until its suppression for alleged indecency in 1872.

Legend has it that the fair originated from the time of King John, when the King was caught making love with the miller's wife in Greenwich. To appease the miller, the King is said to have offered him a grant of all the land he could see in one direction and to have consented to walk the bounds of the miller's new estate once a year with a pair of buck's horns on his head.

Modern historians, though – always ready to spoil a good legend – suggest that the fair originated instead from the parish's patron saint, St Luke, on whose feast day the fair was held.

Hurlingham Park

Hurlingham Road, SW6 *(20 acres)*

The public park was originally part of the private grounds of the exclusive Hurlingham Club which now occupies the thirty-nine acres between here and the river. The club was originally founded by Frank Heathcote in 1869 for pigeon shooting but, following shifting fashions, it later became the headquarters of English polo and now caters mostly for tennis and croquet.

The public park was laid out on the site of the club's original no. 1 polo ground and pony stables following the compulsory purchase of this part of the estate by the London County Council in 1951. Hurlingham Park was opened to the public the following year.

Island Gardens

Saunders Ness Road, E14 *(3 acres)*

This small garden on the Isle of Dogs is situated at the northern end of a footway tunnel under the Thames, providing a novel and convenient form of access from Greenwich Pier. The site of the present garden was practically engulfed by wharf building in response to the rapidly developing dock trade of the 1830s, but the park's acquisition was later made possible by a slump in the Thames shipbuilding trade some fifty years later. After laying-out work, Island Gardens was enthusiastically opened to the public on 3 August 1895.

John Innes Park

Church Path, SW19 *(4½ acres)*

Originally the gardens of the Manor House, the park has some interesting trees and shrubs: deodar cedars, an old mulberry tree and a collection of some forty-two varieties of holly, including three specimens of the rather unusual and fascinating hedgehog holly. The park is the former site of the John Innes Horticultural Institute which undertook research into fruit production and growing media. John Innes, after whom a range of modern potting composts is also named, was a merchant banker and keen amateur horticulturalist.

Jubilee Gardens

Belvedere Road, SE1 *(4½ acres)*

This is the former site of the Dome of Discovery – the chief exhibition feature of the Festival of Britain which in 1951 attracted eight and a half million visitors. The flagpole – a donation from the British Columbia government – is a relic of this. Twenty-five years later, the land was laid out as a riverside park and opened by Queen Elizabeth II, as part of the celebrations of her Silver Jubilee, on 9 June 1977.

Jubilee Park

Thornet Wood Road, Bromley *(49 acres)*

Until the Second World War this was the site of the West Kent Golf Club, where golfers from all over the world (including the American Bobby Jones) played. Though the club house was then destroyed by a parachute mine, many of the old bunkers can still be seen, while the concrete access road and foundations are left-overs from the war itself, when three nests of anti-aircraft guns were based here.

When planning applications were lodged in 1968, and again in 1973, to build some 500 houses on the site, the Petts Wood Residents Association voiced strong opposition. Fortunately, Bromley Council agreed to refuse further loss of green belt land here and their decision was upheld by the Environment Secretary at a public inquiry in 1974.

Since 1981, when the park was opened to the public, over 500 trees have been planted as part of the council's plans to encourage wildlife.

Access is from Crest View Drive, Southborough Lane and Thornet Wood Road.

Kelsey Park

Manor Way, Beckenham *(32 acres)*

As an estate, the park's history can be traced right back to its ownership by the Kelsey family during the reign of Henry III. The original estate was, of course, far larger, extending even in the 1820s to over 150 acres, but gradually diminishing to its present size through the sale or letting of land on building leases.

The first twenty-four acres were purchased by Beckenham Urban District Council in 1912 and in May the following year Kelsey Park was formally opened to the public, with an extension of about seven acres being added in 1936.

The park's most attractive features are its two long interconnected lakes fed by the river Beck and encircled by a woodland belt interrupted occasionally by sloping lawns and some fine specimen trees.

Kenley Common

Golf Road, Kenley *(135 acres)*

This is one of a group of properties, known as the Coulsdon Commons, which were bought by the Corporation of the City of London in February 1883 in order to resolve a legal dispute between the local commoners and the Lord of the Manor, Squire Byron. On a modern map this particular common assumes a rather curious straggling shape – a fact which is due to most of the plateau having been conveyed to the Air Ministry for use as an aerodrome during the First World War. Seventy years later this is still in use, in spite of the original condition of transfer that the land be later returned to the public. However, this agreement also included, by way of compensation, the exchange of a similar acreage of adjoining farmland, so that the common has in the process merely shifted rather than diminished.

Keston Common

Fishponds Road, Keston *(55 acres)*

Keston Common's central feature is an attractive series of ponds, dug originally for John Ward at the beginning of the nineteenth century to provide a water supply for his home, Holwood House. Through the gift of a subsequent owner, the Earl of Derby, the two upper ponds were incorporated into Keston Common in 1926.

At the top end of the ponds, encircled by a low brick wall is 'Caesar's Well', a small spring which in the eighteenth century was used as a public cold bath. The water had the reputation of 'possessing the virtue of curing persons afflicted with weak or rheumatic limbs'.

The land around the ponds is of particular interest to ecologists as being one of the best areas of relict heathland in Greater London and, in recognition of this, has been designated by the Nature Conservancy Council as a Site of Special Scientific Interest (SSSI). The common supports any amount of heather and several clumps of broom – the plant after which nearby Broomleigh (Bromley) is named. Other plants of interest here include both of Britain's insect-eating plants – sundew and butterwort – along with bog asphodel, purple orchid and, on the ponds themselves, some beautiful white and yellow water lilies. A botanical survey carried out here in 1950 recorded a total of over 300 plant species.

In 1981 the fifty-five-acre common was effectively further extended by the twenty-seven-acre addition of Ravensbourne Open Space, given to Bromley Council by Ferndale Homes Ltd.

Kilburn Grange Park

Grangeway, NW6 *(8 acres)*

Formerly part of the Grange estate, eight and a half acres of which the London County Council bought in 1910, originally 'for parks, education and tramway purposes'. Priorities changed, and in May 1913 all but half an acre of this was opened to the public as a park. Today, the grounds include an attractive Old English garden surrounded by flowering shrubs, arrived at through an arbour of roses, wisteria and clematis.

King Edward Memorial Park

The Highway, E1 *(8½ acres)*

Acquired by the London County Council in 1912 and opened by King George V on 24 June 1922 in commemoration of the life and reign of his predecessor, King Edward VII, this park was laid out on the site of the former Shadwell fish market. The park's particular attraction is its proximity to the Thames, the entrance to the Rotherhithe tunnel and the historic riverside pub, The Prospect of Whitby.

King George's Park

Buckhold Road, SW18 *(49 acres)*

The park was opened by King George V and Queen Mary in 1923, on a site previously known as Southfields Park.

The park's most attractive area is the small section north of Mapleton Road, featuring colourful flowerbeds, mature trees and an ornamental lake fed by the Wandle. In this same area also is a scented rose garden designed originally for the blind and partially sighted and, near the northern entrance, a pets' corner with, amongst other animals, some rare sheep breeds. By contrast, the southern section of the park consists mostly of rather bleak-looking playing fields.

Lammas Park

Culmington Road, W13 *(25 acres)*

The park's name comes from the one-time use of the larger part of it as lammas lands – that is, land to which common grazing rights applied for part of the year starting on Lammas Day (1 August by the old calendar). The season for communal grazing lasted each year for eight months, while for the remaining months (April to August) the rights to the soil and grazing were limited to the land's owners.

These ancient lammas rights were bought out when the land was purchased in 1881, two years before the opening of Lammas Land as a public park.

Larkswood

Larkshall Road, E4 *(60 acres)*

The survival of this large area of woodland is the result of petitioning by a local committee in 1925. The land was formally opened to the public on 21 October 1933 with the declaration that it would thereafter be 'preserved in its natural state'.

Lavender Pond Ecological Park

Rotherhithe Street, SE16 *(2 acres)*

This is one of the city's new ecological parks, which was laid out on part of the former Lavender Dock and opened to the public in July 1982.

The site, which is managed by the Ecological Parks Trust, is used primarily for nature study and education, although the general public are also welcome to use the park as a place of relaxation. The site's focal point is a one-acre pond where children are encouraged to study such creatures as dragonflies, pond-snails, mayflies and water boatmen.

Schools are invited to contact the teacher in charge here to discuss the park's educational potential both for art and environmental studies (telephone 01-232 0498).

Limehouse Churchyard

Three Colt Street, E14 *(2 acres)*

The churchyard of St Anne, Limehouse, was opened as a public garden in 1887 as part of a move by the Metropolitan Public Gardens Association to acquire disused churchyards in central London as areas of recreation.

Lincoln's Inn Fields

WC2 *(7 acres)*

Under its old name of Ficetsfeld, or Ficket's Field, this apparently was originally common land, but in the seventeenth century this part was enclosed to provide what, at the time, was described as being one of the largest and finest squares in the world. It is still the largest in London, though in 1843 it was almost lost when Sir Charles Barry designed new Law Courts to be built here. By 1890, however, the move to reacquire the private square for public recreation had begun, and four years later the London County Council finally succeeded in purchasing the land –

having been prevented from so doing first by the House of Commons and later by the House of Lords.

Lincoln's Inn Fields was formally (re)opened to the public by Sir John Hutton, the then Chairman of the LCC, on 23 February 1895.

Littleheath Wood

Littleheath Road, South Croydon *(64 acres)*

The property which today goes by this name, and which was acquired for public use in 1932, consists of several woodland and farmland plots. The plot on the eastern side, around the large water tower, is Foxearth Wood which was originally an old hunting ground – hence the laurel and privet bushes planted as cover for the pheasants. The south-western corner with its three old ponds is the Gee Wood plot, reckoned to be an area of ancient woodland, whereas the woodland of the original 'Little Heath' to the north of this would appear from its nineteenth-century name to be of much more recent origin.

Lloyd Park

Coombe Road, Croydon *(114 acres)*

In July 1931 twenty-three acres of the present Lloyd Park – originally part of the Coombe House estate – were dedicated to the public in memory of Frank Lloyd, a local landowner and benefactor. The park is almost entirely rolling grassland with a narrow strip of lime and hawthorn along its northern boundary and a scattering of mature trees elsewhere – mostly lime, sycamore, horse chestnut and beech.

Lloyd Park

Winns Terrace, E17 *(36 acres)*

Named after the family of Frank Lloyd who donated the house and ornamental grounds (about ten acres) to the council for use as a public park in 1898. This gift was made on condition that a similar area of adjoining land be purchased then by the council for use as playing fields. Lloyd Park was opened to the public in 1900 and the garden for the blind – one of the first of its kind – was opened in 1957.

London Fields

Martello Street, E8 *(31 acres)*

Up until the last century this was part of Hackney's common lammas lands and as such was used as grazing for sheep and cattle. The fields have also long been a centre for entertainment. In July 1813 there was an amusing and novel contest of 'Extraordinary Pedestrianism' held on the common between a Thomas Dudley, aged seventy-four, who had 'acquired great celebrity in the sporting world by running on stilts', and a sailor who was 'equally noted for a short heat'. To the great amusement of the assembled crowd, the old man (who was given a fifty-yard start) won the 100-yard race in ten seconds.

By 1866, though, London Fields was being described as having become 'the run of the riff-raff and vagabonds', leading the Metropolitan Board of Works to take the land over as a public park in 1872.

Lyle Park

Bradfield Road, E16 *(5 acres)*

Lyle Park was the gift of the golden syrup manufacturers whose factory was first established nearby at Plaistow Wharf by Abram Lyle in 1881. Lyle Park was opened to the public in 1924.

Manor House Gardens

Manor Lane, SE12 *(9 acres)*

The attractive old Manor House, now used as a public library, dates from between 1770 and 1778. Both this and the adjoining park belonged to the Baring family from 1796 until the London County Council purchased the property from Sir Francis Baring (later Lord Northbrook) in 1901. The present gardens were formally opened as a public park on Whit Monday, 1902.

With its gently sloping grounds, ornamental lake and good variety of shrubs and trees, Manor House Gardens is one of the most attractive of London's smaller parks. Several of the trees date from the time when this was Sir Francis Baring's private garden and a number, for example the hop tree and white mulberry, are not commonly met with in London's parks. In the park's north-western corner are the remains of the old ice-house, the mound of which is formed from the earth excavated when the ornamental lake was first dug in around 1834.

Marble Hill Park

Richmond Road, Twickenham *(66 acres)*

Marble Hill House, which was built in the 1720s for Henrietta Howard, is a particularly attractive and well-preserved example of the Palladian style of architecture – that is, a style of architecture introduced by Andrea Palladio (1518–80).

The Palladian park which surrounds the house was originally laid out between 1719 and 1728 by Charles Bridgeman and Alexander Pope. Though much of the original detail has since been lost, the ice-house and at least one of the original trees – a magnificent ninety-two-foot black walnut – have survived, and the original grotto has just recently been excavated. Of the park's noted range of trees, horse chestnuts are still a dominant feature and several of the Lombardy poplars are among the tallest in Great Britain.

The park and house were both almost destroyed in 1900 following their purchase by William Cunard, a member of the shipping family. Building preparations were already underway when a preservation campaign finally succeeded in saving the property. The campaign, which was fought chiefly on the grounds that the destruction of the estate would detract from the famous and spectacular view from Richmond Hill, led eventually to the acquisition of both the park and house by the London County Council in July 1902.

Though the park is open every day of the week, Marble Hill House itself is closed to the public on Fridays. (Wheelchair-accessible toilets are adjacent to the house.)

Mayesbrook Park

Lodge Avenue, Dagenham *(104 acres)*

Named after Mayes brook, the eastern branch of which feeds the park's lake, while the western branch runs now mostly underground.

The park and playing fields were laid out as part of the development of the Becontree housing estate, after being presented by the London County Council to Barking Borough Council in 1934. The Italian-style sunken garden near the south-eastern corner was finally abandoned after repeated vandalism in 1978, though the grand concrete steps and walls remain. Today the park's most attractive features are the two lakes which cater for fishing and boating.

Mayow Park

Mayow Road, SE26 *(18 acres)*

The name comes from the previous owner of the land, Mr Mayow Wynell Adams, once officially regarded as the Squire of Sydenham. It was opened in 1877, making this Lewisham's second oldest public open space.

The park has an unusually good variety of trees, including tulip tree, western red cedar, dawn cypress, monkey puzzle and a grand cedar of Lebanon. In the flowerbeds at the eastern end are winter-flowering and tree heathers and, on the southern side of the park, an aviary which is popular with children.

Meanwhile Gardens

Elkstone Road, W10 *(3½ acres)*

First conceived by a young sculptor, Jamie McCullough, in 1976, Meanwhile Gardens is a successful attempt at creating a community park from a canalside strip of urban wasteland. With the help of donations from a wide range of community groups, private companies and public bodies, along with a good deal of vision and personal sacrifice, this strip of land has been laid out with a skateboard track, outdoor stage, pottery, fish pond and scented courtyard garden. Also provided here are an under-fives play hut and boat club (telephone 01-960 4600/8641).

Meath Gardens

Usk Street, E2 *(10½ acres)*

Back in the mid-1800s this land formed one of the city's private cemeteries, but by the end of that century maintenance here had deteriorated to such an extent that it had become 'a disgrace and a scandal . . . the resort of the loafers and roughs of the East End, who came here to gamble and amuse themselves by the wanton destruction of the decaying property.'

To remedy the situation the Metropolitan Public Gardens Association took over the grounds in 1891 and, with the help of substantial private donations, laid out the old burial ground as a public park. The grounds were duly opened in 1894 by the Duke of York and renamed in honour of the association's founder, the Earl of Meath.

Mile End Park

Grove Road, E3 *(60 acres)*

This new park was inspired by the wartime County of London Plan (1943), in which it was envisaged that a strip of open space could be created connecting Victoria Park along the eastern bank of the Regent's Canal to the river Thames. The park, which today provides a pleasant buffer from the traffic for those using the Regent's Canal towpath, is still gradually being developed as old houses are demolished. Incorporated within the park is King George's Field which was opened in 1952, and whose main feature is the East London Stadium.

Millfields (North and South)

Lea Bridge Road, E5 *(64 acres)*

The once-famous corn mills after which the fields are named were situated down by the Lea Bridge. In 1791, when these old mills were up for sale, they were recorded as being capable of grinding almost seventy-five tons of corn a week. Just five years later, though, the entire mills were destroyed by a fire thought to have been caused by a flour-weigher leaving a lighted candle between two sacks of meal.

Millfields themselves were lammas lands in the same way as London Fields, Hackney Downs, Hackney Marsh and Well Street Common, being subject to the same seasonal common grazing, lopping and soil rights. The former use of at least part of North Millfields and part of the adjoining land as brickfields resulted in some interesting archaeological finds, including the bones of a woolly-haired rhinoceros and even elephant bones. Following legal wrangles with the lord of the manor, the Metropolitan Board of Works eventually succeeded in extinguishing all brick earth rights to the land, enabling the board finally to confer protection to Millfields as a public open space in 1884.

Moat Mount Open Space

Barnet Way, NW7 *(217 acres)*

Although the acreage is large, most of this area is in use as farmland. Adjoining the farm, however, is a small but attractive stretch of public woodland known as Nut Wood, the entrance to which leads off Barnet

Way up to a quiet woodland pond.

Along with the 150-acre golf course across the road, this property once formed part of the Moat Mount estate which was put up for sale in 1930 and advertised then as 'ripe building land'. Fortunately, Hendon Council had the foresight to purchase the property for public recreation.

Local historians may be interested to know that during excavations at Moat Mount in 1769 and subsequently, evidence of Roman habitation was found in the form of coins and lamps of the period.

Morden Park

London Road, Morden *(98 acres)*

This is the grounds of a fine Georgian mansion, Morden Park House, former home of John Ewart and Edward Polhill, and subsequently – for a time – the headquarters of Merton Borough's Recreation and Arts Department. The park itself contains two ancient archaeological features: a stretch of the famous Roman road, Stane Street (now covered over), and, near the centre of the park, a native British pagan burial mound, thought to have been erected shortly after the Roman Conquest.

Mountsfield Park

Stainton Road, SE6 *(28 acres)*

The park is named after the Mountsfield mansion, once owned by Henry Stainton, an eminent nineteenth-century entomologist whose name is commemorated by the eastern boundary road. Most of the original house was demolished when the park was being laid out, though the former stables, library and billiard room survived to form the present park offices and café.

When originally opened by the London County Council in 1905 the grounds covered only six acres and it was not until 1925 that the park reached its present size.

In the north-eastern corner there is a number of interesting and attractive trees including the New Zealand kowhai, tulip tree, Kentucky coffee tree and balsam poplar. Though the park's highest point is considerably lower than that of Hilly Fields, there are excellent views out to the west which take in the Telecom and Crystal Palace towers.

Myatt's Fields

Knatchbull Road, SE5 *(12½ acres)*

Some of the finest strawberries in London were grown here in the early nineteenth century by a market gardener named Myatt, whose name at one time was well known all over London and which lives on in an improved strain of spring cabbage – 'Myatt's Offenham compacta'.

The present park, which is all that now remains of the original estate, was donated to the public for use as a garden by William Minet and was laid out by the Metropolitan Public Gardens Association with the help of a grant from the Lord Mayor of London's fund for the unemployed.

Myatt's Fields was duly opened to the public in May 1889. Interestingly, the bandstand which was originally built here in 1894 still survives in good condition.

New River Walk

Canonbury Grove, N1 *(4½ acres)*

Opened in 1954, New River Walk is named after the artificial watercourse whose banks it follows. The old name has survived, in spite of the fact that the original canal was constructed by Sir Hugh Myddelton back in the early seventeenth century to supply water to London from springs in Amwell and Chadwell in Hertfordshire.

A large part of the rockeries and waterfalls for the walk were constructed from Westmoreland stone and, when steel was short, old Belisha beacon poles were used as piping for circulating water through the pumping system to the waterfalls.

Norbury Park

Craignish Avenue, SW16 *(8½ acres)*

The grounds of a locally listed building, Norbury Hall, this park is today a virtual arboretum, with over 700 trees, including many fine old cedars and a swamp cypress. The mansion itself – the one-time home of the Hobbs family (including a Mayor of Croydon) – was rebuilt within the established parkland setting in 1804 and acquired along with the grounds by the local borough in 1956. Norbury Hall was turned then into an old people's home, with most of its remaining grounds being thrown open as a public park. In its days of private ownership the major features of the grounds were its bog garden and lake, the latter being opened during cold weather for public skating in aid of charity, with many visitors arriving via Norbury station from as far away as central London. Though both the lake and bog garden have sadly since had to be sacrificed to management expediency, many of the estate's old garden walls do still survive, as does a Victorian gazebo and the former coach house.

Norwood Park

Salter's Hill, SE19 *(33 acres)*

The park's name derives from the fact that this was at one time a part of North Wood, a large common which once extended to between 1300 and 1400 acres. North Wood was not entirely cut down until the end of the eighteenth century, but by 1903 the site of the present park was the only land of any size left undeveloped. This was purchased from the Ecclesiastical Commissioners by the London County Council in 1909 and opened as a public park two years later.

The park today is largely open grassland on a north- and west-facing hill, with a fairly good variety of trees and, near the top of the hill, a children's paddling pool which proves immensely popular during hot summers.

The Oaks Park

Woodmansterne Road, Carshalton *(74 acres)*

The park's name comes from a nearby grove of large oaks, known as 'Lambert's Oaks' after its owners, an old Banstead land-owning family. The Oaks had been the home of the founder of the Derby races, the twelfth Lord Derby, and was the name given to the first of this type of short race for younger horses held at nearby Epsom.

Legend has it that the present name for the Derby race came about through a discussion between Sir Charles Bunbury and Lord Derby in which they elected to toss a coin to decide after which of them the new race should be named. If there is truth to the story, the resulting toss apparently decided in Lord Derby's favour, against the race being christened the Bunbury Stakes.

The original mansion, which contained items designed by Robert Adam, was purchased by Surrey County Council in the 1930s and sold to Carshalton UDC, who demolished it in the late 1950s. The original grotto and stable block, however, still survive and were listed in 1981, while set among the trees is a modern café.

Among the park's trees are many fine specimens, and the woodland areas are particularly noted for their spring flowers.

Oakwood Park

Oakwood Park Road, N14 *(64 acres)*

Originally part of Enfield Chase, the park's name derives from a converted nineteenth-century farmhouse known as Oak Lodge. Samuel Sugden, who had lived in the lodge since its conversion, died in 1905 leaving his estate in the hands of trustees, and it was from them in 1927–8 that Southgate Council bought the first fifty acres of the present park.

One Tree Hill

Honor Oak Park, SE23 *(15 acres)*

Also known as Honor Oak Hill, this stretch of woodland rises to some 300 feet above the Thames, offering extensive views across the city. Both names refer to an oak (long since dead) which once served as a boundary marker between the parishes of Camberwell (in Surrey) and Lewisham (in Kent).

At the beginning of last century the summit was the site of a semaphore-like station used by the East India Company to signal the appearance of their ships in the Channel and later requisitioned by the Admiralty at the time of Napoleon Bonaparte's threatened invasion of England.

In 1896 the historic hill was enclosed with a six-foot fence by the local golf club, thereby blocking at least five traditional public rights of way – an act which was to lead to considerable protest. In fact, by the following year local indignation had grown to such an extent that on 10 October a crowd of 15,000 protesters gathered on the hill to assert their rights collectively by breaking down the new fence. The following week, the crowd returned to the hill – this time numbering between 50,000 and 100,000 – and were confronted in a rather tense scene by a contingent of some 500 police who had been called in to restrain them. This local sense of injustice simmered on until 1904 when finally the borough council ended the eight-year-old dispute by buying the wooded hill and declaring it freely open to the public 'for ever'.

Paddington Recreation Ground

Randolph Avenue, W9 *(27 acres)*

Only one small hedged area of this serves as a garden, but Paddington Recreation Ground is notable none the less as being the earliest public athletic ground of its kind in London. It was formed by a body of public-spirited local residents, including Lord Randolph Churchill (father of Sir Winston Churchill), who together raised the funds for the land's purchase and laying out. The ground was opened in 1888, its cycle track being subsequently used for a race of the first bicycles ever to be fitted with Dunlop pneumatic tyres.

Parsloes Park

Gale Street, Dagenham *(147 acres)*

The park's name comes from its one-time owners, the Passelewe family, who held land in Dagenham as far back as 1250. In 1901, the Essex Amateur Trotting Club opened a trotting track in the park which was in use up until about 1923, when the manor house and grounds were acquired by the London County Council. Unfortunately, soon after this – in 1925 – the old manor house had to be demolished due to its bad condition, but the park itself was opened to the public ten years later as part of a ceremony marking the completion of the council's new Becontree housing estate. Ownership passed to Barking and Dagenham in 1980.

Of Parsloes Park's total acreage, only thirty-two acres are enclosed, the remainder being flat, open grassland serving as playing fields. This 'inner park' is attractively laid out with an avenue of flowering cherry trees and, around the lake, an excellent use of shrubs including gorse, broom and roses.

Parson's Green

Parson's Green Lane, SW6 *(3 acres)*

As common waste land of the Manor of Fulham, this village green was named after the parsonage or rectory house which, until 1882, stood about midway along the western side of the green.

Before its acquisition by the Metropolitan Board of Works in 1881, Parson's Green was used as a bowling green and as the site of a once popular annual fair founded here in around 1600; like many similar fairs elsewhere, it was suppressed as illegal by the magistrates in the early nineteenth century.

Perivale Park

Hicks Avenue, Greenford *(109 acres)*

Perivale Park was owned by the Ecclesiastical Commissioners and used by the Perivale Park Golf Club, but when, in 1934, the land was threatened with building development, Ealing Town Council (with help from Middlesex) bought the land in order to preserve it as an open space.

Today, the northern half of the park serves as playing fields with tennis courts and a putting course, while the southern end, bordering the river Brent, has remained a golf course. The whole park now forms an integral part of the 850-acre Brent River Park.

Petersham Common

Star and Garter Hill, Richmond *(17 acres)*

Blending to the north into Terrace Gardens and overlooking the Thames to the west, this fine oak woodland was saved in 1902 as part of a move to preserve the famous landscape view from Richmond Hill. The Lord of the Manor, Lord Dysart, had, by means of a Private Member's Bill, been attempting to acquire the right to enclose and build over a large part of the local lammas land in exchange for a gift to the relevant councils of Petersham and Ham Commons, and Petersham Meadow. It was, in fact, a private Inclosure Bill, cunningly introduced under the innocent title of the Petersham and Ham Lands and Footpaths Bill (1896), but fortunately it was heavily defeated in Parliament, largely through the influence of the Commons Preservation Society. As a result of this, the commons and lammas lands along the Thames riverbank (along with the Marble Hill estate) were all subsequently protected under one Act of Parliament – the Richmond Hill, Petersham, and Ham Act (1902) – in what is believed to have been the first statute to permit the purchase of land by a local authority to preserve a landscape view.

Pitshanger Park

Meadvale Road, W5 *(53 acres)*

This park's intriguing name derives from two Old English words, *pyttel* and *hangra,* meaning respectively 'hawk' and 'wooded slope', hence 'wooded slope frequented by hawks'. Pitshanger Park was acquired in two stages, the first part east of Bellevue Road in 1905 and the western end including Scotch Common in 1913. In the eighteenth century this common (previously known as Empscroft Wood) was to become the last significant area of woodland in central Ealing to be destroyed.

Apart from its sports facilities, Pitshanger Park offers the opportunity for a pleasant walk along the banks of the Brent river and now forms part of the interesting and new 850-acre Brent River Park.

Plashet Park

Shrewsbury Road, E7 *(18 acres)*

Although the name comes from the fourteenth-century Plashet estate, the park itself does not form part of this. It was, in fact, formerly the grounds of Wood House which the Vicar of East Ham and J.H. Bethell (to whom East Ham owes many of its parks) acquired for use as a public park in 1889. A reminder of this late eighteenth-century weather-boarded house (which once stood just west of the High Street) is the street name on the park's eastern side – Woodhouse Grove.

Plashet Park was opened to the public in 1891.

Priory Gardens

Church Hill, Orpington *(14 acres)*

The land where the Priory now stands was given to the Priory of Christchurch, Canterbury, by Badsy on entering the priesthood in 1032 as a gift 'for the good of his soul'. The Priory building itself was originally a typical early thirteenth-century manor house, with major extensions made in the late fourteenth, fifteenth and sixteenth centuries, and is considered to be one of the few pre-Reformation rectories to have survived to the present day. Today the building serves as a museum, with a modern extension at the southern end serving as a public library.

The property was first purchased in 1947 but because of a lack of funds it was not until 1960 that laying-out work began. It was then that the park's present eighteenth-century wrought-iron gates were brought here from the High Elms Estate and installed at the High Street/Court Road entrance. Priory Gardens was formally opened to the public in May 1962.

Priory Park

Middle Lane, N8 *(16 acres)*

Originally, when the park was bought in 1891 and 1892, it was known as Middle Lane Pleasure Grounds and covered only eight acres. The low land was first used as a shoot for rubble and was said to have more than paid for itself by 1900 through this use alone, by which time most of the grounds had been permanently laid out. Today the park contains ornamental gardens, bowling green and tennis courts.

Purley Beeches

Beech Avenue, South Croydon *(18 acres)*

This is a mostly wooded area with access from both Purley Oaks Road and Beech Avenue with, as its name suggests, a good number of mature beech trees. In 1823 it was known as Purley Common and in 1860 as Purley Downs – Purley meaning 'a wood with or near pear trees'.

Purley Beeches was saved as a beauty spot through money raised by public subscription and the Sanderstead Parish Council in 1907.

Pymmes Park

Silver Street, N18 *(53 acres)*

Originally known as Pymmes Farm, the land was owned in the sixteenth century by Lord Burghley and later by Robert Cecil, Earl of Salisbury. In the 1870s the Nabob Nazim of Bengal lived here, having apparently been obliged to leave India because he had aroused 'the displeasure of the British Government'.

Initially the land for the park (or at least thirty-three acres of it) was leased only, but this part was opened to the public in 1897. Then, as part of the celebrations for Queen Victoria's Diamond Jubilee, funds for the park's purchase were raised partly through public donations, and Pymmes Park as we know it today was opened to the public on 16 June 1906. The house itself burned down in 1940.

The Queen's Gardens

Katharine Street, Croydon *(2 acres)*

In part, these are the original Town Hall Gardens, laid out on the site of the former Central Croydon railway station in 1894–5, but to which access was at that time permitted only at the discretion of the mayor.

The present gardens, having undergone considerable change, were opened by Her Majesty Queen Elizabeth II on 21 June 1983.

Queen's Park

Harvist Road, NW6 *(30 acres)*

The land for this park was offered along with Highgate Wood to the Corporation of the City of London as a gift by the Ecclesiastical Commissioners 'for preservation as open spaces for ever' in 1885. Though quite content to accept the gift of Highgate Wood, the corporation was, because of the anticipated maintenance costs, not so keen to take on Queen's Park. Fortunately for Kilburn, though, the Commissioners insisted that it was both or nothing.

The corporation's income for open space preservation was at that time very limited (consisting solely of a tax of three-sixteenths of a penny on every hundredweight of grain imported for sale into the Port of London). However, the park's acquisition was finally made possible through the generous bequest of a William Ward of a sum of money 'for the creation of some fund for the benefit of the poorer classes'.

On the opening day there were fears of a 'probable invasion of Kilburn by the cream of London ruffianism' but, according to a contemporary account, the 'great majority of the vast crowd [several thousands] was composed evidently of the respectable class'. Queen's Park was formally opened by the Lord Mayor 'for the free use and enjoyment of the public for ever' and named in honour of Queen Victoria's golden jubilee in 1887.

Radnor Gardens

Cross Deep, Twickenham *(5 acres)*

Named after John Robartes, 4th Earl of Radnor (1686–1757), who built his house here, probably in the 1720s, connecting part of his garden with the Thames by a tunnel under the road. His apparently excessive love of statues and the other embellishments with which he filled the garden led one of his neighbours, Alexander Pope, to write: 'My Lord Radnor's baby houses lay eggs every day and promise new swarms.'

Radnor House was destroyed by a bomb in 1940, though the small summerhouse facing the river has survived.

Richmond Green

Greenside, Richmond *(11 acres)*

Situated at the heart of Richmond, this stretch of grass was, in Tudor and Stuart times, the site for royal tournaments, joustings and pageants. For at least the last three centuries the green has been used also for cricket – a fact celebrated in the name of the adjacent Cricketers public house, whose sign depicts a nineteenth-century match in progress here.

Riddlesdown

Riddlesdown Road, Purley *(100 acres)*

This strip of grass and woodland runs along a steep south-west-facing slope of the North Downs. It was purchased, along with the other Coulsdon Commons, by the Corporation of the City of London in 1883 in order to resolve a legal dispute over common rights with the Lord of the Manor, Squire Byron. A thirty-seven-acre extension was later made by Croydon Borough Council in 1937, though the best part (twenty-five acres) of this is presently under lease to a tenant farmer.

Along the ridge of the down runs a track which once formed part of the old London to Brighton road, thought to be of Roman origin. There have also been an abundance of Neolithic finds including flint scrapers, flakes and cores, and evidence too (just north of the café) of ancient earthworks.

In more recent years the down has been declared by the Nature Conservancy Council to be a Site of Special Scientific Interest (SSSI).

Roding Valley Linear Park

Roding Lane South, Ilford *(209 acres)*

This is a continuous strip of open spaces running north from Redbridge underground station, through the Borough of Redbridge, following the M11 motorway and Roding river valley, out to the edge of Greater London. The park provides riverside walks and bridleways, with some sports facilities and landscaped areas.

Roundshaw Park

Foresters Drive, Wallington *(106 acres)*

The original Roundshaw Park – just a small plot of land on the Foresters/Mollison Drive corner – was purchased in 1928. Only recently has the name been used to refer to the development of a much larger park, stretching from here to Purley Way across the site of the historic Croydon Aerodrome.

Often described as the 'cradle of British civil aviation', and at one time London's only international airport, Croydon Aerodrome was first used for national purposes in 1915 and finally closed down in 1959.

The park itself offers an attractive vantage point for views towards the skyscrapers of central Croydon.

Roundwood Park

Longstone Avenue, NW10 *(35 acres)*

Once a part of the grounds of Roundwood House belonging to the Furness family, Roundwood Park was purchased with the help of private donations and formally opened to the public in May 1895. Five miles of drainage and two miles of paths had first to be laid and 14,500 trees planted as part of the transformation which was described at the time as being from 'a kind of Dartmoor, without the granite' to a 'veritable Garden of Eden, without the serpent'. The opening speeches were devoted largely to emphasizing that the park was now permanently protected from development – even when all 'the beautiful green fields' they could see around them had been built over.

Royal Hospital South Grounds

Royal Hospital Road, SW3 *(6 acres)*

Since 1913, this has been the venue for the Royal Horticultural Society's famous annual Chelsea Flower Show, though the grounds' horticultural history in fact dates back much further – to 1687, when work on the gardens for the new military hospital began.

In Wren's original design, these grounds were laid out in grand and formal style with an eighty-foot-long elevated causeway flanked by formal canals and avenues. Sadly, though, hardly a trace of this early elegance and grandeur survives today.

Burton's Court to the north and Ranelagh Gardens to the east were part of these historic grounds, the former being later cut off by the laying of the Royal Hospital Road and the latter subsequently developed by the Earl of Ranelagh as private pleasure gardens. These pleasure gardens were at one time a favourite resort of the fashionable world, and enjoyed a popularity which, between 1742 and 1803, is said to have rivalled that of the famous pleasure gardens at Vauxhall.

Royal Victoria Gardens

Pier Road, E16 *(10 acres)*

This is the site of the once famous North Woolwich private pleasure gardens which were opened here in 1851, and which were in their day as popular as those at Vauxhall and Cremorne. At the height of their popularity, North Woolwich Gardens attracted large crowds who came to drink and dance until the early hours of the morning, to visit the small permanent menagerie or to see the occasional 'barmaid' and 'monster baby' shows.

Towards the end of the 1880s the gardens were acquiring an undesirable reputation – which was doubtless not helped when the manager, William Holland, took off from here in a balloon to escape (as he said) 'the unpleasant attentions of a process-server'.

Local landowners pressed to have the gardens' dancing and drinking licence rescinded and a committee was then formed to purchase the gardens as a public park. The Royal Victoria Gardens were finally opened as such in 1890.

Russell Square

WC1 *(6 acres)*

Part of the Bloomsbury estate of the Russell family, Dukes of Bedford, this large square was laid out at the beginning of the nineteenth century after the fourth Duke began to develop the family property. (A statue of the fourth Duke is to be found on the south side of the square.) The Russell family moved to Bloomsbury originally in 1700, having acquired the manor through the marriage of Lord William Russell to the heiress.

Russia Dock Woodland

Redriff Road, SE16 *(35 acres)*

Part of the new Surrey Commercial Docks redevelopment, Russia Dock Woodland is a long, thin strip of parkland stretching from Redriff Road at the southern end to Salter Road to the north. Part of the new park has been built over the old Russia Dock, once the property of the Baltic Dock Company which traded in timber and pitch here from 1809.

Since 1980, over 1000 trees both deciduous and evergreen have been planted and several ponds created as part of a programme to encourage wildlife. At the northern end, a short fitness trail and some rustic play equipment have also been provided.

St Chad's Park

Park Lane, Romford *(35 acres)*

St Chad's is Barking and Dagenham's oldest park, originating in 1831 when four acres of ancient heathland were given by the Crown as allotments for the poor. Further additions were made in 1866, when the heath was enclosed, and again in 1928 with the purchase of Blackbush Farm.

St George's Garden

Handel Street, WC1 *(2 acres)*

Once known as Nelson's Burying Ground after the first person to be buried here, the famous religious writer Robert Nelson (1665–1715). Garden paths wend their way between trees and shrubs to a rockery and scented garden for the blind, passing several of the historic memorials which have been retained in the garden's new design.

Among others buried here are Zachary Macaulay (1768–1838), one of the founders of the Clapham Sect, which was responsible for the abolition of slave-trading within the former British Empire.

St John's Wood Church Grounds

Wellington Road, NW8 *(5 acres)*

Until its opening as a public garden in 1886, this was the burial ground of the neighbouring St John's Wood Parish Church. It is today perhaps Westminster's most attractive public park, with extensive shrubberies, mature London planes, a striking specimen of weeping ash and memorials to a host of famous people, including Joanna Southcott, the prophetess, and John Sell Cotman, one of the great topographical artists of the Norwich School.

St Luke's Garden

Sydney Street, SW3 *(3 acres)*

This was the churchyard of St Luke's, the parish church of Chelsea, until the disused burial ground was opened as a public garden in 1887. During the Second World War, as in a number of other London parks and gardens, the flowerbeds here temporarily disappeared when council gardeners used the grounds to grow vegetables.

St Pancras Gardens

Pancras Road, NW1 *(5½ acres)*

The name of the Norman church of old St Pancras comes from a Christian martyr in Rome at the time of Diocletian. It is from this St Pancras churchyard and burial ground of St Giles-in-the-Fields that the present public gardens were formed in 1877. The memorial stones include those of Sir John Soane (architect of the original Bank of England) and Johann Christian Bach (also known as the 'English Bach', the youngest son of Johann Sebastian Bach).

St Paul's Cray Common

St Paul's Cray Road, Chislehurst *(72 acres)*

The common forms a mile-long woodland strip practically surrounded by other woodland and farms – a fact which encourages breeding birds and increases the likelihood of seeing unusual vagrant birds. The great spotted woodpecker breeds here and possibly the green and lesser spotted too, along with the tawny owl, turtle dove and stock dove. Kestrels are seen quite often and woodcocks, reed warblers and reed buntings have all been known to visit the common.

Over the past century or more, the vegetation has changed quite markedly from what was once predominantly an open habitat of gorse and heather. One of the reasons for this transformation was the serious fire that the common suffered in 1870, which burned for a whole fortnight and completely destroyed the existing vegetation. Birch seedlings soon flourished, however, in the potash-enriched soil and these have since largely given way to oak, beech and other trees, along with some interesting flowering plants such as alder buckthorn and butcher's broom.

Of particular historical interest at the very northern tip of the common is the site of the old village stocks and cage once used for punishing local criminals.

St Paul's Cray Common was protected in 1888 for public recreation by the same Act of Parliament as Chislehurst Common, in which the present form of management by a Board of Conservators was constituted.

Sanderstead Plantation

Addington Road, South Croydon *(22 acres)*

The name Sanderstead means simply 'sandy place' – a reference to the soil of the area. Sanderstead Plantation is entirely wooded – predominantly with beech, but also with oak, horse chestnut, sycamore and sweet chestnut. In May the wood is particularly noted for its bluebells, especially after coppicing. A mound by a bend in the footpath at the western end marks the site of an old reservoir demolished here in 1969.

Access to the woodland is from both Addington Road and from a footpath by 61 Church Way.

Scratchwood Open Space

Barnet Way, NW7 *(183 acres)*

Most people know Scratchwood as being the name of the first service station on the M1 motorway, though few would suspect the existence of the ancient oak and hornbeam wood nearby after which it is named.

Just under a quarter of the total area of the property is Scratch Wood proper, the rest being divided into a site for the flying of model aircraft, and a motorists' picnic site.

In 1923, when this land still formed part of the Moat Mount estate, it was up for sale and advertised as 'a most choice Building Proposition being some 400ft above Sea Level, with a South-East slope. Magnificent Views are obtained over the surrounding country for many miles.' Fortunately for us, the local council was awake to the opportunity and Scratch Wood, with its adjoining land, was purchased for protection as part of what was to become known as the green belt. That this land should have been saved from building development is particularly fortunate, since Scratch Wood itself is one of the few remaining portions of the ancient Forest of Middlesex and as such has an ancestry which can be traced right back to the last Ice Age.

Shepherd's Bush Common

Shepherd's Bush Green, W12 *(8 acres)*

This was the old village green of Shepherd's Bush and is the place where

Miles Syndercombe planned to assassinate Oliver Cromwell as he passed by on his way to Hampton Court in January 1657. Before Syndercombe managed to complete the deed, however, one of his accomplices betrayed his plans and Syndercombe was sentenced to 'be hanged on a gallows until he be half dead, and then cut down, and his entrails and bowels taken out and burnt in his face or sight, and his body divided into four quarters, and be disposed of as his Highness shall think fit.'

Shoulder-of-Mutton Green

Bellegrove Road, Welling *(4 acres)*

This was the old village green of Wickham parish and was purchased in 1877 by the Metropolitan Board of Works along with Plumstead Common, following a bitter struggle between the commoners and Queen's College, Oxford, who had been continuously selling off parts of the common as building land. At the height of these struggles, in 1876, there was a meeting of 30,000 people on Plumstead Common burning effigies of their adversaries, in celebration of the release from prison of their campaigner, John de Morgan.

The green's name refers to its irregular shape.

Shrewsbury Park

Plum Lane, SE18 *(33 acres)*

This park is situated near the top of a steep rise just south of Plumstead Common. At 345 feet above sea level, it offers fine views out over the Thames and Plumstead marshes and eastward towards Bostall Woods. Shrewsbury Park itself is mostly oak and silver birch woodland with pleasantly sheltered grassy areas, picnic benches and a refreshment kiosk.

The park once formed part of the grounds of Shrewsbury House in Bushmoor Crescent. Its most distinguished occupier was Frederick Winsor, who built the first gasholder here in order to light the rooms of his house. Winsor's original house, which became famous for its rooms flooded with a remarkable light that neither flickered nor grew dim, was demolished in 1923 and Shrewsbury Park itself was purchased for public use, by the London County Council, in 1928.

Sidcup Place

Chislehurst Road, Sidcup *(37 acres)*

Sidcup Place is thought to have been built in 1743 and was constructed originally in the shape of a 'star fort with angle bastions' – a fact which accounts for the peculiar shape of the south-western part of the present building.

The house was twice used as a school before it and the surrounding estate were sold to a building developer in 1933. Sidcup and Chislehurst Urban District Councils, however, quickly persuaded the builder to resell and on 19 May 1934 the grounds were opened to the public as a park.

Many features of the original estate have survived, notably the ha-ha ditch constructed to keep animals from the house without obstructing the view across the Cray valley.

South Norwood Lake and Grounds

Avenue Road, SE25 *(28 acres)*

The park's main attraction is its seven-acre lake which is used for fishing and by the Croydon Sailing Club. This 14½-million-gallon reservoir, which now forms Croydon's only large expanse of open water, was originally constructed for feeding six locks on the old Croydon Canal which once connected Croydon with the Thames. The canal, which carried coal and other goods from London with boats returning to the City carrying agricultural produce, timber and lime, was opened in 1809. With the advent of the railways, however, much of the old canal bed was taken over for the laying of the new railway track – West Croydon station being built on the canal basin.

Spring Park

Woodland Way, West Wickham *(51 acres)*

Although situated in the London Borough of Bromley, eleven miles from the City, Spring Park has remained in the care of the Corporation of the City of London, to whom about thirty-five acres of woodland were donated by Colonel Sir Henry Lennard in 1924. A subsequent purchase of more open land extended the park to Addington Road in 1927.

Stanmore Country Park

Dennis Lane, Stanmore *(78 acres)*

This is part of the former estate attached to the Jacobean-style Warren House, once owned by Sir Robert Smirke, architect of the British Museum. The land for the park was acquired in 1940 by the Middlesex County Council as part of its green belt policy.

The park's chief attraction today lies in its proximity to Stanmore underground station (access via Kerry Avenue), for it has not yet been developed for its eventual purpose as a country park. The land is rough and undulating, with many patches of gorse and hawthorn, amid mature and regenerating oaks, patches of birch and a few beech, with an area of adjoining farmland rising to 475 feet above sea level and offering unobstructed views south over London.

Stepney Churchyard

Stepney High Street, E1 *(7½ acres)*

This was the disused churchyard of St Dunstan, the parish church of Stepney, when it was acquired in the late nineteenth century by the Metropolitan Public Gardens Association. It was laid out by them as a garden and opened by the Duchess of Leeds on 18 July 1887.

Stoke Newington Common

N16 *(5 acres)*

This flat area of grass, divided in two by a railway cutting and surrounded by large plane trees, has changed a good deal in size, shape and appearance over the centuries. Its present appeal is a far cry from its more rural days when it is said that this was a good spot for hearing cuckoos and nightingales. But perhaps the greatest change to come about here was through the passing in 1864 of the Metropolitan Station and Railways Act. This Act gave the go-ahead for the Great Eastern Railway Company to lay its line across the common on condition either that the line was covered over or that the company gave to the lord of the manor an equal area of adjoining land. Presumably the cheaper option was to buy more land, for in 1873, in exchange for the strip taken for the laying of the new railway, Stoke Newington Common was extended to the south-west.

Sutcliffe Park

Kidbrooke Park Road, SE23 *(52 acres)*

Sutcliffe Park was largely reclaimed from an area of swamp land known as Harrow Meadow. The park was formally dedicated 'to the public use for ever' in May 1937 and named in memory of the Woolwich Borough Engineer, Mr J. Sutcliffe, who had directed the laying-out of the park, but who died before its completion.

Sydenham Wells Park

Wells Park Road, SE26 *(19 acres)*

The park's name derives from the once famous medicinal wells discovered here in the seventeenth century. The healing waters were then variously described as performing 'great cures in scrofulous, scorbutic, paralytic and other stubborn diseases' or as being 'a certain cure for every ill to which humanity is heir'. The precise site of the original wells has not been established, though two of them are known to have been covered over by the church of St Philip the Apostle.

Sydenham Wells Park consists of attractively undulating grassland, beautifully planted with a good variety of trees and shrubs. The stream and lake have a wide range of waterfowl, the most notable of which must surely be the pink Chilean flamingos. As a walking route, the park provides an attractive link between Sydenham Hill Wood and Crystal Palace Park.

The Tarn

Court Road, SE9 *(10½ acres)*

This was part of the Royal Manor of Eltham, granted by King Charles II in 1660 to Sir John Shaw, in whose family it remained until 1830. The Tarn was purchased by Woolwich Borough Council in 1935 and opened as a public park after extensive landscaping and restoration work.

The Tarn's main features are its bird sanctuary and lake – once known as the Long Pond, earlier still as Starbucks Pond. In fact, the park's name comes from the Old Norse word for a small lake – *tjorn* – though since the use of this term was historically confined to the north of England, the name is thought to have been applied here only in modern times.

Telegraph Hill Park

Kitto Road, SE14 *(10½ acres)*

The park's name comes from an old semaphore-like signalling station which once stood on the site of the present tennis courts. This signalling device was one of a series of such stations which connected the Admiralty via West Square, Kennington, Telegraph Hill, Shooter's Hill and so on through to Deal, and which made possible the signalling to London of Wellington's victory at Waterloo in 1815. The station consisted of a small wooden hut with six shutters mounted on top within two frames; by opening and closing different combinations of these it was possible to send sixty-three different signals.

The present park, which consists of two separate plots, was opened to the public on 6 April 1895. The larger plot to the north of Kitto Road includes a willow-banked pond, while the southern plot (the site of the old telegraph station) includes an area of flower gardens.

Ten Acre Wood

off Charville Lane, Hayes *(10 acres)*

This square of oak woodland by Westways Farm is maintained by the London Wildlife Trust as a nature reserve. A guide to the numbered nature trail is available from Hillingdon Public Libraries.

Terrace Gardens

Richmond Hill, Richmond *(10 acres)*

Terrace Gardens, on the slopes of Richmond Hill, is best known for its famous view out over the Thames and six counties, from Windsor to the North Downs. The present gardens have been created from three private estates – those of Lansdowne House, Cardigan House and Buccleuch House – together now forming a strip of lawns, flowerbeds, flowering shrubs and trees that connect via Terrace Field and Petersham Common to Richmond Park.

The gardens were opened to the public on 23 May 1887.

Thamesmead Parks

Thamesmead *(182 acres total)*

This is the collective name of a network of largely interlinked parks forming part of the new Thamesmead housing development, situated between Woolwich and Erith.

In 1967, on what had largely been marshland lying below the Thames high-water level, the Greater London Council began the new development which by 1992 is expected to provide homes for more than 40,000 people.

The major parks here are Southmere Park (41 acres), containing the first and largest of the Thamesmead lakes, complete with its own sailing centre; Birchmere Park (38 acres), whose lake is particularly popular with anglers and windsurfers; and Woodland Way (43 acres).

Tower Hamlets Cemetery

Southern Grove, E3 *(28 acres)*

This disused cemetery functions today as a combined park and wilderness area for wildlife. It was originally established as a cemetery in 1841 and was to become the most working-class of London's early Victorian burial grounds. As a cemetery it became increasingly unprofitable during the mid-1900s until it was finally closed for burials in November 1965 and taken over for use as a public park by the Greater London Council the following year.

Town Park

Cecil Road, Enfield *(23 acres)*

Purchased for the public in 1903, Enfield Town Park originally formed the grounds of Chase Side House which once stood on the site of the present library in Cecil Road. The river which borders the park's western side is the so-called 'New River', dug between 1609 and 1613 to bring clean water into London from springs at Amwell.

Tradescant Garden

Lambeth Palace Road, SE1 *(½ acre)*

This tiny garden is part of the newly-founded Museum of Garden History, housed in the adjacent church of St Mary-at-Lambeth. The museum, which is the first of its kind in the world, was inspired by the fact that the two famous seventeenth-century plant collectors and royal gardeners, John Tradescant (father and son), were both buried here. Following the closure of the church in 1972, the historic landmark would otherwise have been destined for demolition.

The garden itself was designed by the Marchioness of Salisbury, using only those plants known to have been grown by the Tradescants in their famous garden at Lambeth, and was formally opened to the public by Her Majesty Queen Elizabeth the Queen Mother in May 1983.

Apart from establishing the garden, the Tradescant Trust's aims are to conserve plants and to hold exhibitions and lectures related to gardening. There is also a gift shop and tea and coffee are available. Opening hours for the museum and garden are 11.00 a.m.–3.00 p.m. Monday to Friday, 10.30 a.m.–5.00 p.m. on Sunday; closed during the winter months. (For further details, telephone 01-261 1891 between 11.00 a.m. and 3.00 p.m., otherwise 01-373 4030 before 9 a.m.)

Tylers Common

Nags Head Lane, Upminster *(69 acres)*

The name of this piece of ancient common land refers to the earth here which was particularly suitable for the manufacture of tiles and bricks.

It is one of the many anomalies of parks ownership that, although the common is situated well inside the Greater London boundary and maintained by the London Borough of Havering, it is in fact owned by Essex County Council.

Valence Park

Becontree Avenue, Dagenham *(28 acres)*

This park contains the only remaining manor house of Dagenham – now the Valence House Museum and Gallery – along with part of its original moat and gardens. The centre of the park is occupied by the offices, workshops and stores of the council Building Works Department. The London County Council purchased the whole manor in 1921 and sold the park and house to Dagenham Council in 1926.

Vauxhall Park

Fentiman Road, SW8 *(8 acres)*

John Cobeldick bought this land in the late 1880s with the purpose of property speculation, but the Kyrle Society successfully persuaded him the following year to sell the site instead to the Metropolitan Board of Works for the creation of a new public park. Vauxhall Park was finally opened by the Prince of Wales on 7 July 1890.

Victoria Embankment Gardens

Villiers Street, WC2 *(11 acres)*

These gardens were laid out on land reclaimed from the Thames following the building of the Victoria Embankment in the late 1860s. Though the idea to build the embankment appears to have originated with Sir Christopher Wren as part of redevelopment plans following the Great Fire of London in 1666, it was not until 1864 that work finally began under the Metropolitan Board of Works.

Across the road from the gardens, by the riverbank, is the famous Cleopatra's Needle – an ancient monolith from Egypt, dedicated originally to the sun god by the Pharaoh Thothmes III in about 1500 BC. The story of its life over the past 3500 years is well described in inscriptions at its base.

Victoria Tower Gardens

Millbank, SW1 *(5½ acres)*

On the upstream side of the Houses of Parliament are the Victoria Tower Gardens, which were laid out here between 1912 and 1913. Up until the Second World War, these gardens were overlooked by shabby terraced houses, since replaced by Abingdon Street Gardens which itself contains an interesting ancient Jewel Tower, built in 1365–6 as a treasury for Edward III. Both gardens are now administered by the Department of the Environment.

Walpole Park

Mattock Lane, W5 *(30 acres)*

The Walpole family had lived in the area for nearly one hundred years, this land having been owned by them for nearly sixty years. The park was purchased from Sir Spencer Walpole in 1899–1900 and opened on May Day 1901 for 'the public use and convenience of the people of Ealing for ever' by Lord George Hamilton, the then Secretary of State for India.

Wandle Park

Baltic Close, SW19 *(9½ acres)*

Two acres of this are owned by the National Trust and are known as Millpond Gardens, in reference to the large triangular pond (since filled in) which once formed part of the waterworks for the eighteenth-century Merton corn mill. The land was donated to the trust by Mrs Richardson Evans in memory of her brother, Mr John Feeney, and opened to the public on 11 July 1907.

Today, although the trust retains ownership of this section of the park, the whole nine and a half acres is managed by the London Borough of Merton.

Wandle Park

Waddon New Road, Croydon *(21 acres)*

Named from the river which once flowed through the park, but which was culverted beneath it in 1967. Some evidence of the river's original course is still to be seen, as are traces of the once popular boating lake. The park has been formed from two river meadows, known as Frog Mead and Stubbs Mead – the former name being a reminder of the poor drainage which has plagued the park until quite recent times.

Wandle Park was purchased in 1889, making it one of Croydon's oldest public open spaces.

Wandsworth Park

Putney Bridge Road, SW15 *(20 acres)*

Apart from its three commons (Wandsworth Common, Putney Heath and Garratt Green) Wandsworth had also three common fields: Bridge Field, North Field and South Field. It was from part of one of these – North Field – that the land for the present riverside park was acquired. Funds for its purchase were raised in 1898 in commemoration of Queen Victoria's Diamond Jubilee and the park formally opened to the public in February 1903.

Well Hall Pleasaunce

Well Hall Road, SE9 *(12 acres)*

This was the home of Margaret Roper, daughter of St Thomas More. Her original house was replaced by an eighteenth-century building which in 1899 became the home of E. Nesbit, author of *The Railway Children*, and of her husband, Hubert Bland, who helped to found the Fabian Society. The old farmyard has since been grassed over and only the large moat, rose garden walls and barn (now an art gallery and restaurant) remain, along with many mature trees and beautiful flowerbeds.

Well Street Common

Gascoyne Road, E9 *(21 acres)*

It seems possible that the original Hackney Common, as this was at one time known, extended as far as the Well Street after which the common now takes its name. The original well, situated by the old Cottage Place, is thought to have been a therapeutic mineral spring or perhaps a spring with a holy reputation in connection with the palace of the Priors of St John of Jerusalem.

Today the common's attractions are mainly its new fitness trail and its function as an extension to neighbouring Victoria Park.

West Ham Park

Ham Park Road, E15 *(77 acres)*

As a private estate, the history of West Ham Park can be traced back to the sixteenth century, with the local Rooke family occupying Rooke's Hall here. The estate's most notable period, however, was from 1762 to 1780 when it was owned by the Quaker physician and botanist Dr John Fothergill, who enlarged the estate to something like its present size and established famous botanical gardens here.

After his death, the estate continued in Quaker ownership – first by James Sheppard and then by Samuel Gurney, the banker and philanthropist, whose sister, Elizabeth Fry, spent the last fifteen or sixteen years of her life conducting her campaign for penal reform from a house adjacent to the estate.

The idea of turning the property into a public park was first put forward in 1869 by John Gurney, and in 1872 he offered to sell the land for that purpose for a generously low price. The Gurney family capped this generosity by subscribing two-fifths of the purchase price and, after a similar donation by the Corporation of the City of London and substantial public subscriptions, the park was opened in 1874.

Though well outside 'the square mile', West Ham Park has remained to this day under the ownership and management of the City Corporation.

West Wickham Common

Gates Green Road, West Wickham *(25 acres)*

It was the rapid disappearance of West Wickham Common that led to neighbouring Hayes Common being the first common to be protected under the new Metropolitan Commons Act of 1866. Originally about one hundred acres in area, West Wickham Common was at that time fast being sold off as building plots by the Lord of the Manor, Sir John Lennard. Since Sir John kept denying that the land was in fact a common, it fell to the local inhabitants to find at least one property to which undisputed common rights still belonged.

The local branch of the Commons and Footpaths Preservation Society was finally successful in tracing such a property, but in spite of strong local feeling that it should fight the Lord of the Manor in the Law Courts, a compromise was reached with Sir John by paying him the sum of £2000 for the land. Three-quarters of this was raised by local subscription, the balance being met by the Corporation of the City of London who, as conservators, now own and maintain the common.

The formal opening ceremony was held in November 1892.

Wimbledon Park

Home Park Road, SW19 *(45 acres)*

This public park, with the neighbouring world-famous All England Lawn Tennis Club grounds, are small remnants of the original private estate of Wimbledon Park House – one-time home of the Spencer family, who employed 'Capability' Brown to landscape the property.

In 1914, Wimbledon Council bought the lake and a large area around it, with the intention of selling most of it for building development. Partly due to pressure from Wandsworth Council, these plans were amended and several years later the land was instead laid out as a public park, cricket ground and golf course. The golf course and twenty-two-acre lake are on a twenty-year lease to the golf club, leaving forty-five acres as a public park.

Woodland Walk

Oakridge Road, Bromley *(5 acres)*

This delightful mile-long woodland strip zig-zags behind the houses from the corner of Oakridge Road and Bromley Road to the corner of Woodbank Road and Whitefoot Terrace.

The Woodland Walk was acquired by the London County Council as part of the development of the Downham housing estate and opened to the public in 1931. Today it forms a part of the sixteen-mile Green Chain Walk which links the banks of the Thames with Cator Park in Beckenham. Its most attractive stretch is the western streamside section which passes between rows of mature oaks and which provides a suitable route for wheelchairs.

Woolwich Common

Academy Road, SE18 *(106 acres)*

Originally a common in the true and legal sense of the word, Woolwich

Common was once much larger, extending as far as Charlton. Since the arrival of the military in the latter half of the eighteenth century, the common has been steadily built upon, but not without considerable public protest. Local residents argued that, even though the commoners' rights had been legally extinguished under an 1803 Act of Parliament, the spirit of this agreement was to make it easier for the army to exercise here, not actually to exclude the general public. With each new enclosure, local residents asserted what they believed to be their moral claim to the common, and yet in spite of all the protests Woolwich Common remains today the property of the Ministry of Defence and technically the public have no legal right of way. As Lord Eversley wrote in 1910: it appears to be 'a most unfortunate and regrettable fact that one of the only serious inclosures, made and maintained, during the last forty years, in respect of any common, within fifteen miles of London, should be by a public authority such as the War Office.'

Wormwood Scrubs

Scrubs Lane, W10 *(191 acres)*

Wormwood Scrubs was, like Oak Common, oak woodland open to manorial tenants as common grazing land for pigs and cattle. From as early as 1812, right up until 1962, parts of it were occupied by the army for military training and even today user rights over a large area are retained by the Ministry of Defence.

In 1910 this was the starting point for the famous London to Manchester aeroplane race, and in 1923 it was being seriously considered as the site for a London airport.

Today, however, Wormwood Scrubs is one of London's main sporting centres with its West London Stadium and other sports facilities built where the old wartime guns and military stores depot used to be. Otherwise, the Scrubs' main asset is its size, for it is the largest open space for almost two miles. It is in other respects, though, rather bleak and unattractive, consisting mostly of playing fields, with an industrial skyline dominated by the old prison.

Yeading Brook Open Space

Charville Lane, Hayes *(127 acres)*

This two-mile strip of meadowland stretches along the banks of the Yeading brook, from the Ten Acre Wood at the end of Charville Lane to the Grand Union Canal footbridge leading to the municipal sports ground at the end of West Avenue. Most of the land consists of playing fields and grassy children's playgrounds linked together by the hawthorn-lined brook.

Yeading Walk

The Ridgeway, Harrow *(23 acres)*

This is a little-known long narrow strip of parkland stretching along the banks of the Yeading brook. The more formal stretch, extending either side of The Ridgeway, was first laid out in the 1930s and occupies seven acres of the total. The wilder remaining section is sometimes referred to as the Streamside Reservation.

The willows, which dominate the walk, date back to long before the park was created and were probably pollarded when this was still farmland; some of the oaks are believed to be 200 or more years old. Many ornamental trees have since been planted, including at least six cornelian cherry trees (which bear beautiful bright yellow flowers in early February), several Japanese maples, paper birch, weeping birch, southern beech and sweet gum.

York House Gardens

Riverside, Twickenham *(5 acres)*

These beautiful riverside gardens, to the south of York House, are pleasantly secluded and quite easily missed if approaching the house from the landward York Street side. The gardens took on much of their present appearance in about 1897, when the Duke of Orleans enclosed what had until then been riverside grazing land. Many improvements were made by a later resident, Sir Ratan Tata – one of these being the setting out in 1906 of the beautiful Italian fountain and statues which, though since subjected to vandalism, still survive.

The southern approach to the house from the gardens is quite spectacular as one climbs the steps of the stone bridge leading over Riverside, and suddenly York House comes into view across a classically formal lawn. The mansion, which dates back to the 1690s, now houses the council offices of the London Borough of Richmond upon Thames.

Green Walks

Some of London's larger parks offer excellent opportunities for long circular walks – a walk around the whole of either **Richmond Park** or **Hampstead Heath**, for example, covers over eight miles, and a walk around **Trent Park** (from Oakwood to Cockfosters tube stations) covers just under five. With a little imagination it is not hard also to link some of the clusters of adjoining parks to make interesting linear walks. Such possibilities exist in some of the most unlikely places – as in Central London, where **St James's Park**, **Green Park**, **Hyde Park** and **Kensington Gardens** provide an almost rural three-mile link between Westminster and Queensway tube stations. The possibilities are really endless, and the following are just a few of the more interesting ones.

ɔn to Boston Manor tube station – 5 miles*

n walk south to Perivale Lane and turn right, into Stockdove Way and under the railway into walk continues via Greenford Bridge, more or less ks of the river till it meets the Grand Union Canal ll Flight of Locks. The path then follows the eastern side veers across playing fields to Boston Manor station. For ad and directions there is a booklet entitled *Walks in the Brent River* available for a small charge from Jenny Vallance, 17 Sutherland Road, Ealing, W13 (01-998 9785).

Canalside Walk

from Limehouse to Rickmansworth – 34 miles

It is now possible to walk some forty miles along the towpaths of the Grand Union Canal and Regent's Canal. Six of these forty miles represent the Brentford Arm of the Grand Union, while the remainder forms a continuous route from Limehouse (access to the towpath via Tomlins Terrace, E14) to Rickmansworth (on the Metropolitan tube line). The route takes in the new Mile End Park, **Victoria Park**, **Regent's Park** and **Primrose Hill**, Meanwhile Gardens, **Horsenden Hill** and seven miles of the **Colne Valley Park**. For detailed maps and directions (as far as Uxbridge) there is a small booklet entitled *London Is Canal Walks*, available from the London Tourist Board.

Epping Forest Centenary Walk

from Manor Park railway station to Epping tube station – 15 miles

It is perhaps not well known that Epping Forest extends so far into London – the walk follows almost the forest's entire length, from Wanstead Flats to Epping. Starting at Manor Park station, the walk crosses Wanstead Flats, goes through Bush Wood, Leyton Flats, Gilbert's Slade, Walthamstow Forest, Higham's Park and along the banks of the river Ching to the Epping Forest Museum at Queen Elizabeth's Hunting Lodge on Ranger's Road. From here the forest widens considerably and becomes more densely wooded. The path continues past Connaught Water to the Epping Forest Conservation Centre by the King's Oak public house at High Beach. From here the route passes through Little and Great Monk Wood, past Ambresbury Banks, through Bell Common to Epping town. For detailed route maps and directions there is a small booklet entitled *Epping Forest Centenary Walk* by Fred Matthews and Harry Bitten available for 15p from the Epping Forest Conservation Centre, High Beach, Loughton, Essex (01-508 7714).

Green Chain Walk (i)

from Thamesmead to Cator Park, New Beckenham – 16 miles

The Green Chain is the name given to a string of parks, woods, playing fields and golf courses which stretch in an arc through south-east London from Thamesmead to Beckenham, through the boroughs of Bexley, Greenwich, Lewisham and Bromley. Along its length run several connecting signposted walks. This one starts by the windmill sculpture on the Thamesside Walk (riverside promenade) at Thamesmead, and runs through Southmere Park, **Lesnes Abbey Woods**, **Bostall Heath and Woods** and East Wickham Open Space to **Oxleas Wood**, before joining the alternative route (below) to continue through to Beckenham.

Green Chain Walk (ii)

from the Thames Flood Barrier to Cator Park, New Beckenham – 14 miles)
Starting just east of the Thames Flood Barrier, this walk passes through **Maryon Park and Maryon Wilson Park**, Charlton Park, Woolwich and Eltham Commons, Castle Wood and Jackwood to **Oxleas Wood**, where the alternative route (above) joins the path. With further occasional signposted options of route, the path continues via Conduit Meadow, Eltham Palace and **Beckenham Place Park** to Cator Park and Kent House railway station. For detailed route maps and directions, there is a series of four booklets entitled *Green Chain Walks* 1 to 4, available from the Green Chain Working Party, John Humphries House, Greenwich, London SE10 (01-853 0077 ext. 259).

Lee Valley Walk

from Clapton railway station to Ware railway station – 21 miles
This walk follows the river Lee towpath through the **Lee Valley Park**, from Lea Bridge Road to the edge of Greater London and beyond to the town of Ware. Few people would perhaps want to walk the whole route in one day, but it can be tackled in sections, returning by train along the line which follows the west side of the valley. Those more energetic might, on the other hand, consider *extending* the walk by starting at Mile End tube station and approaching the valley via Mile End Park, **Victoria Park**, the Red Path, Mabley Green and Hackney Marsh. A map of the route is available from the Publicity Department, Lee Valley Park, PO Box 88, Enfield, Middlesex (Lea Valley 717711).

Parkland Walk

from Finsbury Park station to Alexandra Palace station – almost 5 miles
A short walk through **Finsbury Park** brings one to this disused railway line, which is accessible from the old footbridge opposite Oxford Road. The route follows the old railway to Holmesdale Road, and then via a footpath by the library in Shepherd's Hill to Priory Gardens and down another alleyway into **Queen's Wood**. Continuing via **Queen's and Highgate Woods**, the railway path resumes from the junction of Cranley Gardens and Muswell Hill Road, to reach **Alexandra Park** – and thence to the Alexandra Palace railway station. (See the main parks text for further details.) For a detailed map and directions there is a booklet, entitled *The Parkland Walk*, available from The Warden, Parkland Walk Information Centre, 73c Stapleton Hall Road, N4 (01-341 3582).

Thames Riverside Walk

from Kew Bridge railway station to Kingston station – 9 miles
Cross Kew Bridge to follow the Thames towpath by **Kew Gardens**, the Old Deer Park, **Ham Riverside Lands** and Canbury Gardens to Kingston station. It is worth making a slight detour to take in Terrace Gardens and **Ham House Grounds**.

Useful Addresses

Organizations with an active interest in the provision and conservation of London's parks and woodlands

British Trust for Conservation Volunteers (BTCV) (London Region) 2 Mandela Street, London NW1 (01-388 3946). The trust, which has over twenty local groups in London, organizes practical conservation tasks, training volunteers of all ages, and provides conservation advice to other bodies.

Ecological Parks Trust The Old Loom House (4th Floor), Back Church Lane, London E1 1LS (01-481 0893). Interested in all aspects of urban ecology, but best known for its pioneering work in setting up ecological parks, the first of which – William Curtis Ecological Park – was set up in 1977 just a few yards from Tower Bridge (though since closed to make way for building development).

Enbro (Environment Bromley) 300 Baring Road, London SE12 0DS (01-857 5258). A voluntary organization locally active in the conservation and interpretation of the environment.

Friends of the Earth 377 City Road, London EC1V 1NA (01-837 0731). Some local groups of this national organization have set up nature reserves within the city's smaller parks.

Green Heritage Service 3 Mayfield Road, Thornton Heath, Croydon, Surrey CR4 6DN (01-689 4197). Set up specifically to foster the study and appreciation of London's open spaces. The organizers have a wide range of study material and put on informal talks on the city's parks for local amenity or hobby groups.

London Wildlife Trust London Ecology Centre, 80 York Way, London N1 9AG (01-278 6612/3). Founded in 1981, the trust has already been instrumental in the creation or protection of over thirty nature reserves across the capital, including the Gunnersbury Triangle in West London. Worth joining for its newsletter alone – *Wild London*.

Metropolitan Public Gardens Association 4 Carlos Place, London W1Y 5AE (01-493 6617). One of the bodies to which we owe many of our older open spaces; most significant was its contribution to the passing of The Disused Burial Grounds Act, 1884, which obliged local authorities to turn the city's graveyards into public open spaces. Though less active today, the association continues to make some grants towards open spaces, helping to provide seats and trees to deserving areas.

The Open Spaces Society 25A Bell Street, Henley-on-Thames, Oxon RG9 2BA (0491 573535). More formally known as the Commons, Open Spaces and Footpaths Preservation Society, this organization has played a crucial role in the saving of London's commons, and continues today to campaign for the protection of common land, village greens, open spaces and public paths throughout the country.

Royal Society for the Protection of Birds (RSPB) The Lodge, Sandy, Beds SG19 2DL (0767 80551). Has fourteen member groups in London which, apart from organizing meetings and excursions, take an interest in local aspects of nature conservation.

The Tradescant Trust 74 Coleherne Court, London SW5 0EF (01-261 2891 or 01-373 4030). The trust has converted the St Mary-at-Lambeth Church, Lambeth Palace Road, to house the new Museum of Garden History, which provides a venue for exhibitions and lectures related to gardening.

Managing bodies and owners of London's major parks and open spaces

London's parkland is administered by over fifty different bodies, a complete list of which has never, to my knowledge, been published.

The thirty-two London boroughs: Barking and Dagenham, Barnet, Bexley, Brent, Bromley, Camden, Croydon, Ealing, Enfield, Greenwich, Hackney, Hammersmith and Fulham, Haringey, Harrow, Havering, Hillingdon, Hounslow, Islington, Kensington and Chelsea, Kingston upon Thames, Lambeth, Lewisham, Merton, Newham, Redbridge, Richmond upon Thames, Southwark, Sutton, Tower Hamlets, Waltham Forest, Wandsworth and Westminster.

Brent River and Canal Society 17 Sutherland Road, London W13 0DX (01-998 9785).

Chislehurst and St Paul's Cray Commons Conservators Clerk to the Board, Old Fire Station, Hawkwood Lane, Chislehurst

(01-467 1886).

Church Commissioners 1 Millbank, London SW1P 3JZ.

Colne Valley Regional Park Authority County Hall, Aylesbury, Bucks HP20 1UX (0296 5000).

The Corporation of the City of London Guildhall, London EC2 (01-236 6920).

The Crown – *see* Department of the Environment.

Curators of Monken Hadley Common 19, 23 and 25 Wood Street, Barnet, Herts.

Department of the Environment Royal Parks Office, 2 Marsham Street, London SW1P 3EB (01-212 3434).

Duke of Northumberland – *see* Syon Park Garden Centre.

Ecological Parks Trust The Old Loom House (4th Floor), Back Church Lane, London E1 (01-481 0893).

English Heritage 23 Savile Row, London W1X 2HE (01-734 6010).

Essex County Council Estates and Valuation Department, Clarendon House, Parkway, Chelmsford CM2 0NT (0245 267222).

Forestry Commission (East Forest District Office), Brook House, Cranbrook Road, Hawkhurst, Kent TN18 5EE (05805 3757).

Inner London Education Authority County Hall, London SE1 7PB (01-633 5000).

Lee Valley Regional Park Authority Myddelton House, Bulls Cross, Enfield, Middlesex EN2 9HG (Lea Valley 717711).

London Residuary Body County Hall, London SE1 7PB.

London Wildlife Trust London Ecology Centre, 80 York Way, London N1 9AG (01-278 6612/3).

Ministry of Defence Main Building, Whitehall, London SW1A 2HB (01-218 9000).

Mitcham Common Conservators c/o London Borough of Merton, Education and Recreation Department (01-543 2222).

The National Trust 36 Queen Anne's Gate, London SW1H 9AS (01-222 9251).

Petersham Common Conservators c/o London Borough of Richmond upon Thames, Parks and Recreation Department (01-940 8351).

Syon Park Garden Centre Brentford, Middlesex (01-568 0882).

The Tradescant Trust 74 Coleherne Court, London SW5 0EF (01-261 2891 or 01-373 4030).

The Trustees of Chelsea Physic Garden 60 Royal Hospital Road, London SW3 4HS (01-352 5646).

The Trustees of the Royal Botanic Gardens Kew, Richmond, Surrey TW9 3AB (01-940 1171).

Wimbledon and Putney Commons Conservators Manor Cottage, Wimbledon Common.

Further Reading

Guides to London Parks

London County Council. *London Parks and Open Spaces: being one of a series of Popular Handbooks on the LCC and what it does for London.* Hodder and Stoughton, London, 1924.

London County Council. *Open-Air London: An illustrated guide to some 480 open spaces in and around London including the Green Belt.* LCC and London Transport, 1939.

London County Council. *Open-Air London: A guide to the parks and open spaces of London and London's Country.* LCC and London Transport Executive, 1952.

Sexby, Lieut-Col. J.J. *The Municipal Parks, Gardens, and Open Spaces of London: Their History and Associations.* Elliot Stock, London, 1905 (reprint of 1898 edition).

Management of Parks for Wildlife

Flint, Rosamund. *Encouraging Wildlife in Urban Parks: Guidelines to Management.* London Wildlife Trust, 1985.

Greater London Council. *Ecology and Nature Conservation in London* (Ecology Handbook No. 1). Greater London Council, 1984.

London Cemeteries and Churchyards

Hackman, Harvey. *Wates's Book of London Churchyards: A Guide to the Old Churchyards and Burial-grounds of the City and Central London.* Collins, London, 1981.

Meller, Hugh. *London Cemeteries.* Avebury, Godstone, Surrey, 1983.

London Squares

Chancellor, Edwin Beresford. *The History of the Squares of London: Topographical and Historical.* Kegan Paul, Trench & Trubner, London, 1907.

Index